Introduction

Chemistry for You is designed to introduce you to the basic ideas of Chemistry. It will show you how these ideas help to explain about the materials in our world, and how they can be changed. From your trainers to the space shuttle, chemists work to develop new materials.

Chemistry for You aims to be interesting and help you pass your exams, whether you are using it to study Double Science (Co-ordinated or Modular), Single Science or Chemistry at GCSE.

The book is carefully laid out so that each new idea is introduced and developed on a single page or on two facing pages. Words have been kept as simple and straightforward as possible. Pages with an orange stripe in the top corner are the more difficult pages, needed to achieve grade B or above in the Higher Tier exam.

Throughout the book there are many experiments for you to do. A safety sign means your teacher should give you further advice (for example to wear safety glasses). Plenty of guidance is given on the results of these experiments, in case you don't actually do a particular practical or are studying at home.

Each new chemical word is printed in **heavy type** and important points are placed in a box. There is a summary of important facts at the end of each chapter.

There are questions at the end of each chapter. They always start with an easy fill-in-the-missing-words question useful for revision and writing notes. At the end of each of the 6 main sections you will find plenty of further questions taken from recent GCSE papers.

Calculations are covered in the Extra Section at the end of the book. You will also find advice on practical work, careers, revision and examination techniques in this section.

Throughout the book, cartoons and rhymes are used to help explain ideas. The 'Chemistry At Work' pages will also show you how Chemistry is useful to us in everyday life.

However, above all I hope that you will find Chemistry easier to understand and that using the book will be fun!

I would like to thank my family (Judy, Nina and Alex) for their amazing support and understanding throughout this project.

Lawrie Ryan

D0719612

Contents

Chemists make new materials
that change the world
in many ways ...

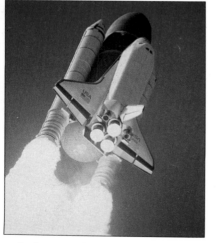

From everyday materials, such as cosmetics

... to the materials used in the space shuttle.

The following chapters may be required for a Single Science GCSE course:

chapter 1

STATES OF MATTER

Most of us know about solids, liquids and gases.
We know that wood is a solid, that water is a liquid,
and that air is a gas. But how many people could
answer the question:
'What are the physical *states* of wood, water and air?'
It's tricky if you don't know what physical state means!

There are **3 states of matter** – solid, liquid and gas.
Look at the table below:
It shows the properties of the 3 states of matter.

Solids	Liquids	Gases
have their own shape	take the shape of their container	take the shape of the whole container
stay where they are put	can be poured	spread out quickly
are difficult to pass through	are quite easy to pass through	are very easy to pass through
can't be compressed (squashed)	are very difficult to compress	are easy to compress

Models

Scientists like to make models which help to explain
the things we see. So how can we explain the
differences we see between solids, liquids and gases?
First of all, we must imagine that solids,
liquids and gases are made up from particles.
In our model, these particles are like tiny marbles!

Now try these experiments:

Experiment 1.1   Explaining solids, liquids and gases
Solid

Tilt your tray slightly. Pour your marbles into one corner.
● How are the particles arranged in a solid?

Liquid

Keep your tray slightly tilted. Now start to shake it gently.
● Can you see the particles slipping and sliding
   past each other?

Gas

Now put your tray level. Shake it more quickly.
● What happens to the distance between particles
   compared to your solid and liquid models?

Particles in solids, liquids and gases

In the last experiment, how did you move the tray to increase the distance between particles?

Our model of solids, liquids and gases describes
1. the distance between particles, and
2. the movement of the particles.

Look at the diagrams and poems below:

Solid

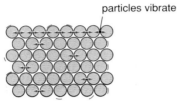

particles vibrate

Solid

Squashed together, the particles are tight,
Some think they're still – but that's not right.
Even though you can't see them shaking,
Believe it or not – they are vibrating!

Liquid

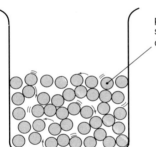

particles slip and slide over each other

Liquid

Particles mingling and inter-twined,
There's not much room in here to find!
The forces of attraction are still quite strong,
But particles are free to move slowly along.

Gas

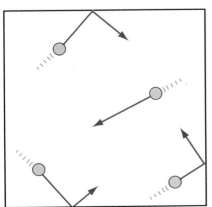

particles move very quickly in all directions; as the particles bash against the walls of the container, they exert a force that causes pressure

Gas

Particles whizzing everywhere,
Moving randomly, they just don't care!
Speeding left and speeding right,
With space in between, they're amazingly light.

▷ Invisible particles

The ancient Greeks were the first to suggest that everything is made up from particles.

Scientists still believe this now. Yet these particles are too small to be seen.
Even if you use the most powerful microscopes, you still can't really 'see' them. So why are we so sure that they exist?

Nowadays, scientists have developed special probes that can measure very small forces.
These probes can be used to detect particles, and even position them where you want.

Around 400BC Democritus put forward his ideas about particles – but most people didn't believe him

Diffusion

If somebody spills some perfume in your classroom, you soon know about it. The smell quickly spreads through the room. However, you don't **see** any perfume in the air. Yet your nose tells you that it really is there.

The perfume gives off invisible particles of itself. These particles mix with the gas particles in the air. When particles mix like this it is called **diffusion.**

Diffusion happens by itself. You don't need to mix or stir the substances.
You can see for yourself in the next experiment:

Perfume particles spread (diffuse) through the air particles

Experiment 1.2   Diffusion through a liquid

Use tweezers to pick up a few potassium manganate(VII) crystals.
Gently place them at the bottom of a beaker of water.
Observe the beaker for a few minutes.
● What do you see happen?

Leave your beaker until next lesson.
Draw a diagram to show your results.
● Explain what you think happens to the purple particles.
  Use the words **particles** and **diffuse** in your answer.

⚠ potassium manganate(VII)

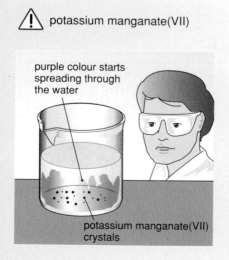

purple colour starts spreading through the water

potassium manganate(VII) crystals

Demonstration 1.3   Diffusion through a gas

cotton wool soaked in
ammonia solution (concentrated)

cotton wool soaked in
hydrochloric acid
(concentrated)

Watch what happens when the stoppers from bottles of
ammonia and hydrochloric acid are brought near each other.
Your teacher will set up the apparatus
as shown above.

⚠️

concentrated acid and alkali

- What do you see in the long tube where the acid and
  ammonia particles meet?
- Which particles diffuse faster, ammonia or acid?
  How can you tell?

Small particles move faster than large ones.

Small, light particles diffuse faster than large, heavy ones.

- In the experiment above the particles meet
  nearer the acid end of the tube.
  Which particles are lighter, acid or ammonia?

More evidence for particles

As you know, the particles in solids, liquids
and gases can't be seen under a microscope.
However, you can see some effects of the
particles using a microscope.

*Small particles move faster than
large ones!*

Experiment 1.4   Brownian motion

Focus your microscope on a smoke cell, as shown:
The smoke contains bits of dust which you
can see under the microscope.
Look at the pieces of dust carefully.
- What do you see?
- Can you explain the shaky movements?

You can try the same experiment using milk.
Put a drop of milk under a cover-slip on a
microscope slide.
This time look for tiny blobs of fat jiggling
about in the milk.
This movement is called **Brownian motion.**

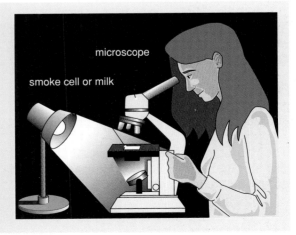

microscope

smoke cell or milk

▷ Changing state

We all like a cool drink on a hot day.
Have you noticed what happens to the
size of the ice cubes in your glass?

The ice slowly melts into your drink.

When you heat up a solid, like ice,
it turns into a liquid. It *changes state*.

If you carry on heating, the liquid turns into a gas.

These changes are **physical changes**.
No new substances are made when substances
change state. You can also reverse the change quite easily.

Can you think of any other everyday changes of state?

Look at the changes of state below:

Ice melting is a physical change

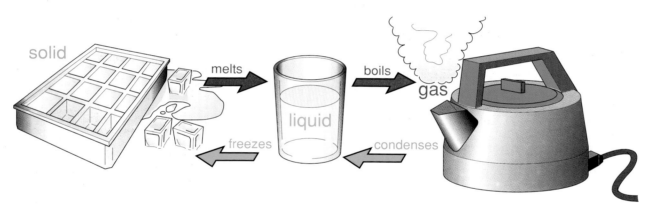

As we heat a **solid,** its particles
vibrate more and more quickly.
The solid expands.

Eventually, the particles shake about so much
that they begin to break free from each other.
The solid starts melting. It turns into a **liquid**.

If we carry on heating, the particles in the liquid
move around more quickly. Some particles at the
surface have enough energy to escape as a **gas**.

The liquid **evaporates**. With more heating,
the liquid eventually boils.

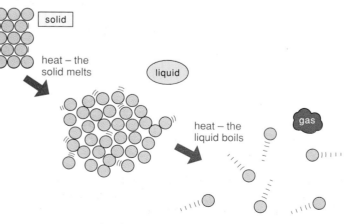

Experiment 1.5 Melting

In this experiment you can look at the energy changes when a solid turns into a liquid. Set up the apparatus as shown in diagram. Record the temperature every minute as the stearic acid heats up.

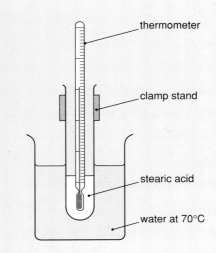

Time (mins)	Temperature (°C)
0	
1	

- What is the temperature when you notice the solid starting to melt? Show this in your table.

Keep recording until the temperature reaches about 70 °C.

Experiment 1.6 Freezing

Use the clamp stand to lift the tube from the hot water in experiment 1.5, as shown:

Record the temperature every minute as the stearic acid cools down.
Use a table like the one above.
- Note in your table when you see the first signs of solid forming.
Keep recording until the temperature drops to about 50 °C.

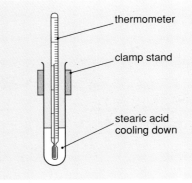

- Plot line graphs of your results for both experiments. Put time along the bottom and temperature up the side.
- Label your graphs to show where stearic acid is a solid, a liquid, or present in both states.
- What is the melting point of stearic acid?
- What is the freezing point of stearic acid?

You will have noticed that both your graphs have a flat section. The temperature stays the same for a while. At this temperature both solid and liquid are present. It is the melting point or freezing point of the stearic acid.

Even though you carry on heating the stearic acid, its temperature does not go up as the solid melts. This is because, at its melting point, the energy is being used to separate its particles from each other.

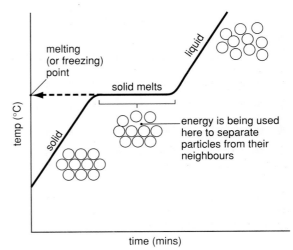

Investigation 1.7   Does temperature affect the rate of diffusion?

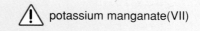

Look at the potassium manganate(VII) experiment on page 8.

- What do you think will happen if you change the temperature of the water?

- Explain why you think this will happen.
  Use your ideas about particles.

- Plan an investigation to test your prediction.
  Make sure it is a fair test and that your method is safe.

- Let your teacher check your plan before you start.

Investigation 1.8   What affects the rate of evaporation?

Water soaked into a damp paper towel slowly **evaporates**
(turns from a liquid into a gas).
As it does, the paper towel loses mass.

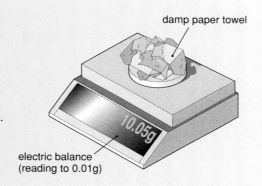

damp paper towel

electric balance
(reading to 0.01g)

- What could affect how quickly the water evaporates?

- Predict what will happen.
  Try to explain your prediction using ideas about particles.

- Can you think of a way to investigate your ideas?

- Let your teacher check your plan before you start.

Summary

- Everything is made up from tiny particles.
- **Diffusion** is the movement of particles of one substance through another.
- Small, light particles diffuse faster than large, heavy ones.

- There are 3 states of matter – solid, liquid and gas.
- The particles in a **solid** are packed tightly together.
  The particles are stuck in position, but do vibrate.
- The particles in a **liquid** have a little more space between them.
  They can move around within the liquid, slipping and sliding over each other.
- The particles in a **gas** have lots of space between them.
  They zoom around very quickly.

- When a substance **changes state**, it takes energy to increase
  the distance between particles.
  Examples are solids melting or liquids boiling.

▶ Questions

1. Copy and complete:
   There are 3 states of matter – a) . . . . , b) . . . .
   and c) . . . . . The particles in a solid are packed
   . . . . together. The particles are fixed in position,
   but they do . . . . . The particles in a . . . . can
   move around, but there is still
   very little . . . . between them. In a gas,
   particles move around very . . . . .
   There are large . . . . between particles.

   When particles get closer together, for example
   when a gas c_ _ _ _ _ _ _ _ , energy is given out.
   On the other hand, we need to supply . . . . to
   increase the distance between particles. An
   example is when a solid . . . . .

2. a) What do we call these changes:
      i)   solid ——▶ liquid
      ii) liquid ——▶ gas
      iii) gas ——▶ liquid
      iv) liquid ——▶ solid.
   b) Which of the changes in a) require us to
      provide energy, and which give out energy?

3. Describe the movement of the particles in a
   solid substance as it is heated to its boiling point.

4. Imagine that you are a particle of sugar.
   Describe your adventures as you leave the sugar
   bowl to sweeten a cup of tea.

5. Look at the apparatus below:

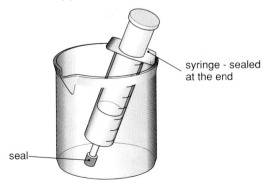

   a) What happens if you pour hot water into the
      beaker?
   b) Explain why. Mention pressure and the
      movement of the air particles.

6. Look at this cooling curve for substance X as it
   turns from a liquid to a solid.

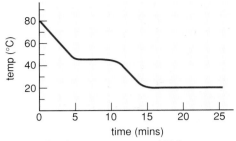

   a) What is the freezing point of X?
   b) What is the melting point of X?
   c) What was the room temperature that day?

7. The density of a substance is worked out using
   this formula:

$$\text{density} = \frac{\text{mass}}{\text{volume}}$$

   a) An 8 cm³ block of iron has a mass of 62.88 g.
      Work out the density of iron in (g/cm³).

   Look at the densities in the table below:

Element	Density (g/cm³)
oxygen	0.001 33 (at room temp. and pressure)
copper	8.92
zinc	7.14
nitrogen	0.001 17 (at room temp. and pressure)

   b) What is the physical state of each element in
      the table at 25 °C?
   c) Explain the big differences in the densities of
      the elements shown. Mention particles in
      your answer.
   d) Why is the temperature and pressure
      important when giving the density of oxygen
      and nitrogen?

8. Explain each of the statements below in terms
   of particles:
   a) You can smell a fish and chip shop from
      across the road.
   b) Sugar dissolves faster in hot water than cold
      water.
   c) Condensation forms on the inside of your
      windows in winter.

Further questions on page 37.

chapter 2

▶ Atoms

Scientists believe that everything is made from tiny particles.

But what are these particles like?

This is a difficult question because nobody has *ever* seen one. They are too small.
So scientists have had to think up ideas which explain the things they *can* see.

Around 1805 John Dalton put forward his ideas.
He thought that the smallest particles were like tiny, hard snooker balls. They could not be split.
He called these **atoms**.

Dalton suggested that there were just a few dozen different types of atom. He made up a list from substances which could not be broken down at that time.

He explained the millions of different substances on Earth quite simply. The atoms could join together in different combinations to make new substances.

Many of Dalton's ideas are still useful today.
Can you think of any things he got wrong?

There are 92 different types of atom found naturally on Earth. Your body is made up from just 26 of these!

John Dalton (1766–1844) was born in Cumbria. For most of his life he taught in Manchester.

All these words in this dictionary... from just 26 different letters!

All those substances in this person... from just 26 types of atom!

Symbols

Each atom has its own name and chemical symbol.
Most symbols are taken from the English names.
Some are based on their Latin names.

Look at the table opposite:
• Which atoms have symbols based on their Latin names?
• Why is helium's symbol He, and not H?

Notice that you always use a capital letter for the first letter of a symbol.
If the symbol has a second letter, it is always a small letter.

Atom	Symbol
Hydrogen	H
Helium	He
Nitrogen	N
Neon	Ne
Oxygen	O
Chlorine	Cl
Iron	Fe
Copper	Cu
Lead	Pb

Can you see where the word 'plumber' came from? Water pipes used to be made of lead. Why don't we use it now?

▶ Molecules

Atoms are nature's building blocks.
When atoms are joined together by
chemical bonds they make **molecules**.

A hydrogen molecule

> **Molecules are groups of 2 or more atoms bonded together.**

Atoms are nature's building blocks.

Chemical formula

Can you guess the most well-known
chemical formula in the world?
It's H_2O – a molecule of water.
Lots of people know the formula,
but many have no idea what it means.

Chemists use a kind of short-hand
to describe molecules.
It's called the **chemical formula**.

The formula tells you which atoms
are in the molecule by looking at
the symbols. It also tells you how many
of each atom there are by small numbers
after each symbol.
Notice that if there is no number after
a symbol, it means there is
just one of those atoms in the molecule.

So, look at the molecule of water:
It is made from 2 hydrogen atoms and
just 1 oxygen atom.

This table shows some common molecules.

A formula helps chemists who can't spell!

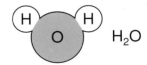

A water molecule.

nitrogen	N_2	
ammonia	NH_3	
hydrogen chloride	HCl	
chlorine	Cl_2	

▶ Elements

Some substances can't be broken down
into anything simpler.
This is because all the atoms in them
are the same type.
These are the chemical **elements**.

> **Elements contain only one type of atom.**

You might remember from page 14,
that there are 92 different types of atom
found naturally on Earth.
So how many natural elements could there be?
Look at these examples of elements:

Elements just can't be split into simpler substances!

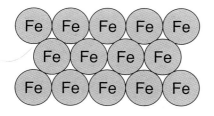

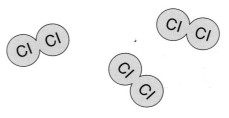

Iron is an element
(it is a solid, made from only Fe atoms)

Chlorine is an element
(it is a gas, made from Cl_2 molecules)

Can you see how we can have *molecules* of elements?

▶ Compounds

There are only 92 elements in nature,
and therefore 92 different types of atom.
However, there are millions of different substances.
So as you can imagine, most substances must
be made from more than one element. They must contain
more than one type of atom!

These substances are called **compounds**.

> **Compounds contain 2 or more types of atom (chemically bonded together).**

Many of us use gas to cook with or to heat our homes.
This gas is a compound called methane.
Its formula is CH_4.
It is made from 1 carbon atom and
4 hydrogen atoms bonded together.
So there are 2 elements in CH_4 – carbon and hydrogen.

Look back to the table on page 15.
● Which substances are elements?
● Which substances are compounds?

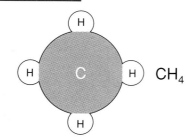

A molecule of methane (a compound)

Experiment 2.1 Making a compound

In this experiment you can look at the difference
between a compound and the elements it is made from.

A. Collect a spatula of iron filings on a piece of paper.

- Describe what is looks like.

Collect a spatula of sulphur powder.

- Describe what it looks like.

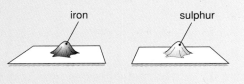

iron   sulphur

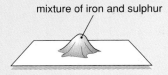

mixture of iron and sulphur

B. Mix the iron and sulphur together with a spatula.
This is called a **mixture**.

Use a hand-lens to look closely at your mixture.

- What does the mixture look like?
- How could you separate the iron and sulphur?
  Can you think of 2 ways?
  If you have time, try out your ideas.

C. Put your mixture into a small test-tube.
Heat it strongly in a fume-cupboard.

⚠ Take care to keep your flame away from
the mouth of the tube. If sulphur catches fire
toxic sulphur dioxide gas is given off.
Stop heating once the reaction starts.

- What do you see happen in your test-tube?

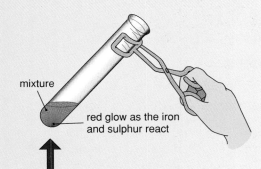

mixture

red glow as the iron
and sulphur react

heat

D. Give your test-tube to your teacher when it has cooled down.
Your teacher can wrap the tube in a cloth
and crack it carefully to get your new compound out.

- What are the differences between the mixture
  of iron and sulphur and the new compound you have made?

The compound made from the elements, iron and sulphur,
is called iron sulphide.
The reaction can be shown by a **word equation**:

iron + sulphur ⟶ iron sulphide
  reactants   product

The things that we start with before the reaction are called **reactants**.
The substances made in reactions are called **products**.
Can you name the reactants and product in the word equation above?

▷ Separating mixtures

In the last experiment you mixed iron and sulphur.
Before you heat the mixture, you can still separate
the iron and sulphur. For example, you can use
a magnet to attract the iron.

Why can't you separate the iron and sulphur after
they are heated?

Look at the differences between a mixture and a compound:

Mixture	Compound
the amount of each substance can vary	the amount of each element is always fixed
has the properties of each substance in the mixture	has completely different properties from the elements in the compound
the substances can be easily separated from each other	it is not easy to separate the elements from the compound (it needs a chemical reaction)

Let's look at some different ways to separate mixtures:

Filtration

We use filtration to separate an insoluble solid
from a liquid or solution.
Do you like the smell of coffee? We can filter
a mixture of fresh coffee and hot water.
The insoluble bits of the coffee grains are left on
the filter paper. The dark brown solution
passes through.

The insoluble bits of the coffee grains are left on the filter paper

Let's try separating the mixture below:

Experiment 2.2   Separating sand and salt

You are given a mixture of sand and salt.
Sand does not dissolve in water, but salt does.

Add water to your mixture and stir.
Filter your mixture as shown:
- What is left on the filter paper?
- If you leave the sand to dry, will it be pure?

Wash the sand with distilled water.
Then leave it to dry.
This rinses away any salt solution from the sand.

- How can you get the salt from the salt solution?

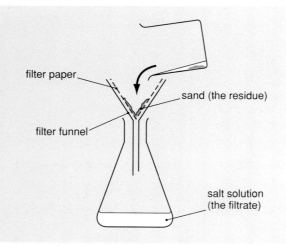

filter paper

sand (the residue)

filter funnel

salt solution (the filtrate)

Evaporation

Experiment 2.3   Evaporation of a solution

Pour your salt solution into an evaporating dish.
Set up the water bath as shown:
The dish is heated by the steam from
the water in the beaker.

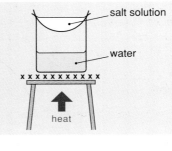

- What do you see inside the dish?
- Explain how this happens.

Distillation

In the last experiment you got salt from
a mixture of salt and water.
What happened to the water? If we want
to collect it, we can distil the mixture.
We evaporate the water. The steam given off
is condensed and collected as pure water.
What happens to the salt?

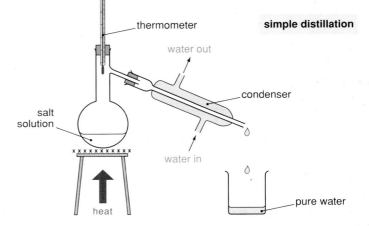

Experiment 2.4   Simple distillation

This is used to collect the liquid from
a solution. The solid stays in the flask.

Set up the apparatus as shown:
Gently boil the salt solution.

You collect pure water in the beaker.

Demonstration 2.5   Fractional distillation

This is used to separate two or more liquids that are mixed.
Look at the apparatus opposite:
What is the difference between it and the apparatus
we use for simple distillation?

Watch the distillation.

Ethanol boils at 78 °C.
- What is the boiling point of water?
- Which liquid is collected first?
Try lighting a few drops of the ethanol collected
on a watch glass.

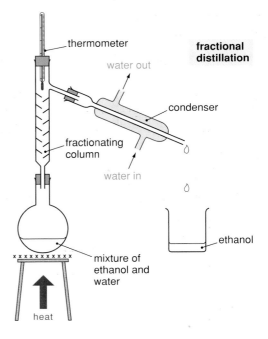

We need the fractionating column when the liquids
have **similar boiling points.**
As the mixture is heated, both liquids evaporate.
However, the liquid with the higher boiling point
condenses on the glass inside the column.
Then it drips back into the flask.

Chromatography

We can use chromatography to separate
small amounts of dissolved solids.
For example, we can separate the dyes in inks.

Let's try to separate the dyes in food colourings:

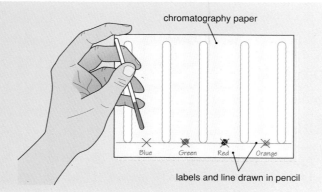

Experiment 2.6   Chromatography
Set up a piece of chromatography paper
as shown:

Let the water soak up the paper until
you have separated the colours.
Leave it to dry and stick the paper,
called a chromatogram, into your book.

Make a table to show which colours
make up each food colouring.

- Which food colourings contain only one dye?

The more soluble a substance, the
further up the paper it is carried by the water.
The soluble substance is called the **solute**.
The water is called the **solvent**.
Other solvents, such as ethanol, can also be used.
Do you think you would get the same results?

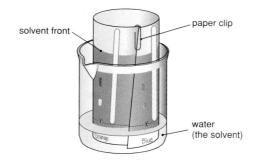

Chromatography can also be used to identify
unknown substances.
We can look at chromatograms for substances
we know. We compare these with one for the
unknown substance.
Look at the example shown below:
This has led to use in hospitals and in
forensic science.
When might chromatography be useful for
a doctor or in police work?

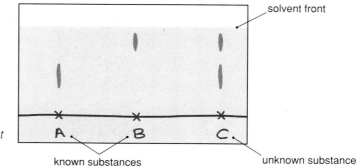

*This chromatogram shows that
the unknown substance C is a
mixture of A and B*

▷ Chemistry at work : Useful mixtures

Emulsions

Have you ever noticed the two layers
of liquid in a bottle of salad dressing?
What can you do to the bottle to mix
the oil and water together?

Oil floats on top of water.
The liquids are **immiscible.** They only
mix when you shake them up. Then the oil
and water mix as tiny blobs.
This type of mixture is called an **emulsion**.

What happens when you leave the
emulsion to stand for a while?

Salad cream is an emulsion.
Does it separate out into two layers,
like salad dressing?
You don't have to shake a bottle of
salad cream to mix it. It has egg yolk added.
This is an **emulsifying agent.** It stops
the oil and water separating into layers.
Many food additives (E numbers) are
emulsifying agents. Just look on a
bar of chocolate!

You can see the oil and water layers in the salad dressing.
Salad cream is an emulsion. Why don't the oil and water
separate into layers?

Oil and water are mixed in paints.

Foams

A **foam** is a mixture of a gas spread through
a liquid or a solid.
Can you think of any examples of solid foams?
Why do we need special rules about
the type of foam used in furniture.

Look at the photo
opposite:
Do you use any
liquid foams?

This bar of chocolate contains a solid foam.

▶ Chemical reactions

Do you remember from experiment 2.1, how iron reacts with sulphur? It forms iron sulphide.

This change was shown by a word equation. However, a **chemical** (or **symbol**) **equation** gives you more detail. It shows you the formula of each substance in the reaction:

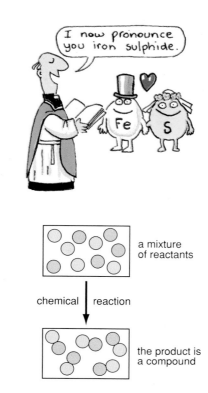

iron + sulphur ⟶ iron sulphide **Word equation**

Fe + S ⟶ FeS **Symbol equation**

This tells us that 1 atom of iron reacts with 1 atom of sulphur. They make iron sulphide, which contains 1 iron atom for each sulphur atom.

The atoms have been chemically bonded together. The new compound, iron sulphide, is not like iron or sulphur at all. It has totally different properties. A new substance has been made.

It is also difficult to get the iron and sulphur back from the iron sulphide. This is typical of a **chemical change** or **reaction**.

a mixture of reactants

chemical | reaction

the product is a compound

Another example of a chemical change is the reaction between sodium and chlorine:

sodium **+** chlorine ⟶ sodium chloride

 **+**

Sodium is a highly reactive, dangerous metal. Chlorine is a toxic gas.

Yet when they react together, they make something as harmless as sodium chloride.

You know sodium chloride better as common salt. So luckily its properties are very different from sodium or chlorine!

Sodium and chlorine were pretty wild when they were single. Now they've 'tied the bond', they're totally different!

22

Classifying changes

Chemical changes are very different from
the physical changes, such as melting, described on page 10.
Remember separating different mixtures on pages 18 and 19?
Were these physical changes or chemical changes?

Can you list some chemical changes in everyday life?
Which of these changes are useful and which are not?

Chemical change	Physical change
new substance(s) made	no new substances made
not easily reversed	easily reversed

In the next experiment you can try to classify
some changes for yourself:

*Is baking a cake a physical
change or a chemical change?*

Experiment 2.7   Physical and chemical changes

Heat each substance in a test-tube, gently at first.
If there is no sign of change, you can heat it
more strongly.

Observe carefully what happens as you are heating.
Record this and what is left after heating
in a table:

Substance tested	Observations	
	During heating	**After heating**
copper carbonate		
salol		
zinc oxide		
copper foil		
paraffin wax		
copper sulphate		
sand		

Your teacher might show you some other changes.
- Which changes do you think are physical changes?
- Do any substances show no signs of change?
- Which are chemical changes? Explain how you decided.

► Balancing equations

You are used to working with equations
in maths lessons.
You know that each side of an equation
must balance. They are equal.

It is the same in chemical equations.
The number of atoms on either side of
the equation must be equal. Remember that
no new atoms can be made or destroyed in
a chemical reaction.

mass of reactants = mass of products

▲

*A balanced equation. The same number and type
of atoms are on both sides of the equation.*

Let's look at an example.
Do you know the test for hydrogen gas?
A lighted splint 'pops'.

The hydrogen (H_2) reacts with oxygen molecules (O_2)
in the air.
They make the compound called water (H_2O).

Word equation: hydrogen   +   oxygen ⟶ water (hydrogen oxide)

Using formulas: H_2 + O_2 ⟶ H_2O

        left-hand side   right-hand side

✓

✗

But this equation is **not balanced.**

Counting atoms

If you count the atoms on either side of the equation,
they are not equal.

On the left-hand side (reactants):   we have two H atoms
                                     and two O's (from the O_2 molecule).
On the right-hand side (products):   we've got 2 H's (that's good),
                                     but only one O atom.

This can't be correct because you know that
an oxygen atom cannot just disappear in
the reaction.

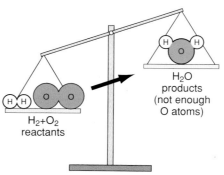

Not balanced

Get the balance right !

So how do you go about balancing the equation ?

Well, you need 1 more O atom
on the right-hand side.
Unfortunately, you can't simply change the
formula of water from H_2O to H_2O_2 !

But you can change the number of H_2O's
made in the reaction.
For each O_2 molecule, you can make **2** H_2O's
(because you start with 2 oxygen atoms).
Let's try that :

$$H_2 \ + \ O_2 \ \longrightarrow \ 2\,H_2O \qquad \text{✗}$$

This has now solved the oxygen problem.
You have 2 on each side.
Unfortunately, in doing this, you now
need 2 extra H's on the left-hand side.

But that's easy to put right :

$$2\,H_2 \ + \ O_2 \ \longrightarrow \ 2\,H_2O \qquad \text{✓}$$

This is the **balanced equation**.

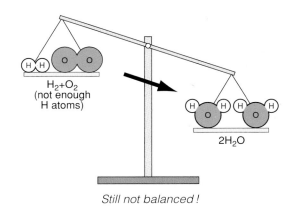

Still not balanced !

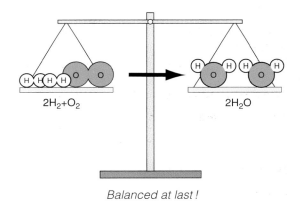

Balanced at last !

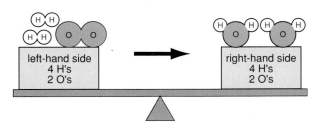

The equation reads : 2 hydrogen molecules plus 1 oxygen molecule
gives 2 molecules of water.

Remember you should **never change a formula** when
balancing an equation. You can only put numbers
in front of a formula.

- Now you can try to balance these equations.

    i) $H_2 \ + \ Cl_2 \ \longrightarrow \ HCl$

    ii) $Ca \ + \ O_2 \ \longrightarrow \ CaO$

    iii) $Na \ + \ Cl_2 \ \longrightarrow \ NaCl$

▶ State symbols

Sometimes we find it useful to add even more information to our equations. We can show the **state** of reactants and products. Remember that there are 3 states of matter – solid, liquid and gas. It is also useful to know if any substances in the equation are dissolved in water.

Chemists use a short-hand called state symbols to show these things:

		state symbol
solid	=	(s)
liquid	=	(l)
gas	=	(g)
solution (dissolved in water)	=	(aq)

(aq) comes from the Latin word for water, aqua.

*A balanced equation,
Now what shall we do?
I know, we'll put in state symbols too.*

*States of matter
there are three,
we'll show them by an s, l and g.*

Look at this equation with all 4 state symbols:

sodium + water $\longrightarrow$ sodium hydroxide + hydrogen
$2\,Na(s) + 2\,H_2O(l) \longrightarrow 2\,NaOH(aq) + H_2(g)$

It tells us that solid sodium reacts with liquid water. They form a solution of sodium hydroxide and hydrogen gas.

State symbols are also useful when substances in equations are not in their normal state at room temperature. For example,

$Mg(s) + H_2O(g) \longrightarrow MgO(s) + H_2(g)$

Which substance in the equation is not in its usual state? The state symbols tell us that the magnesium has reacted with steam. Notice that the H_2O in the equation is a gas, not a liquid.

*Dissolved in water?
Now this one is new.
I know!
It's shown by the letters aq!*

Summary

- All substances are made from tiny particles called **atoms**.
- Groups of 2 or more atoms chemically bonded together are called **molecules**.
- Some substances contain only one type of atom. These are **elements**. Elements can't be broken down into simpler substances.
- If a substance contains more than one type of atom, it is a **compound**. The different elements in a compound can't be separated easily (they are chemically bonded together), unlike the substances in a mixture.
- Chemical changes make new substances, but physical changes don't.
- We can show chemical changes (called reactions) by equations. We use either words or chemical symbols (and formulas).
- Symbol equations must be balanced. New atoms are not created or destroyed in a chemical reaction.
- State symbols – (s), (l), (g) or (aq) – can give us extra information about a reaction.

▷ Questions

1. Copy and complete:
   a) The smallest part of an element is called an ..... All the .... in an element are the same. Elements can't be broken down into .... substances.
   b) Atoms joined, or bonded, together chemically are called ..... If a substance is made from more than one type of atom, it is called a .....
   c) In a .... change, new substances are formed. However, no new substances are made in a .... change.

2. Look at this candle burning:

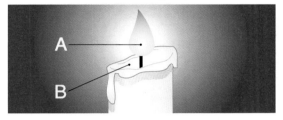

   Which label (A or B) shows a chemical change and which shows a physical change?
   Explain your answer.

3. Look at the boxes below:

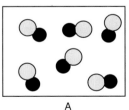
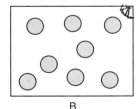

A   B

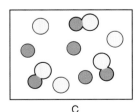
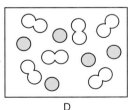

C   D

   Which box contains:
   a) one element
   b) a mixture of elements
   c) a pure compound
   d) a mixture of elements and a compound?
   What might be happening in this box?

4. Describe how you could separate and collect the first substance (in **bold**) from each mixture:
   a) **salt** and sand
   b) **iron filings** and sugar
   c) **water** and salt
   d) **sand** and sugar
   e) **blue dye** and red dye
   f) **ethanol (alcohol)** and water.

5. When 2 liquids don't mix, they are called **immiscible**. The liquids can be separated in a separating funnel, like the one shown here:

a separating funnel

   a) Draw the funnel, containing oil and water. How do you separate the two liquids?
   b) What is an emulsion?
   Look at these bottles and their labels:

   c) Which bottle contains an emulsion?
   d) Which substance is acting as an emulsifier (or emulsifying agent)?

6. Some rescue flares contain aluminium (Al) powder. It reacts with oxygen (O_2) in the air to form aluminium oxide (Al_2O_3) – a white solid.
   a) Is this a physical or a chemical change?
   b) Write a word equation for the change.
   c) Now write a balanced symbol equation. Include state symbols.

7. Balance these equations:
   a) $H_2 + F_2 \longrightarrow HF$
   b) $CaCO_3 + HCl \longrightarrow CaCl_2 + CO_2 + H_2O$
   c) $CH_4 + O_2 \longrightarrow CO_2 + H_2O$
   d) $NaNO_3 \longrightarrow NaNO_2 + O_2$

Further questions on page 38.

chapter 3

ATOMIC STRUCTURE

▶ History of the atom

The word atom comes from a Greek word meaning something which can't be split.
This fits in nicely with Dalton's ideas about atoms. However, as you probably already know, atoms can be split !

In the late 1800s and early 1900s, scientists had to think up new pictures of atoms to explain new observations.

For example, in 1897 J.J. Thomson put forward his 'plum pudding' theory. He thought atoms were balls of positive charge with tiny negative particles stuck inside. The negative particles were called **electrons**. He said they were like the currants in a bun or Christmas pudding.

This model explained Thomson's experiments with electricity very well. However, later experiments using radioactive particles needed a new picture. By 1915, scientists, like Ernest Rutherford and Niels Bohr, had developed a model that is still useful today.

400 BC	Democritus suggests that all things are made of particles (see page 8).
1805	John Dalton's atomic theory. Atoms of the same element are all alike. They combine to make compounds. (See Chapter 2.)
1897	J.J. Thomson finds the electron (see page 29).
1909	Ernest Rutherford discovers the proton (see page 29).
1911	Ernest Rutherford discovers the nucleus (see below).
1913	Niels Bohr suggests that electrons are found in shells around the nucleus (see page 30).
1932	James Chadwick proves that neutrons exist (see page 30).

▶ Inside the atom

There are 3 types of particle inside an atom. These are **protons**, **neutrons** and **electrons**.

The protons and neutrons are found squashed together in the middle of the atom.

The middle, called the **nucleus**, is incredibly small and dense.

The tiny electrons whizz around this nucleus.

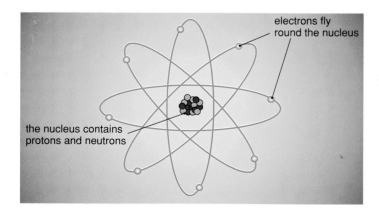

electrons fly round the nucleus

the nucleus contains protons and neutrons

This table shows the charge and mass of the particles in an atom.

Particle	Charge	Mass (in atomic mass units)
proton	1+	1
neutron	0	1
electron	1−	0 (almost)

Things to notice :

- protons and neutrons have the same mass.

- the electrons are so light that you can ignore their mass.
  In fact it takes almost 2000 electrons to weigh the same as a proton or a neutron.

- remember the charge on each particle like this :
  - **p**rotons are **p**ositive,
  - **neut**rons are **neut**ral,
  - (so electrons must be the negative ones).

Protons

*I'm Penny the **Proton** and I'm pretty large,
I'm considered a plus, with my **positive charge**.
My friends and I, **in the nucleus** we huddle,
It's nice and cosy **with neutrons** to cuddle!*

Neutrons

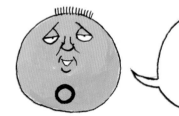

*I'm Ned the **Neutron** and I'm pretty **heavy**,
I'm fat and lazy and take things steady.
You could call me 'cheap' – I've **no charge** at all,
I really am just a dense, **neutral** ball!*

Electrons

*I'm Elvis the **Electron** and I'm pretty quick,
I fly round the nucleus at a fair old lick!
The protons and I, we tend to attract,
I'm **negative** you see and that's a fact!*

▷ Electron shells

The electrons in the atom are arranged in **shells** around the nucleus. The shells are sometimes called orbitals or energy levels.

The **first shell** (nearest to the nucleus) can hold just **2 electrons**.
The **second shell** can hold up to **8 electrons**.
The **third shell** can also hold **8 electrons**.

Electrons go round the nucleus in shells !

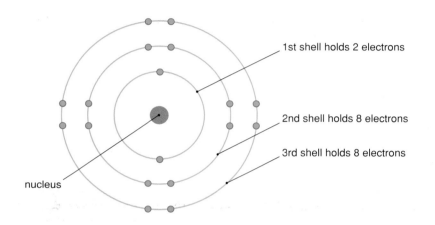

1st shell holds 2 electrons

2nd shell holds 8 electrons

3rd shell holds 8 electrons

nucleus

Filling the shells

The electrons start filling up the shells from the inner shell outwards. They like to get as close to the nucleus as possible.

You can see this from the examples below :

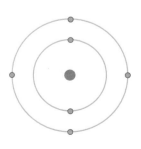

helium
(has 2 electrons)

carbon
(has 6 electrons)

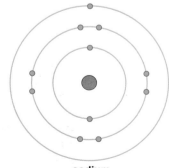

sodium
(has 11 electrons)

▷ Describing atoms

You don't need to draw pictures of
atoms every time. You can use a short-hand
called the **electronic structure**.
This just shows the number of electrons in each shell,
working outwards from the nucleus.

So the examples drawn on the previous page can be shown as:

helium   2   carbon   2, 4   sodium   2, 8, 1

- Can you write down the electronic structures of
  a) nitrogen (with 7 electrons)   b) neon (with 10 electrons)
  c) aluminium (with 13 electrons)   d) calcium (with 20 electrons – the last 2 electrons start filling
                                         the 4th shell)?

Atomic number (or proton number)

Each element has its own **atomic number**,
sometimes called the proton number.
It tells us how many protons there are in
one atom of that element.
(All the atoms of a particular element have
the same number of protons.)

| **Atomic number**   =   the number of protons (which is the same as the number of electrons) |

Atoms are neutral. The positive charges are cancelled out
by an equal number of negative charges.

So the number of protons (+) in an atom
must always equal the number of electrons (−).

Mass number

You already know that protons and
neutrons are the heavy particles which
make up an atom's mass.
The mass number tells us how many
of these protons and neutrons there
are in an atom.

| **Mass number**   =   the number of protons   +   the number of neutrons |

You can work out the number of
neutrons from this, as long as you know
the atomic number as well.

Number of neutrons   =   mass number − number of protons
                     =   mass number − atomic number

▶ Using atomic numbers and mass numbers

We can use the atomic number and mass number
to build up a complete picture of an atom.

Let's look at an example:

Example

Lithium's atomic number is 3. Its mass number is 7.
a) How many protons, neutrons and electrons are in a lithium atom ?
b) Draw a diagram of a lithium atom.

a) The atomic number = 3, so there are 3 protons and 3 electrons.
   The mass number = 7
   Therefore, 7 = number of protons + number of neutrons.
   We know there are 3 protons, so   7 = 3 + the number of neutrons.
   It follows that the number of neutrons must be 4.
   Or you might just remember:

   number of neutrons = mass number − atomic number
                       =   7   −   3
                       =   4
Answer : 3 protons, 3 electrons and 4 neutrons.

b)

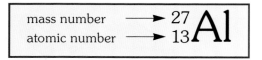

lithium   3 protons and
                 4 neutrons

More short-hand !

The atomic number and mass number can be
shown using chemical short-hand.
The information about lithium in the example above
can be shown as:

$$^{7}_{3}\text{Li}$$

The top number is the mass number.
The bottom number is the atomic number.

mass number ⟶	$^{27}_{13}\text{Al}$
atomic number ⟶	

- Can you work out the number of protons, neutrons and electrons in
  $^{16}_{8}\text{O}$, and $^{31}_{15}\text{P}$?   Now show how the electrons are arranged.

▶ Isotopes

There are often stories about nuclear power and
atomic weapons on television. So you might
have heard the phrase 'radioactive isotopes'.
But what is an **isotope**?

Some elements are made up of atoms with different masses. The
number of protons in atoms of the same element is always the same.
So isotopes must have *different numbers of neutrons.*

*These Easter eggs look the same, but
one is heavier. Why? (See below.)*

Let's look at this example:

Example

Carbon's atomic number is 6.
Most carbon atoms have a mass number of 12.
A few have a mass number of 14. Draw the two isotopes of carbon.

6 protons and
6 neutrons

6 protons and
8 neutrons

$^{12}_{6}$C

$^{14}_{6}$C

Two isotopes of carbon

You can see that the isotopes are exactly
the same, apart from their numbers of neutrons.

Isotopes of an element have the *same chemical reactions*.
This is because their electrons are arranged in exactly
the same way.
(Chemical reactions only involve electrons. The protons and
neutrons in the nucleus take no part in chemical reactions.)

*Isotopes are a bit like Easter eggs which have
the same chocolate shell, but different numbers
of sweets inside!*

Isotopes are sometimes written showing just
their mass numbers. In the example above
the isotopes can be written as carbon-12 and carbon-14.

**Isotopes are atoms with the same number of protons,
but different numbers of neutrons.**

- Can you find the number of protons, neutrons and
  electrons in these two isotopes of chlorine?

  $^{35}_{17}$Cl   and $^{37}_{17}$Cl

▷ Relative atomic mass (R.A.M.)

Each type of atom has a different mass.
However, the mass of an atom is too small to measure.
So we compare their masses on a scale which gives
the lightest element of all, hydrogen, a mass of 1.
This gives us a number called the **Relative Atomic Mass (R.A.M.)**,
sometimes given the symbol A_r.

Each element has a R.A.M. !

Let's look more closely at the hydrogen atom:
Hydrogen's atomic number is 1. Its mass number is also 1.
This means that a hydrogen atom has 1 proton, 1 electron,
but no neutrons.
You can see why it is so light!

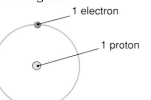

the hydrogen atom –

the lightest of
all atoms

1 electron

1 proton

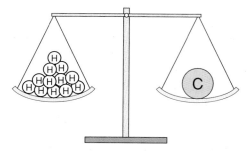

A carbon atom is 12 times as heavy as a hydrogen atom. Its R.A.M. is 12.

You might think that there is no point having
Relative Atomic Masses and mass numbers.
Both seem to tell us how heavy atoms are.
However, look at the R.A.M.s in the table opposite:

Do you notice anything strange?
Could you ever get a mass number that was not
a whole number? You can't have fractions of
protons or neutrons in atoms.

Element	R.A.M.
chlorine	35.5
copper	63.5
iron	55.8

In fact, the Relative Atomic Mass of an element
takes into account the element's **different isotopes**.
Some elements are found as mixtures of their isotopes.
The R.A.M. is their average mass, taking into account
the **different proportions** of each isotope in the natural mixture.

Example

On the last page, you worked out the difference between
chlorine-35 and chlorine-37 . (Chlorine-37 has 2 more
neutrons than chlorine-35.)
Any sample of chlorine gas is a mixture of the 2 isotopes –
75 % is chlorine-35 and 25 % is chlorine-37 .

So if you have 100 chlorine atoms, 75 will be chlorine-35 and
25 will be chlorine-37 .
We can work out the total mass of the 100 atoms
(relative to a hydrogen atom):
$(75 \times 35) + (25 \times 37) = 3550$
Therefore, the average mass (or Relative Atomic Mass) of chlorine
$= 3550 \div 100 = \underline{35.5}$

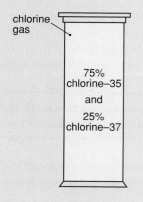

chlorine
gas

75%
chlorine–35

and

25%
chlorine–37

▷ Relative Formula Mass

Once you have a list of relative atomic masses,
you can work out the relative mass of any molecule.
You just need to know the chemical formula.

Let's look at carbon dioxide as an example:

The formula of carbon dioxide is CO_2.
It's molecules are made up of 1 carbon atom and 2 oxygen atoms.
The R.A.M. of carbon is 12.
The R.A.M. of oxygen is 16.

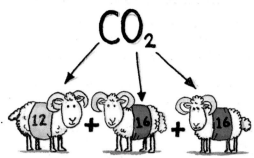

Add up the R.A.M.s to get the Relative Formula Mass

If we add up the R.A.M.s as in the formula,
we get the **relative formula mass (or molecular mass)**,
sometimes given the symbol M_r.
So for CO_2 we have:

1 carbon $= 1 \times 12 = 12$
2 oxygen $= 2 \times 16 = \underline{+32}$
44

Therefore the relative formula mass of carbon dioxide is 44.

How many times heavier than a hydrogen atom is
a molecule of carbon dioxide?

These masses are useful to chemists when
working out the masses of reactants and products
in chemical reactions. (See page 329.)

Now let's try a harder example:

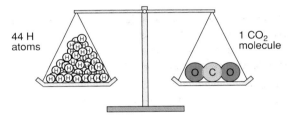

44 H atoms   1 CO_2 molecule

CO_2 is 44 times as heavy as one H atom.

Example

What is the relative formula mass (or molecular mass) of
aluminium sulphate, $Al_2(SO_4)_3$?
(R.A.M.s: $Al = 27$, $S = 32$, $O = 16$)

Sometimes a formula has a number outside a pair of brackets.
This tells us that all the atoms inside the brackets
are multiplied by the number outside.
So in aluminium sulphate, we have:
2 aluminiums, 3 sulphurs and 12 oxygens.

Now let's add up their R.A.M.s to get the answer:

2 Al $= 2 \times 27 = 54$
3 S $ = 3 \times 32 = 96$
12 O $= 12 \times 16 = \underline{+192}$
342

Therefore the relative formula mass of aluminium sulphate is 342.

Formula masses help us to do calculations (see pages 223 and 311).

Summary

- Atoms contain **protons**, **neutrons** and **electrons**.
- Protons are positively charged. Electrons are negatively charged.
  Neutrons have no charge. They are neutral.
- Protons and neutrons are the heavy particles in an atom.
  They each have a mass of 1 atomic mass unit, and are found in the **nucleus** (centre) of an atom.
  We can ignore the tiny mass of the electrons.
- The electrons orbit the nucleus in shells.
  The 1st shell can hold 2 electrons
  The 2nd shell can hold 8 electrons, as can the 3rd shell.
- The **atomic number** = the number of protons (which equals the number of electrons).
- The **mass number** = the number of protons + the number of neutrons.
- Isotopes are atoms with the same number of protons, but different numbers of neutrons.

▶ Questions

1. Copy and complete:
   There are 3 types of particle found inside
   atoms: a) ...., b) .... and c) .....
   This table shows their mass and charge:

Sub-atomic particle	Charge	Mass (atomic mass units)
proton	....	....
....	0	1
....	....	0 (almost)

   The protons and neutrons are found in the ....
   of the atom, called the nucleus.
   The .... zoom around the nucleus in shells.
   The 1st shell, which is .... the nucleus, can
   hold .... electrons, whereas the 2nd and 3rd
   shells can hold .... electrons.

2. a) What is the **atomic number** of an atom?
   b) What is the **mass number** of an atom?
   c) What is the atomic number of the atom below?
      What is its mass number?

   $$^{40}_{18}Ar$$

3. Give the numbers of protons, electrons and
   neutrons in the atoms below:
   a) $^{14}_{7}N$ b) $^{20}_{10}Ne$ c) $^{19}_{9}F$
   d) $^{39}_{19}K$ e) $^{60}_{27}Co$ f) $^{235}_{92}U$

4. Draw fully labelled diagrams of the atoms below:
   a) $^{4}_{2}He$ b) $^{9}_{4}Be$ c) $^{27}_{13}Al$ d) $^{40}_{20}Ca$

5. Copy this table and fill in the gaps.
   Use Table 1 on pages 342 and 343 to help you.

Element	Atomic number	Electronic structure
lithium	....	2, 1
....	14	....
....	19	....

   Do you have to look up the atomic number of
   lithium, given the information in the table above?
   Explain your answer.

6. Hydrogen (atomic number 1) has 3 isotopes.
   They can be shown as $^{1}_{1}H$, $^{2}_{1}H$ and $^{3}_{1}H$.
   a) What are **isotopes**?
   b) What is the difference between the 3 isotopes?
   c) Hydrogen reacts with chlorine in sunlight,
      forming hydrogen chloride:
      $$H_2 + Cl_2 \longrightarrow 2\,HCl$$
      Would you expect the same reaction for each
      isotope of hydrogen? Why?
   d) Chlorine exists naturally as 2 isotopes.
      75 % is $^{35}_{17}Cl$, and 25 % is $^{37}_{17}Cl$.
      Show why the relative atomic mass of
      chlorine is 35.5.
   e) The element chlorine is a gas. Its formula is
      Cl_2. How many different masses of the Cl_2
      molecule would you expect to find in a
      sample of chlorine gas? Explain your answer.

7. Work out the relative formula mass of:
   a) H_2O b) C_2H_5OH c) Na_2SO_4
   (R.A.M.s: H = 1, O = 16, C = 12, Na = 23,
   S = 32)

Further questions on page 40.

▶ States of matter

1. Use some of these words to complete the following sentences.

water	melts	sublimes
gas	evaporates	condenses
liquid	solid	

a) When ice is heated it .... to form water.
b) Steam is a ....
c) Ice is a .... [3] (ULEAC)

2. Use the following words to label the changes a) to d) below:

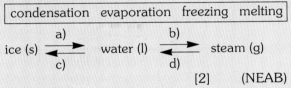

condensation evaporation freezing melting

a)
ice (s) ⇌ water (l) b)
⇌ steam (g)
c)   d)
[2] (NEAB)

3. Mary has some calcium carbonate and water in a bottle. The calcium carbonate does not dissolve in the water.
The arrangement of calcium carbonate particles is shown below. Draw diagrams to show the arrangement of particles in air and water. [4]

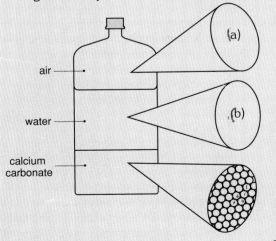

air
water
calcium carbonate

(a)
(b)

c) Why is it easier to compress air than water ?
[1] (MEG)

4. a) The following experiment was set up:

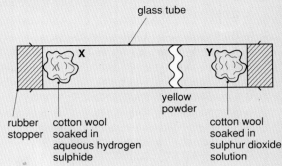

glass tube
X
Y
yellow powder
rubber stopper   cotton wool soaked in aqueous hydrogen sulphide   cotton wool soaked in sulphur dioxide solution

At **X** hydrogen sulphide gas is released.
At **Y** sulphur dioxide gas is released.
The yellow powder formed where the gases met.
  i) Which particles travelled the fastest ? [1]
  ii) Describe the path you would expect a hydrogen sulphide particle to follow down the tube. [1]
  iii) What would happen if the experiment was repeated at a higher temperature ? [1]
  iv) What scientific principle does the experiment demonstrate ? [1]

b) A biologist named Brown noticed that when he examined tiny particles of pollen floating on water under a microscope, the particles moved around in a haphazard fashion.
When the pollen was examined on its own no movement was observed.
Explain these observations. [2] (WJEC)

5. a) A pure substance was melted and then allowed to cool. The temperature of the substance was measured every minute as it cooled down. The results are given in the table below.

Time (min)	0	1	2	3	4	5	6	7	8
Temperature (°C)	75	59	55	55	55	55	53	50	47

  i) Plot a graph of temperature against time. [3]
  ii) What is the melting point of the substance ? [1]
b) Explain in terms of particles what happens when the substance is heated until it melts. [4] (ULEAC)

Further questions on classifying materials

▷ Elements, mixtures and compounds

6. In the boxes below different atoms are represented by ● and ○

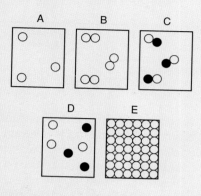

Match the letter on the box to the following descriptions :
a) a mixture of gases
b) a solid
c) a gaseous compound
d) oxygen (O_2)
e) a pure gas made up of single atoms.
[5]   (WJEC)

7. The list below contains three elements and three compounds.

aluminium	copper
ammonia	sulphur
carbon dioxide	water

Say which are elements and which are compounds.   [3]   (NEAB)

8. Choose words from this list to complete the sentences below.

hundreds	tens
millions	thirty
ninety	twenty

There are about . . . . naturally occurring elements.
From these elements . . . . of different substances are made.   [2]   (NEAB)

9. Iron is a metal and sulphur is a non-metal. Explain why it is easier to separate iron from a mixture of iron and sulphur than from a compound of iron and sulphur.
[2]   (SEG)

10. The fertiliser a farmer uses is based on ammonium nitrate (NH_4NO_3).
Is this substance an element or a compound ? Explain your answer.   [2]   (NEAB)

11. Four test tubes contain different substances as shown in the diagram.

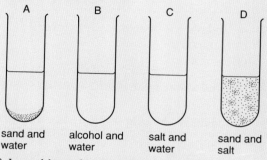

a) I would use filtration to separate the substances in tube . . . .   [1]
b) I would use **simple** distillation to separate the substances in tube . . . .   [1]   (NEAB)

12. Choose **from the list** the most suitable method for each of the following separations:

chromatography	dissolving
distillation	evaporation
filtration	fractional distillation

a) To separate the mixture of liquids in crude oil.
b) To obtain some solid salt from a solution of salt in water.
c) To separate a mixture of different coloured inks.
d) To obtain a sample of pure water from some tap water.   [4]   (NEAB)

13. Two bottles have been accidentally knocked off a store room shelf. The two white powders were collected and the broken glass removed. Both chemicals are expensive so it is worth separating them. One, silver nitrate, is soluble in water. The other, silver chloride, is insoluble in water. Describe how you would obtain dry samples of each chemical from the mixture.
[5]   (WJEC)

14. J, K, L, M and **N** are five food colourings. The dyes in these food colourings are separated by chromatography. This chromatogram shows the results.

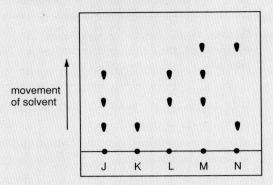

The food colouring **J could be** a mixture of
A   K and L
B   K and M
C   K and N
D   L and N   [1]   (SEG)

15. The figure shows laboratory apparatus which can be used to produce almost pure alcohol from a mixture of alcohol and water.

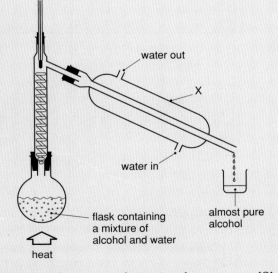

a) Name the process being used.   [2]
b) What does part X do ?   [1]
c) What will be left in the flask at the end of the process ?   [1]
                                    (ULEAC)

16. A student was investigating the ink in a felt tip pen. The diagram shows the chromatogram he made.

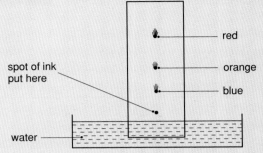

What does this experiment tell him about this ink ?   [2]   (NEAB)

17. Which one of the following is an example of a chemical change ?
A   Separating iron from sulphur with a magnet
B   Filtering copper from sodium chloride solution
C   Heating ice to form water
D   Frying an egg.   [1]   (SEG)

18. a) Balance these chemical equations.
   i) $H_2 +$ $O_2 \longrightarrow$ H_2O [1]
   ii) $Al +$ $O_2 \longrightarrow$ Al_2O_3 [1]
b) Briefly explain why an unbalanced chemical equation cannot fully describe a reaction.
                              [2]   (NEAB)

19. The reaction between sodium and water may be represented by the following equation :

$$2Na(s) + 2H_2O(l) \longrightarrow 2NaOH(aq) + H_2(g)$$

Write down the meaning of **each** of the state symbols in brackets above.   [2]   (WJEC)

20. Which one of the following chemical equations is correctly balanced ?
A $Fe_3O_4 + 2H_2 \longrightarrow 3Fe + 2H_2O$
B $H_2O \longrightarrow H_2 + O_2$
C $H_2O_2 \longrightarrow H_2O + O_2$
D $Mg(OH)_2 \longrightarrow MgO + H_2O$
E $2Na + H_2O \longrightarrow 2NaOH + H_2$
                              [1]   (MEG)

▷ Atomic structure

21.

Element	Atomic number	Mass number
Oxygen	8	16
Chlorine	17	35
Gallium	31	70
Zinc	30	65
Tungsten	74	184

Use the table above, where necessary, to help you to answer these questions.
a) How many protons would you expect to find in an atom of oxygen ?
b) Where in the atom would the protons be found ?
c) How many neutrons would you expect to find in an atom of zinc ?
d) Which element in the table above has atoms which contain the same number of protons as neutrons ?   [4]   (ULEAC)

22. Copy the table below and fill in the missing numbers.

Element symbol	Proton number (Atomic number)	Mass number	Number of protons	Number of neutrons	Electron arrangement
He	2	a)	2	2	2
Na	11	23	11	b)	2,8,1
P	15	31	c)	d)	2,8,5
Ca	e)	40	20	20	f)
Cl	17	37	17	g)	h)

[8]   (WJEC)

23. a) The element argon exists as single atoms. Use the information from the Periodic Table on page 344 to find the number of protons, neutrons and electrons in an argon atom.   [3]
b) Draw a diagram to show how the electrons are arranged in an atom of argon.   [1]
(ULEAC)

24. Give the information required below for an atom of the chlorine isotope $^{35}_{17}Cl$.
a) Number of protons
b) Number of neutrons
c) Number of electrons
d) Electron structure   [4]   (ULEAC)

25. Use the information given about a sodium atom to complete the table.

mass number $^{23}_{11}Na$
proton (atomic) number

In one atom of sodium	the number of protons is	a)
	the number of neutrons is	b)
	the number of electrons is	c)

[3]   (NEAB)

26. a) A diagram of the nucleus of an atom is shown below.

8p
8n

i) Draw a diagram to show the electronic arrangement of this atom.   [1]
ii) What is the mass number (nucleon number) of this atom ?   [1]
b) Copy and complete the table shown below.

Name	Relative charge	Relative mass
proton	i)	1
ii)	zero (0)	iii)
electron	negative (-ve)	$\frac{1}{1840}$

[3]   (SEG)

27. $^{222}_{86}Rn$ is an isotope of the noble gas radon. How many protons, neutrons and electrons are there in one atom of the radon isotope $^{222}_{86}Rn$?   [3]   (ULEAC)

28. Which two particles **W, X, Y** and **Z** represent different isotopes of the same element ?

	Number in one particle		
Particles	Protons	Neutrons	Electrons
W	1	1	1
X	1	2	1
Y	9	10	9
Z	9	10	10

[1]   (SEG)

29. Refer to the Periodic Table of elements on page 344 and draw the electronic arrangement in an aluminium atom and an oxygen atom.

[6] (NEAB)

30. Three isotopes of hydrogen are shown in the diagram:

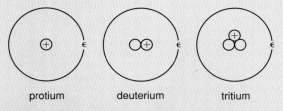

| protium | deuterium | tritium |

Which of these symbols best represents protium ?

A $^1_1$H   **B** $^2_1$H

C $^3_1$H   **D** $^2_2$H   [1]   (SEG)

31. Two isotopes of iron are ^{56}Fe and ^{59}Fe. Copy and complete the following table by putting in the missing numbers.

Isotope	Mass number	Number of protons	Number of neutrons
^{56}Fe	56	26	a)
^{59}Fe	59	b)	c)

[3]   (WJEC)

32. The two carbon atoms represented below are isotopes.

ISOTOPE 1   **ISOTOPE 2**

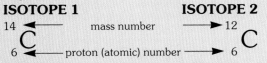

14 ← mass number → 12

C   C

6 ← proton (atomic) number → 6

The atoms of both isotopes have six protons.
a) Describe **one other** way in which the isotopes are similar. [1]
b) Describe **two** ways in which they are different. [2]   (NEAB)

33. a) The formula for ammonia is NH_3. What does the formula tell you about each molecule of ammonia ? [3]
b) Ammonia is used to make nitric acid (HNO_3). Calculate the formula mass (M_r) for nitric acid. (Show your working.)
($H = 1$, $N = 14$, $O = 16$) [3]   (NEAB)

34. Look at the table.
It gives some relative atomic masses (A_r).

Atomic symbol	Relative Atomic Mass (A_r)
H	1
O	16
S	32
Zn	65

Sulphuric acid has the formula, H_2SO_4.
It has a relative formula mass (M_r) of 98.
Zinc sulphate has the formula $ZnSO_4$.
Work out its relative formula mass (M_r). [2]
(MEG)

35. Look at the table.

Substance	Formula	Relative Formula Mass (M_r)
decane	$C_{10}H_{22}$	142
ethene	C_2H_4	
octane	C_8H_{18}	

The relative atomic mass (A_r) of hydrogen is 1 and the relative atomic mass of carbon is 12. Work out the relative formula mass (M_r) of ethene and octane. [2]   (MEG)

36. Boron is a non-metallic element.
The table shows information about two types of boron atom.

atom	symbol	protons	electrons	neutrons
boron–10	$^{10}_5$B			5
boron–11	$^{11}_5$B			

a) Copy and complete the table. [3]
b) The relative atomic mass of boron measured precisely is 10.82. What does this tell you about the relative amounts of the two different boron atoms in a sample of boron ? (No calculation required.) [1]
c) What is the electron arrangement in a boron atom ? [1]   (MEG)

chapter 4

The Periodic Table

Sorting out the elements

Scientists like to find patterns.
Around 200 years ago, scientists were discovering lots of new elements. However, they struggled to find any links between the different elements.

Look at the picture opposite :

At the time, some substances, which were thought to be elements, were in fact compounds.
Other elements had not yet been discovered.
No wonder finding a pattern was tricky !

Finding the pattern

Real progress was made around 1865
by John Newlands.
He put the elements in order of their atomic mass.
He found that every eighth element was similar.

Unfortunately, his pattern only worked for the first 15 elements known at that time. After that, he could see no links between the rest of the elements.
Other scientists made fun of his ideas. They suggested that he could have done better by sorting the elements into alphabetical order !

In 1869 the problem was solved by a Russian called Dmitri Mendeleev.
He also tried putting the elements in order of their atomic mass.

He made a table of elements.
New rows were started so that elements which were alike could line up together in columns.
He wanted a table of regular (periodic) patterns.

However, Dmitri was not afraid to take risks.
When the pattern began to go wrong, he would leave a gap in his table. He claimed that these gaps were for elements that had not yet been discovered.
He even changed the order round when similar elements didn't line up.

As you might expect, people doubted his 'Periodic Table'.
However, he used his table to predict the properties of elements which could fill the gaps.
In 1886, the element germanium was discovered.
The new element matched Dmitri's predictions.
Finally other scientists accepted his ideas.

How would you like to do a jig-saw with no picture to work from ? Some pieces are missing and others don't belong in this jigsaw ! This was the state of chemistry at the start of the 1800s.

Dmitri was a chemistry teacher in Russia !

▶ The Periodic Table

Although Mendeleev's table was accepted, there was
one thing that he could not explain.
Why did he sometimes need to change the order of
atomic masses to make the pattern carry on?
The answer lies inside the atoms. The atoms of elements
in the Periodic Table are not arranged in order of mass.
It is their number of protons (atomic number)
which really matters.

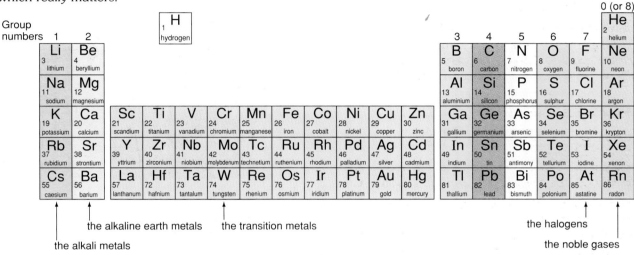

the alkaline earth metals   the transition metals

the alkali metals

the halogens

the noble gases

*Each colour shows a chemical family of similar elements.
You can see the full Periodic Table on page 344*

Groups

There are 8 groups in the Periodic Table.
A group is a **vertical column**.
All the elements in a group have similar properties.
They are a 'chemical family'.

Look at the Periodic Table above:
Some groups have special 'family' names.
Can you find Group 7? What is the group called?
Have you met any elements from this 'family' before?
Other groups are just known by their group number.
Notice that the transition metals form a block on their own.

*Groups are families of elements. The members of
the family are similar but not exactly the same.*

Periods

Periods are the **rows across** the Periodic Table.
You read the table like a book. Start at the top,
and work your way down, reading from left to right.
So there are 2 elements in the 1st period, H and He.
The 2nd period has 8 elements, starting with Li.
Which is the last element in the 2nd period?
Can you count how many elements are in the 3rd period?

> *Example*
>
> **C** is in Group 4.
> It is in the 2nd period.
> **Al** is in Group 3.
> It is in the 3rd period.

▶ Metal and non-metal elements

92 elements are found naturally on Earth.
Most can be sorted into 2 sets –
the **metals** and the **non-metals**.
Let's look at their properties.

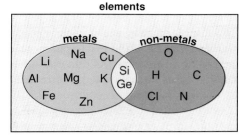

Most of the elements are metals. There are
about 20 non-metals. A few elements, like
silicon, are called semi-metals or metalloids.

Metals

Over three quarters of the elements are metals.
The experiments below show us some typical
properties of metals.

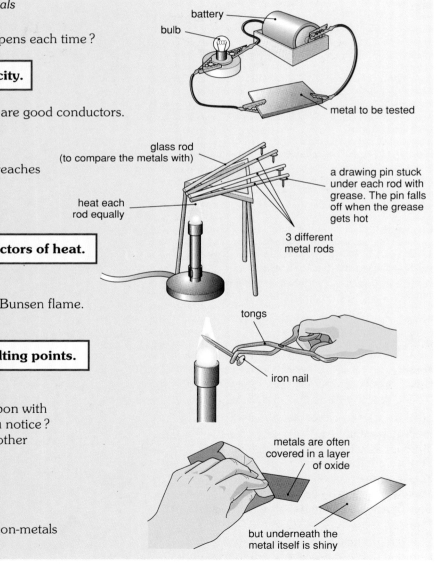

Experiment 4.1   Looking at metals

1. Set up this circuit:
   Try different metals. What happens each time?

   All metals conduct electricity.

   Page 256 explains why metals are good conductors.

2. Set up this apparatus:
   What happens when the heat reaches
   the end of the rod?
   How can you tell which metal
   is the best conductor of heat?

   All metals are good conductors of heat.

3. Heat an iron nail strongly in a Bunsen flame.
   Does the iron melt?

   Most metals have high melting points.

4. Rub a piece of magnesium ribbon with
   some sand-paper. What do you notice?
   Do the same thing with some other
   'tarnished' metals.

   All metals are shiny.

The properties of metals and non-metals
are shown on the next page.

Properties of metals

All the properties shown below are **physical properties**.
They describe the metal itself, not its chemical reactions.
Metals are important in all our lives. Can you think of
a use to match each property shown below?

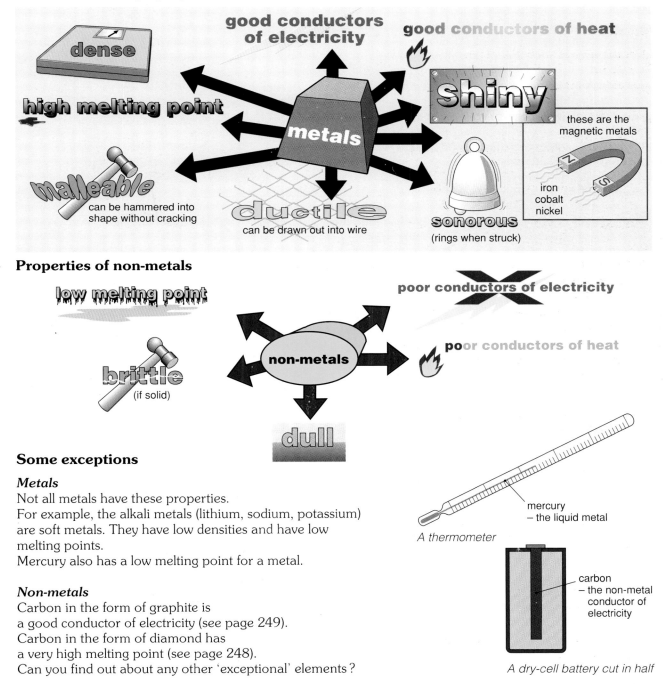

dense

good conductors of electricity

good conductors of heat

high melting point

shiny

malleable
can be hammered into
shape without cracking

ductile
can be drawn out into wire

sonorous
(rings when struck)

these are the
magnetic metals

iron
cobalt
nickel

Properties of non-metals

low melting point

poor conductors of electricity

non-metals

poor conductors of heat

brittle
(if solid)

dull

Some exceptions

Metals
Not all metals have these properties.
For example, the alkali metals (lithium, sodium, potassium)
are soft metals. They have low densities and have low
melting points.
Mercury also has a low melting point for a metal.

Non-metals
Carbon in the form of graphite is
a good conductor of electricity (see page 249).
Carbon in the form of diamond has
a very high melting point (see page 248).
Can you find out about any other 'exceptional' elements?

mercury
– the liquid metal

A thermometer

carbon
– the non-metal
conductor of
electricity

A dry-cell battery cut in half

► Oxides of metals and non-metals

You have seen the physical properties of metals and non-metals. Now let's look at some **chemical properties**. The chemical properties of a substance describe its reactions.

We can make oxides by reacting elements with oxygen.

Experiment 4.2   Burning elements in oxygen
Collect 4 large test-tubes of oxygen gas.

Use tongs or a combustion spoon to heat your element in a Bunsen flame.
Then plunge it into one of your tubes of oxygen gas.
When the reaction has finished, add a few drops of universal indicator solution.
Then shake the tube gently.
(See page 141 to revise pH.)

Record your results in a table:

- Which oxide is slightly alkaline?
- Which oxides are acidic?

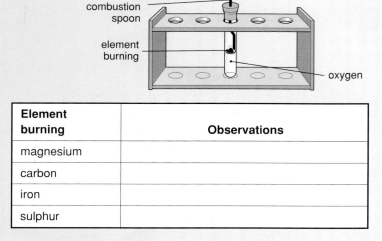

⚠️ burning magnesium
sulphur dioxide gas (fume cupboard)

Element burning	Observations
magnesium	
carbon	
iron	
sulphur	

The elements burn more fiercely in pure oxygen than in air. This is because only about 20 % of the air is made up of oxygen.

Metals burning

The metal oxides made are solids. For example,

magnesium + oxygen ⟶ magnesium oxide
$$2\,Mg(s) \ + \ O_2(g) \ \longrightarrow \ 2\,MgO(s)$$

- Can you write the word equation for iron reacting with oxygen?

Non-metals burning

When non-metals burn, their oxides are often gases. For example,

carbon + oxygen ⟶ carbon dioxide
$$C(s) \ + \ O_2(g) \ \longrightarrow \ CO_2(g)$$

- Try to write the word and symbol equations for sulphur reacting with oxygen.
  (The product is sulphur dioxide gas. Its formula is SO_2.)

Sparks fly when iron reacts with oxygen. The metal gets oxidised.

Sulphur dioxide and carbon dioxide cause pollution. Find out how they are formed and the pollution they cause. (See pages 178 and 179.)

Basic and acidic oxides

In the next experiment, you can test
the pH of more oxides.
The oxides have been dissolved in water for you.

Experiment 4.3   Testing the pH of oxides

Collect 2 cm^3 of each oxide solution in separate test-tubes.

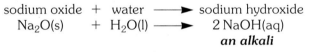 acid and alkali

Add 3 drops of universal indicator solution to each oxide solution.
Record your results in a table like the one below:

Oxide	Colour of universal indicator	pH number	Acid, alkali or neutral ?
nitrogen oxide sodium oxide potassium oxide phosphorus oxide calcium oxide			

- Which compounds in the table are metal oxides?
- What do you notice about your results for the metal oxides?
- What can you say about your results for the non-metal oxides?

Metal oxides

If a metal oxide dissolves in water, it makes
an alkaline solution. For example,

sodium oxide + water $\longrightarrow$ sodium hydroxide
$\quad$ Na$_2$O(s) $\quad$ + H$_2$O(l) $\longrightarrow$ $\quad$ 2 NaOH(aq)
$\qquad\qquad\qquad\qquad\qquad$ ***an alkali***

Some metal oxides do not dissolve in water.
Iron oxide is insoluble. These metal oxides test neutral
with universal indicator.
However, they do react with acid.
Insoluble metal oxides are called **bases**.
Look at the diagram opposite:
Another common base is copper oxide (see page 144).

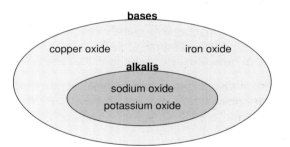

All metal oxides are bases.
The soluble ones are alkalis.

Non-metal oxides

Most non-metal oxides dissolve in water to form **acids**. For example,

carbon dioxide + water $\longrightarrow$ carbonic acid
$\quad$ CO$_2$(g) $\qquad$ + H$_2$O(l) $\longrightarrow$ $\quad$ H$_2$CO$_3$(aq)

One exception is the oxide of hydrogen.
What do we call this oxide? What is its pH?
However, ***in general*** we can say:

> **Metal oxides are basic. Non-metal oxides are acidic.**

► Metals, non-metals and the Periodic Table

As you know from page 43, the Periodic Table has 8 groups, or families, of elements. Groups 1 and 2 are all metals, whereas Groups 7 and 0 contain only non-metals.

However, the elements in the middle groups start with non-metals at the top, but finish with metals at the bottom.

For example, look at Group 4 :

C	carbon		non-metal
Si	silicon	}	silicon and germanium are called **semi-metals** or **metalloids**. They are on the borderline between metals and non-metals
Ge	germanium		
Sn	tin		metal
Pb	lead		metal

Silicon is a semi-metal

Silicon is the most well-known semi-metal.
It behaves like a metal in some ways,
but like a non-metal in others. For example,
it is shiny like a metal, but brittle like a non-metal.
Tin oxide reacts like a metal oxide, but also
reacts like a non-metal oxide !
It is an **amphoteric** oxide (behaves like an acid and a base).

This shows us that science is not always 'black and white'.
The semi-metals are a 'grey' area.
However, we can draw an imaginary line
in the Periodic Table to divide the metals and non-metals.
You can think of the line as a staircase.
Below stairs you find metals, above stairs you find non-metals.

Silicon is used in the micro-electronic industry. The silicon chip has made it possible to make circuits incredibly small.

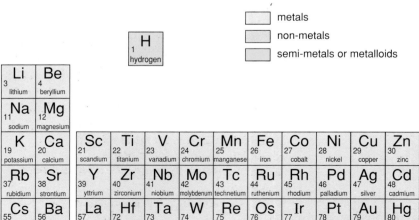

metals

non-metals

semi-metals or metalloids

Summary

- The **Periodic Table** arranges the elements in order of atomic number.
- Elements with similar properties line up in vertical columns. These columns are called **groups**.
- There are 8 groups in the Periodic Table.
- A row across the Periodic Table is called a **period**.
- The elements can be divided into **metals** and **non-metals** (with a few semi-metals or metalloids in between).
- Metals are good conductors of heat and electricity. They are shiny, malleable (can be hammered into shapes) and ductile (can be drawn out into wires). Most are hard, dense and have high melting points.
- Iron, cobalt and nickel are the magnetic metals.
- Most non-metals are gases. They have low melting and boiling points. They are poor conductors of heat and electricity. If solid, they are usually dull and brittle.
- In general, metal oxides are **basic**. Non-metal oxides are usually **acidic**.

► Questions

1. Copy and complete:
The elements line up in order of atomic . . . . in the Periodic Table. There are . . . . groups. The elements in each group have . . . . properties. Groups form v _ _ _ _ _ _ _ columns, whereas periods are h _ _ _ _ _ _ _ _ _ rows. Most of the elements can be divided into 2 sets – the . . . . and the non-metals. In general, metal oxides are . . . . , and non-metal oxides are . . . . .

2. Copy and complete this table:

Property	Typical metal	Typical non-metal
conducts electricity ?	Yes	No
conducts heat ?		
dull ?		
low melting point ?		
malleable ?		
ductile ?		

3. Not all metals and non-metals have the properties listed in question 2.
Can you name some exceptions and say why they are unusual ?

4. Yasha and Eric tested solutions of some unknown oxides. Look at their results:

Unknown oxide	pH of solution
A	10
B	2
C	1
D	7

D did not dissolve in water, but did dissolve in dilute acid.
a) Which are the oxides of non-metals ? How can you tell ?
b) Which metal oxide is an alkali and which is a base ? Explain your answer.

5. The numbers in this Periodic Table represent elements.

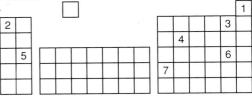

a) Which 2 elements are in the same group ? Give the name and number of this group.
b) Which elements are in the 2nd period ?
c) Which elements are metals ?
d) Which group is element 7 in ? Which period is it in ?
e) Which element is a semi-metal (or metalloid) ?

Further questions on page 71.

chapter 5

Groups of Metals

▶ Group 1 – The alkali metals

The elements in this first group don't have many uses
as the metals themselves. They are too reactive.
However, you will certainly use some of their compounds
every day.
You can read about these on pages 52, 53 and 118.

Li	lithium
Na	sodium
K	potassium
Rb	rubidium
Cs	caesium

You will find the elements in Group 1
an exciting bunch!
They are metals, but they have some very
unusual properties.
You can see for yourself below:

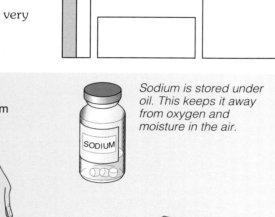

Demonstration 5.1   Looking at sodium

Your teacher will show you a piece of sodium.
What is it stored under? Why?
Does the sodium look like a metal?

⚠ sodium

Sodium is stored under oil. This keeps it away from oxygen and moisture in the air.

SODIUM

Your teacher will cut a piece of sodium with a knife.
• How soft is it? What does it look like inside?
• Is this more like a metal now?

Your teacher will warm a small piece of sodium
gently on a combustion spoon.
• How easily does sodium melt?

sodium melts
at 98 °C

shiny surface

*Sodium can be cut with a knife.
Its like cutting a piece of cheese.*

Now you can see why sodium, and the other
alkali metals, are unusual metals. They have
low melting points and are *very soft*.
For metals, they also have very *low densities*.
You will see in the next experiment that
lithium, sodium and potassium float on water!

Help!

The alkali metals can be cut with a knife

Look at the table opposite:
• Can you see a pattern going down the group?
• Can you predict the melting point of caesium?

Typical metals have much higher melting points.
For example, iron melts at 1540 °C.

Alkali metal	Atomic number	Melting point (°C)
lithium	3	180
sodium	11	98
potassium	19	63
rubidium	37	39
caesium	55	

Reactions of the alkali metals

The alkali metals are the most reactive group of metals in the Periodic Table. They are too dangerous for you to use in experiments. However, your teacher can show you some reactions of lithium, sodium and potassium.

Demonstration 5.2   Lithium with water

Your teacher will drop a small piece of lithium into a trough of water. What do you see happen?
The gas given off can be collected as shown:
Test the gas with a lighted splint.

- Which gas is given off?

Now add a little universal indicator solution to the trough.

- Is the solution left acidic or alkaline?

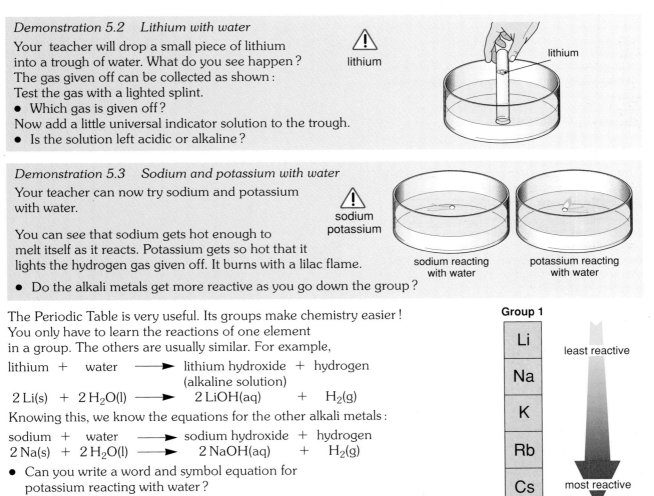

lithium

lithium

Demonstration 5.3   Sodium and potassium with water

Your teacher can now try sodium and potassium with water.

You can see that sodium gets hot enough to melt itself as it reacts. Potassium gets so hot that it lights the hydrogen gas given off. It burns with a lilac flame.

sodium
potassium

sodium reacting with water

potassium reacting with water

- Do the alkali metals get more reactive as you go down the group?

The Periodic Table is very useful. Its groups make chemistry easier! You only have to learn the reactions of one element in a group. The others are usually similar. For example,

lithium + water $\longrightarrow$ lithium hydroxide + hydrogen
(alkaline solution)

$2\,Li(s)\ +\ 2\,H_2O(l) \longrightarrow\ 2\,LiOH(aq)\ +\ H_2(g)$

Knowing this, we know the equations for the other alkali metals:

sodium + water $\longrightarrow$ sodium hydroxide + hydrogen
$2\,Na(s)\ +\ 2\,H_2O(l) \longrightarrow\ 2\,NaOH(aq)\ +\ H_2(g)$

- Can you write a word and symbol equation for potassium reacting with water?

Group 1

| Li |
| Na |
| K |
| Rb |
| Cs |

least reactive

most reactive

This pattern is explained on page 69

> **The alkali metals get more reactive as you go down the group.**

Other reactions

The alkali metals react well with non-metals. For example,

lithium + oxygen $\longrightarrow$ lithium oxide
$4\,Li(s)\ +\ O_2(g) \longrightarrow\ 2\,Li_2O(s)$

sodium + chlorine $\longrightarrow$ sodium chloride
$2\,Na(s)\ +\ Cl_2(g) \longrightarrow\ 2\,NaCl(s)$

► Chemistry at work : Group 1 metals and their compounds

Lithium

Lithium gets its name from the Greek word for 'stone'.
As the metal itself, we use it to strengthen other metals, such as magnesium, in alloys (see page 259).
It is also used in batteries.
Lithium batteries are powerful and lightweight.
In fact you might be nearer than you think to a lithium battery now!
They are suitable for calculators, watches and cameras.
They are also used in heart pace-makers.

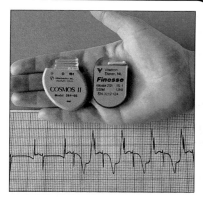

Lithium batteries are used in heart pace-makers.

Lithium compounds

Lithium compounds have been used more and more since the Second World War.
Look at the diagram below.
It shows many of their uses today:

medicine
(lithium carbonate is used to treat mental illness)

kill germs
(lithium hypochlorite kills germs in swimming pools and in hospital laundries)

glass
(lithium carbonate is used in making tubes inside TV's and for lenses which darken in sunlight)

lithium compounds

ceramics
(lithium oxide is added to ceramics, from oven-ware to the nose cones of rockets)

dyes
(lithium hydroxide helps to dye nylon and paper)

YELLOW PAGES

air conditioning
(lithium hydroxide is used in air conditioning systems and on submarines to remove carbon dioxide)

Potassium compounds

Potassium is essential for the healthy growth of plants.
Potassium nitrate is used as a fertiliser. It is also used in making explosives and fireworks (see page 183).

▶ Chemistry at work: Group 1 metals and their compounds

Sodium

The element sodium is used in street lamps
and in nuclear reactors.
You can read about the uses of sodium on page 118.

Sodium compounds

The two most important sodium compounds are
sodium chloride and sodium hydroxide. Their uses
are covered in Chapter 10.

Food additives

Do you eat cereal for your breakfast? If you do,
have you ever read the box?
You will almost certainly find some sodium compounds
in the list of ingredients, even if it's only salt.
Common salt, sodium chloride ($NaCl$), was the first
food additive. You can read about it on page 112.

Nowadays, we use many other sodium compounds
as additives. Sodium sulphite, sodium nitrite and
sodium nitrate are all preservatives. They stop
bacteria growing. Other sodium compounds
improve the texture of foods.

But perhaps the most well-known (or infamous!) additive is
mono-sodium glutamate. It brings out the flavour in foods, and
is used a lot in Chinese restaurants. However, in some people
it can cause dizziness, headaches, nausea and is dangerous
to asthmatics. Not surprisingly, it is banned from baby foods!

Sodium carbonate

The materials needed to make sodium carbonate are
brine (sodium chloride solution), limestone and
ammonia. We make about 26 million tonnes each year!
Look at the diagram showing its uses:

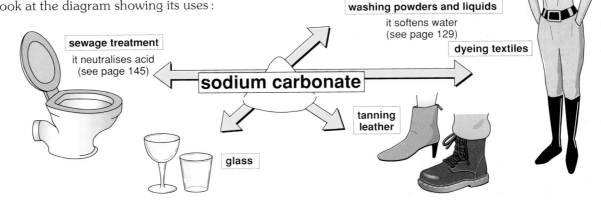

sewage treatment
it neutralises acid
(see page 145)

washing powders and liquids
it softens water
(see page 129)

dyeing textiles

sodium carbonate

glass

tanning leather

► Group 2 – The alkaline earth metals

Be	beryllium
Mg	magnesium
Ca	calcium
Sr	strontium
Ba	barium

Like Group 1, the Group 2 elements are metals.
However, they are not as reactive as their neighbours.
For example, beryllium is not as reactive as lithium.
Magnesium is not as reactive as sodium, and so on.
The Group 2 elements are called the **alkaline earth metals**.
Their compounds are quite common in rocks in the Earth's crust.
Let's look at the two best-known alkaline earth metals
– magnesium and calcium:

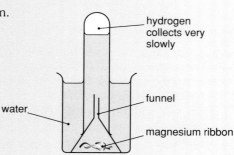

Experiment 5.4   Magnesium with water

Let's compare magnesium with its neighbour in Group 1, sodium.
Look at a piece of magnesium ribbon.
• Does magnesium have to be stored under oil, like sodium?
• Does this give you a clue about which is more reactive?

Clean your piece of magnesium with sand-paper.
• Is it shiny inside, like sodium?

Set up the apparatus as shown:
Leave it for a few days.
Test the gas collected with a lighted splint.
• What happens? Which gas is it?

Think of the reaction between sodium and water (page 51).
This shows us clearly the difference in reactivity
between Group 1 and Group 2 metals.

Group 2 metals are less reactive than their Group 1 neighbours.

Experiment 5.5   Calcium with water

Set up your apparatus as shown, with the test-tube
ready to collect any gas.
Use tweezers to put the calcium in the water.
Test the gas collected with a lighted splint.
• What happens? Which gas is it?
  Add some universal indicator solution to the beaker.
• Is the solution left acidic or alkaline?
  This is why we call the Group 2 elements the *alkaline* earth metals.
• Does calcium react faster than magnesium with water?

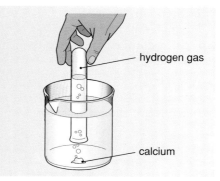

The equations for the reactions are similar to the alkali metals:

calcium +   water ⟶ calcium hydroxide + hydrogen
$Ca(s)$ + $2 H_2O(l)$ ⟶ $2 Ca(OH)_2(aq)$ + $H_2(g)$

• Can you write a word and symbol equation for magnesium and water?

Q. What did the greengrocer
get when she crossed a
barium atom with 2 sodium
atoms?

A. A BaNaNa!

Strontium and barium with water

Strontium and barium both react well with cold water.
Barium gives off hydrogen more quickly than strontium.

What is the solution left after each reaction?
What is the pattern in reactivity as we go down Group 2?
Is this the same as the pattern in Group 1?

Strontium reacting with water

Barium reacting with water

Group 2 metals get more reactive as you go down the group.

Experiment 5.6   Magnesium and calcium with dilute acid

Add a little magnesium and calcium
to dilute hydrochloric acid as shown:
- What do you see happen?
- Which fizzes more quickly?
- Does this agree with the pattern in the box above?

Test the gas given off by adding a little more
magnesium to your first tube.
This time put your thumb over the top.
When you feel the pressure building up,
test with a lighted splint.
- What happens?
- Which gas is given off?

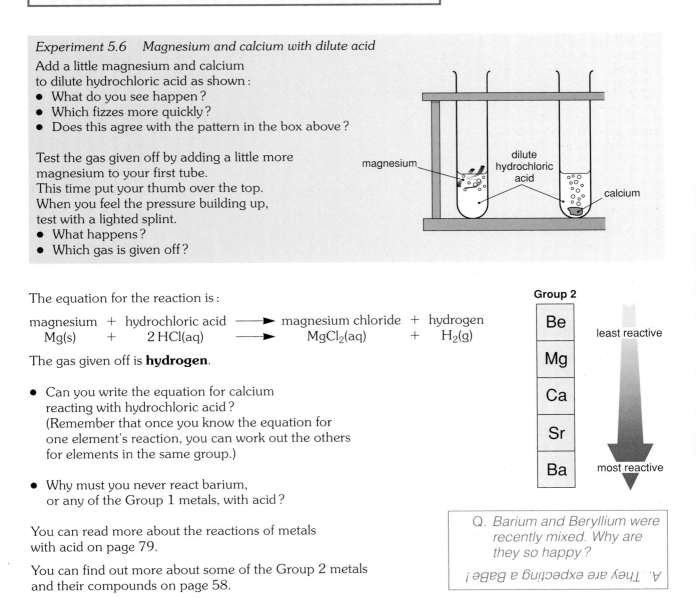

The equation for the reaction is:

magnesium + hydrochloric acid ⟶ magnesium chloride + hydrogen
$$Mg(s) + 2\,HCl(aq) \longrightarrow MgCl_2(aq) + H_2(g)$$

The gas given off is **hydrogen**.

- Can you write the equation for calcium
  reacting with hydrochloric acid?
  (Remember that once you know the equation for
  one element's reaction, you can work out the others
  for elements in the same group.)

- Why must you never react barium,
  or any of the Group 1 metals, with acid?

You can read more about the reactions of metals
with acid on page 79.

You can find out more about some of the Group 2 metals
and their compounds on page 58.

Group 2

Be	least reactive
Mg	
Ca	
Sr	
Ba	most reactive

Q. Barium and Beryllium were
recently mixed. Why are
they so happy?

A. They are expecting a BaBe!

▶ The transition metals

The transition metals lie in between Group 2 and Group 3.
They have many important uses (see page 59).
Some well-known transition metals are iron, copper,
chromium, nickel and gold.

Metals in the whole block have similar
properties. As you know, this is
strange for the Periodic Table. Usually
families of elements line up in
the columns we call groups.

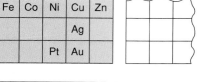

Sc	Ti	V	Cr	Mn	Fe	Co	Ni	Cu	Zn
								Ag	
			W				Pt	Au	

Physical properties

The transition metals are 'typical' metals.

They are hard, dense and shiny. They are good conductors
of heat and electricity. They are also malleable and ductile.
Do you remember these properties from page 45 ?

Why is copper used for water pipes ?

Experiment 5.7   *Magnetic metals*
Try touching different transition metals with a magnet.
● Which ones are attracted to it ?

Iron, cobalt and nickel are the magnetic metals.

Chemical properties

Experiment 5.8   *Heating copper*
Hold a strip of copper foil in some tongs.
Heat it strongly for a few minutes in a Bunsen flame.

copper strip

● Does the copper burst into flames, like magnesium does ?
● What does the copper look like after it has cooled down ?
● Which gas in the air has it slowly reacted with ?
● What do you think the black coating on its surface is called ?

Copper, like many transition metals, only **reacts slowly**
with oxygen in the air.
It forms a layer of black copper oxide on its surface.

copper + oxygen ⟶ copper oxide
$2\,Cu(s)$ + $O_2(g)$ ⟶ $2\,CuO(s)$

Q. *What does an alloy of
nickel and titanium wear in bed ?*

A. a Ni-Ti!

funnel

water

transition metal

The transition metals react very slowly, if at all, with water.
You can read about iron rusting on page 91.

The transition metals are *less reactive* than Group 1 or Group 2 metals.

Transition metal compounds

Look at the compounds of transition metals :
What do they have in common ?

copper(II) chloride   nickel chloride   iron(III) chloride

cobalt(II) chloride   manganese(II) chloride

Transition metals mostly form *coloured* compounds

On the other hand, the compounds of Group 1 and Group 2 metals
are usually white.

Which formula ?

Most transition metals form compounds which can
have more than one formula. For example,
on the last page you saw copper oxide, CuO, formed.
However, there is another form of copper oxide,
whose formula is Cu_2O. The compounds are different colours.
Roman numbers in the names tell us which compound
we mean.
Copper(II) oxide is CuO. Copper(I) oxide is Cu_2O.
Other examples are iron(II) oxide, FeO, and
iron(III) oxide, Fe_2O_3.
You can find out how to work out formulas on page 241.

The presence of chromium (Cr^{3+}) makes this emerald green

Catalysts

We use catalysts in industry to speed up reactions
(see page 198). Look at the table opposite :

Manufacture of ...	Catalyst
ammonia	iron
sulphuric acid	vanadium(V) oxide
nitric acid	platinum / rhodium
margarine	nickel

The transition metals and their compounds are important catalysts.

▶ Chemistry at work : Group 2 metals and their compounds

Magnesium

Do you know what the flame looks like
when we burn magnesium ribbon ?
Magnesium ribbon and powder are very reactive
in air. This leads to their use in rescue flares and
fireworks.

So would you think of making a car engine
from magnesium ? Strange as this idea seems,
Volkswagon 'Beetle' engine parts have been
made from magnesium for many years.

Magnesium does not burn easily in large lumps.
More and more car makers are looking at magnesium
to make a variety of parts for new cars.
In a Porsche 911, there is more than 50 kg of magnesium.
It is much less dense than steel, or even aluminium.
Therefore, you use less fuel, and pollution is reduced.

*The girl is lifting a magnesium VW crankcase ...
try doing this with a cast iron crankcase !*

Magnesium compounds

Magnesium and calcium compounds are common in the
Earth's crust. That is why Group 2 metals are known as
the alkaline **earth** metals.

Magnesium oxide has a very high melting point.
It is used to line furnaces.
Magnesium hydroxide is in 'milk of magnesia'.
It neutralises excess stomach acid, soothing indigestion.
Magnesium sulphate is found in the laxative, Epsom salts.

Calcium compounds

Calcium carbonate is the most common
compound of calcium.
You can read about its uses and
other calcium compounds in Chapter 11.

Calcium phosphate is found in our
teeth and bones.
An adult has about 1 kg of calcium in
their body.

Strontium and barium compounds

Strontium compounds give a crimson red flame,
and are used in fireworks.

Barium compounds are very poisonous. In fact,
barium carbonate is used as rat poison.
However, barium sulphate, which is insoluble,
is used in 'barium meals'. A patient takes it
so that their digestive system will show up on an X-ray.

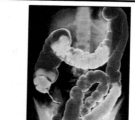

*X-ray after a
'barium meal'.*

▶ Chemistry at work : Transition metals and their compounds

The transition metals and their compounds are widely used in industry and in everyday life.
Iron is the most commonly used metal, mostly as steel.
You can read about its uses on page 92.

Here are some uses of the transition metals around the home :

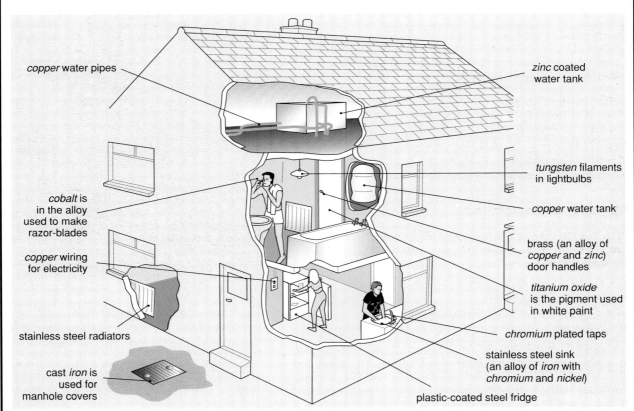

copper water pipes

zinc coated water tank

cobalt is in the alloy used to make razor-blades

tungsten filaments in lightbulbs

copper water tank

copper wiring for electricity

brass (an alloy of *copper* and *zinc*) door handles

titanium oxide is the pigment used in white paint

stainless steel radiators

chromium plated taps

stainless steel sink (an alloy of *iron* with *chromium* and *nickel*)

cast *iron* is used for manhole covers

plastic-coated steel fridge

Other uses

A radioactive isotope of **cobalt** is used to treat patients with cancer.

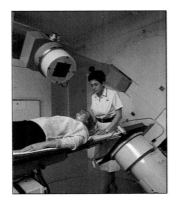

Platinum is used in catalytic converters, fitted to car exhausts. It cuts down the amount of pollution from cars.

Summary

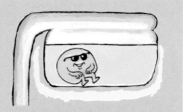

- **Group 1 – The alkali metals**
    - are soft metals, stored under oil
    - have low densities and low melting points
    - quickly tarnish in air, but are shiny when freshly cut
    - are the most reactive group of metals
    - get more reactive as you go down the group.

- **Group 2 – The alkaline earth metals**
    - have higher melting points and densities than Group 1 metals
    - are less reactive than their Group 1 neighbours
    - get more reactive as you go down the group.

- **Transition metals**
    - are hard and dense
    - have high melting points
    - are less reactive than Group 1 or Group 2 metals
    - form coloured compounds
    - can form compounds with more than one formula,
      for example, iron(II) oxide, FeO, and iron(III) oxide, Fe_2O_3
    - are important catalysts in industry.

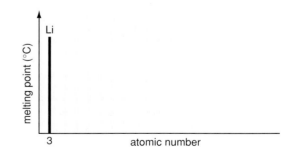

▶ Questions

1. Copy and complete:
   a) Group 1 elements are called the . . . . metals. They have . . . . melting points and . . . . densities. They are the most . . . . group of metals, and are stored under . . . . . Lithium is the . . . . reactive member of the group. They all react with cold water, giving off . . . . gas and leaving an . . . . solution.
   b) Group 2 elements are called the . . . . metals. They are . . . . reactive than Group 1 elements. Like Group 1, they get . . . . reactive as you go down the group.
   c) The . . . . metals are typical metals. They are hard, have . . . . melting points and . . . . densities. They are . . . . reactive than the metals from Groups 1 and 2. They form . . . . compounds, which can often have more than one . . . . .

2. Look at the cartoons in the Summary box above.
   a) Which alkali metal is used in street lights? (see page 53.)
   b) List some uses of named transition metals (see page 59).

3. Use Table 1 on pages 342 and 343 to help you answer this question.
   a) Record the melting points and atomic numbers of the Group 1 metals in a table.
   b) Plot a graph like the one shown below:

   melting point (°C) — Li — atomic number — 3

   c) What pattern do you see going down Group 1?
   d) Look up the melting points and atomic numbers of the Group 2 metals and put them in a table.
   e) Now do another graph, showing the melting points of the Group 2 metals.
   f) Compare your graphs for Groups 1 and 2. How are they alike? How do they differ?

4. a) Describe what you **see** when sodium reacts with water.

b) Write a word equation for the reaction in a).

c) When the reaction in a) has finished what would you add to the solution left to test its pH?

d) What is the pH of the solution left?

e) Which substance makes the solution an alkali?

f) We can collect the gas given off when lithium reacts with water. How can you test that the gas is hydrogen?

g) Why would it be impossible to collect the gas given off when potassium reacts with water?

h) Predict what would happen when rubidium, which is under potassium in Group 1, reacts with water.
Include a word and symbol equation in your answer.

5. Look at the table below showing the densities of the Group 1 and Group 2 metals:

Group 1	Density (g/cm³)	Group 2	Density (g/cm³)
lithium	0.53	beryllium	1.85
sodium	0.97	magnesium	1.74
potassium	0.86	calcium	1.53
rubidium	1.53	strontium	2.6
caesium	1.88	barium	3.59

a) Plot the densities of the Group 2 metals against their atomic numbers (from pages 342 and 343). Draw a graph like the one in question 3.

b) Is there a pattern?

c) On the same graph, plot the densities of the Group 1 metals against their atomic numbers. Use a different colour for your lines.

d) What **general** pattern can you see from your graph for the Group 1 metals?

e) Which group 1 element breaks the pattern?

f) What can we say about the density of Group 1 metals compared to those in Group 2?

6. John claims that strontium is less reactive than lithium because 'Group 2 metals are less reactive than Group 1 metals'.
What do you think about John's idea?
How could you test his idea?

7. The alkali metals, and particularly their compounds, are very useful.
Draw a spider diagram to show their uses. You could make a poster from your research. You will have to refer to information in Chapter 10 to find out more about sodium.

8. a) Where in the Periodic Table do you find the transition metals?

b) Name 5 common transition metals.

c) Make a list of the properties of a typical transition metal.

d) Compare the reactions of sodium (Group 1), magnesium (Group 2), and copper (a transition metal) with air.
What can you say in general about the reactivity of the transition metals compared to metals from Groups 1 and 2?

e) Look at these two compounds:

Which one is the transition metal compound, and which is the alkali metal compound? How can you tell the difference?

9. Make a list of some uses of the Group 2 metals and their compounds (see page 58).

10. Look at this table of data about 4 metals, labelled A, B, C and D.

Metal	Melting point (°C)
A	63
B	1494
C	650
D	98

Use letters A, B, C or D to answer a) to c).

a) Which metal is probably a transition metal?

b) Which metals do you think are from Group 1?

c) One metal is from Group 2. Which one?

d) A column showing the density of each metal would help you to be more certain of your answers above. Why?

Further questions on page 71.

chapter 6

We have looked at some groups of metals. Now let's move across to the other side of the Periodic Table and look more closely at some non-metal elements.

▶ Group 7 – The halogens

F	fluorine
Cl	chlorine
Br	bromine
I	iodine
At	astatine

Halogen molecule	Colour	State (at room temp.)
F_2	pale yellow	gas
Cl_2	yellow / green	gas
Br_2	orange / brown	liquid
I_2	grey / black (violet vapour)	solid

The Group 7 elements are called the **halogens**.
Look at the table above :
Notice that all the halogens' atoms 'go round in pairs'.
They form **diatomic** molecules. In other words,
'two-atom' molecules, like F_2 and Cl_2.

You can also see some patterns in the table
as you go down the group.
Do they get darker or lighter in colour?
Look at their states : What is the pattern?
Do their melting points and
boiling points get higher or lower
as we go down the group?

Using the table, can you make some predictions
about astatine (at the bottom of Group 7)?

Now let's look at some of the reactions of the halogens :

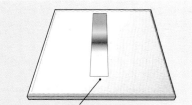

The halogens form 'diatomic' molecules.
(They are atomic twins !)

Q. Why can iodine molecules
see so well?

A. Because they have
two I's !

Experiment 6.1   The halogens with water

In this experiment you will use halogens dissolved in water.
Use a dropper to put a few drops of solution
on to some universal indicator paper as shown :
● What do you see happen?
● Which halogen solution is most acidic?
● Which is the strongest bleach?

solutions of
chlorine and bromine

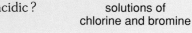

solution of chlorine

Chlorine is used as a bleach (see page 64).
It reacts with water :

chlorine + water ⟶ hydrochloric acid + chloric(I) acid (bleach)
$Cl_2(g)$ + $H_2O(l)$ ⟶ $HCl(aq)$ + $HOCl(aq)$

Bromine is less acidic than chlorine.
It is also a weaker bleach. Iodine is even weaker.

Reactivity of the halogens

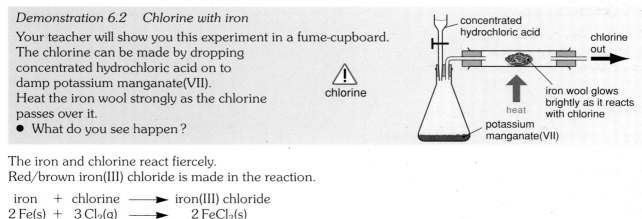

The iron and chlorine react fiercely.
Red/brown iron(III) chloride is made in the reaction.

iron   +   chlorine ⟶   iron(III) chloride
$2\,Fe(s) + 3\,Cl_2(g) \longrightarrow 2\,FeCl_3(s)$

Notice how chlor**ine** changes to chlor**ide** in its compounds.
In general, we say that the halogens form **halides**.
Bromine forms bromides. Iodine forms iodides.
Bromine does not react with iron as quickly as
chlorine. Iodine is even slower.
We find that:

> **The halogens get *less* reactive as you go down the group.**

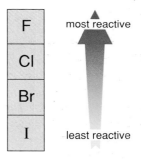

Which is the most reactive of all the halogens?

Halogens in competition

The halogens, like most elements, prefer to be in compounds.
We can put them into competition with each other to see
which is more reactive.

This pattern is
explained on page 69

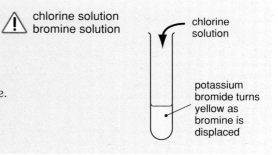

Chlorine is more reactive than iodine or bromine.
It can 'push' (**displace**) bromine and iodine out of solution.

chlorine + potassium bromide ⟶ potassium chloride + bromine
$Cl_2(aq) + 2\,KBr(aq) \longrightarrow 2\,KCl(aq) + Br_2(aq)$

Bromine is more reactive than iodine. Can it displace iodine from solution?
Can you write a word (or symbol) equation for the reaction?

► Chemistry at work : Halogens and their compounds

Fluorine

Fluorine is the most reactive of all the non-metal elements. It even attacks glass! However, some of its *compounds* are useful. Remember that the properties of elements are completely different from those of the compounds they form.

Most toothpastes contain fluoride to prevent tooth decay. Some places have fluoride added to their water supplies (see page 244).

Teflon is a fluorine compound. It is the non-stick lining on pans (see page 167).

Chlorine

Chlorine and its compounds have many uses :

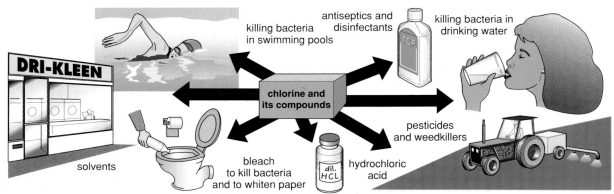

killing bacteria in swimming pools

antiseptics and disinfectants

killing bacteria in drinking water

DRI-KLEEN

chlorine and its compounds

solvents

bleach to kill bacteria and to whiten paper

dil. HCL

hydrochloric acid

pesticides and weedkillers

The most common chlorine compound is common salt, sodium chloride. You can see some products made from it on page 117.

Bromine

Bromine is used in pesticides. It is also used to make medicines. Silver bromide is used in photographic film (see page 244).

Iodine

Iodine is an antiseptic. It is dissolved in alcohol, and put on to cuts.

Iodine can be used before operations

Halogens – working for or against us ?

The halogens and their compounds have had both good and bad effects on the world.

Chlorine has had a bad reputation since it was used as the first chemical weapon in the First World War. Its compounds are also used in biological nerve gases.

However, chlorine's use in killing bacteria in **drinking water** has saved millions of lives around the world. It has greatly reduced the number of cases of cholera. However, about 25 000 people still die around the world every day from diseases spread in water.

There are still many people who have to drink untreated water

Yet even this use is now being questioned. Scientists are carefully measuring the poisonous compounds that the chlorine makes after it is added to our water supply.

These poisons were first noticed in discharges from paper mills. Chlorine is used to make paper white. Paper manufacturers now use less chlorine gas, and are looking for new ways to bleach paper.

Halogen-based **pesticides** have reduced deaths caused by diseases carried by insects, such as malaria. They also reduce the loss of crops in storage. On the other hand, these compounds can affect other wildlife in the food chain.

Halogen compounds are also damaging the **ozone layer**. This layer in the upper atmosphere protects us from harmful ultra-violet rays from the Sun. **CFC**s (chloro-fluoro-carbons) were once hailed as new wonder compounds. They are very unreactive and were thought to be completely harmless to living things. They found uses in aerosols and as coolants in fridges.

This aerosol contains no CFCs

However, scientists in the 1980s discovered a hole in our ozone layer – and it was growing. They predicted that more cases of skin cancer and eye cataracts would soon be observed. This has led to a search for different compounds to do the jobs of the CFCs.

CFCs are now being phased out, as are other halogen compounds used in fire extinguishers, flame-proofing and solvents. However, because they are so long-lasting, CFCs will remain in the atmosphere for many years to come.

▶ Group 0 (or 8) – The noble gases

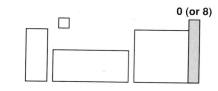

He	helium
Ne	neon
Ar	argon
Kr	krypton
Xe	xenon
Rn	radon

Q. *What do you call a chemical element with no chemistry ?*
A. *A noble gas !*
The most striking thing about this family of elements is their lack of reactivity.
They used to be called the inert gases. Inert means 'having no reactions'.
However, in 1962 their first compound was made.
They were then re-named the **noble gases**.

The noble gases prefer to be alone

As you know, most of the gases we have met so far are made up of molecules. Gases like oxygen, O_2; hydrogen, H_2; and chlorine, Cl_2. However, the noble gases are so unreactive that they are found as the atoms themselves. They are called **monatomic** gases ('one-atom' gases).

The noble gases are 'monatomic'

> **The noble gases are very unreactive.**

Why are the noble gases so unreactive ?

Chemical reactions involve the electrons in the outer shells of atoms. Every atom 'likes' to have its outer shell completely full of electrons. With **full outer shells**, atoms are **stable**.

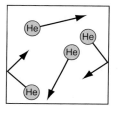
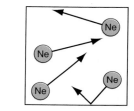

Atoms can swap or share electrons with other atoms to get full outer shells (see Chapters 19 and 20).
So let's look at the atoms of the first 3 noble gases :
(Remember that the 1st shell can hold 2 electrons, the 2nd and 3rd shells can each hold 8 electrons.)

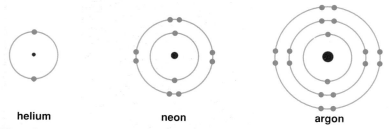

helium   neon   argon

What do you notice about their outer shells ?

> **The noble gases are stable because their outer shells are full.**

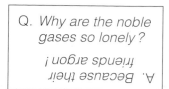

Q. *Why are the noble gases so lonely ?*

A. *Because their friends argon !*

▶ Chemistry at work : The noble gases

Helium

If we cool metals down to very low temperatures, they lose their electrical resistance. They become perfect conductors, or **super-conductors**. Liquid helium is used to cool metals down. It boils at $-269\,°C$! It is used to cool the coils in body scanners. The coils can then make the very strong magnetic fields that scanners need.

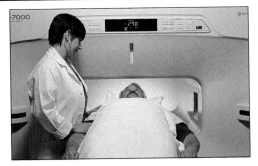

Body scanners use liquid helium

Helium is much lighter than air. It is used in air-ships. The density of the noble gases increases as you go down the group

Divers breathe a mixture of helium and oxygen. This prevents divers getting 'the bends' if nitrogen from the air dissolves in their blood.

Neon

Neon glows red in low pressure tubes which have a voltage applied

Argon

Light bulbs are filled with argon. It won't react with the tungsten filament, even when it is white-hot. It is also used in welding. It acts as a shield around the weld. The argon stops the hot metal reacting with oxygen in the air.

Krypton

Krypton is used in lasers to repair the retina behind the eye

▶ Atomic structure and the Periodic Table

We already know that the elements in the Periodic Table are arranged in order of **atomic number**.
The atoms of each element have one more proton (and electron) than the one before it.

The table below shows the way electrons are arranged in the first 20 elements.
(You don't need to know any more than this.)

Atomic number	Element	Electronic structure	Atomic number	Element	Electronic structure
1	H	1	11	Na	2,8,1
2	He	2	12	Mg	2,8,2
3	Li	2,1	13	Al	2,8,3
4	Be	2,2	14	Si	2,8,4
5	B	2,3	15	P	2,8,5
6	C	2,4	16	S	2,8,6
7	N	2,5	17	Cl	2,8,7
8	O	2,6	18	Ar	2,8,8
9	F	2,7	19	K	2,8,8,1
10	Ne	2,8	20	Ca	2,8,8,2

Can you see any patterns?

Look at these atoms from the groups we have met:

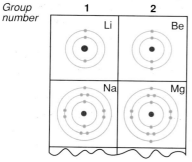

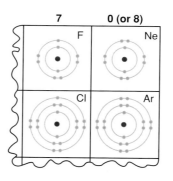

Can you see a link between the group number and the number of electrons in the outer shell?

Group number in the Periodic Table = the number of electrons in the outer shell.

Therefore all the atoms of elements in the same group have the **same number of electrons in their outer shell.**
For example, N – 2,5 and P – 2,8,5 are both in Group 5.

It is the electrons in the outer shell that get swapped or shared in chemical reactions. This explains why elements in the same group have **similar chemical reactions**.

Although iodine has 53 electrons, you know it has 7 electrons in its outer shell because it is in Group 7

Explaining patterns in the Periodic Table

Why are the alkali metals (from Group 1) so reactive?

Like all atoms, they want to react to get a full outer shell.
As elements, they have just 1 electron in their outer shell.
So when they react, they want to lose that 1 electron to
leave a full outer shell.

Group 1 elements are so reactive because it is easy for them
to get rid of just 1 electron.
Why do you think that sodium, from Group 1, is more reactive
than its neighbour from Group 2, magnesium?

Why do the metals get more reactive as we go down Group 1?

The outer electron gets easier to remove
as you go down the group.

Remember that electrons are negative. They are attracted to
the positive protons in the nucleus. As you go down the group,
the atoms get bigger. Therefore the outer electron
gets further away from the attractive force of the nucleus.
This makes it easier for an electron to escape from
a bigger atom (even though the positive charge on
the nucleus is greater).

Why do the halogens get less reactive as we go down Group 7?

An atom of a halogen has 7 electrons in its outer shell.
It needs to gain 1 electron to fill up its outer shell.

A fluorine atom is a lot smaller than an iodine atom.
Therefore, an electron entering the outer shell of
a fluorine atom is nearer to the attractive force
of the nucleus. The electron is attracted more strongly.

Charged particles

Remember that when the alkali metals react,
they lose the electron from their outer shell.

Once the electron is lost, the atom is no longer neutral.
It becomes a charged particle called an **ion**.
It has one more proton than electrons, so its charge is $1+$.

All the elements in a group form ions with the same charge
(for example, Li^+, Na^+ and K^+).

On the other hand, the halogens gain an electron.
How many protons and electrons does fluorine have
after it has gained an electron?
The halogens all form $1-$ ions (F^-, Cl^-, Br^- and I^-).

Sodium is more reactive than lithium

The shielding effect
As well as distance from the
nucleus, another factor affects the
attraction of a nucleus for the
electrons in the outer shell. The
inner shells of electrons **shield** the
outer electrons from the pull of the
nucleus.
Does this fit with the patterns in
reactivity for Group 1 and Group 7?

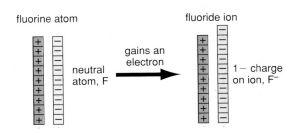

Summary

The elements of Group 7 are called the **halogens**.
They exist as diatomic molecules (F_2, Cl_2, Br_2, and I_2).
They are a reactive group of non-metals.
They get less reactive as you go down the group.

The elements in the last group (numbered 0 or 8) are called the **noble gases**.
They exist as single atoms.
They are all very unreactive.
Their atoms are very stable because their outer shells are full of electrons.

An element's group number in the Periodic Table equals
the number of electrons in the outer shell of its atoms.

▶ Questions

1. Copy and complete:
   The elements in Group . . . . are called the
   halogens.
   Fluorine and . . . . are gases, ... is a liquid and
   iodine is a . . . . . They all exist as . . . . molecules,
   e.g. Cl_2 and Br_2.
   They get . . . . reactive as you go down the
   group. Therefore, ... is the most reactive
   halogen.

   The elements in Group 0 are called the . . . .
   gases. They are the most . . . . group in the
   Periodic Table, having almost no chemistry at
   all. This is because the outer shell of their atoms
   is . . . . of electrons.

   The number of the group an element is in tells
   us how many electrons are in the . . . . shell of its
   atoms. For example, iodine is in Group 7;
   therefore it has . . . . electrons in its outer shell.

2. Copy and complete these sentences about the
   uses of the noble gases:
   a) Helium is used to fill airships and balloons
      because . . . . .
   b) Divers breathe a mixture of helium and
      oxygen because . . . . .
   c) Liquid helium is used in body scanners
      because . . . . .
   d) Neon is used in advertising signs
      because . . . . .
   e) Argon is used inside light bulbs
      because . . . . .

3. Draw a picture in your book, or make a poster,
   showing the uses of the halogens and their
   compounds.

4. a) Draw a table showing the colour and physical
      state of fluorine, chlorine, bromine and iodine.
   b) Which is the *least* reactive of the halogens
      in a)?
   c) You want to collect a gas-jar of chlorine gas.
      Copy and complete the diagram below.
      (Hint: chlorine is more dense than air.)

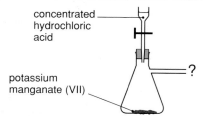

   concentrated
   hydrochloric
   acid

   potassium
   manganate (VII)

   d) Write a word and symbol equation for the
      reaction between chlorine and iron.

5. Sodium (Na) reacts with chlorine (Cl_2), making
   sodium chloride (NaCl).
   a) Write a word equation for this reaction.
   b) Now write a symbol equation. (Don't forget
      to balance your equation.)
   c) Write word and symbol equations for the
      reaction between sodium and fluorine.
   d) How would you expect the reaction with
      sodium to differ if you used fluorine instead
      of chlorine. Explain your answer.

Further questions on page 71.

▶ The Periodic Table

1. Below is the outline of a Periodic Table. The letters represent elements but are **not** their chemical symbols.

Which two elements are in the same period?
A **W** and **X**
B **W** and **Z**
C **X** and **Y**
D **Y** and **Z**   [1]   (SEG)

2. A particular element has these properties:
- floats in water.
- shiny (on cut surfaces).
- melting point is 98°C.
- good conductor of electricity.
- burns in air.

Which **two** of these properties suggest that the element is a metal?   [2]   (NEAB)

3. The table gives some information about three elements.

Element	Physical property
W	Is a grey solid that does not conduct electricity
X	Is a colourless gas at room temperature
Y	Is a shiny solid with a high density

a) Say if each element is a metal or a non-metal.
b) Give another physical property of each element.   [3]   (SEG)

4. Choose words from these lists to answer a), b) and c).
NON-METAL ELEMENTS:
   bromine   chlorine   iodine
METAL ELEMENTS:
   magnesium   mercury   sodium   zinc
a) Which is a non-metal element that is liquid at room temperature?   [1]
b) Which is a metal element that is liquid at room temperature?   [1]
c) Which is a metal element that reacts vigorously with cold water?   [1]   (NEAB)

5. The table below shows some of the properties of five elements. The letters used are **not** the symbols of the elements.

Element	Solubility in water	Melting point (°C)	Electrical conductivity when solid
V	insoluble	1083	good
W	soluble	−101	poor
X	insoluble	114	poor
Y	insoluble	1772	good
Z	slightly soluble	−7	poor

a) Give the letter of **one** of the elements which is a metal. Explain your answer.   [2]
b) Give **two** differences in the properties of metals and non-metals other than those listed in the table.   [2]   (ULEAC)

6. Calcium oxide forms an alkaline solution in water, and carbon dioxide forms an acidic solution.
a) What type of elements usually have:
   i) alkaline oxides?   [1]
   ii) acidic oxides?   [1]
b) Use the Periodic Table on page 344 to suggest another example of an element which forms:
   i) an alkaline oxide   [1]
   ii) an acidic oxide.   [1]   (MEG)

7. The table shows properties of some elements.

element	melting point /°C	boiling point /°C	conduct electricity	reaction with water
bromine	−7	59	no	soluble
potassium	64	760	yes	violent
sodium	98	892	yes	fast
sulphur	113	445	no	insoluble

a) i) Which element is a liquid at room temperature (20°C)?   [1]
   ii) Use the table to choose **two** non-metals. Explain your choice.   [3]
b) Sodium reacts with water to form an alkaline solution.
   i) How can you test that the solution is alkaline?   [1]
   ii) What would you see during your test if the solution were alkaline?   [1]
c) Name the most reactive metal in the table.   [1]   (MEG)

Further questions on the Periodic Table

8. Some oxides dissolve in water to form acid solutions. The following oxides may be present in car exhaust fumes.

carbon dioxide	lead oxide
nitrogen dioxide	sulphur dioxide

Which **one** of these oxides will **not** form an acid solution in rain water? [1]
Explain your answer. [1] (NEAB)

9. The table below shows the formulae, melting points and pH values of aqueous solutions (when soluble) of the oxides of some elements.

Atomic (proton) number of element	11	12	13	14	15	16	17	18
Formula of oxide	Na_2O	MgO	Al_2O_3	SiO_2	P_4O_6	SO_2	Cl_2O	no oxide
Melting point (ºC)	920	2900	2040	1610	24	-75	-20	–
pH of aqueous solution (if soluble)	14	11	insol	insol	3	3	3	–

a) How many of these oxides are solid at a room temperature of 20°C? [1]
b) Why does the element with atomic number 18 not have an oxide? [1]
c) When sodium oxide is added to water, the solution formed has a pH of 14. Explain the reason for this. [2] (ULEAC)

10. The table below lists some of the properties of the element silicon.

Property	Silicon
Appearance	black solid
Melting point	1410°C
Electrical conductivity	medium
Reaction with dilute acid	no reaction
Type of oxide	acidic

It is difficult to classify silicon. Give **two** pieces of evidence, from the table, for silicon being a metal and **two** pieces of evidence for it being a non-metal. [4] (ULEAC)

11. Lithium, sodium, potassium and rubidium appear in this order in Group 1 of the Periodic Table. This table contains data about three of these elements.

Element	Melting point in °C	Boiling point in °C
lithium	180	1330
sodium	98	890
potassium	—	—
rubidium	39	688

Which of **A, B, C** or **D** is most likely to be potassium?

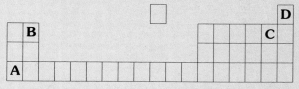

	Melting point in °C	Boiling point in °C
A	34	700
B	64	774
C	83	1007
D	120	817

[1] (SEG)

12. This is an outline of part of the Periodic Table.

The four letters show the positions of four elements. Which letter represents an element with one electron in the outermost shell of each atom? [1] (SEG)

13. The element potassium is in the same group of the Periodic Table as sodium. Potassium reacts with chlorine to make potassium chloride which is sometimes used instead of common salt in cooking.
a) Predict the formula of potassium chloride. [1]
b) By reference to the electronic structures of potassium and sodium, explain why the reaction of potassium with chlorine is similar to the reaction of sodium with chlorine. [1] (NEAB)

14. Sodium reacts violently with cold water.
a) Complete the word equation for the reaction.

sodium + water ⟶ sodium hydroxide + ... [1]

b) Describe in detail what you would **see** when a small piece of sodium is placed in a dish of cold water. [4]

c) At the end of the reaction, the solution in the dish is sodium hydroxide. If universal indicator is added to this solution it turns purple.
  i) What colour is universal indicator in water? [1]
  ii) Explain why the indicator goes purple in sodium hydroxide solution. [2]
  iii) Suggest a likely pH value for sodium hydroxide solution. [1]

d) Name a metal which reacts:
  i) more violently than sodium with water;
  ii) less violently than sodium with water.
    [2]   (ULEAC)

15. a) The diagram shows the electronic structure of a particular element.

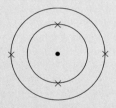

In a similar way, show the electronic structure of another element from the same group in the Periodic Table and name the element you select. [2]

b) The element lithium gives a moderate reaction with cold water, releasing hydrogen and forming a solution of lithium hydroxide. Describe how sodium is
  i) similar to lithium and
  ii) how it is different from lithium,
    in its chemical reaction with cold water.
Explain any similarity or difference in terms of their atomic structure. [5]   (NEAB)

16. The table below shows some properties of the Group 1 metals.

Element	Reaction with water	Melting point (°C)	Density (g/cm³)
Lithium	Floats, forms hydrogen and an alkaline solution. Burns with a crimson flame when lit with a splint.	180	0.53
Sodium	Floats, forms hydrogen and an alkaline solution. Burns with a yellow flame when lit with a splint.	98	0.97
Potassium	Floats, forms hydrogen and an alkaline solution. Burns with a lilac flame. Explosive reaction.	64	0.86
Rubidium	i)	39	1.53
Caesium	Explodes on contact with water. Forms hydrogen and an alkaline solution.	ii)	1.88

a) Use the table to predict:
  i) rubidium's reaction with water; [2]
  ii) caesium's melting point. [1]

b) In terms of electronic structure, what do the Group 1 metals have in common? [1]
    (ULEAC)

17. This label has been taken from a packet of magnesium ribbon.

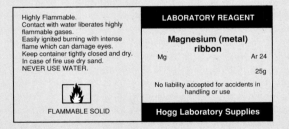

a) Write the symbol for magnesium. [1]

b) Magnesium is a metal. One of its properties is that it conducts electricity.
  i) Describe an experiment to show that magnesium conducts electricity. You may draw a diagram if you wish. [3]
  ii) Give **one** other property of metals. [1]

c) i) Describe what you **see** when magnesium burns in air. [2]
  ii) Name the compound formed. [1]
  iii) Write the word equation which represents the reaction taking place. [1]
    (NEAB)

73

Further questions on the Periodic Table

18. Here is part of the Periodic Table of the elements:

I	II						group						III	IV	V	VI	VII	0
1 H																		2 He
3 Li	4 Be												5 B	6 C	7 N	8 O	9 F	10 Ne
11 Na	12 Mg												13 Al	14 Si	15 P	16 S	17 Cl	18 Ar
19 K	20 Ca	21 Sc	22 Ti	23 V	24 Cr	25 Mn	26 Fe	27 Co	28 Ni	29 Cu	30 Zn	31 Ga	32 Ge	33 As	34 Se	35 Br	36 Kr
37 Rb	38 Sr	39 Y	40 Zr	41 Nb	42 Mo	43 Tc	44 Ru	45 Rh	46 Pd	47 Ag	48 Cd	49 In	50 Sn	51 Sb	52 Te	53 I	54 Xe
55 Cs	56 Ba	57 La	72 Hf	73 Ta	74 W	75 Re	76 Os	77 Ir	78 Pt	79 Au	80 Hg	81 Tl	82 Pb	83 Bi	84 Po	85 At	86 Rn
87 Fr	88 Ra	89 Ac																

a) Which group contains the alkali metals? [1]
b) If the properties of strontium (Sr) and barium (Ba) in Group 2 were **compared**, what should be noticed? [1]
c) Which part of the table is occupied by the non-metals? [1]
d) Look at the thick line of the Periodic Table. What is unusual about the properties of the elements close to the thick line? [3]
(ULEAC)

19. A form of the Periodic Table of the elements is shown below. The elements have been arranged in four sections.

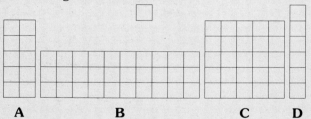

A　　　　**B**　　　　**C**　　**D**

From the four sections, **A** to **D**, choose the one in which the element described would be most likely to be placed:
a) a metal that is magnetic.
b) a colourless gas used to fill weather balloons and airships.
c) a metal that is so reactive it has to be stored under oil.
d) a yellow solid that will not conduct electricity. [4] (MEG)

20. The table below gives information about elements in Group 2 of the Periodic Table.

Element	Atomic number	Reactivity with water	Reactivity with air
Beryllium	4	No reaction	Beryllium turnings burn when strongly heated
Magnesium	12	Reacts very slowly with cold water	Burns with a blinding bright flame on heating
Calcium	20	Reacts slowly with cold water	Reacts slowly without heating
Strontium	38	Reacts quickly with cold water	Reacts quickly without heating
Barium	56	Reacts very quickly with cold water	Can catch fire in air without heating
Radium	88		

Use the information in the table to help you answer the questions.
a) Suggest how radium
   i) reacts with water; [1]
   ii) reacts with air. [1]
b) As a result of your answers to a), suggest how radium should be stored. [1]
c) Suggest a connection between the atomic number and reactivity of the elements with air. [1]
d) Use the information in the table to suggest a use for magnesium. [1] (MEG)

21. Here is some information about the elements vanadium, manganese and cobalt.

	Vanadium	Manganese	Cobalt
Symbol	V	Mn	Co
Atomic number	23	25	27
Density (g/cm³)	6.0	7.2	8.9
Melting point (°C)	1130	1240	1492
Electrical conductivity	good	good	good
Common oxides	V_2O_3 V_2O_5	MnO MnO_2 Mn_2O_7	CoO Co_2O_3

a) Choose **three** properties from the table that show why these three elements are examples of *transition metals*. [3]

b) Give **two** more properties of transition metals or their compounds **not** mentioned in the table above. [2]   (SEG)

22. Describe a test which you could do to show that manganese is a metal.
Include a diagram and state the result of the test in your answer. [4]   (ULEAC)

23. Iron, nickel and platinum can act as catalysts. Several industrial reactions use catalysts to lower the cost of the manufactured products.

a) What type of metals are able to act as catalysts? [1]

b) Name an industrial process that uses a catalyst and name the catalyst. [2]   (SEG)

24. Which of the following represents the electronic structure of three elements in the same group of the Periodic Table?

A 2.1   2.8.1   2.8.8.1
B 2.7   2.8   2.8.1
C 2.8   2.8.1   2.8.2
D 2.8.2   2.8.3   2.8.4   [1]   (SEG)

25. G, H, J and **K** are four elements. These are their electronic structures.

G 2.1   **H** 2.6
J 2.8.1   **K** 2.8.8

Which two elements have similar chemical properties?

A G and **H**
B G and **J**
C H and **J**
D J and **K**   [1]   (SEG)

26. a) Fluorine is the first member of a group called the halogens.
Give the **names** of **two** other halogens in this group. [2]

b) Give **two** properties which the vapours of the halogens have in common. [2]   (WJEC)

27. The table below shows the elements of Group 7 of the Periodic Table.

Symbol	Name	Proton number	Melting point (°C)
F			
Cl			
Br			
I			
	Astatine	85	–

a) Copy the table above. Use Table 1 on page 342 and the Periodic Table on page 344 to help you complete the table . [2]

b) The element astatine does not exist naturally on earth. Draw a suitable graph to enable you to estimate its melting point. [5]

c) Use your knowledge of the properties of the elements in Group 7 to predict:
   i)   the number of electrons in the outer shell (energy level) of an astatine atom
   ii) the formula of a molecule of astatine;
   iii) the electrical charge on an astatide ion. [3]

d) From a knowledge of electronic structure, explain why scientists predict that astatine is the least reactive element in Group 7. [3]
(NEAB)

28. The table shows the name and symbol of four elements.

Name	Symbol
Fluorine	F
Chlorine	Cl
Bromine	Br
Iodine	I

These elements are placed in the same group of the Periodic Table. Explain why [3]
(ULEAC)

Further questions on the Periodic Table

29. Use the Periodic Table on page 344 to help you to answer this question. In the diagram that follows, **e** represents an electron, **n** represents a neutron and **p** represents a proton.

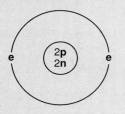

a) Identify the element, the atom of which is drawn above. [1]
b) Name another element that is in the same group. [1]
c) What do the outer electron shells of the other elements in this group have in common with each other ? [1] (SEG)

30. Look at the table below.
It shows some of the noble gases and their atomic number.

Noble gas	Atomic number
helium	2
neon	10
argon	18
krypton	36

a) Write down one use for argon. [1]
b) Write down the name of one **other** noble gas from the table. Write down one use of this gas. [1]
c) Which of the noble gases in the table has the highest density ? [1]
d) What is the meaning of the term atomic number ? [1] (ULEAC)

31. Look at the Periodic Table on page 344.
a) Describe and explain the pattern in the electronic structure of the first 18 elements. [3]
b) Explain why the charge on a sodium ion is +1 but the charge on a chloride ion is −1. [2] (ULEAC)

32. Questions a) to f) concern the position of elements, represented by the letters **A** to **E**, in a part of the Periodic Table shown below. The letters in the table do not represent the symbols of the elements.

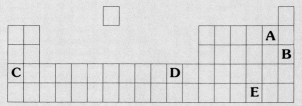

Choose, from **A** to **E**, the element which is
a) an alkali metal [1]
b) in Group 6 [1]
c) a very unreactive gas [1]
d) a transition metal [1]
e) a reactive non-metal [1]
f) a halogen [1] (ULEAC)

33. Nine elements are listed below :

Aluminium   Hydrogen   Xenon
Beryllium   Nitrogen   Yttrium
Chlorine   Potassium   Zinc

In the questions which follow, you may use each element once, more than once, or not at all.
a) Choose from the list above an element which
   i)   is a metal
   ii) is a halogen
   iii) is a gas at room temperature which contains diatomic molecules
   iv) is used to sterilize drinking water. [4]
b) Using the Periodic Table on page 344, choose from the list above an element which
   i)   has an atomic number of 39
   ii) is a transition element
   iii) is in the same group of the Periodic Table as magnesium
   iv) is in the same period of the Periodic Table as calcium
   v)   is a noble (inert) gas
   vi) has five electrons in the outer shell of its atoms. [6] (ULEAC)

Materials from ores and rocks

Chemistry is important in all our lives.
Look at these pictures:
We rely on chemical reactions to make most
of the materials that we all take for granted.
Materials like the steel used to make bicycles,
cars, ships and trains. Or the aluminium
used in making aeroplanes.
We will look at the chemistry involved in getting
these metals from their raw materials, **ores**, in this section.

Ores

Ores are rocks from which we extract metals.
Look at the pictures of ores below
and the metals we get from them:

The metals used above are all extracted from ores

Bauxite contains aluminium oxide.
We extract aluminium from it.

Haematite contains iron(III) oxide.
We extract iron from it.

Rocks

We will also look at the chemicals we get from
the important raw materials, **rock salt** and **limestone**.

 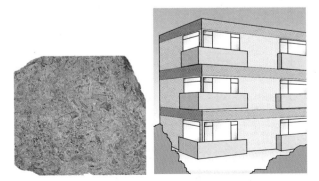

Rock salt is the raw material for making chlorine

Limestone is a raw material for making concrete and glass

77

chapter 7

The Reactivity Series

The metals in ores are chemically bonded to
other elements. So how can we extract the metals?
To answer this we must understand the **Reactivity Series** of metals.
The Reactivity Series is like a 'league table' for metals.
The most reactive metals are at the top of the league.
The least reactive ones are at the bottom.
We can start putting the metals in order by looking at
their reactions with water and dilute acid.

Metals with water

You have already seen how the alkali metals
react with water on page 51. We met lithium,
sodium and potassium. Can you remember which
of these is most reactive?

The order of reactivity is : 1. potassium
                              2. sodium
                              3. lithium

This is the top of the Reactivity Series.

You have also seen how magnesium and calcium
react with water on page 54.
Which was more reactive, magnesium or calcium?
You can add these metals to the league table we started above.
                              4. calcium
                              5. magnesium

Remember how slowly magnesium reacts with water? We can
speed up the reaction by heating up the water to make steam.

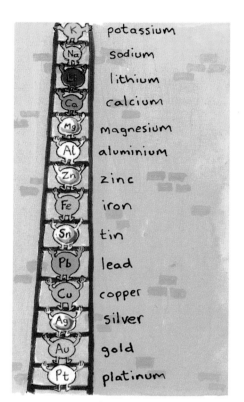

The Reactivity Series

Demonstration 7.1 *Magnesium and steam*

Your teacher will show you this reaction.
Heat the magnesium strongly. Every now and
again, switch the flame briefly to the ceramic wool?
- Why do we heat the ceramic wool?
As the reaction starts, the gas given off can be lit
at the end of the tube, as shown :
- What is the colour of the flame?
- Which gas is burning?

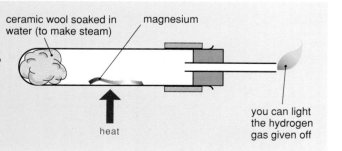

heat

ceramic wool soaked in
water (to make steam)

magnesium

you can light
the hydrogen
gas given off

The magnesium reacts strongly with the steam. It leaves
white magnesium oxide in the test-tube. Hydrogen gas is given off.

magnesium + steam ⟶ magnesium oxide + hydrogen
  $Mg(s)$ + $H_2O(g)$ ⟶ $MgO(s)$ + $H_2(g)$

The oxygen atom in H_2O has 'swapped partners'!
It starts off with hydrogen, but ends up with magnesium.

*Magnesium 'takes' the oxygen from
hydrogen!*

Zinc and iron also react with steam.

Metals	Reaction with water	Reaction with steam
potassium sodium lithium calcium	fizz, giving off **hydrogen** gas and leaving an alkaline (**hydroxide**) solution	explode
magnesium aluminium zinc iron	very slow reaction (aluminium is protected by a layer of aluminium oxide on its surface)	react, giving off **hydrogen** gas and forming the **metal oxide**

Metals with acid

Look at the metals below calcium in the table above.
We can't use the reaction with water to judge their reactivity.
The reactions are too slow. However, metals react
more quickly with **dilute acids**. We can compare them
by seeing how quickly they give off hydrogen gas.

Watching magnesium, aluminium, zinc and iron react with water would be very boring

Experiment 7.2   Metals with dilute acid

Clean the metals with sand-paper.
Set up the boiling tubes as shown : ⚠ acid

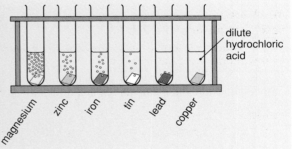

- How can you test that any gas given off is hydrogen ?
  If you see no bubbles, you can warm the tube *gently* in
  a beaker of hot water. See if any gas is given off now.
  Record your results in a table.
- Do your results agree with the order in the table below ?

Notice that copper does not react with dilute acid.
However, the other metals tested do react. For example,

magnesium + hydrochloric acid ⟶ magnesium chloride + hydrogen
$$Mg(s) + 2\,HCl(aq) \longrightarrow MgCl_2(aq) + H_2(g)$$

- Why do we never add potassium, sodium or lithium to acid ?

Metals	Reaction with dilute acid
calcium magnesium aluminium zinc iron	fizz, giving off **hydrogen** gas (aluminium is protected by a tough layer of oxide on its surface)
tin lead	give off **hydrogen** very slowly (the acid needs to be warmed up)
copper	no reaction

▷ Displacement reactions

We have now seen how the metals react with water and with acid. We have used these reactions to get an order of reactivity.
We can also judge reactivity by putting the metals into competition with each other.

In the next two experiments the metals will 'fight' each other to 'win their prize' – oxygen. The more reactive metal will win the fight.

Experiment 7.3   Metals in competition – iron v copper

Mix a spatula of iron filings and copper oxide in a test-tube. Heat the mixture strongly.
● Is there a reaction? Look for a red glow spreading through the mixture.
When the tube has cooled, empty it into a dish.
● Can you see any pink copper metal left?

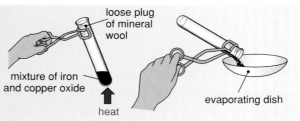

loose plug of mineral wool

mixture of iron and copper oxide

heat

evaporating dish

Copper starts off with the oxygen in copper oxide. However, iron is more reactive, so it takes the oxygen away from copper. You see a reaction take place, and copper is left by itself.
We say that iron has **displaced** ('kicked out') the copper.

copper oxide + iron ⟶ iron oxide + copper

This is a **displacement reaction**

It shows us that iron is more reactive than copper. Why wouldn't you expect to see a reaction between iron oxide and copper?

iron oxide + copper ⟶̸ no reaction

You can now try some other displacement reactions.

The winner!

Experiment 7.4   Displacement reactions

Try heating the mixtures of metals and oxides shown in the table:
Look for any signs of a reaction.
✓ = a reaction   ✗ = no reaction
(Be careful when looking for signs of a reaction. Zinc oxide turns yellow when you heat it by itself. It turns white again when it cools down.)

Metal \ Metal oxide	zinc oxide	iron oxide	copper oxide
zinc	✗		
iron		✗	✓
copper			✗

● Why can you put some ✗'s in the table before you do the experiment?
● Write word equations for the reactions you have ticked.

We find that:

> **a more reactive metal can displace a less reactive metal from its oxide.**

Your teacher may show you some more displacement reactions:

Demonstration 7.5   More displacement – magnesium v the rest
These reactions must be demonstrated in a fume-cupboard.

Mix magnesium powder with each of these:
1. zinc oxide
2. iron oxide
3. copper oxide.
Place each mixture on a tin lid and heat strongly.

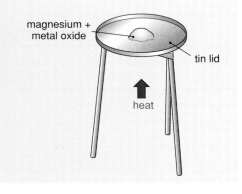

- Is magnesium more reactive than the other metals?
  How can you tell?
- Write word equations for the reactions.

Magnesium is more reactive than zinc, iron and copper.
Therefore it can displace these metals. For example,

magnesium + zinc oxide $\longrightarrow$ magnesium oxide + zinc
$$Mg + ZnO \longrightarrow MgO + Zn$$

Zinc has been **displaced** by magnesium.

Magnesium and zinc both want the oxygen

Magnesium wins the 'tug-of-war'

Thermit reaction

Look back to the Reactivity Series on page 78.
Would you expect aluminium to displace iron
from its compounds?

The reaction between aluminium and iron oxide
gives out lots of heat. It is called the thermit reaction.
(Your teacher might demonstrate this spectacular reaction.)

iron oxide + aluminium $\longrightarrow$ aluminium oxide + iron
$$Fe_2O_3 + 2\,Al \longrightarrow Al_2O_3 + 2\,Fe$$

This displacement reaction has found a use in
repairing railway tracks.

The heat given out in the reaction melts the iron formed.
The molten iron runs down between the tracks
and welds them together.

*These railway workers are using the reaction
between aluminium and iron oxide to weld rails
together*

▷ Displacement from solution

You have seen metal and metal oxide powders
in displacement reactions.
Metals can also 'compete' with each other in solution.

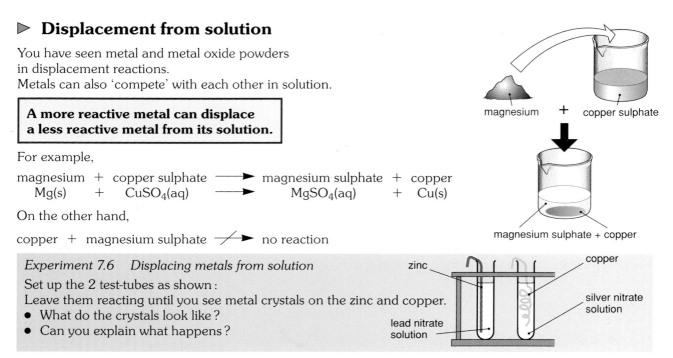

magnesium   +   copper sulphate

magnesium sulphate + copper

> **A more reactive metal can displace
> a less reactive metal from its solution.**

For example,

magnesium + copper sulphate ⟶ magnesium sulphate + copper
$\quad$ Mg(s) $\quad$ + $\quad$ $CuSO_4$(aq) $\quad$ ⟶ $\quad$ $MgSO_4$(aq) $\quad$ + $\quad$ Cu(s)

On the other hand,

copper + magnesium sulphate ⟶̸ no reaction

Experiment 7.6 *Displacing metals from solution*

Set up the 2 test-tubes as shown:
Leave them reacting until you see metal crystals on the zinc and copper.
- What do the crystals look like?
- Can you explain what happens?

zinc $\qquad$ copper

silver nitrate
solution

lead nitrate
solution

Zinc is more reactive than lead. It is higher up the Reactivity Series.
Therefore zinc displaces lead from the solution:

$\quad$ zinc + lead nitrate ⟶ zinc nitrate + lead
$\quad$ Zn(s) + $Pb(NO_3)_2$(aq) ⟶ $Zn(NO_3)_2$(aq) + Pb(s)

You see the lead forming as crystals on the zinc.

Now you can use the Reactivity Series to predict reactions:

Experiment 7.7 *Predicting reactions*

Copy and fill in the table below.
Predict which will react (✓) and which won't (✗).
Try out the reactions on a spotting tile.

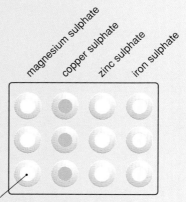

magnesium sulphate $\quad$ copper sulphate $\quad$ zinc sulphate $\quad$ iron sulphate

Metal / Solution	magnesium	copper	zinc	iron
magnesium sulphate	✗			
copper sulphate		✗		
zinc sulphate			✗	
iron sulphate				✗

add metals

- Write word equations for any reactions in your table.

Once again, the more reactive metal displaces one lower in the Reactivity Series.
For example,

zinc + copper sulphate ⟶ zinc sulphate + copper
Zn(s) + $\quad$ $CuSO_4$(aq) ⟶ $\quad$ $ZnSO_4$(aq) $\quad$ + $\quad$ Cu(s)

▷ Hydrogen in the Reactivity Series

We can use displacement reactions to give
hydrogen a place in the Reactivity Series.
Do you remember the metals reacting with
acid? Look back to the table at the bottom
of page 79.
Which metals can displace hydrogen from solution?
Hydrogen slots in the Series just above copper.

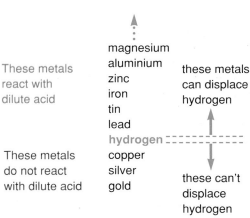

These metals
react with
dilute acid

magnesium
aluminium
zinc
iron
tin
lead
hydrogen

these metals
can displace
hydrogen

Cells

So far we have used our observations to work out
the order of metals in the Reactivity Series.
No measurements have been made. However,
the experiment below lets us *measure*
the *difference* in reactivity between metals.
Our Reactivity Series is like a league table,
without the points. It gives us the order,
but does not tell us the size of the differences
between metals.

These metals
do not react
with dilute acid

copper
silver
gold

these can't
displace
hydrogen

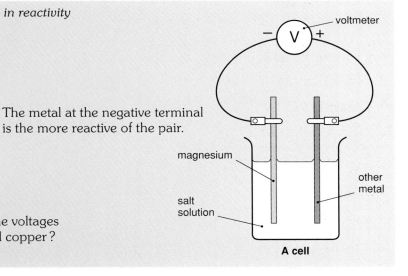

Experiment 7.8   *Measuring differences in reactivity*

Set up the apparatus as shown:
Record the voltage in a table:

Pair of metals Negative – Positive	Voltage (V)
magnesium – zinc	
magnesium – iron	
magnesium – lead	
magnesium – copper	

The metal at the negative terminal
is the more reactive of the pair.

voltmeter

magnesium

salt
solution

other
metal

A cell

- Do you get the order you expect?
- Can you use your results to predict the voltages
  between other pairs, such as zinc and copper?
  Try out your predictions.

All metals want to form positive ions.
This makes them more stable (see page 69).
To form positive ions the metal atoms lose electrons.
The more reactive a metal, the more easily it loses electrons.

$$Mg \longrightarrow Mg^{2+} + 2e^-$$

Magnesium atoms lose 2 electrons
to form magnesium ions

The voltmeter measures the difference
in the ability of 2 metals to lose electrons.
The voltage gives us a measure of the difference
in reactivity. Can you think of a use for this?

Summary

- The **Reactivity Series** lists metals in order of reactivity.
- You can use the Reactivity Series to make predictions about reactions:
  A more reactive metal can **displace** a less reactive metal from its compounds. For example,
  copper oxide + zinc ⟶ zinc oxide + copper
- Here is a table which summarises the reactions of metals:

Order of reactivity	Reaction when heated in air	Reaction with water	Reaction with dilute acid
potassium sodium lithium	burn brightly, forming oxide	fizz, giving off hydrogen; alkaline solutions (hydroxides) are formed	explode
calcium magnesium aluminium zinc iron		react with steam, giving off hydrogen; the metal oxide is made	fizz, giving off hydrogen
tin lead copper	oxide layer forms without burning	only a slight reaction with steam	react slowly with warm acid
silver gold platinum	no reaction	no reaction, even with steam	no reaction

- Hydrogen is placed just above copper in the Series.

▷ Questions

1. Copy and complete:
   a) The Reactivity Series puts the . . . . in order of
      . . . . .
   b) The highly reactive metals react with cold water, giving off . . . . gas and leaving an . . . . solution.
   c) Metals of medium reactivity only react very . . . . with cold water, but they react well with . . . . . These metals fizz with dilute . . . . giving off . . . . gas.
   d) Metals of low reactivity, such as . . . . , silver, ... and platinum do not react with water or dilute . . . . .
   e) A more reactive metal can . . . . a less reactive metal from its compounds. For example,
      zinc + copper sulphate ⟶ . . . . + ...

2. Zinc reacts with dilute sulphuric acid. It gives off hydrogen gas. Design some apparatus which can be used to collect the gas.

3. This apparatus can be used to react iron with steam:

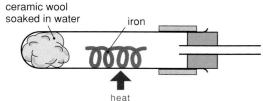

ceramic wool soaked in water   iron

heat

   a) Which gas is given off in the reaction?
   b) What does the iron change to?
   c) Write a word equation for the reaction.
   d) How can you change the apparatus above to collect the gas given off? Draw a diagram.
   e) How could you test the gas you collect?

4. You have 3 unknown metals – A, B and C.
   You know that:
   C displaces B from its oxide when heated.
   However, there is no reaction when C is heated with the oxide of A.
   Put the 3 metals in order (most reactive first).

5. The Reactivity Series is like a league table of metals.
   a) Put the metals into 3 'divisions'. How did you decide on your divisions?
   b) Here is the draw for the quarter-finals of the Metals' Cup:

                                              Final

   Iron Wanderers *v* Potassium City ⎯⎯⎯
   Magnesium Rovers *v* Calcium Athletic ⎯⏋
   Sodium United *v* Zinc City ⎯⎯⎯⎯
   Lithium Town *v* Aluminium Aces ⎯⎯⏌

   Predict the winners of the matches.

   What would happen in the semi-finals, and then the final.

6. Decide which of the pairs below will react. If they do react complete the word equations:
   a) zinc + copper oxide
   b) zinc + iron nitrate
   c) iron + magnesium oxide
   d) magnesium + copper sulphate
   e) copper + silver nitrate
   f) copper + lead nitrate

7. Complete these word and symbol equations:
   a) magnesium + zinc oxide ⟶
      $Mg(s)$ + $ZnO(s)$ ⟶
   b) zinc + copper sulphate ⟶
      $Zn(s)$ + $CuSO_4(aq)$ ⟶
   c) zinc + lead nitrate ⟶
      $Zn(s)$ + $Pb(NO_3)_2(aq)$ ⟶
   d) magnesium + iron nitrate ⟶
      $Mg(s)$ + $Fe(NO_3)_2(aq)$ ⟶
   e) magnesium + copper chloride ⟶
      $Mg(s)$ + $CuCl_2(aq)$ ⟶
   f) lead + silver nitrate ⟶
      $Pb(s)$ + $AgNO_3(aq)$ ⟶

8. Look at these metals reacting with dilute hydrochloric acid:

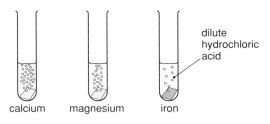

   calcium   magnesium   iron

   a) What is the gas given off?
   b) Complete this word equation:
      magnesium + hydrochloric acid ⟶ ?
   c) Draw 2 test-tubes, showing what happens when i) zinc and ii) copper are added to dilute hydrochloric acid.

9. Explain these facts:
   a) Gold, silver and platinum are used to make jewellery.
   b) Potassium, lithium and sodium are stored in jars of oil.
   c) Food cans are plated in tin, but not zinc.
   d) Aluminium is quite high in the Reactivity Series, but can be used outdoors for things such as window frames.

10. Here is a message from the Lonely Hearts section of the 'Zoos of the World'!

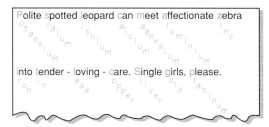

   Polite spotted leopard can meet affectionate zebra into tender - loving - care. Single girls, please.

   Can you make up your own sentence to help you remember the Reactivity Series?

Further questions on page 133.

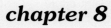

EXTRACTION of METALS

chapter 8

In Chapter 7 you learned about the Reactivity Series.
You can now start to understand how we get metals
from their ores. This includes the most widely used
of all metals, iron.

▷ **Metals of low reactivity**

Most metals are found naturally in rocks called ores.
They are in compounds, chemically bonded to other elements.
However, the unreactive metals at the bottom of the
Reactivity Series can be found as the elements themselves.
We say that they are found **native**.

We can find copper, silver, gold, and platinum
as the metals in nature. (Copper and silver are also
mined as ores.)
Look at the photograph :

Gold is found as the metal itself

● Why can gold be found native ?
Gold is very expensive because it is difficult to find.
For example, there is plenty of gold in the sea.
Unfortunately, it is spread all round the world.
This makes it too costly to extract from sea-water.

Roasting ores

Many metal ores contain oxides or sulphides of the metal.
Copper is found in an ore called chalcocite. This has
copper(I) sulphide in it.
We can get the copper from this ore just by
heating it in air.
Look at the equation below :

$$\text{copper(I) sulphide} + \text{oxygen} \xrightarrow{heat} \text{copper} + \text{sulphur dioxide}$$
$$\text{Cu}_2\text{S(s)} + \text{O}_2\text{(g)} \longrightarrow 2\,\text{Cu(s)} + \text{SO}_2\text{(g)}$$

Care must be taken to stop sulphur dioxide
gas escaping from the furnace. This gas causes
acid rain (see page 178).

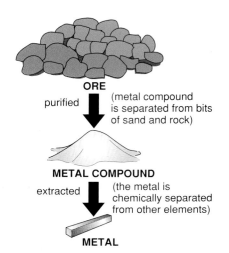

In this chapter, we will see how we extract metals

These people are 'panning' for gold in Brazil

The copper in this ore is chemically bonded to sulphur and iron. We must heat it to extract the copper.

ORE
purified (metal compound is separated from bits of sand and rock)

METAL COMPOUND
extracted (the metal is chemically separated from other elements)

METAL

▷ Metals of medium reactivity

The metal above copper in the Reactivity Series is lead.
Lead can be extracted from an ore that contains
lead sulphide. Look at the experiment below:

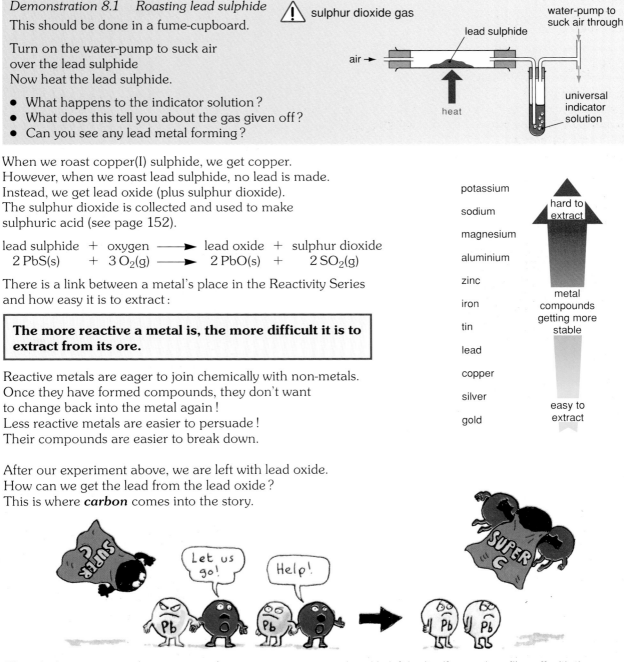

Demonstration 8.1   Roasting lead sulphide
This should be done in a fume-cupboard.

⚠ sulphur dioxide gas

Turn on the water-pump to suck air
over the lead sulphide
Now heat the lead sulphide.

- What happens to the indicator solution?
- What does this tell you about the gas given off?
- Can you see any lead metal forming?

When we roast copper(I) sulphide, we get copper.
However, when we roast lead sulphide, no lead is made.
Instead, we get lead oxide (plus sulphur dioxide).
The sulphur dioxide is collected and used to make
sulphuric acid (see page 152).

lead sulphide + oxygen ⟶ lead oxide + sulphur dioxide
$$2\,PbS(s) \;+\; 3\,O_2(g) \longrightarrow 2\,PbO(s) \;+\; 2\,SO_2(g)$$

There is a link between a metal's place in the Reactivity Series
and how easy it is to extract:

> **The more reactive a metal is, the more difficult it is to
> extract from its ore.**

Reactive metals are eager to join chemically with non-metals.
Once they have formed compounds, they don't want
to change back into the metal again!
Less reactive metals are easier to persuade!
Their compounds are easier to break down.

potassium

sodium

magnesium

aluminium

zinc

iron

tin

lead

copper

silver

gold

hard to extract

metal
compounds
getting more
stable

easy to
extract

After our experiment above, we are left with lead oxide.
How can we get the lead from the lead oxide?
This is where ***carbon*** comes into the story.

The whole story is on the next page!

Lead is left by itself as carbon flies off with the oxygen!

▷ Extracting metals with carbon

Carbon and the Reactivity Series

Carbon is a non-metal. However, we can put it into
our league table of metals. It slots in between
aluminium and zinc. This means that carbon can displace
any metal below aluminium in the Reactivity Series.

We get carbon from coal. Coal is cheap
and there's plenty of it at present.
Therefore, extracting metals with carbon
is not too expensive.

You can try to extract the lead from lead oxide
in the next experiment:

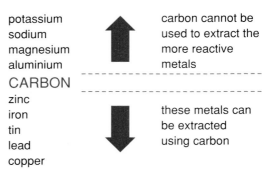

potassium
sodium
magnesium
aluminium

CARBON

zinc
iron
tin
lead
copper

carbon cannot be
used to extract the
more reactive
metals

these metals can
be extracted
using carbon

Experiment 8.2   Extracting lead and copper

Mix a spatula of carbon powder with
a spatula of lead oxide.   ⚠️   lead oxide
Set up the apparatus as shown:
Heat it gently at first, then more strongly.
Look for signs of a reaction in the test-tube.
● Can you see any silvery beads left after the reaction?
This is lead metal.

Try the same experiment, using carbon and copper oxide.
● Can you see any copper metal (a pinkish brown powder)?

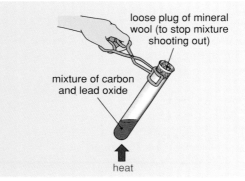

loose plug of mineral
wool (to stop mixture
shooting out)

mixture of carbon
and lead oxide

heat

Carbon is more reactive than lead.
Therefore, it can displace lead from lead oxide.

lead oxide + carbon ⟶   lead + carbon dioxide
  $2\,PbO(s)$ + $C(s)$ ⟶ $2\,Pb(s)$ + $CO_2(g)$

Reduction and oxidation

Look at the equation above.
The lead oxide loses its oxygen. We say that
lead oxide is **reduced**.
The carbon gains oxygen. We say that
carbon is **oxidised**.

REDUCTION is the LOSS of OXYGEN	–O
OXIDATION is the ADDITION of OXYGEN	+O

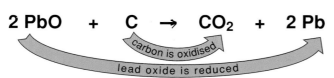

$$2\,PbO \quad + \quad C \quad \rightarrow \quad CO_2 \quad + \quad 2\,Pb$$

carbon is oxidised
lead oxide is reduced

*Reduction and oxidation are chemical
opposites. (For more details see page 309.)*

▷ Extraction of iron

Carbon is important in the extraction of iron.
We use a giant **blast furnace** to get the iron
from its ore. The raw materials are fed into the top
of the furnace. The raw materials are:

- **iron ore** (mainly haematite, iron(III) oxide),
- **coke** (a cheap form of carbon, made from coal),
- **limestone** (to get rid of sandy waste).

Look at the diagram:
Can you see why it is called a **blast** furnace?
It's a bit like a huge barbecue. The temperature
gets above 1500 °C.

Reactions in the blast furnace

1. The coke (carbon) reacts with oxygen in the
   hot air to make carbon dioxide.

   $$C(s) + O_2(g) \longrightarrow CO_2(g)$$

2. This carbon dioxide reacts with more hot coke
   to make **carbon monoxide** gas.

   $$CO_2(g) + C(s) \longrightarrow 2CO(g)$$

3. The carbon monoxide then **reduces**
   the iron oxide to iron.

   $$Fe_2O_3(s) + 3CO(g) \longrightarrow 2Fe(l) + 3CO_2(g)$$

4. Limestone gets rid of the sandy bits (acidic
   impurities) in the iron ore. They form a liquid **slag**.

Notice that the iron oxide is reduced to iron
by carbon monoxide gas in step 3.

$$Fe_2O_3 + 3CO \longrightarrow 2Fe + 3CO_2$$

We say that carbon monoxide is the **reducing agent**.

Reducing agents take away oxygen.

At the high temperatures in the furnace,
the iron formed is molten (a liquid). It sinks
to the bottom of the furnace.
The iron is run off into moulds.

The molten slag floats on top of the iron.
The slag is tapped off, cooled and
used for making roads.

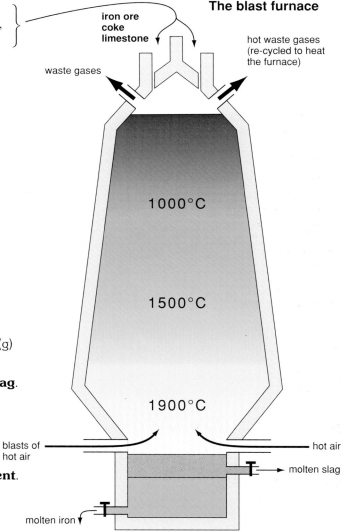

The blast furnace

iron ore
coke
limestone

hot waste gases
(re-cycled to heat
the furnace)

waste gases

1000°C

1500°C

1900°C

blasts of
hot air

hot air

molten slag

molten iron

▷ Iron into steel

The iron from the blast furnace is impure.
It contains 3 % to 4 % carbon, plus some other non-metals.
The impure iron is very brittle. It smashes easily.
Most of it gets turned into steel which is much tougher.

Steel is mainly iron (over 98 %). It has a tiny amount
of carbon left in it. Other metals can also be added.
There are 2 main steps in turning iron into steel:

1. Removing carbon
This is done by blowing oxygen into molten iron
from the blast furnace. The carbon burns
and escapes as carbon dioxide gas.

2. Adding other metals
Small amounts of other metals give the steel
special properties. For example, we make
stainless steel by adding a little chromium
and nickel. This type of steel does not rust.
It is used to make cutlery.

You can find out more
uses of steel on page 92.

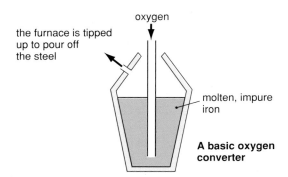

oxygen

the furnace is tipped
up to pour off
the steel

molten, impure
iron

A basic oxygen converter

*Iron is turned into steel. The oxygen burns off the
carbon and other non-metal impurities.*

*Stainless steel
does not rust*

▷ Corrosion of iron

The rusting of iron costs us millions of pounds
every year.
Rust forms on the surface of iron (or steel).
Unfortunately, it is a soft, crumbly substance.
It soon flakes off, then more iron rusts.
Let's find out what causes iron to rust:

Changing a rusty exhaust

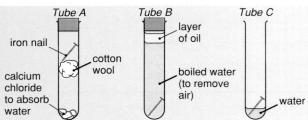

Experiment 8.3   What causes iron to rust?

Set up the test-tubes as shown:
Tube A tests to see if air alone will make iron rust.
Tube B tests to see if water alone will make iron rust.
Tube C tests to see if air and water will make iron rust.
Leave the tubes for a week.
● What do you see in each test-tube?

Tube A

iron nail

cotton
wool

calcium
chloride
to absorb
water

Tube B

layer
of oil

boiled water
(to remove
air)

Tube C

water

Rust is a form of iron(III) oxide. It has water
loosely bonded to it.
It is called **hydrated iron(III) oxide**.

> **Both air (oxygen) and water are
> needed for iron to rust.**

*In order for iron to rust
Both air and water's a must.
Air alone won't do
Without water there too,
So protect it, or get a brown crust!*

Experiment 8.4   Speeding up rusting

Set up the test-tubes as shown:
Leave the tubes for a week.

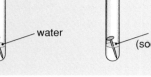

- Which tube has more rust in it?

Salt speeds up the rusting of iron.
Car owners who live near the sea
should wash their cars regularly. Why?
Why is salt a problem for car owners
in winter? What can they do
to reduce the problem?

Preventing rust

We know that air and water are needed for iron to rust.
Therefore, if we can keep these away from iron,
it can't rust.
We can do this by coating the iron or steel with:
1. paint   2. oil or grease   3. plastic
4. a less reactive metal, or   5. a more reactive metal.

Let's look at how good these methods are:

How has the fence around these tennis courts been protected?

Experiment 8.5   Stop the rust

Set up the test-tubes as shown:
The rust indicator turns blue at the first signs of rust.
Look at your test-tubes every few minutes.

- Which method is best at preventing rust?

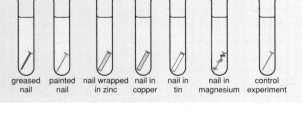

Most methods for preventing rust rely on
keeping the iron away from air and water.
The iron will rust if there is even a tiny gap
in the coating.
Then the rust soon spreads under the coating.

However, this does not happen if you use
a more reactive metal. Even if the coating is scratched,
the iron does not rust.
Zinc is often used to protect iron.
We say that the iron is **galvanised**.

*If the tin coating is broken, the can will rust
– harmful bacteria will then get to the food.
Why can't we use zinc to coat food cans?*

The zinc is more reactive than the iron. Therefore,
any water or oxygen reacts with the zinc rather than the iron.
This is called **sacrificial protection**.
The zinc sacrifices itself to protect the iron (see page 93).

▷ Chemistry at work : Uses of steel

Steel is used more than any other metal.
It is very important in the building industry.
It is used for girders and for the rods inside
reinforced concrete.
You will have seen the steel tubes, called scaffold,
used when buildings are made or repaired.

Workers erecting steel scaffold

Different types of steel

As you know from page 90, steel is made mainly
from iron. It has a small amount of carbon in it.
The amount of carbon affects its properties.
Look at this table :

Carbon steels

Type of steel	Amount of carbon	Hardness	Uses
mild steel	0.2%	can be easily shaped	car bodies, wires, pipes, bicycles
medium steel	0.3% to 0.6%	hard	girders, springs
high-carbon steel	0.6% to 1.5%	very hard	drills, hammers, other tools

- What happens to the hardness of the steel as we
  increase the amount of carbon ?
- Why do you think that mild steel is used to make cars ?

Why don't we use mild steel for rail tracks ?

Alloy steels

You can change the properties of steel
by adding small amounts of other metals.
For example, tungsten in steel keeps it
hard **and** tough, even when it gets very hot.
It is used to make high-speed cutting tools.

Mixtures of metals are called **alloys**.
You can read more about alloys in Chapter 21.

*How can steel cutting tools be
used to shape steel objects ?*

▷ Chemistry at work : Preventing rust

Unfortunately, iron and steel rust.
However, we have found some very effective
ways to fight against rust.

You have just read about alloy steels.
If chromium and nickel are added to steel,
you get **stainless steel**, a steel which
does not rust.
Stainless steel is expensive, but is used for
small items, such as knives and forks.
Why don't we make cars from stainless steel?

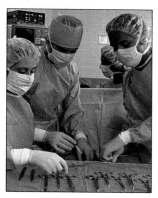

*Stainless steel is used to make a
surgeon's instruments. It is
important that they do not rust.*

*Magnesium bars are bolted onto this
ship's hull*

Sacrificial protection

You have seen on page 91 that iron
can be coated in zinc (galvanised). This
works even if the coating gets scratched.
How does this method work?

Magnesium can be used instead of zinc.
It is used in harsh conditions.
Look at the photos:
Why are these things likely to rust very quickly
without the protection of magnesium?

*This pier is
built on
steel legs*

Shocking rust !

Concrete is the most widely used building
material.

It is reinforced by steel rods which make it
much stronger. However, some concrete
buildings and bridges are showing signs of
weakness. The steel inside the concrete is
rusting away!

Rust takes up much more space than steel so
the concrete cracks!

Scientists have found a way to stop this.

A small electric current passing through the
steel will protect it. Many new structures will be
protected this way.

▷ The highly reactive metals

The highly reactive metals are the most difficult
to extract from their ores. These metals are found
in very stable compounds.

Reduction by carbon won't work. You know
carbon's place in the Reactivity Series. It lies
just under aluminium. Therefore carbon can't displace
the highly reactive metals from their ores.

However, we do have a way to get these metals.
It is called **electrolysis**. We will look at this
in more detail in the next chapter. You will see
how sodium and aluminium are extracted by electrolysis.
Once you have separated the metal compound from the ore,
the next 2 steps are:

1. *melt* it, then
2. *pass electricity* through it.

Both steps use up a lot of energy.
Therefore highly reactive metals are expensive to extract.

Reactive metals form stable compounds. This makes them difficult to extract!

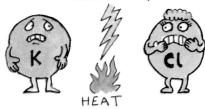

It takes a lot of energy to split up compounds of reactive metals, like potassium

Summary

The way we extract a metal from its ore
depends on its place in the Reactivity Series.
The more reactive a metal is, the harder it is to extract.

Look at the list of metals below:

Order of reactivity	Method of extraction
potassium (K) sodium (Na) lithium (Li) calcium (Ca) magnesium (Mg) aluminium (Al)	**Electrolysis** The metal compound is: 1. melted, then 2. has electricity passed through it.
zinc (Zn) iron (Fe) tin (Sn) lead (Pb)	**Reduction** by carbon For example, $ZnO + C \longrightarrow Zn + CO$ Carbon monoxide is formed when we extract zinc. (If the ore is a sulphide, it is roasted first to get the oxide.)
copper (Cu) silver (Ag) gold (Au) platinum (Pt)	These metals can be found uncombined, as the metal itself. We say that they are found **native**. (Copper and silver are often found as ores but they are easy to extract by roasting the ore.)

difficult
to
extract

easy to
extract

▷ Questions

1. Copy and complete:
   The method used to extract a metal from its ore depends on its position in the ....:
   a) Metals of low reactivity can be found ...., as the metal itself.
   b) Metals of medium reactivity must be extracted from their ores by heating with ..... The metal oxide has its oxygen .... by the carbon. We say that it has been .... by the carbon. Iron is extracted in a .... furnace. Carbon, in the form of ...., is mixed with iron ore and ..... The main reducing agent in the furnace is .... gas.
   c) Highly reactive metals are extracted by ..... There are 2 main steps:
      1. the metal compound is ..., then
      2. .... is passed through it.

2. This table shows when some metals were discovered:

Metal	Known since:
potassium	1807
sodium	1807
zinc	before 1500 in India and China
copper	ancient civilisations
gold	ancient civilisations

   a) What pattern can you see between a metal's place in the Reactivity Series and its discovery?
   b) Can you explain this pattern?

3. Lead is found in the ore galena. The lead is in a compound called lead sulphide, PbS.
   To extract the lead, we first roast the ore. It is then reduced by carbon.
   a) Write word and symbol equations to show what happens when lead sulphide is roasted in air.
   b) Explain what happens in the reduction with carbon.

4. Look at this table which shows how much some metals cost:

Metal	Cost ($ per tonne)
lithium	61 500
magnesium	2250
aluminium	1650
zinc	980

   a) Can you see a pattern between the position of these metals in the Reactivity Series and their cost?
   b) Can you explain this pattern?
   c) Gold costs $12 300 000 per tonne. Platinum costs about the same as gold.
      i) Is your pattern from a) true for the whole Reactivity Series?
      ii) Can you explain the high cost of gold and platinum?

5. a) Copy this diagram of a blast furnace and fill in the blanks:

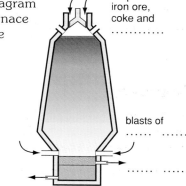

iron ore, coke and ....

blasts of ....

....

....

   b) Describe the 4 main reactions that happen in a blast furnace.
   c) What is the main impurity in the iron we get from a blast furnace?
   d) How is iron turned into steel?
   e) List some uses of steel.

6. a) How could you show in an experiment that both **air** and **water** are needed for iron to rust?
   b) List 5 ways to prevent iron rusting.
   c) *Explain* which method is best to protect i) a bicycle chain, and ii) a dustbin.

Further questions on page 135.

chapter 9

We met the word **electrolysis** in the last chapter.
You've probably seen it in adverts for beauty shops.
It can be used to remove unwanted hair.
More importantly for us, it is the way that we extract
highly reactive metals from their compounds.

Electrolysis is the break-down of a substance by electricity.

Now we will find out more about electrolysis.

> ### Electrolytes

Experiment 9.1   Electrolysis

Set up the circuit as shown :

This can be shown
in a circuit diagram
like this :

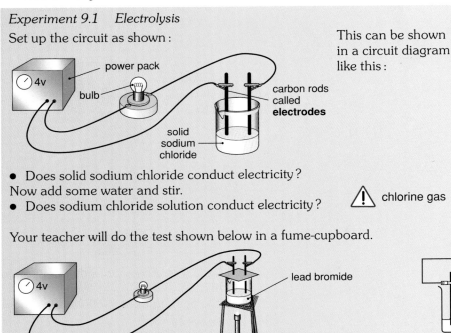

* Does solid sodium chloride conduct electricity ?
Now add some water and stir.
* Does sodium chloride solution conduct electricity ?

⚠ chlorine gas

Your teacher will do the test shown below in a fume-cupboard.

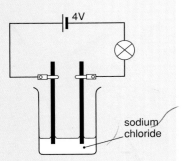

* Does solid lead bromide conduct ?
Now heat the lead bromide until it melts.
* Does molten lead bromide conduct ?
* Do you think electrolysis can happen in solids ?

⚠ bromine gas

We find that electrolysis only happens in liquids.
Substances which can be electrolysed are called **electrolytes**.

**Electrolytes are compounds which don't conduct electricity when
solid, but do conduct when molten or dissolved in water.**

Experiment 9.2   Which substances are electrolytes?

The substances in the table below have been dissolved in water.
You can test which conduct electricity.

Set up the circuit as shown:
Do not breathe in any gases given off.

Make sure you don't let the electrodes touch each other.
Rinse your beaker and electrodes well after each test.
Put your results in a table like this:

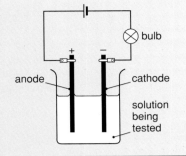

Solution	Does it conduct?	What do you see at each electrode?	
		+ (anode)	– (cathode)
potassium chloride (KCl)			
sucrose ($C_{12}H_{22}O_{11}$)			
ethanol (C_2H_5OH)			
sodium iodide (NaI)			
zinc bromide ($ZnBr_2$)			
calcium hydroxide ($Ca(OH)_2$)			
dilute sulphuric acid (H_2SO_4)			
glucose ($C_6H_{12}O_6$)			
copper sulphate ($CuSO_4$)			

- Which solutions are conductors?
These dissolved compounds are the **electrolytes**.
- Did you see the reactions at the electrodes?
Electrolytes are usually compounds of metals and non-metals.
- Which is the exception in the table above?

When electrolytes conduct, we see reactions at the electrodes.
The reactions at the electrodes are explained later in the chapter.

Why do electrolytes conduct?

Most electrolytes contain metals and non-metals.
These compounds are all made up of **ions**.
We have met ions before on pages 69 and 83.
Remember that ions are **charged particles**.

We saw in experiment 9.1 that solid compounds
don't conduct electricity.
Solids like sodium chloride contain ions,
but they are fixed in position.
Their ions can't move to the electrodes.
However, when they are melted or dissolved in water,
the **ions become free to move** around.

> **Electrolytes are made up of ions.**
> **When molten or dissolved in water, the *ions are free*
> *to move*.**

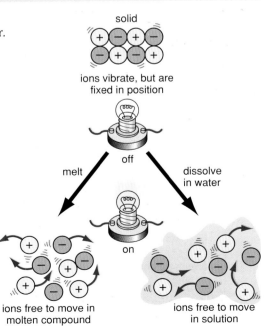

▷ Moving charges

We know that liquids containing ions conduct electricity.
Yet solids which contain ions don't conduct.
We think it must be the **movement** of ions
in liquids that is important in electrolysis.
Let's look at some evidence for the theory
of the moving ions:

In order to make your lamp bright,
You need an elec-tro-lyte.
The ions must flow,
Through liquids they go,
In solids they're just packed too tight!

Experiment 9.3   *Ions on the move*

We can use coloured ions to see which way
ions move during electrolysis.

a) Potassium manganate(VII)

Set up the apparatus as shown:
Use tweezers to place the potassium manganate(VII)
in the middle of the damp filter paper.
Leave the power pack on for 20 minutes.

The potassium ions are **colourless**.
The manganate(VII) ions are **purple**.

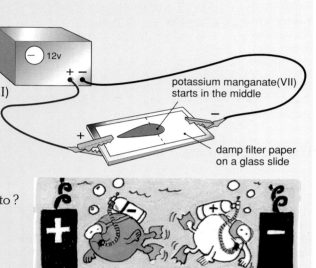

potassium manganate(VII)
starts in the middle

damp filter paper
on a glass slide

- What happens on the filter paper?
- Which electrode do the manganate(VII) ions move to?
  How can you tell?
- Do you think the manganate(VII) ions carry
  a positive or negative charge? (Remember that
  opposite charges attract.)
- Which way do you think the potassium ions move?

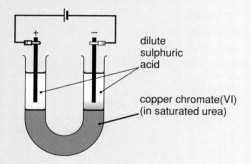

Ions carry their charge to the electrode

b) Copper chromate(VI)

Your teacher will set up this apparatus:
Leave the power on until you can see colours
near the electrodes.

Copper ions are **blue**.
Chromate(VI) ions are **yellow**.

dilute
sulphuric
acid

copper chromate(VI)
(in saturated urea)

- Which colour can you see near the positive electrode?
- Which ion is attracted to the positive electrode?
- Which colour can you see near the negative electrode?
- Which ion is attracted to the negative electrode?

In general we can say that:

metal ions are positive

non-metal ions are negative

For example, Na^+, K^+, Ca^{2+}, Al^{3+}
(exceptions: H^+, hydrogen ions
and NH_4^+, ammonium ions).

For example, Cl^-, Br^-, I^-, O^{2-}
(exceptions: complex transition metal ions, like the ones in
the experiment above, MnO_4^-, CrO_4^{2-}).

Cations and anions

We know that metal ions are positive.
We also know that opposite charges attract.

Therefore, as we have seen on the last page:

> **metal ions are always attracted to the negative electrode (cathode).**

Positive ions are sometimes called **cations**.
This comes from the word cathode – a negative electrode.

Negative ions are attracted to
the positive electrode (anode).
These ions are sometimes called **anions**.
Why are they called anions?

Cat-ions are 'pussytive'!
Cations go to the cathode.
When they get there they
receive electrons
(see page 101).

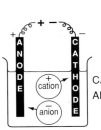

CATions → CAThode
ANions → ANode

Why are ions charged?

Lithium fluoride is made up of ions.
Let's look at the difference between the atoms
of lithium and fluorine and their ions:

Can you remember your work on atomic structure
in Chapter 3?
Atoms have the same number of protons (+) as electrons (−).
Therefore atoms have no charge. They are neutral.

The charge in an atom is balanced

Lithium **atom**, Li		Fluorine **atom**, F	
number of protons = 3+		number of protons = 9+	
number of electrons = 3−		number of electrons = 9−	
overall charge = 0		overall charge = 0	

However, in ions there are different numbers of
protons and electrons. Metals lose electrons
and non-metals gain electrons. You can read about
why this happens on page 238.

Now count the electrons (−) around each ion below:
Look at the positive charge in each nucleus.
Can you see why lithium is positively charged?

The charge on an ion is un-balanced.
Can you draw see-saws for F and F⁻?

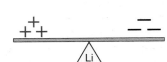

Lithium **ion**, Li^+		Fluoride **ion**, F^-	
number of protons = 3+		number of protons = 9+	
number of electrons = 2−		number of electrons = 10−	
overall charge = 1+		overall charge = 1−	

Magnesium ions have a 2+ charge.
How many more protons than electrons does an Mg^{2+} ion have?

▷ Electrolysis of copper chloride

We know that ions are attracted to
oppositely charged electrodes.
But what happens to the ions when they
get to the electrode? The next experiment
will help us to find out.

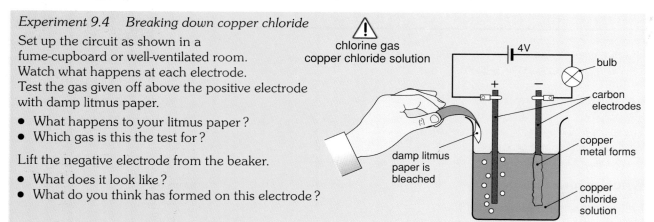

Experiment 9.4   Breaking down copper chloride

Set up the circuit as shown in a
fume-cupboard or well-ventilated room.
Watch what happens at each electrode.
Test the gas given off above the positive electrode
with damp litmus paper.

- What happens to your litmus paper?
- Which gas is this the test for?

Lift the negative electrode from the beaker.

- What does it look like?
- What do you think has formed on this electrode?

Copper metal forms on the negative electrode (cathode).
Chlorine gas is given off at the positive electrode (anode).
The copper chloride is **electrolysed**.
It is broken down into its elements, copper and chlorine.

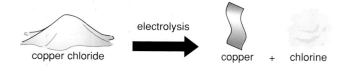

copper chloride   → electrolysis →   copper + chlorine

Explaining electrolysis

To understand how copper chloride is broken down,
we need to know how electricity flows around a circuit.
An electric current is the flow of electrons.
Look at the diagram opposite:
Remember that electrons are tiny negative particles.
They are 'pushed out' of the negative end of the battery.
Then they travel around the wire, and are 'sucked back'
into the positive end of the battery.

During electrolysis, the electrons from the battery
go to the negative electrode. Here they meet the
positive ions. The **ions** then change into neutral **atoms**.

In our experiment above, copper ions changed into
copper atoms.

This carbon electrode has been coated with
copper metal

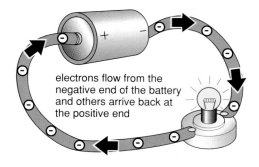

Electrons flow through the wires and bulb. This
is an electric current.

Negative ions gather at the positive electrode.
The ions are negatively charged because they carry
extra electrons. (Look back to the example
of the fluoride ion on page 99.)
Their extra electrons are removed at the positive electrode.
These get 'sucked back' into the battery. In our experiment
we saw bubbles of chlorine gas on the positive electrode.

Look at the cartoon opposite:
Electrons leave the negative end of the battery.
Electrons arrive back at the positive end of the battery.
Therefore we have a complete circuit.
A bulb in the circuit will light up.

However, no free electrons pass through the electrolyte.

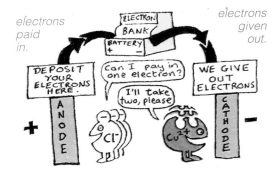

Electrolysis works like a bank. The ions are the customers. The electrons are the money. Electrons flow to and from the battery but not between the electrodes.

> **Ions carry charge through electrolytes. No free electrons pass through.**

Half-equations

We can describe what happens at the electrodes
using **half-equations**.
These show what happens to the ions during electrolysis.

Let's look at the electrolysis of copper chloride
in more detail:

Copper ions have a 2+ charge. They have lost 2 electrons.
(See the example of the lithium ion on page 99.)
At the negative electrode they gain 2 electrons.
The ion is no longer charged. It becomes a copper atom.
This can be shown by a half-equation:

> $$Cu^{2+} + 2e^- \longrightarrow Cu \quad \text{(at the cathode)}$$

At the positive electrode, the chloride ion, Cl^-,
loses its extra electron:

$$Cl^- - e^- \longrightarrow Cl$$

A chlorine atom is formed.
However, chlorine does not exist as Cl atoms,
but as Cl_2 molecules. So two Cl atoms
join together and we see chlorine gas:

$$Cl + Cl \longrightarrow Cl_2$$

These changes at the positive electrode (anode)
can be shown like this:

> $$2\,Cl^- - 2e^- \longrightarrow Cl_2 \quad \text{(at the anode)}$$

AT THE CATHODE
The copper ion is feeling blue. It's lost two electrons. But help is available at the cathode.

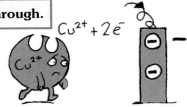

Copper's in the pink. It gets two electrons and changes from an ion to an atom.

AT THE ANODE
electrons go back
to the
battery

Two Cl^- ions each lose their extra electron and make a Cl_2 molecule.

▷ Electrolysis of molten compounds

In experiment 9.1 we saw that **solid** lead bromide does not conduct. However, it does when we **melt** it. Can you remember why?
The **ions must be free to move** to the electrodes before we get electrolysis.
In the next experiment you can look more closely at the electrolysis of a molten compound.

Demonstration 9.5   *Electrolysis of lead bromide*

Your teacher will set up the apparatus as shown in a fume-cupboard.

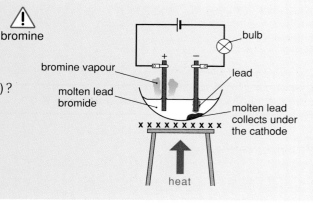

- When does the bulb light up?
- What do you see at the positive electrode (anode)?

After a few minutes, carefully pour off the molten lead bromide using tongs.

- What is left in the bottom of the dish?
- What has lead bromide turned into?

The electrolysis of lead bromide starts as soon as it melts.
The ions are then free to move between the electrodes.
The lead bromide breaks down into its elements:

lead bromide → (electrolysis) → lead + bromine

At the cathode (−) $Pb^{2+} + 2e^- \longrightarrow Pb$	**At the anode (+)** $2\,Br^- - 2\,e^- \longrightarrow Br_2$
Lead ions, Pb^{2+}, gain 2 electrons. They form lead atoms	Two bromide ions, Br^-, each lose their extra electrons. They form Br_2 molecules

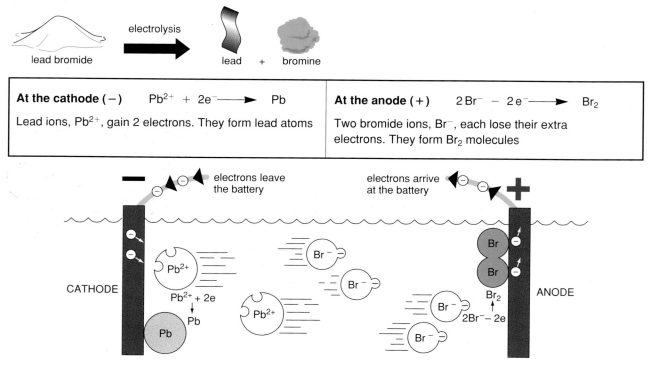

▷ Extraction of aluminium

As you know, highly reactive metals are extracted by electrolysis.
The most important of these metals is **aluminium**.
Aluminium has many useful properties.
It conducts heat and electricity well. It has a low density
for a metal. It does not corrode. You might remember
the oxide layer on its surface which protects it (see page 79).
Look at the pictures opposite:
Can you explain why aluminium is chosen
to make each thing?

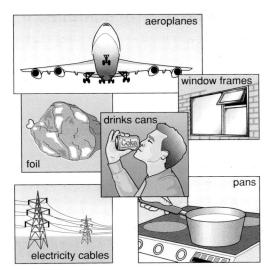

Getting the ore

Aluminium is extracted from its ore **bauxite**.
This is mainly **aluminium oxide**.
The impurities are removed before aluminium
is extracted.
Large amounts of bauxite are dug up in Jamaica.
Look at the photo opposite:
What effect does the aluminium industry have
on our environment?   Will *recycling* help?

Electrolysis of aluminium oxide

The aluminium oxide is *melted*, then *electrolysed*.
Why do we need to melt the aluminium oxide?
Energy is saved by dissolving the oxide in molten *cryolite*.
This lowers its melting point.
The electrolysis is done in cells like the one shown:

Open-cast mining in Jamaica

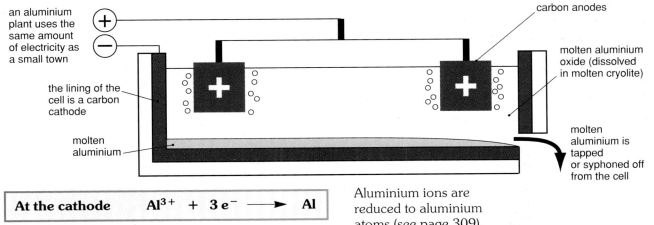

an aluminium plant uses the same amount of electricity as a small town

carbon anodes

the lining of the cell is a carbon cathode

molten aluminium

molten aluminium oxide (dissolved in molten cryolite)

molten aluminium is tapped or syphoned off from the cell

At the cathode	$Al^{3+} + 3e^- \longrightarrow Al$

Aluminium ions are
reduced to aluminium
atoms (see page 309).

At the anode $\qquad 2O^{2-} - 4e^- \longrightarrow O_2$

The oxygen gas reacts with the carbon anodes.
It makes carbon dioxide gas. This burns away
the anodes, which must be replaced quite often.

▷ Electrolysis of solutions

To get a highly reactive metal from its compounds
we must melt the compound before we can electrolyse it.
Don't you think it would be cheaper and easier
to just dissolve the compound in water, then electrolyse it?
After all, solutions have free ions, just like molten compounds.
However, you can't get any reactive metals
from their solutions by electrolysis.

When electrolysing solutions, we have to think about
the **water** molecules in the electrolyte.
Water (H_2O) can affect what is formed at each electrode.
Let's test some of the products we get from
the electrolysis of solutions:

You can't extract sodium from sea-water
(sodium chloride solution)

Experiment 9.6   Electrolysing solutions

Set up the apparatus as shown:
See if you can identify any of the products shown below.
Do not breathe in any gas given off.

Solution	Cathode (−)	Anode (+)
potassium iodide (KI)	hydrogen	iodine
potassium nitrate (KNO_3)	hydrogen	oxygen
magnesium bromide ($MgBr_2$)	hydrogen	bromine
sodium carbonate (Na_2CO_3)	hydrogen	oxygen
calcium nitrate ($Ca(NO_3)_2$)	hydrogen	oxygen
lithium chloride (LiCl)	hydrogen	chlorine
copper sulphate ($CuSO_4$)	copper	oxygen
sodium hydroxide (NaOH)	hydrogen	oxygen

- Which gas is given off at the cathode instead of the reactive metal?
- Where do you think this gas has come from?
- What happens with a less reactive metal, like copper?

Look at the table above:
You can see that the **reactive metals stay in solution**.
Hydrogen gas is given off instead. The hydrogen comes from H_2O.

> **When you electrolyse a solution of a highly reactive metal,
> hydrogen – not the metal – is given off at the cathode.**

The half-equation is:
$$H^+ + e^- \longrightarrow H$$
A hydrogen ion, H^+, gains an electron to form a hydrogen atom, H.
Then two H atoms join together to make an H_2 molecule:
$$H + H \longrightarrow H_2$$
These 2 steps are usually shown as:

$$\boxed{2\,H^+ + 2\,e^- \longrightarrow H_2}$$

Hydrogen (not sodium) is given off when we
electrolyse sodium chloride solution

Why is hydrogen given off?

Let's take a solution from the last experiment as an example. Let's look at calcium nitrate solution:

In any solution there are a few water molecules which have split up:

$$H_2O(l) \rightleftharpoons H^+(aq) + OH^-(aq)$$

They form hydrogen ions, H^+, and hydroxide ions, OH^-.

Let's think what happens at the cathode $(-)$.
Both calcium ions and hydrogen ions are attracted towards the cathode.
However, calcium ions are more stable than hydrogen ions.
Remember how calcium reacted with acid (page 55)?
Calcium displaced H^+ ions from the acid solution.

So given a choice between H^+ and Ca^{2+} at the cathode, it's H^+ ions that have to leave the solution!

At the cathode	$2 H^+(aq) + 2 e^- \longrightarrow H_2(g)$

What happens at the anode?

Hydroxide ions, OH^-, and nitrate ions, NO_3^-, are both attracted to the anode $(+)$.
But which of the two ions is 'kicked out' (or **discharged**) from the solution?

Look at the 'order of discharge' opposite:
If the negative ion is above the hydroxide in the list, it stays in solution. So nitrate (NO_3^-) ions stay in solution. Hydroxide ions from water are discharged.
When this happens, we get oxygen gas (O_2).
Here is the half-equation:

Order of discharge

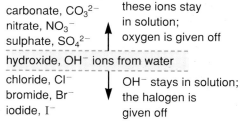

carbonate, CO_3^{2-} — these ions stay in solution;
nitrate, NO_3^-
sulphate, SO_4^{2-} — oxygen is given off

hydroxide, OH^- ions from water

chloride, Cl^- — OH^- stays in solution;
bromide, Br^- — the halogen is
iodide, I^- — given off

At the anode	$4 OH^-(aq) - 4 e^- \longrightarrow 2 H_2O(l) + O_2(g)$

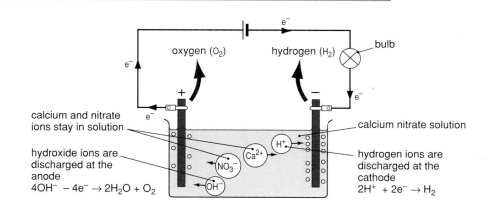

calcium and nitrate ions stay in solution

hydroxide ions are discharged at the anode
$4OH^- - 4e^- \rightarrow 2H_2O + O_2$

oxygen (O_2) hydrogen (H_2) bulb

calcium nitrate solution

hydrogen ions are discharged at the cathode
$2H^+ + 2e^- \rightarrow H_2$

▷ Active electrodes

We have now seen how electrolysis can be used to extract highly reactive metals, like aluminium. The other uses of electrolysis depend on electrodes which react – **active electrodes**.

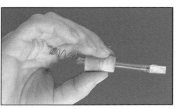

Platinum is used to make inert electrodes. Why do you think we've used carbon but not platinum electrodes in our experiments?

In all our experiments so far, we have used carbon electrodes. These are called 'inert' electrodes. They take no part in the electrolysis. The carbon electrodes just carry electrons to and from the electrolyte.

However, some metal electrodes do take part in electrolysis.
These are called **active** electrodes.

Let's look at copper as an example of an active electrode. We will electrolyse copper sulphate solution.

These metals form 'active' electrodes!

Experiment 9.7   Electrolysis of copper sulphate solution using copper electrodes

Make sure your copper electrodes are clean and shiny. Use a pencil to mark one electrode + and the other −. Weigh them with an accurate balance.

Set up the apparatus as shown:

After 10 minutes, rinse the electrodes with distilled water. Dry them by dipping in propanone and letting it evaporate. When dry, re-weigh the electrodes.
● What do you find?

Look back to the electrolysis of copper sulphate solution on page 104.
● What difference do you notice at the anode (+)?

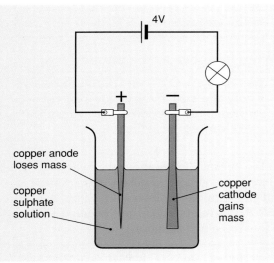

copper anode loses mass

copper sulphate solution

copper cathode gains mass

When we electrolyse copper sulphate solution using copper electrodes the mass of both electrodes changes. Remember that metals are always formed at the cathode (−). So not surprisingly, the cathode gets heavier. The strange thing is that the anode loses mass. The copper anode is an **active electrode**. We find that:

> **loss in mass at the anode = gain in mass at the cathode**

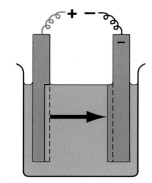

The anode's loss is the cathode's gain

Comparing inert and active electrodes

Let's compare the electrolysis of copper sulphate solution using carbon and copper electrodes:

	Carbon electrodes	Copper electrodes
At the cathode (−)	$Cu^{2+} + 2e^- \longrightarrow Cu$	$Cu^{2+} + 2e^- \longrightarrow Cu$
	the reactions are the same	
At the anode (+)	$4\,OH^- - 4e^- \longrightarrow 2H_2O + O_2$ oxygen gas is given off	$Cu - 2e^- \longrightarrow Cu^{2+}$ no oxygen is seen; copper atoms from the anode lose 2 electrons and enter the solution as Cu^{2+} ions

The copper anode is an active electrode.
As copper atoms form on the cathode,
copper atoms are lost from the anode.
As copper ions leave the solution at the cathode,
they are replaced in the solution at the anode.

Copper ions, Cu^{2+}, make copper sulphate solution blue.
What do you think would happen to the colour
of the copper sulphate solution using carbon electrodes?
Why won't the colour fade using copper electrodes?

As copper ions enter the solution at the anode, copper ions leave the solution at the cathode

Getting pure copper

Have you ever wired a plug or seen inside an electric cable?
The metal wire is copper.
Copper is an excellent conductor of electricity. However,
it must be very pure to do its job well.

Copper extracted from its ores is not pure enough
to be used for electrical wiring.
It can be made pure using electrolysis.

Look at the diagram opposite:
In industry a thin cathode of pure copper is used.
The anode is made of impure copper.
What do you think happens at each electrode?

The cathode slowly gets bigger as the anode
gets smaller and smaller.

The impurities from the anode drop
to the bottom of the cell. This sludge contains
valuable metals, like gold and silver.

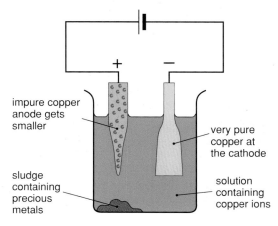

impure copper anode gets smaller

very pure copper at the cathode

sludge containing precious metals

solution containing copper ions

Many of these cells operate at the same time in industry.
The cathodes are removed after about two weeks.

107

▶ Electroplating

Do you ride a bike, eat tinned foods or
have any inexpensive jewellery? These all
involve electroplated objects.
Look at the photos on the next page:
We all use things which have been electroplated
every day of our lives.

> **An electroplated object is coated with a thin
> layer of metal by electrolysis.**

Electroplating is used to make objects look
attractive and shiny. The object can also
be protected against corrosion.
Some metals used in electroplating are nickel,
chromium, tin, silver, and gold.

*Can you think why steel cans are coated with tin?
Why is jewellery silver-plated or the handlebars on
your bike chrome-plated?*

Experiment 9.8   Nickel-plating

Clean a piece of copper foil with sandpaper.
Your teacher will gently melt a tray of wax.
Holding your copper with tongs, dip it into
the tray of molten wax. Let the wax set.

⚠️
hot wax
nickel sulphate

Scratch a simple design on your copper foil.
Make sure you remove all the wax from
the area to be coated.

Set up the apparatus as shown:

You get better results if you use a small current
for a long time. When you finish, rinse your
copper and scrape off the rest of the wax.

- What does your copper foil look like?
- Can you explain what happens?

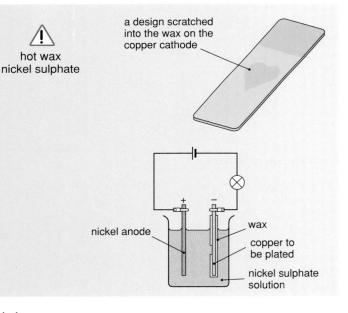

a design scratched
into the wax on the
copper cathode

nickel anode

wax

copper to
be plated

nickel sulphate
solution

In the experiment, we plate the copper foil with nickel.

At the **cathode (−)** $Ni^{2+}(aq) + 2e^- \longrightarrow Ni(s)$
this coats the foil

The nickel anode is an active electrode.
As nickel plates the foil, it is replaced in the solution
from the anode.

At the **anode (+)** $Ni(s) - 2e^- \longrightarrow Ni^{2+}(aq)$

- Can you design a circuit to coat a 'silver' coin
  with copper?

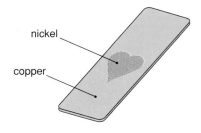

nickel

copper

▷ Chemistry at work : Electroplating

Chromium-plating

Most metal objects are made from iron or steel.
As you know, rusting is a problem.
Chromium is a hard, shiny metal which resists corrosion.
However, chromium does not stick very well to steel.
The objects are first electroplated with copper. A layer
of nickel goes on top of this. Now the chromium has
a good base to stick to. The final layer of chromium
makes the object beautifully shiny !

Object at the cathode	$Cr^{3+}\ +\ 3\,e^-\ \longrightarrow\ Cr$

Silver-plating

Silver is a precious metal. Pure silver is expensive
Therefore plating objects with silver saves us money.
Cutlery and tea services are often silver-plated.
These may be stamped with the letters EPNS.
This stands for electroplated nickel silver.

Object at the cathode	$Ag^+\ +\ e^-\ \longrightarrow\ Ag$

Tin-plating

'Tin cans' have very little tin in them !
Cans are made from steel, with a very thin
coating of tin. The tin layer, which is only a few
thousandths of a millimetre thick, stops the steel
from rusting.
Steel sheet passes quickly through a plating solution,
with anodes made from blocks of tin.

Steel at the cathode	$Sn^{2+}\ +\ 2\,e^-\ \longrightarrow\ Sn$

If the coating is scratched, the can will soon corrode.
This lets in bacteria from the air which cause food poisoning.
Several people have died in Britain from botulism.
This was traced back to faulty cans of tuna fish.
They had rusted through at the seam and let in
the harmful bacteria.

Investigation 9.9 Investigate electrolysis !

You can now use your ideas about electrolysis to find out:

Which factors affect the rate of electrolysis ?

You can investigate copper sulphate solution.
Think about these things :
- How can you speed up the electrolysis of copper sulphate ?
- Use your ideas about ions to explain why it is speeded up.
- How can you measure or judge how quickly it happens ?
  (Hint: an ammeter might be useful).
- How can you make it a fair test ?
- Is your plan safe ?

Show your plan to your teacher before you start.

Summary

- **Electrolysis** is the break-down of a substance using electricity.
  For example,   copper chloride ⟶ copper + chlorine
- **Ions** are charged particles. Metal ions are positive. Non-metal ions are negative.
- The negative electrode is called the **cathode**. The positive electrode is the **anode**.
- Solid compounds made from ions cannot be electrolysed.
  They must be melted or dissolved in water first.
  The ions then become free to move to the electrodes.
- Metals form at the cathode ($-$).
  Non-metals form at the anode ($+$).
  For example, in the electrolysis of copper chloride :
  at the cathode $Cu^{2+} + 2e^- \longrightarrow Cu$
  at the anode $2Cl^- - 2e^- \longrightarrow Cl_2$
- In solutions, reactive metals are not formed at the cathode.
  They stay in the solution and **hydrogen** (from the water) is given off :
  at the cathode $2H^+ + 2e^- \longrightarrow H_2$
- Reactive metals are extracted from **molten** compounds.
  For example, aluminium is extracted by electrolysing molten aluminium oxide.
- Other uses of electrolysis are purifying copper and electroplating.

▷ Questions

1. Copy and complete :
   When we break down a substance using
   electricity it is called . . . . .
   The . . . . electrode is called the cathode.
   The . . . . electrode is called the anode.
   The ions in a . . . . are not free to move.
   However, when they are molten or . . . . in water,
   electrolysis can take place.

   Metals form at the . . . . , and non-metals at the
   . . . . . For example,
   at the cathode $Pb^{2+} + 2e^- \longrightarrow Pb$
   at the anode $2Br^- - 2e^- \longrightarrow Br_2$
   When solutions of reactive metal compounds are
   electrolysed . . . . is formed at the cathode, not the
   metal. Electrolysis is used in industry to extract
   . . . . metals, to purify . . . . and for electro– . . . . .

2. Liz and Jabeen set up the experiment below:

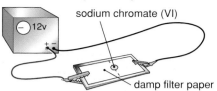
sodium chromate (VI)

12v

damp filter paper

They left it for 15 minutes.
Sodium ions are positively charged. They are colourless.
Chromate(VI) ions are negatively charged. They are yellow.

a) What did they **see** happen?
b) Explain the results of their experiment.

3. What do these words mean:
   a) cathode, b) anode, c) cation, d) anion?

4. Copy and complete this table:

Substance electrolysed	What is formed at cathode?	What is formed at anode?
molten lead bromide	?	?
?	potassium	chlorine
calcium nitrate solution	?	?
copper chloride solution	?	?
?	aluminium	oxygen
sodium iodide solution	?	?

5. Copy and complete these half-equations at the **cathode**:
   a) $Na^+ + \ldots \longrightarrow Na$
   b) $Li^+ + e^- \longrightarrow \ldots$
   c) $Mg^{2+} + \ldots \longrightarrow Mg$
   d) $\ldots + 2e^- \longrightarrow Ca$

6. Copy and complete these half-equations at the **anode**:
   a) $2Cl^- - \ldots \longrightarrow Cl_2$
   b) $\ldots - 2e^- \longrightarrow Br_2$
   c) $2I^- - 2e^- \longrightarrow \ldots$
   d) $2O^{2-} - 4e^- \longrightarrow \ldots$

7. Jo and Tim set up this experiment:

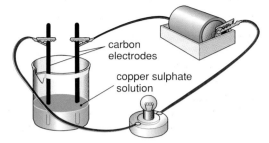
carbon electrodes

copper sulphate solution

a) Draw a circuit diagram of their apparatus.
b) What did they **see** at the cathode?
c) Complete this half-equation at the cathode:
   $Cu^{2+} + \ldots e^- \longrightarrow Cu$
d) What did they **see** at the anode?
e) Jo and Tim did the experiment again, but this time they used **copper** electrodes instead of carbon. What differences did they notice between their two experiments?

8. Look at the experiment below:

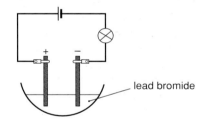
lead bromide

a) The bulb does not light up when you dip the electrodes into the solid lead bromide. Explain why not. (Use the word **ions** in your answer).
b) You want to electrolyse the lead bromide. Which apparatus is missing from the diagram.
c) Copy and complete:
   .... moving through the wires make the bulb light up, whereas .... carry the charge through the lead bromide.

9. Explain why reactive metals can't be extracted from their solutions by electrolysis.

10. a) Draw a labelled diagram to show how you could nickel-plate a spoon.
   b) How would you change your apparatus to silver-plate the spoon?

Further questions on page 133.

111

SALT

chapter 10

Do you like a little salt on your food ?
Even if you don't add it yourself, just look at the labels
on the packets and tins at home.
Salt is added to many foods to bring out the flavour.

It can also help to preserve food. Early explorers,
like Captain Cook, took meat rubbed
in salt on their long voyages.

> **The chemical name for salt is sodium chloride.
> Its formula is NaCl.**

Have you ever been swimming in the sea ? If you have,
you will know how salty sea-water is. Imagine how
much salt must be dissolved in the world's oceans !
It's no wonder that chemists call salt '**common salt**' !

In hot countries salt is extracted from sea-water.
The sea-water is left in huge shallow lakes.
Then the Sun's energy evaporates the water.
Why don't we get much salt this way in Britain ?

Fortunately, we have found thick layers of salt
under the ground in this country. Most salt lies under
the Cheshire countryside. How do you think it got there ?
Salt is a very useful raw material. It has attracted
the chemical industry into Cheshire.

So how do we get the salt up to the surface ?
There are two methods :

1. *digging from mines*, and
2. *pumping up salt solution* (brine).

First of all, let's look at mining salt.

Salt mining

The salt is found about 300 m below ground.
In its natural, impure form it is called **rock salt**.
It is drilled and blasted out, then brought to the surface.
The underground caverns formed do not cave in
if pillars of rock salt are left in place.

The rock salt is sold to councils around the country.
It is used to grit roads in winter.
Why is rock salt put on roads ? Can you remember
its disadvantage for car owners ? (see page 91.)

*People think that millions of years ago there was
an inland sea where Cheshire is today. It
dried up leaving salt behind. The seam is up to
2000 metres thick !*

Rock salt can be dug from underground

Experiment 10.1   Melting ice

Set up the 2 beakers as shown:
Record the lowest temperature in each one.
- What is the normal melting point of ice?
- In which beaker is ice melting below 0 °C?

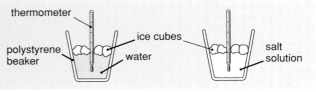

0 °C is the melting point of ice. It is also
the freezing point of pure water.
However, when salt is dissolved in the water,
it **lowers the freezing point**. The salt makes it
more difficult for bonds to form between water molecules.
So ice will form at a lower temperature than normal.

Salt from rock salt

The salt used to grit roads does not need to be pure.
However, sometimes we do need pure salt.

We can get rid of bits that don't dissolve in water
by **filtration**.

Salt lowers the freezing point of water

Experiment 10.2   Purifying rock salt

Follow steps 1 to 4 to get a purer sample of salt.

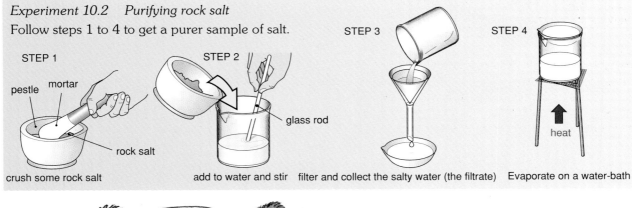

crush some rock salt   add to water and stir   filter and collect the salty water (the filtrate)   Evaporate on a water-bath

There was a young man called Walt,
Who tried to purify salt.
The solution he got,
Was it clear? It was not!
Though he claimed it was never his fault!

- What did Walt do wrong?

▷ Extraction of sodium

We saw in the last chapter that reactive metals
are extracted by *electrolysis*. Do you remember
where sodium is in the Reactivity Series? (See page 84.)
Sodium is a very reactive metal.

We extract sodium from *molten sodium chloride*.
The molten salt is electrolysed.
As well as sodium, what else do you think will
be formed?

The electrolysis is done in a Down's Cell.
Look at the diagram below:

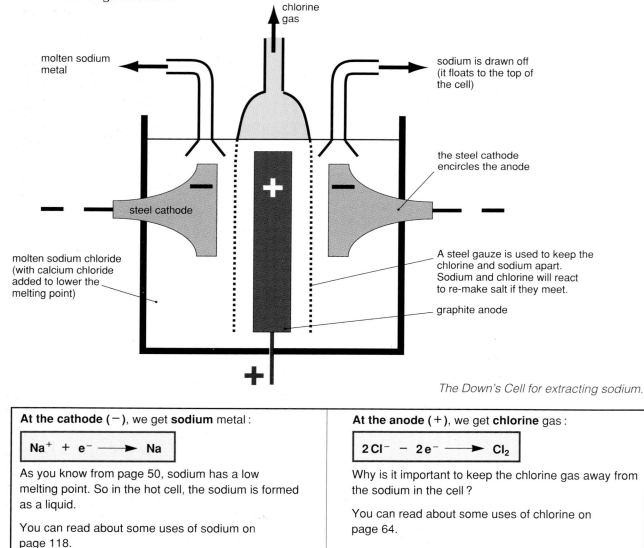

chlorine gas

molten sodium metal

sodium is drawn off (it floats to the top of the cell)

the steel cathode encircles the anode

steel cathode

molten sodium chloride (with calcium chloride added to lower the melting point)

A steel gauze is used to keep the chlorine and sodium apart. Sodium and chlorine will react to re-make salt if they meet.

graphite anode

The Down's Cell for extracting sodium.

At the cathode (−), we get sodium metal:

$$Na^+ + e^- \longrightarrow Na$$

As you know from page 50, sodium has a low
melting point. So in the hot cell, the sodium is formed
as a liquid.

You can read about some uses of sodium on
page 118.

At the anode (+), we get chlorine gas:

$$2\,Cl^- - 2e^- \longrightarrow Cl_2$$

Why is it important to keep the chlorine gas away from
the sodium in the cell?

You can read about some uses of chlorine on
page 64.

▷ Brine (salt solution)

We have seen how rock salt is mined on page 112.
The second way that we can get
salt from the ground is **solution mining**.
This method relies on salt dissolving in water.
Look at the diagram below:

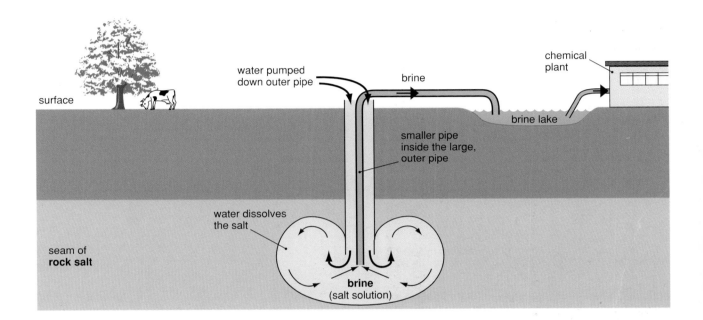

Hot water is pumped down the outer pipe.
It dissolves the salt. The salt solution is then
forced up the smaller, inner pipe
by the pressure of water.

The salt solution is called **brine**.
The brine is stored in lakes until it is needed.
It is then pumped straight to the chemical plant.

When mining in an area has finished,
the holes left under the ground must be filled.
If not the land above can collapse and slide
into the old mines. This is called subsidence.
Look at the old photograph opposite:

Subsidence used to be more of a problem in
Cheshire. Nowadays the holes are carefully
spaced out.

Subsidence was a problem in Cheshire

▷ Electrolysis of brine

We have now seen how brine (salt solution)
is brought to the surface.
At the chemical plant it is electrolysed (broken down
by electricity).
You can try this yourself in the next experiment:

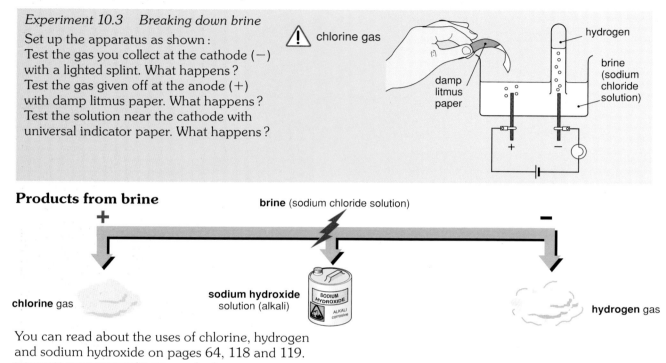

Experiment 10.3   Breaking down brine

Set up the apparatus as shown:
Test the gas you collect at the cathode (−)
with a lighted splint. What happens?
Test the gas given off at the anode (+)
with damp litmus paper. What happens?
Test the solution near the cathode with
universal indicator paper. What happens?

⚠ chlorine gas

hydrogen

brine (sodium chloride solution)

damp litmus paper

Products from brine

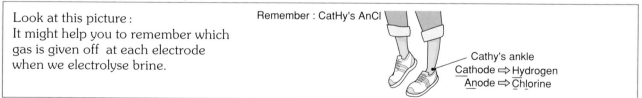

brine (sodium chloride solution)

+

−

chlorine gas

sodium hydroxide solution (alkali)

SODIUM HYDROXIDE
ALKALI corrosive

hydrogen gas

You can read about the uses of chlorine, hydrogen
and sodium hydroxide on pages 64, 118 and 119.

Look at this picture:
It might help you to remember which
gas is given off at each electrode
when we electrolyse brine.

Remember: CatHy's AnCl

Cathy's ankle
Cathode ⇨ Hydrogen
Anode ⇨ Chlorine

In industry

There are several types of cell used in industry.
The most modern is called a membrane cell.
Look at the diagram opposite:
A plastic membrane divides the cell in two.
This keeps the chlorine and hydrogen gas apart and stops
chlorine reacting with the sodium hydroxide.
The gases leave from the top of the cell.

Only sodium ions can pass through the membrane.
Chloride ions can't get through. This gives us
sodium hydroxide on the negative side of the cell.

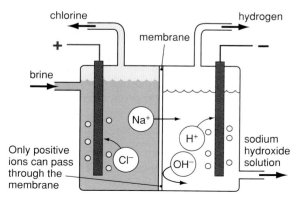

chlorine

hydrogen

+

membrane

−

brine

Only positive
ions can pass
through the
membrane

Na^+

H^+

Cl^-

OH^-

sodium
hydroxide
solution

Explaining the electrolysis of brine

Let's see if we can work out how we get hydrogen, chlorine and sodium hydroxide from brine.

You might have read about the electrolysis of solutions on page 104. It explains why reactive metals, such as sodium, are not freed from solutions during electrolysis.
Remember that brine is sodium chloride solution. Instead of sodium we get hydrogen forming at the cathode ($-$).

Can you recall where the hydrogen comes from?
H^+ ions come from the water (H_2O) in the solution. A few water molecules split up into hydrogen ions (H^+) and hydroxide ions (OH^-):

$$H_2O(l) \rightleftharpoons H^+(aq) + OH^-(aq)$$

Therefore, in a solution of sodium chloride we have 4 different ions:

sodium Na^+, hydrogen H^+, chloride Cl^-, and hydroxide OH^-

The H^+ and Cl^- ions are discharged at the electrodes.
Hydrogen comes off at the cathode ($-$):

$$\boxed{2\,H^+(aq) + 2\,e^- \longrightarrow H_2(g)}$$

Chlorine comes off at the anode ($+$):

$$\boxed{2\,Cl^-(aq) - 2\,e^- \longrightarrow Cl_2(g)}$$

The Na^+ and OH^- ions stay in solution.
They form **sodium hydroxide** solution in the cell.
Sodium hydroxide is a very important alkali.

Look at the diagram:

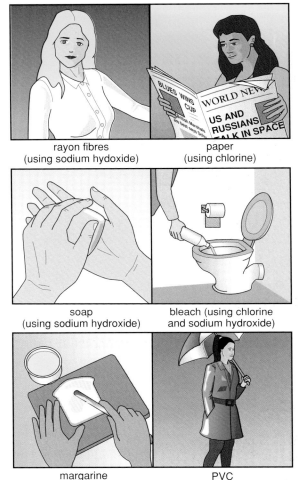

rayon fibres
(using sodium hydoxide)

paper
(using chlorine)

soap
(using sodium hydroxide)

bleach (using chlorine
and sodium hydroxide)

margarine
(using hydrogen)

PVC
(using chlorine)

These are some everyday products made using salt as a raw material

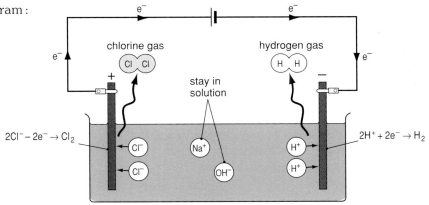

$2Cl^- - 2e^- \rightarrow Cl_2$

chlorine gas

stay in solution

hydrogen gas

$2H^+ + 2e^- \rightarrow H_2$

▷ Chemistry at work : Products from salt

Here are the chemicals we can
get from salt :

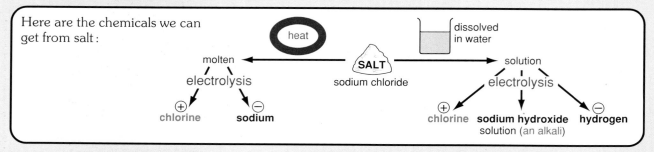

Uses of sodium

Street lamps
Have you ever noticed the yellow glow
at night in a lit-up area ?
We can thank sodium for this effect.
A small amount of sodium vapour
is inside the yellow street lamps.

Sodium vapour is used in street lamps

Heat transfer
Sodium is also used in some nuclear reactors.
You might think it is strange to use
such a reactive metal in a nuclear power plant.
However, sodium has some useful properties.
It is a good conductor of heat and has a low melting point.
This is why it is used to transfer heat
from the reactor to the steam generators.
It is pumped around the power plant in sealed pipes.

Why is it important to keep the pipes sealed ?
Why can't a safer, less reactive metal, such as copper,
be used to transfer the heat ?

Sodium is used in nuclear reactors

Uses of hydrogen

Making margarine
Margarines are made from vegetable oils.
The oils are liquids which are too runny to spread on bread.
The problem has been solved by reacting hydrogen with
the natural oil molecules. This makes the oils thicker.
The larger molecules formed have higher melting points.
A nickel catalyst is used to speed up the reaction.
Chemists have to judge just the right amount of hydrogen to add.
If they add too much, the margarine will be too hard to spread
when it comes out of the fridge. If they don't add enough,
the margarine will be soft and runny if left out of the fridge !

*Hydrogen reacts with oils to
make margarine with the right
consistency*

▷ Chemistry at work : Products from salt

Hydrogen as a fuel

Can you remember the test for hydrogen gas?
Hydrogen reacts explosively with the oxygen in air.
When a lighted splint pops in hydrogen,
it reacts with oxygen to make water (steam).

$$\text{hydrogen} + \text{oxygen} \longrightarrow \text{water}$$
$$2H_2(g) + O_2(g) \longrightarrow 2H_2O(g)$$

One of the first uses of hydrogen was in airships.
Hydrogen is the lightest of all gases. However, its
violent reaction with oxygen led to disasters.
Which safer gas is used in airships today? (see page 67.)

Scientists are very interested in using hydrogen
as a fuel. Look at the equation above:
Do you think hydrogen makes any pollution when it burns?
What problems do you think hydrogen-powered cars have?
Chemists are looking for ways to store the gas
on the surface of transition metals. This would be safer
and take up less room in the car.

Hydrogen has played a big part in space travel.
It can be used as rocket fuel. The liquid hydrogen
is stored in tanks, ready to react with liquid oxygen.
It has also been used inside space-craft to power
fuel cells. A fuel cell is an efficient way of reacting
hydrogen with oxygen. It transfers the energy from
the reaction directly into electrical energy.

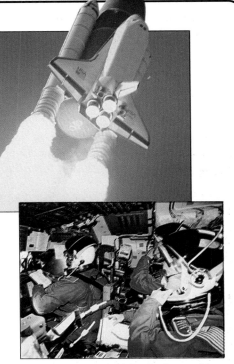

Hydrogen is one of the fuels used in rockets. It is also used in fuel cells to provide electricity for the astronauts in space.

Uses of sodium hydroxide

The salt industry is known as the **'chlor-alkali'** industry.
The alkali, sodium hydroxide, is the most important
of the products from salt.
Look at the range of things it is used to make:

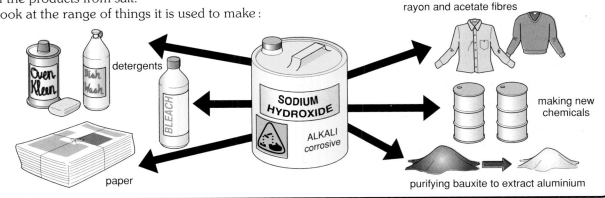

detergents

rayon and acetate fibres

BLEACH

SODIUM HYDROXIDE

ALKALI corrosive

making new chemicals

paper

purifying bauxite to extract aluminium

Summary

- Common salt is **sodium chloride, NaCl**.
- It is found in the sea or in underground seams.
- Salt is dug up from mines as **rock salt**. It is also pumped to the surface as a solution. Salt solution is called **brine**.
- When *molten* sodium chloride is electrolysed we get:
  sodium at the cathode ($-$), and
  chlorine at the anode ($+$).
- When a *solution* of sodium chloride (brine) is electrolysed we get:
  hydrogen at the cathode ($-$),
  chlorine at the anode ($+$), and
  sodium hydroxide solution (*an alkali*) formed.

▷ Questions

1. Copy and complete:
   The chemical name for common salt is . . . .
   Its chemical formula is . . . . . When molten
   sodium chloride is electrolysed, ... metal forms
   at the . . . . ($-$) and . . . . gas is given off at the
   anode ($+$).
   Salt solution is called . . . . When it is electrolysed
   . . . . gas forms at the cathode ($-$) and . . . . gas at
   the anode ($+$). The solution becomes an . . . . as
   sodium . . . . is left.

2. Copy and complete this flow diagram. It shows
   the chemicals we can get from salt:

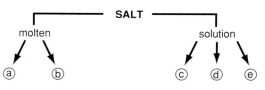

3. This diagram shows the solution mining of salt.

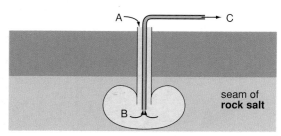

   seam of
   rock salt

   Copy the diagram and explain what happens at
   A, B and C.

4. Sodium metal is extracted in a Down's Cell.
   a) Copy this diagram and fill in the labels:

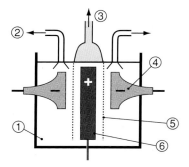

   b) Complete this word equation to describe
   what happens in the Down's Cell:
   sodium chloride $\xrightarrow{\text{electrolysis}}$ . . . . + ...
   c) It takes a lot of energy to melt the sodium
   chloride.
   i)   Why can't we use sodium chloride
        solution to get the sodium metal?
   ii) Which substance is added to the sodium
        chloride to lower its melting point?
        Explain why sodium would cost more to
        buy if this substance was not added.
   d) Why is there a barrier between the positive
   and the negative electrodes?

5. a) Describe how brine is electrolysed in
   industry. Include a diagram in your answer.
   b) Imagine you are a sodium ion, Na^+, in a
   seam of rock salt. Describe your adventures
   on the way to finding yourself as sodium
   hydroxide in an oven cleaner.

Further questions on page 133.

chapter 11

Calcium carbonate

Have you ever seen the 'white cliffs of Dover'?
If you have, you've seen lots of **calcium carbonate**.
Chalk is one form of calcium carbonate.

You might also find other forms of calcium carbonate
around your school. Some schools are built of it!
Limestone is the most important form of calcium carbonate.
It is a common building material. It might
be spread on the school roads or roofs as chippings.

The third form of calcium carbonate is **marble**.

A school built from limestone

> ### The chemical formula of calcium carbonate is $CaCO_3$.

All forms of calcium carbonate are formed from
the shells of sea creatures that died millions of years ago.
Yet chalk, limestone and marble are very different.
How does their hardness differ? The 3 forms have been
heated and squashed underground by different amounts.
You can read Chapter 23 for more details about
different types of rock and how they were formed.

Limestone is a raw material for making concrete and glass

Limestone

Have you ever visited the Peak District or the
Yorkshire Dales? If you have, you will have
enjoyed the beautiful views from the limestone hills.
You might have been pot-holing or visited the caves there.
These caves have been worn out of the limestone
by rain-water. Rain-water is slightly acidic
because carbon dioxide dissolves in it as it falls.
You can see how limestone reacts with acid on page 190.

Limestone is a common rock in Britain. It is blasted
from the hillsides in huge quarries.
Look at the photograph:

Why do you think that many people are against
any plans for new quarries?
These arguments have to be balanced against the benefits.
Limestone is a vital raw material for industry.
Look at its uses on pages 124 and 125.
New jobs and money are created for the area.
What are your views on quarrying?

A limestone quarry 'scars' the landscape

▷ Looking at limestone

Once limestone is quarried, it is changed into many useful materials.
Is your home made from bricks? If it is, they are fixed in place by mortar. Mortar is mixed using cement, which we get from limestone.
Or perhaps you live in a building made mainly from concrete? The raw material for concrete is also limestone.

In this experiment you can make some new substances from limestone:

Limestone and its products are used a lot in the building industry

Experiment 11.1 Changing limestone

Follow the steps shown below.
Write down what happens as you go along.

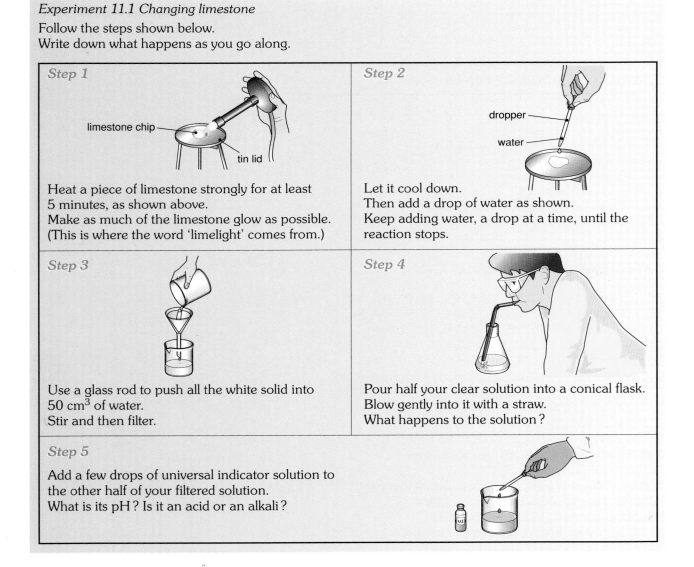

Step 1

limestone chip

tin lid

Heat a piece of limestone strongly for at least 5 minutes, as shown above.
Make as much of the limestone glow as possible.
(This is where the word 'limelight' comes from.)

Step 2

dropper

water

Let it cool down.
Then add a drop of water as shown.
Keep adding water, a drop at a time, until the reaction stops.

Step 3

Use a glass rod to push all the white solid into 50 cm^3 of water.
Stir and then filter.

Step 4

Pour half your clear solution into a conical flask.
Blow gently into it with a straw.
What happens to the solution?

Step 5

Add a few drops of universal indicator solution to the other half of your filtered solution.
What is its pH? Is it an acid or an alkali?

▷ Reactions of limestone

The reactions in the last experiment can be shown like this:

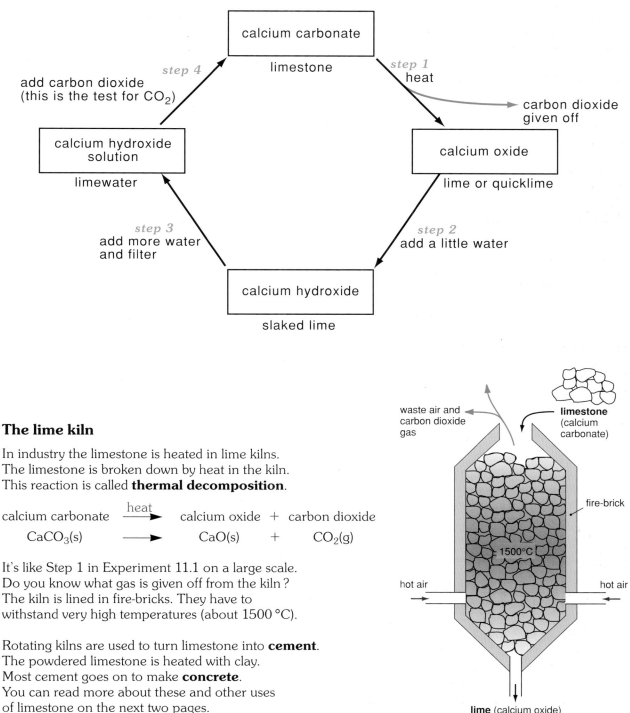

The lime kiln

In industry the limestone is heated in lime kilns.
The limestone is broken down by heat in the kiln.
This reaction is called **thermal decomposition**.

calcium carbonate $\xrightarrow{\text{heat}}$ calcium oxide + carbon dioxide

$$CaCO_3(s) \longrightarrow CaO(s) + CO_2(g)$$

It's like Step 1 in Experiment 11.1 on a large scale.
Do you know what gas is given off from the kiln?
The kiln is lined in fire-bricks. They have to
withstand very high temperatures (about 1500 °C).

Rotating kilns are used to turn limestone into **cement**.
The powdered limestone is heated with clay.
Most cement goes on to make **concrete**.
You can read more about these and other uses
of limestone on the next two pages.

123

▷ Chemistry at work : Uses of limestone

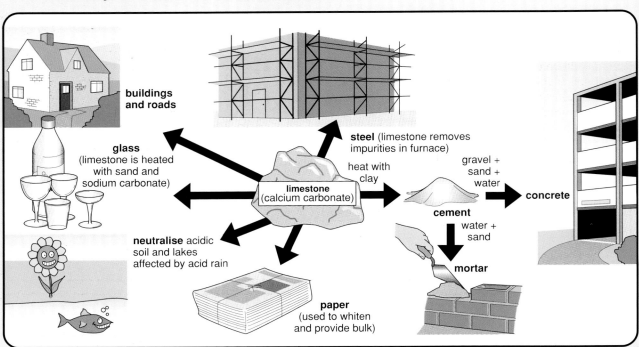

buildings and roads

glass (limestone is heated with sand and sodium carbonate)

steel (limestone removes impurities in furnace)

heat with clay

limestone (calcium carbonate)

gravel + sand + water

cement

concrete

water + sand

mortar

neutralise acidic soil and lakes affected by acid rain

paper (used to whiten and provide bulk)

Cement

Have you ever watched brick-layers at work? They use a mixture of cement and sand, with water added to make a thick paste. This is called **mortar**. It takes a lot of skill to set the bricks in the right position. What do you think would happen if their mortar was too runny? What if it was too dry?

Cement is made by heating limestone and clay (or shale). They are ground up and heated in kilns which rotate. A little gypsum (calcium sulphate) is added. This stops the cement from setting as soon as you add water.

Cement sets as it reacts with water. The reactions are complex. We can think of it as 'fingers' of crystals growing out from each grain of cement. These interlock and bind the mixture together. Mortar will set overnight. However, it carries on reacting and getting stronger for several months.

Investigation 11.2   Mortar   ⚠ cement

Why don't you try some brick-laying yourself! Experiment with different mixtures of cement and sand. See which mixture makes the best mortar.

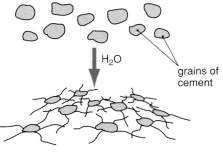

H_2O

grains of cement

Crystal fingers (of calcium hydroxide) hold the structure together as it sets

▷ Chemistry at work : Uses of limestone

Concrete

What are the paths around your school made from?
Some will be made from concrete.
Concrete is made by mixing cement, sand and small stones.
If you look closely, you will see the small stones
set in position.

Concrete is the most widely used building material
in the world. That explains why we produce about
1000 million tonnes of cement in the world every year!

Investigation 11.3   Concrete

⚠ cement

You can test different mixtures of cement, sand,
and gravel to see which makes the strongest concrete.
You can make your mixtures in yoghurt pots.
● Do you know how we can make concrete even stronger?

Limestone in paper !

Will your chemistry book be around in another 100 years?
That depends on whether it has acidic or alkaline paper!

Paper is made mainly from wood pulp.
Acid is used to help break down the wood.
We also add other things to the pulp.
It needs to be made white and opaque.
It also has fillers added to give it bulk.
This uses up less wood.

For over a century this treatment of the wood
has resulted in paper which is acidic!
The acid slowly attacks the fibres of wood pulp.
Some books over 40 years old are starting to fall apart.
The paper becomes too brittle to touch.

However, we now know how to make alkaline paper!
This involves replacing old whiteners and fillers
by a fine powder of calcium carbonate.

The reaction of limewater with carbon dioxide gives us
fine, evenly shaped particles of calcium carbonate.
And at last we have a use for 'the test for CO_2'!

Calcium carbonate filler reduces the amount of wood needed to make paper

As well as longer-lasting paper, re-cycling recovers
more of the wood fibre than before.
You also don't need as much wood to make the paper
because limestone is such a good filler.
This is all good news for trees!

▷ Hard water

Do you know what **hard water** is?

If you live in an area which has hard water
you certainly will!

You'll find it difficult to make a lather with soap.
Bits of white scum will float around in the water
when you use soap.
However, it does have its advantages.
Look at this table:

Disadvantages of hard water	Advantages of hard water
Difficult to form lather with soap. Scum forms in a reaction which wastes soap. Scale (a hard crust) forms inside kettles. This wastes energy when you boil your kettle. Hot water pipes 'fur up' on the inside. The scale formed can even block up pipes completely.	Some people prefer the taste. Calcium in the water is good for children's teeth and bones. Helps to reduce heart illness Some brewers like hard water for making beer.

Let's see if we can find out why some water is hard:

Experiment 11.4   What causes hardness in water?

Use 10 cm^3 of each solution.
Add 1 cm^3 of soap solution to your boiling-tube.
Put a bung in and shake.
See if you get a good lather (one that lasts 30 seconds).
A good lather means that the solution is **soft**.
A poor lather and white bits (scum) in your solution
means that it is **hard**.

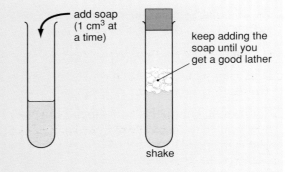

Record your results in a table like this:

Solution	Volume of soap to get a good lather (cm^3)	Hard or soft?
sodium chloride calcium chloride potassium chloride magnesium chloride		

- Which substances make the water hard?
- Is it the metal or the chloride ions in these solutions which make the water hard? How can you tell?

What makes water hard?

If your water supply has flowed through chalk
or limestone (**calcium carbonate**) it will be hard.
Other rocks which contain calcium or magnesium,
also cause hardness. Gypsum (**calcium sulphate**)
is an example.

**Calcium (or magnesium) compounds dissolved in
water make it hard.**

Calcium sulphate is slightly soluble in water. When a river
flows over gypsum, it dissolves some of the rock.
Therefore, calcium gets into the water.

However, calcium carbonate is not soluble in water.
Water does not dissolve chalk or limestone rock.
But do you remember from page 121 how
limestone caves are formed?

People often think that rain-water is the purest water
you can get. This isn't quite true.
On its way down, gases dissolve in the rain.
One of these gases is carbon dioxide – a weakly acidic gas.
It's the bubbles you see in fizzy drinks:

water + carbon dioxide $\longrightarrow$ carbonic acid (a weak acid)
$H_2O(l)$ + $CO_2(g)$ $\longrightarrow$ $H_2CO_3(aq)$

This weakly acidic solution dissolves away the limestone or chalk:

calcium carbonate + carbonic acid $\longrightarrow$ calcium hydrogencarbonate
$CaCO_3(s)$ + $H_2CO_3(aq)$ $\longrightarrow$ $Ca(HCO_3)_2(aq)$

Look at the state symbols in the equation above.
You can see that the **calcium hydrogencarbonate** formed
is soluble in water. Therefore the calcium gets into
the water, making it hard.

You can test water from different places
to see how hard it is.

Water flowing over gypsum (calcium sulphate)
becomes hard

*Limestone reacts with the weakly
acidic rain and river water.
Eventually underground caverns
can be formed as the rock is
worn away.*

Experiment 11.5   How hard?

Add 1 cm³ of soap solution to 10 cm³ of the water
being tested. Stopper the test-tube and shake.
Repeat this until you get a good lather
(one that lasts at least 30 seconds).

Test different samples.
Record your results in a table:

Water tested	Volume of soap needed to get a good lather (cm³)
distilled water	
local tap water	
hard tap water	

▷ Removing hardness

You have now seen how hard water is formed.
The calcium or magnesium in the water
is present as charged particles called ions (see page 69).
The most common cause of hardness is
the calcium ion, Ca^{2+} **(aq)**.

These calcium ions react with ions from soap
(sodium stearate) to form **scum** :

calcium ions (aq) + stearate ions (aq) ⟶ calcium stearate (s)
    hard water   +   soap   ⟶   scum

If we can remove these Ca^{2+} ions from the water
we will get rid of the hardness.

Temporary hardness

Do you remember how calcium ions from
insoluble calcium carbonate get into hard water ?
Limestone reacts with acidic rain-water. It forms
a solution of calcium hydrogencarbonate.
Calcium ions are now in solution.

This is called **temporary** hardness.

When this solution is boiled,
calcium hydrogencarbonate breaks down.
It turns back into the insoluble calcium carbonate.
Therefore *calcium ions are removed* from the water.

calcium hydrogencarbonate ⟶ calcium carbonate + carbon dioxide +   water
    $Ca(HCO_3)_2(aq)$ ⟶ $CaCO_3(s)$ + $CO_2(g)$ + $H_2O(l)$

The calcium carbonate formed is the **scale**
you get inside kettles and hot-water pipes.

Temporarily hard water can be softened by boiling.

Do you think this is a cheap way to get rid of hardness ?
Imagine your heating bills if you
had to boil all your water before
you could use your washing machine !

However, not all hard water can be softened by boiling.
Other calcium compounds, such as calcium sulphate
from gypsum, are not removed by boiling.
These form **permanently** hard water.

There was a young boy called Arthur
Who tried to make a good lather
But try as he might
His bubbles weren't right.
"It's hard, soft lad !" said his father.

Scale on the heating element in a kettle

This hot water pipe has been
almost blocked by scale (or lime-scale)

Removing all types of hardness

We have seen how we can soften temporarily hard water by boiling. But permanent hardness can also be removed. Permanent means forever, but all types of hardness can be removed from water.

1. Washing soda (sodium carbonate)

When you add washing soda to hard water, the calcium ions are removed. They react with the carbonate ions from the washing soda. This forms *insoluble* calcium carbonate:

Washing soda removes hardness

calcium ions + carbonate ions $\longrightarrow$ calcium carbonate

$$Ca^{2+}(aq) + CO_3^{2-}(aq) \longrightarrow CaCO_3(s)$$

(in hard water)   (from washing soda)   precipitate (insoluble)

This is called an **ionic equation**. It only shows the ions which are affected in the reaction.

> **If a solid forms when two solutions are mixed, it is called a precipitation reaction.**

Most modern washing powders have their own water softeners added.

2. Ion-exchange column

This method is more suitable for large-scale treatment of hard water.
Look at the diagram opposite:
The column is filled with a resin which holds plenty of sodium ions.
Hard water goes in at the top. On the way down, the calcium ions are swapped for sodium ions.
The calcium ions get stuck on the resin.
Sodium ions, which don't cause hardness, come out in the water at the bottom.

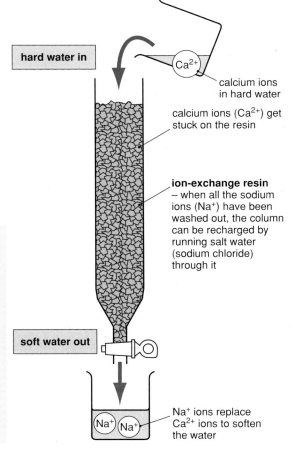

hard water in

calcium ions in hard water

calcium ions (Ca^{2+}) get stuck on the resin

ion-exchange resin – when all the sodium ions (Na^+) have been washed out, the column can be recharged by running salt water (sodium chloride) through it

soft water out

Na^+ ions replace Ca^{2+} ions to soften the water

Experiment 11.6   Removing hardness

Look back to experiment 11.5 on page 127.
Use that method to test the hardness of your water samples before and after treatment:

1. Test some temporarily hard water.
   Now boil a fresh sample of the water and re-test it.

2. Test some permanently hard water.
   Now add a spatula of washing soda to a fresh sample.
   Make sure it dissolves, then re-test.

3. Test your samples of the hard water after they have passed through an ion-exchange column.

▷ Chemistry at work : Glass

Limestone is one of the materials that we use to make **glass**.
Glass is important in all our lives.
Think of all the things we use every day
that are made from glass.
Look at the photos :
Can you think of any other things made from glass ?

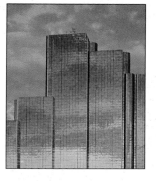

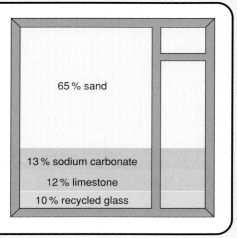

What is glass ?

Glass is a strange material. Can you remember the 3 states of matter (page 6) ?
Some people call glass the 4th state of matter. It's like a 'solid liquid' !
The raw materials (see below) are heated to 1500 °C. At this high temperature,
they melt and react to form molten glass. As it cools down,
the glass turns into a solid. However, the particles don't form a regular pattern.
It's as if the particles in the molten glass are frozen in place.
Look at the diagram :
Can you see how the structure is jumbled up ?

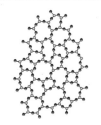

The disorderly structure in borosilicate glass

What's in glass ?

Did you know that glass is made mainly from sand ?
Glass has been around for a long time. It was probably discovered
by accident in the sand underneath an ancient fire !
The first glass object has been dated at about 4500 BC.
The Egyptians used glass containers around 3000 BC.

As well as **sand** (SiO_2), the other raw materials are
limestone ($CaCO_3$) and **sodium carbonate** (Na_2CO_3).
You have seen some of the uses of common salt (sodium chloride)
on pages 118–119. Sodium carbonate is another useful product
made from salt.
Re-cycled glass (cullet) is becoming more important.
It can make up to 30 % of some glass-making mixtures.

65 % sand

13 % sodium carbonate

12 % limestone

10 % recycled glass

▷ Chemistry at work : Glass

Different types of glass

Have you ever seen a car window that's been smashed?
The bits of glass look very different from the pieces
you get when a bottle smashes.
Bottles and car windows are made from different types of glass.

There are many different types of glass. Scientists have
tried changing the glass-making mixture. They've also
found ways of treating the glass to change its properties.
For example, windscreens are usually made like a
glass sandwich – with a thin sheet of plastic as the filling!
This is called laminated glass.
How does this help if a stone hits your windscreen?
Look at the table below:
Do all these types of glass have any properties in common?

This glass had not been laminated

Type of glass	Use
soda-lime	windows
boro-silicate	test-tubes, beakers, etc. (heat-proof, chemical resistant)
lead-crystal	decorative glasses, bowls and vases
glass fibres	fibre optics, fibreglass
optical glass	lenses in spectacles, cameras, projectors, etc.
glass ceramic	opaque oven-ware

These glass fibres carry information in the form of light. A single fibre can carry 10 000 phone calls at once.

Coloured glass

Have you taken any glass to be re-cycled at a bottle-bank?
The bottles are sorted out into different colours.
What are the most common colours of glass bottles?
Green and brown bottles get their colour from iron impurities
in the sand that it is made from.
On page 57 we found out that the **transition metals**
form coloured compounds. Adding small amounts
of their oxides makes glass coloured.

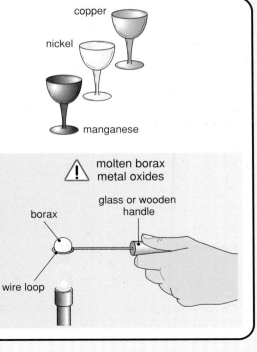

copper

nickel

manganese

Experiment 11.7   Make your own glass

1. Sugar, like sand, is made of crystals.
   You can make sugar-glass (toffee) by melting some sugar.
   Heat it until its colour is pale brown.
   Then cool it quickly to make a clear, hard toffee.

2. Heat some borax on a wire loop as shown:
   This melts to form a structure like glass.
   When molten, dip it in a *tiny* amount
   of a transition metal oxide.
   This will make a bead of coloured glass when cool.

⚠ molten borax
metal oxides

glass or wooden
handle

borax

wire loop

131

Investigation 11.8 Thermal decomposition

You have seen on page 122 what happens when we heat calcium carbonate. The reaction is called thermal decomposition. Now investigate this problem.

Which carbonates break down most easily?
You can investigate some of the carbonates of:
calcium, magnesium, sodium, potassium, copper, and zinc.
Plan a fair test to find out which of these decomposes most quickly.
• How can you make it safe?
Ask your teacher to check your plan before you try it.

carbonate being tested
limewater
heat

Summary

• Calcium carbonate ($CaCO_3$) is mainly found in nature as limestone, chalk and marble.
• It is broken down by heat (thermal decomposition), to give calcium oxide and carbon dioxide.
• Calcium ions cause hardness in water.
• We can remove temporary hardness by boiling the water. Permanent hardness can be removed by adding washing soda or passing the water through an ion-exchange column.

▷ Questions

1. Copy and complete:
   The chemical name for limestone is ....
   Its formula is .....
   When heated, limestone breaks down in a reaction called .... decomposition. The products formed are .... and carbon dioxide.
   .... ions cause hardness in water. Boiling will get rid of .... hardness. However, permanent hardness must be treated by adding sodium carbonate (known as ....), or by passing it through an ....-.... column.

2. Draw a table with 2 columns. In the table show the advantages and disadvantages of starting a limestone quarry in a National Park.

3. Limestone is roasted in a lime kiln.
   a) Write a word and symbol equation for the reaction in a lime kiln.
   b) What do we call this type of reaction?
   c) Draw a diagram of the apparatus you could use to show that carbon dioxide gas is given off when calcium carbonate is heated.

4. Anna tested 3 samples of water with soap solution. She recorded how much soap was needed to get a permanent lather, before and after boiling:

Water sample	Soap solution added (cm³)	
	before boiling	after boiling
sample A	8	7
sample B	1	1
sample C	7	2

   What can you deduce about each sample of water?

5. Limestone is insoluble in water. However, water flowing over limestone becomes hard.
   a) Explain how calcium ions get into water that has passed over limestone rock.
   b) List the advantages and disadvantages of hard water.
   c) Explain how adding washing soda removes hardness from water.

6. Make a spider diagram of the useful products that we can make from limestone.

Further questions on page 139.

▷ The Reactivity Series

1. Wendy did an experiment to find out how reactive five different metals are.
   She tested small amounts of each metal with cold water.
   She tested small amounts of some of the metals with hot water and steam.
   Some tests she did not try.
   She wrote down what happened in this table.

metal	cold water	hot water	steam
A	no reaction	reacts slowly	burns if heated in steam
B	no reaction	no reaction	no reaction
C	reacts very vigorously	not tried	not tried
D	no reaction	no reaction	slow reaction
E	reacts slowly	rapid reaction	not tried

   a) Arrange the metals, **A, B, C, D** and **E** in order of decreasing reactivity. [1]
   b) Suggest why she did not try metal **C** in hot water or steam. [1] (MEG)

2. a) Describe how the elements magnesium and iron react with dilute sulphuric acid. [2]
   b) Predict how readily, if at all
      i) platinum,
      ii) calcium,
      would react with dilute sulphuric acid. [2]
   c) i) What changes would you expect to **see** if a piece of zinc were left in some blue copper(II) sulphate solution? [2]
      ii) Name the substances formed in the reaction. [1] (WJEC)

3. Space explorers found the metals **X, Y** and **Z** on another planet.
   a) The table shows their reactions with water and with dilute acid.

metal	with cold water	with dilute acid
X	no reaction	slow reaction
Y	fast reaction	violent reaction
Z	no reaction	no reaction

   Arrange the three metals in order starting with the most reactive. [1]

b) Another test is tried on metal **X**.

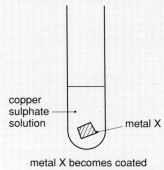

metal X becomes coated in a red/brown substance

Explain as fully as you can, the results of this test. [2] (NEAB)

4. A pupil grew some lead crystals by displacing lead from a solution of lead nitrate.

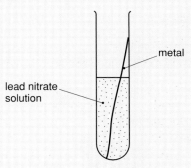

The pupil dropped a piece of metal into the lead nitrate solution. The metal displaced the lead from the lead nitrate solution and shiny, dark crystals of lead were formed.
a) What information above suggests that lead crystals are metal? [1]
b) i) Which **one** of the following metals would displace lead from lead nitrate solution? (You may find it helpful to use page 84.)
      copper   platinum
      gold   silver
      lead   zinc   [1]
   ii) Explain why you have chosen this metal. [1] (NEAB)

Further questions on products from metal ores and rocks

5. The results of two experiments are summarised in the following word equations:

zinc + nickel oxide ⟶ zinc oxide + nickel
nickel + copper oxide ⟶ nickel oxide + copper

Use the results to place the **three** metals in order of **decreasing** reactivity. [1] (WJEC)

6. You may find page 84 helpful in answering this question.
When a piece of zinc foil is placed in a solution of blue copper sulphate, it becomes covered with a brown layer.
When a similar piece of zinc foil is placed in a solution of magnesium sulphate, there is no change.
Explain the results of the two experiments. [3]
(NEAB)

7. a) Window frames made from iron corrode faster than those made from aluminium. This observation does **not** follow the order of the reactivity series. Explain the reasons for this.

[3]

b) The diagram shows how railway lines are welded together. The reaction of aluminium with iron oxide (Fe_2O_3) forms molten iron which is run between the lengths of railway line.

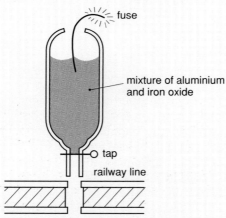

i) Explain how aluminium reacts with iron oxide to form iron. [2]
ii) Why does this reaction form molten iron? [2]
iii) Give a balanced symbolic equation for this reaction. [1] (SEG)

8. The following experiments were carried out to investigate the reactivity of the metals copper, magnesium and sodium.

a) **Experiment 1**
An excess of magnesium powder was shaken with copper(II) sulphate solution. The solution became colourless and a red-brown powder was seen.
i) Name the red-brown powder. [1]
ii) Name the colourless solution. [1]
iii) Write a word equation for the reaction. [1]

b) **Experiment 2**
A small piece of sodium was put into a trough containing water. The sodium floated on the surface, forming a silver-coloured ball. The ball fizzed around. It got smaller and smaller, then disappeared. The gas given off popped with a lighted splint. Universal Indicator solution turned blue when added to the water.
i) Name the gas given off. [1]
ii) Name the substance that turned the Universal Indicator blue. [1]
iii) Write a word equation for the reaction between sodium and water. [1]

c) **Experiment 3**
Magnesium reacts very slowly with cold water. It was reacted with steam in the apparatus shown below.

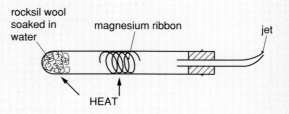

The magnesium and rocksil wool were heated. A bright light was seen inside the test tube. A lighted splint was applied to the jet and then a flame was seen. A white powder was left in the test tube.
i) Name the white powder. [1]
ii) Name the gas burning at the jet. [1]
iii) Write a word equation for the reaction in the test tube. [1] (NEAB)

▷ Extraction of metals and Electrolysis

9. The flow diagram shows how iron is produced in the blast furnace.

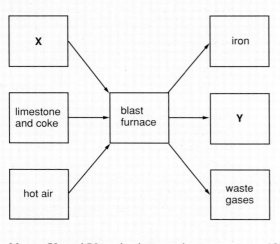

Name **X** and **Y** in the boxes above.   [2]
(MEG)

10. Iron ores are mined and shipped to blast furnace plants. The iron ore (mainly iron oxide) reacts with carbon monoxide formed in the furnace. The equation is given below:

$$Fe_2O_3(s) + 3CO(g) \longrightarrow 2Fe(s) + 3CO_2(g)$$

   a) What is the function of carbon monoxide in this reaction?   [1]
   b) Discuss the factors that would influence the choice of a site for a new blast furnace.   [3]
   c) The iron formed is used in making alloys. Name and give a use of an alloy containing iron.   [2]   (MEG)

11. Iron is produced in the blast furnace. A mixture of iron ore, limestone and coke is fed into the top of the furnace and hot air is blown in near the bottom.
   a) What is the purpose of the limestone?   [1]
   b) State **two** functions of the coke.   [2]
(MEG)

12. The diagram shows a blast furnace for the extraction of iron.

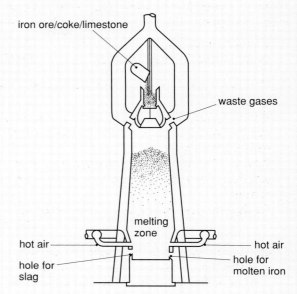

Hot air is blown into the furnace. Its main purpose is to
A react with the coke.
B react with the iron ore.
C react with the limestone.
D remove the excess coke.
E remove the waste gases.   [1]   (MEG)

13. The main ore present in a certain mine is malachite. Malachite has the formula $Cu_2CO_3(OH)_2$ and is converted into copper oxide on heating. The copper oxide is then converted into copper in a furnace.
   a) Give the name of the chemical process which takes place when copper oxide is converted into copper.   [1]
   b) Suggest the name of a substance which might be used in the furnace to convert the copper oxide into copper.   [1]
   c) Limestone is also put into the furnace when copper oxide is converted into copper. Suggest a reason for this.   [1]   (ULEAC)

Further questions on products from metal ores and rocks

14. The test tubes below were part of an investigation on rusting.

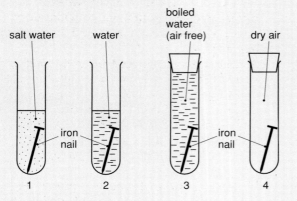

salt water   water   boiled water (air free)   dry air

iron nail   iron nail

1   2   3   4

a) Why do the nails **not** rust in test tubes 3 and 4? [2]

b) The iron hull of a ship is painted to stop it rusting.
   i) How does paint stop the iron rusting? [1]

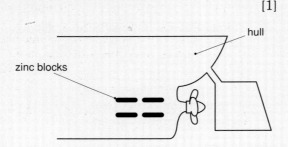

hull

zinc blocks

   ii) The picture shows zinc blocks attached to the hull of the ship. Use the Reactivity Series on page 84 to explain why the zinc blocks corrode away instead of the iron hull. [1]

c) Why might a ship in sea-water rust faster than one that is only used in a large freshwater lake? [2]   (NEAB)

15. In which one of the following sets are all the metals so reactive that they all have to be extracted by electrolysis?

A	Ca	Cu	Pb	
B	Ca	Mg	Na	
C	Cu	Mg	Zn	
D	Cu	K	Mg	
E	Mg	Pb	Zn	[1] (MEG)

16. Tungsten is used for the manufacture of filaments for light bulbs. Tungsten may be obtained by heating its oxide, WO_3, in hydrogen. The equation for this reaction is:
$$WO_3(s) + ... H_2(g) \longrightarrow W(s) + ... H_2O(g)$$
a) What is the chemical symbol for tungsten used in the above equation?
b) Balance the above equation.
c) What does $H_2O(g)$ in the equation suggest about the temperature of the reaction?
d) What is **reduced** in this reaction?
e) What is **oxidised** in this reaction? [6]
f) Do you think that the above method would be suitable for the extraction of potassium from potassium oxide? Explain why. [2]
(ULEAC)

17. a) A student was trying to extract the metals from lead oxide and aluminium oxide. She heated each oxide with carbon in a fume cupboard:

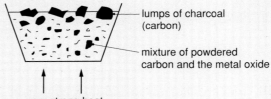

lumps of charcoal (carbon)

mixture of powdered carbon and the metal oxide

very strong heat

She was able to extract lead from lead oxide but not aluminium from aluminium oxide.
   i) Explain the results of these experiments. [4]
   ii) Complete this word equation for the reaction between lead oxide and carbon.
   lead oxide + carbon $\longrightarrow$ .... + ... [1]
b) Copper can be extracted as shown below.

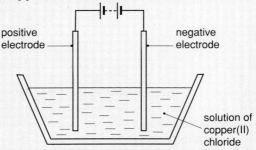

positive electrode

negative electrode

solution of copper(II) chloride

Copper chloride is an ionic compound. State where the copper would collect and explain your answer fully. [2]   (NEAB)

18. Aluminium is a very useful metal.
  a) Give **two** properties of metals. [2]
  b) Aluminium is found in the Earth's crust as its ore. The ore is called bauxite. Bauxite is an impure form of aluminium oxide and so it has to be purified before the aluminium can be extracted.
  The pure aluminium oxide is melted and electrolysed.

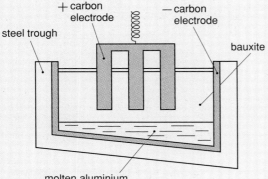

  i) Explain why aluminium is **not** obtained from its ore by heating the ore with carbon. You may find it helpful to use the table on page 88. [1]
  ii) Aluminium oxide is a solid with a very high melting point. It does not conduct electricity when it is solid. However, when it is melted it does conduct electricity.
  What does this tell you about the particles from which aluminium oxide is made? [1]
  iii) The word equation for the reaction in which aluminium is deposited at the electrode is:

aluminium ions + electrons ⟶ aluminium atoms

  Write this as a symbol equation and balance it. [3]
  iv) What is produced at the other electrode when aluminium oxide is electrolysed? [1]
  v) Write a word equation to describe the reaction at this electrode. [2] (NEAB)

19. Magnesium metal is manufactured by electrolysis of the salt magnesium chloride. This salt is obtained from sea water.
Before electrolysis, magnesium chloride is mixed with sodium chloride and the mixture is heated to melt it.
Adding sodium chloride lowers the melting point of the magnesium chloride without affecting the products of the electrolysis.
  a) i) What is the state of magnesium chloride in sea water? [1]
    ii) What is the state of magnesium chloride during the electrolysis process? [1]
  b) i) What **type** of particle is present in magnesium chloride which allows it to be electrolysed? [1]
    ii) At which electrode will magnesium metal be formed during electrolysis? [1]
    iii) Name the substance formed at the other electrode. [1]
  c) Sodium chloride lowers the melting point of magnesium chloride so less energy is needed to melt the magnesium chloride. Suggest **two** advantages of using less energy. [2] (ULEAC)

20. Copper sulphate solution can be electrolysed. What forms at the cathode?
  A Copper
  B Hydrogen
  C Oxygen
  D Sulphur [1] (SEG)

21. Aluminium is manufactured from the naturally occurring substance bauxite. The bauxite is purified to produce aluminium oxide. The aluminium oxide is converted to aluminium by passing electricity through it at about 900°C in molten form. The electric current decomposes (breaks down) the aluminium oxide.
  a) Name the raw material used to make aluminium. [1]
  b) Name the process of decomposing (breaking down) substances using electricity. [1]
  c) Name the **other** main product of the process. [1] (WJEC)

22. a) Name **one** metal that is commonly
   extracted by electrolysis from a solution
   formed from its ore   [1]
   b) In the electrolytic cell used in part a) above,
   what material is the positive electrode
   (anode) made from?   [1]   (SEG)

23. Electrolysis of copper(II) sulphate solution can
be carried out using carbon electrodes.
The diagram shows the apparatus which is
used.
A red-brown solid forms on the negative
electrode.

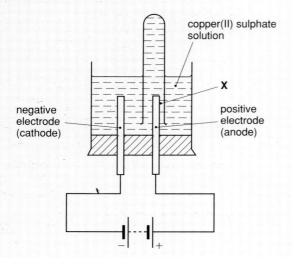

copper(II) sulphate
solution

X

negative
electrode
(cathode)

positive
electrode
(anode)

a) What is the name of the red-brown
   solid?   [1]
b) What would you see at **X** during
   electrolysis?   [1]
c) Copper(II) sulphate solution contains Cu^{2+},
   SO_4^{2-}, H^+ and OH^- ions.
   Copy and complete the ionic equations for
   the reactions which take place at each
   electrode.

   cathode: $Cu^{2+} + \ldots \longrightarrow Cu$
   anode: $4OH^- - 4e^- \longrightarrow \ldots + \ldots$ [3]
                                          (MEG)

▷ **Salt**

24. Look at the diagram.
It shows how sodium hydroxide solution can
be manufactured. It is manufactured by the
electrolysis of sodium chloride solution.

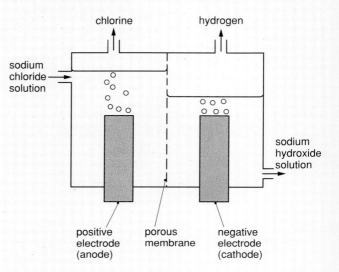

chlorine   hydrogen

sodium
chloride
solution

sodium
hydroxide
solution

positive
electrode
(anode)

porous
membrane

negative
electrode
(cathode)

a) What is the meaning of the word
   'electrolysis'?   [2]
b) Sodium hydroxide is produced when
   sodium chloride solution is electrolysed.
   Give the names of the other **two** products.
                                           [2]
c) Sodium chloride solution contains particles
   called ions.
   Explain how sodium chloride solution
   conducts electricity.   [1]
d) The cost of making sodium hydroxide
   includes the cost of the raw materials used.
   Write down **three** other costs involved in
   making sodium hydroxide.   [3]
e) The electrolysis of sodium chloride solution
   can also be carried out in the laboratory.
   Describe what you would observe at the
   positive electrode.   [1]   (MEG)

25. The diagram in the previous question shows an electrolysis cell used in the chlor-alkali industry. Sodium chloride solution is placed in the cell and the products are sodium hydroxide, chlorine and hydrogen.
a) i) Write a symbol equation to show what happens at the anode (positive). [2]
ii) Write a symbol equation to show what happens at the cathode (negative). [2]
b) Use your answer to a) to explain how sodium hydroxide solution is made during this electrolysis reaction. [2] (ULEAC)

26. The diagram below shows the electrolysis of sodium chloride solution, in the laboratory.

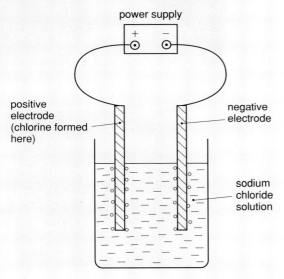

power supply

positive electrode (chlorine formed here)

negative electrode

sodium chloride solution

a) Which gas forms at the negative electrode? [1]
b) Explain why chlorine gas forms at the positive electrode. [2]
c) State **one** use of chlorine gas. [1]
(NEAB)

27. a) Explain why you **cannot** get pure water by filtering sea-water. [1]
b) One pupil suggested that you can get pure water from sea-water by electrolysis. Explain why this is not true! [1]
c) If you do electrolyse sea-water, how can you test the gas at the negative electrode to show that it is hydrogen? [2] (SEG)

▷ **Limestone**

28. Lime (calcium oxide) is used in agriculture to reduce the acidity of soils.
Describe, as fully as you can, the reaction by which lime is made.
Name any other product(s). [3] (NEAB)

29. a) Limestone is a very useful material which is readily available in the United Kingdom. When it is heated, it is broken down into simpler substances. What is the name for this type of chemical reaction? [1]
b) Limestone can be used for many purposes. Some uses are shown below.

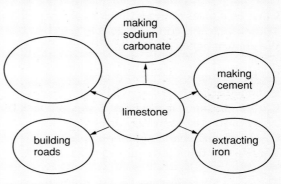

making sodium carbonate

making cement

limestone

building roads

extracting iron

Name **one** more use of limestone. [1] (SEG)

30. Limestone is heated with sand (silicon dioxide) and soda ash (sodium carbonate) to make glass.
a) Describe how atoms are arranged in glass. [2]
b) Glass can be used to make oven doors. Explain, in terms of structure, **one** property of glass which makes it suitable for this use. [2]
c) Limestone (calcium carbonate) was formed in the tourist area now called the Peak District, about 300 million years ago. Today limestone is mined near Buxton, in one of the largest limestone quarries in the United Kingdom.
Suggest **three** social or environmental issues which might be involved in the mining of limestone in the Peak District. [3] (MEG)

chapter 12

ACIDS AND ALKALIS

Acids all around

What do you think of when you hear the word **acid**?
Most people think of a fuming, corrosive liquid
which is very dangerous.

However, not all acids are like this. Most of us
like a little acid on our fish and chips!
Look at the cartoon on page 112.
Which acid does vinegar contain?

Vinegar has the sharp, sour taste of acids.
(The Latin word for sour is acidus.)
Citric acid gives oranges and lemons their sharp taste.
These fruits also contain ascorbic acid.
We know it better as vitamin C!

We have already seen that even rain-water
is slightly acidic (see page 121).
Carbon dioxide gas dissolves in the rain as it falls.
This is also the gas in fizzy drinks, such as
cola, beer and sparkling mineral water.
Why do you think these drinks taste tangy?

These are all examples of **weak acids** that we meet every day.

Acids in the lab

You will have used acids in your science lessons.
The 3 common acids found in school are:

hydrochloric acid	**HCl**
sulphuric acid	**H$_2$SO$_4$**
nitric acid	**HNO$_3$**

These are **strong acids**.

Did you know that we all have one of
these strong acids in our stomachs?
Hydrochloric acid is used to break down
our food into smaller molecules.

You can read more about sulphuric acid on page 152.
Nitric acid is on page 221.

These teenagers are enjoying a little ethanoic acid on their chips!

Fizzy drinks are acidic

We all have hydrochloric acid in our stomachs

▷ Neutralisation

Have you ever had indigestion? The 'burning' feeling
comes from too much hydrochloric acid in your stomach.
You can cure the pain quickly by taking a tablet.
The tablet contains an **alkali** which gets rid of the acid.

Acids and alkalis are chemical opposites.
They react together and 'cancel each other out'.

If we mix just the right amount of acid and alkali together,
we get a neutral solution.

These tablets can neutralise excess acid in your stomach

> **The reaction between an acid and an alkali is called neutralisation.**

The pH scale

You have used universal indicator before to measure pH.
Do you know the pH of a neutral solution?
Here is a reminder of the pH scale:

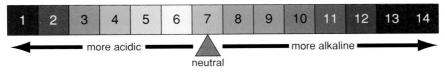

| 1 | 2 | 3 | 4 | 5 | 6 | 7 | 8 | 9 | 10 | 11 | 12 | 13 | 14 |

◄━━━ more acidic ━━━ neutral ━━━ more alkaline ━━━►

In the next experiment you can neutralise some hydrochloric acid.
You will react the acid with an alkali, sodium hydroxide:

Experiment 12.1   Get the balance right!

Collect 10 cm³ of dilute hydrochloric acid in a small flask.
Add 5 drops of universal indicator solution.
What colour is the solution? What is its pH?

Measure out 9 cm³ of sodium hydroxide solution in
a measuring cylinder. Add it to the acid in the flask.
You can also use a burette to add the acid.
What colour is the solution now?

As you can see, the solution is still strongly acidic.
You will need to add the next sodium hydroxide
a drop at a time. Use a dropper or a burette.
Swirl the flask as you add each drop of alkali.

Try to get a **neutral solution**.
Look at the pH scale above.
What colour are you aiming for?

If you add too much alkali, you don't have to start again.
What can you add, a drop at a time, to neutralise
the alkali? It's a bit like balancing a see-saw!

You can keep your neutral solution for the next experiment.

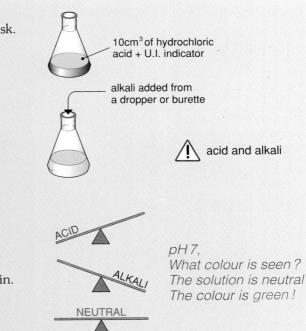

10cm³ of hydrochloric
acid + U.I. indicator

alkali added from
a dropper or burette

⚠ acid and alkali

ACID

ALKALI

NEUTRAL

pH 7,
What colour is seen?
The solution is neutral
The colour is green!

▷ Salts

In the last experiment you neutralised an acid
with an alkali.
If you ever get stung by a bee,
you will be grateful for that reaction!
A bee's sting is acidic. It can be neutralised by
an alkali. The pain is eased by treating it with
bicarbonate of soda (a weak alkali).
Why shouldn't you use sodium hydroxide on the sting?

But what is made when an acid and alkali react together?
In general we can say:

*A bee's sting is acidic.
A wasp's sting is alkaline.
How would you treat a
wasp sting? (see page 154.)*

---

acid + alkali ⟶ a salt + water

Let's look at the equation for the reaction in experiment 12.1:

hydrochloric acid + sodium hydroxide ⟶ sodium chloride + water
$$HCl(aq) \quad + \quad NaOH(aq) \quad \longrightarrow \quad NaCl(aq) \quad + \quad H_2O(l)$$

The salt, sodium chloride, is dissolved in water.
Can you think how we can get it from its solution?

You can try this out in the next experiment:

Experiment 12.2   Preparing sodium chloride

Have you got your neutral solution from the last experiment?
If not, follow the method for experiment 12.1.

Add a spatula of charcoal powder to the green solution.
Stir it with a glass rod.
The charcoal takes the colour out of the solution.

⚠ **acid and alkali**

Filter the mixture.
You should get a clear, colourless solution.
Put the solution into an evaporating dish.
Now heat it on a water bath as shown:

Stop heating when you see some white crystals
around the edge of the solution.
Leave your evaporating dish for a few days.
The rest of the water will evaporate off slowly.
Slow evaporation gives bigger crystals.

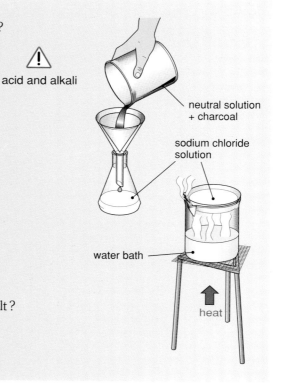

neutral solution
+ charcoal

sodium chloride
solution

water bath

heat

- What is the chemical name for the salt you have made?
- Can you write the equation for the reaction to make the salt?
- What do we call this type of reaction?
- What shape are your salt crystals?
- Can you think of any reactions that we use in everyday life
  to neutralise acids?

What is a salt?

You already know a lot about one salt. We have looked at common salt, sodium chloride, in Chapter 10. We have also made some crystals of it in the last experiment.

But chemists use the word **salt** to describe any *metal compounds that can be made from acids.*

Can you remember the formulas of the strong acids from the start of the chapter?
Look back to page 140 if you can't think of them.
Which element do they all contain?

We find that, *all acids contain hydrogen.*

> **When we replace the hydrogen in an acid by a metal, we get a salt.**

▷ Naming salts

Each acid has its own salts. Look at this table:

Acid	Its salts	Example
hydro**chlor**ic acid, HCl ⟶	**chlorides**	sodium chloride, NaCl
sulphuric acid, H_2SO_4 ⟶	**sulphates**	copper sulphate, $CuSO_4$
nitric acid, HNO_3 ⟶	**nitrates**	potassium nitrate, KNO_3

Naming a salt is like naming a person.
Look at the examples in the table above.
A salt gets its first name from the metal,
and its surname from the acid.

Sodium chloride is 'common salt'. There are thousands of other compounds called salts.

Sodium chloride is a salt from hydrochloric acid, HCl. Why would we never make sodium chloride by adding sodium to hydrochloric acid? (see page 79.)

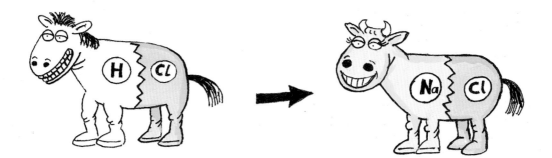

An acid turns into a salt! Hydrogen in the acid is replaced by a metal in the salt.

▷ Preparing salts

You have now seen how to make a salt by
reacting an acid with an alkali.
But alkalis are part of a larger group of compounds
called **bases**.
We've already met some bases – the metal oxides –
on page 47.

Can you remember the difference between an alkali
and a base?
An alkali is just a base that can dissolve in water.

Do you think bases will react with acids, as alkalis do?
The general equation is:

acid + **base** ⟶ **a salt** + **water**

For example,

sulphuric acid + zinc oxide ⟶ zinc sulphate + water
$H_2SO_4(aq)$ + $ZnO(s)$ ⟶ $ZnSO_4(aq)$ + $H_2O(l)$

As in all neutralisation reactions, a salt is made.
What is the name of the salt in the reaction above?

*Salts have many uses. This farmer is treating
his vines with copper sulphate to kill pests.
Why must grapes be washed well before we
eat them?*

Experiment 12.3   Making a salt from an acid and a base

1. Put 25 cm³ of sulphuric acid in a small beaker.
   Add black copper oxide and stir with a glass rod.
   Keep adding the copper oxide until
   no more will dissolve (react).
   - How do you know when all the acid has reacted?
   - Can you work out what is formed in the reaction?

2. Filter the mixture in your beaker.   ⚠ acid
   You should get a clear, blue solution.
   - What should you do if you still have
     some black powder in your solution?

3. Pour your solution into an evaporating dish.
   Then heat it on a water bath as shown:
   Stop heating when you see some crystals around the
   edge of the solution.
   Leave the solution for a few days to crystallise slowly.
   - What is the name of your salt?
   - What do the crystals look like?

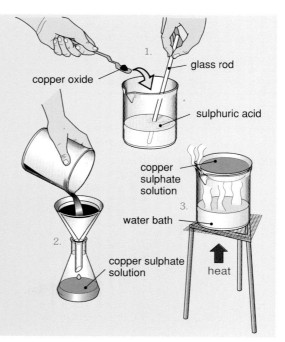

The sulphuric acid is neutralised by the base, copper oxide:

sulphuric acid + copper oxide ⟶ copper sulphate + water
$H_2SO_4(aq)$ + $CuO(s)$ ⟶ $CuSO_4(aq)$ + $H_2O(l)$

More soluble salts

Acids can also be neutralised by reacting them
with carbonates. You have already seen how
limestone (calcium carbonate) reacts with acid.
In general we can say:

| acid + a carbonate ⟶ a salt + water + carbon dioxide |

How is this different from the equation for
an acid reacting with a base?
How could you test for the gas given off?

We can use the same method as experiment 12.3
to prepare a salt from a carbonate. This is because
most carbonates are insoluble in water.

This lake has become acidic.
It is being neutralised by
calcium carbonate.

Experiment 12.4   Preparing a salt from an acid and a carbonate

Collect 25 cm^3 of hydrochloric acid in a small beaker.
Add a spatula of copper carbonate.
- What happens? What is the gas given off?

Add more copper carbonate until it stops fizzing.
Filter to remove the un-reacted copper carbonate.
Repeat step 3 from the end of Experiment 12.3
to get some crystals of your salt.
- What is your salt called?
- What do its crystals look like?

⚠
acid
copper carbonate

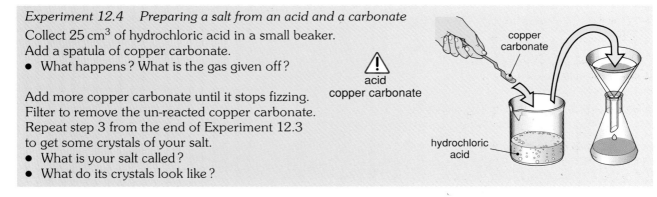

The hydrochloric acid is neutralised by copper carbonate:

hydrochloric acid + copper carbonate ⟶ copper chloride + water + carbon dioxide

$$2\,HCl(aq) \quad + \quad CuCO_3(s) \quad \longrightarrow \quad CuCl_2(aq) \quad + \quad H_2O(l) \quad + \quad CO_2(g)$$

Metals and acid

We have already seen how some metals react with acid.
Can you remember which gas is given off?
Do all metals react with acid? (See the table on page 79.)
If a metal does react, the general equation is:

| acid + a metal ⟶ a salt + hydrogen |

You can use the method from experiment 12.3 to prepare the salt.
Why would it be dangerous to use this method
to prepare sodium chloride?
Which acid and metal would you start with to
make magnesium sulphate?

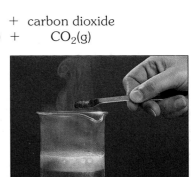

Here is magnesium reacting with
dilute sulphuric acid. How can
you remove any excess
magnesium after the acid has
been neutralised?

145

▷ Acids need water !

All the acids we have used so far have been solutions.
The acid molecules are dissolved in water.
Acids need water before they can show their acidic properties.
Let's look at citric acid (the acid in oranges) as an example :

Experiment 12.5   Testing citric acid

You can compare solid citric acid (which has
no water added to it) to a solution of the acid.
Write down your results in a table like this :

⚠ acid

Test	Results for pure citric acid	Results for citric acid solution
blue litmus paper sodium carbonate magnesium ribbon does it conduct electricity ?		

- How does water affect the properties of citric acid ?
- Can you think of another test to show if a substance is acidic ?

Without water, substances are not acidic.
Look at these properties of a typical acidic solution :
- turns litmus red, and has a pH less than 7,
- reacts with a base,
- fizzes with a carbonate, giving off carbon dioxide,
- fizzes with a metal, such as magnesium, giving off hydrogen.

Let's see what difference the water makes :
In water, the acid molecules split up.
We can look at hydrogen chloride, HCl, as an example :
Hydrogen chloride is a gas. It only shows
its acidic properties when we dissolve it in water.
We call the solution formed hydrochloric acid :

$$HCl(g) \xrightarrow{\text{dissolve in water}} H^+(aq) + Cl^-(aq)$$

Remember that all acids contain hydrogen.
When dissolved in water, the hydrogen is released
into the solution as **H^+(aq) ions**.

> **It is H^+(aq) ions that make a solution acidic.**

Explaining neutralisation

When we neutralise an acid, the H^+(aq) ions
are removed from the solution.
Alkaline solutions contain hydroxide ions, OH^-(aq) :

> **H^+(aq) + OH^-(aq) $\xrightarrow{\text{neutralisation}}$ H_2O(l)**

The H^+ and OH^- ions 'cancel each other out'.

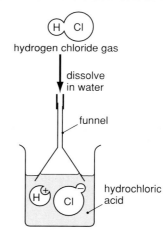

The hydrogen chloride gas splits up (dissociates) in
water into ions. The solution is called hydrochloric
acid. (The gas is very soluble in water.)
Why is a funnel used when dissolving the gas ?

*Acid plus alkali gives salt and water,
H^+ ions are led to the slaughter !*

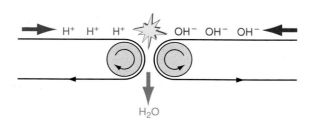

146

▷ Solubility of salts

Do you remember how we get a soluble salt
from its solution?
If we heat the solution, water evaporates off.
Small crystals of the salt start to form.
This is called the **point of crystallisation**.

We now have a **saturated** solution.
No more salt can dissolve in the solution.
As more water evaporates, the crystals
of the salt grow bigger.

Solubility curves

We measure how soluble a salt is by seeing
how much dissolves in 100 g of water.
(100 cm³ of water has a mass of 100 g.)
For example, the solubility of copper sulphate
is 19 g per 100 g of water, at 15 °C.

Notice that the value for the solubility above
is given at 15 °C.
Do you think that temperature affects
how soluble a salt is?

Look at the graph:

- Which of the 3 salts is most soluble at 20 °C?
- Which salt is most soluble at 60 °C?

We call the lines on the graph **solubility curves**.
They show us how much salt dissolves
at different temperatures.

*You can get the salt from sea-water in hot countries. As the
water evaporates, the solution becomes saturated. Then
salt crystallises and is collected.*

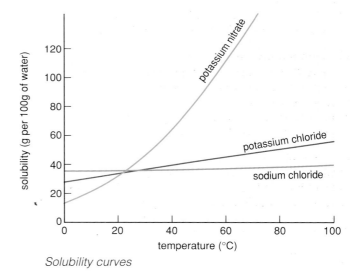

Solubility curves

Investigation 12.6   Which salt is most soluble?

You can test the solubility of these salts:
copper sulphate, sodium chloride, calcium chloride and zinc sulphate.

Plan a fair test to see which of these salts is most soluble.
Use 10 cm³ of water for each test?
- What other things must be the same for a fair test?
- How can you tell when your solutions are saturated?
- How will you measure how much of each salt dissolves?
Your teacher will check your plan before you start.

Investigation 12.7   Which factors affect the solubility of copper sulphate?
Your teacher will check your plan before you start.

▷ Making insoluble salts

The salts we have made so far are all soluble
in water. To get the salt, we crystallise it
from its solution.
However, some salts are **insoluble**.

We can prepare an insoluble salt
by a precipitation reaction.
Can you remember what a precipitate is? (see page 129.)
Sometimes, when we mix two solutions
we get an insoluble solid formed.
The solid is a **precipitate**.

Look at the cartoon below:
It explains what happens in a precipitation reaction.

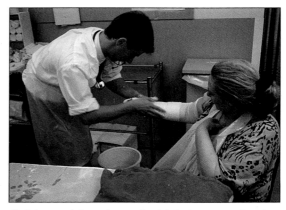

Calcium sulphate is a salt which does not dissolve
well in water. It is used to make plaster casts

A and D have swapped partners and formed a precipitate

Experiment 12.8   Making an insoluble salt by precipitation

1. Take 5 cm³ of lead nitrate solution in a test-tube.
   Add 10 cm³ of sodium iodide solution.
   - What happens?
   - What is the precipitate called?
   - How can we separate the precipitate from the solution?

   ⚠ lead salts

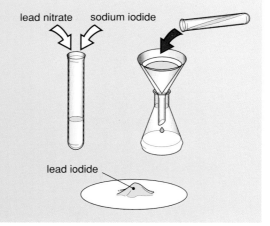

2. Filter your mixture.
   The solid lead iodide is left on the filter paper.
   Rinse it with distilled water.
   - Why must we rinse the lead iodide?

3. Scrape the salt made on to some fresh filter paper.
   Leave it to dry.

The lead nitrate and sodium iodide react to make
a precipitate, lead iodide.

lead nitrate (aq) + sodium iodide (aq) ⟶ lead iodide (s) + sodium nitrate (aq)

The lead iodide must be rinsed with water to wash away any soluble salts.

▷ Precipitation

In the last experiment we made an **insoluble** salt
from two **soluble** salts.
To help us choose which salts to mix,
we need to know which salts dissolve in water.
Look at the table below:

$$AB(aq) \; + \; CD(aq) \longrightarrow AD(s) \; + \; CB(aq)$$
A precipitation reaction

Salt	Solubility
chlorides	soluble (except for lead chloride, silver chloride)
sulphates	soluble (except for barium sulphate, calcium sulphate, lead sulphate)
nitrates	all soluble

Any salts of lithium, sodium or potassium are also soluble.

● Which two salt solutions could you mix to make
  barium sulphate?
● Which acid would you add to barium nitrate solution
  to make barium sulphate?

Look at the word equation for the last experiment.
The balanced equation is:

$$Pb(NO_3)_2(aq) \; + \; 2\,NaI(aq) \longrightarrow PbI_2(s) \; + \; 2\,NaNO_3(aq)$$

We can also show what happens like this:

$$Pb^{2+}(aq) \; + \; 2\,I^-(aq) \longrightarrow PbI_2(s)$$

You have seen an equation like this on page 129.
It is called an **ionic equation**.

It shows us which ions stick together
in the precipitation reaction.
The sodium ions, $Na^+(aq)$, and the nitrate ions, $NO_3^-(aq)$,
stay in the solution. They are not changed, so they
don't appear in the ionic equation.
They are called **spectator ions**.

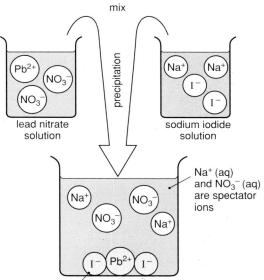

mix

lead nitrate
solution

sodium iodide
solution

precipitation

Na^+ (aq)
and NO_3^- (aq)
are spectator
ions

precipitate of
lead iodide

A precipitation reaction

The centrifuge

The solids in precipitation reactions
are formed as very small grains.
The mixture is called a **suspension**.
A centrifuge is a machine which spins test-tubes
around at high speed.
What do you think happens to the fine particles
of the precipitate? Think about what happens to you
on a ride that spins around quickly at a fairground!

*A centrifuge spins
test-tubes at high
speed*

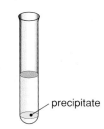

precipitate

*After centrifuging the solid is
packed at the bottom. The
solution above can be poured
off (decanted).*

▷ Testing salts

We can use precipitation reactions to test for
some negative ions.
We can see if a salt is a

- chloride,
- bromide,
- iodide, or
- sulphate, by the tests below:

Look at the table below:
You dissolve the salt in dilute nitric acid,
then do the test shown:

Type of salt (ion)	Test	Result
chloride (Cl^-)	silver nitrate solution ⟶	a white precipitate of silver chloride
bromide (Br^-)	silver nitrate solution ⟶	a cream precipitate of silver bromide
iodide (I^-)	silver nitrate solution ⟶	a pale yellow precipitate of silver iodide
sulphate (SO_4^{2-})	barium nitrate solution ⟶	a white precipitate of barium sulphate

Let's use these tests to find out about some unknown salts:

Experiment 12.9   Identifying salts

Your teacher will give you 5 unknown salts,
labelled A to E.

⚠ acid

salts dissolved in
dilute nitric acid

You can find out which salts are chlorides, bromides,
iodides or sulphates.

You will have to dissolve each salt in
dilute nitric acid before you do the tests.
We will use the tests from the table above.

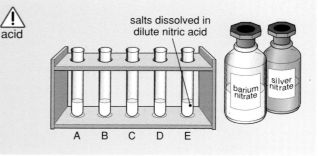

A B C D E

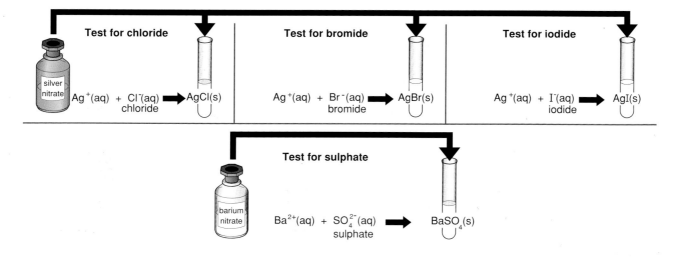

Test for chloride

silver nitrate

$Ag^+(aq) + Cl^-(aq) \longrightarrow AgCl(s)$
chloride

Test for bromide

$Ag^+(aq) + Br^-(aq) \longrightarrow AgBr(s)$
bromide

Test for iodide

$Ag^+(aq) + I^-(aq) \longrightarrow AgI(s)$
iodide

Test for sulphate

barium nitrate

$Ba^{2+}(aq) + SO_4^{2-}(aq) \longrightarrow BaSO_4(s)$
sulphate

Metals in salts

The tests on the last page tell us
which is the negative ion in some salts.
Remember that salts also contain a metal.
The metal part of a salt is always a positive ion.

We can also identify
some metals using a **flame test**.

*The colours in these
fireworks are
made by metal ions
(see page 184)*

Experiment 12.10   Flame tests for metals
You can test the unknown salts from experiment 12.9.

Take the colour out of a Bunsen flame by opening
the air-hole slightly.
Heat a piece of nichrome wire in the flame to clean it.

Put the loop at the end of the wire into some water.
Then dip it into one of the unknown salts.
Hold the wire in the edge of the flame.

Record the colour.
Clean the wire again and test the other salts.

- Use the flame colours shown below
  and your results from Experiment 12.9
  to name salts A to E.

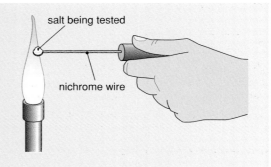

salt being tested

nichrome wire

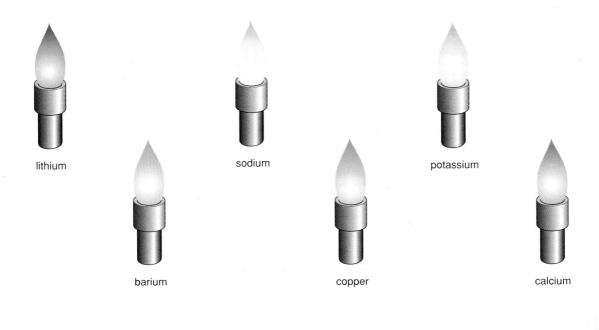

lithium   sodium   potassium

barium   copper   calcium

▷ Chemistry at work : Sulphuric acid, H_2SO_4

Uses of sulphuric acid

Sulphuric acid is one of the most important
products of the chemical industry.
Look at its uses below :
Which products made from sulphuric acid
have you used today?

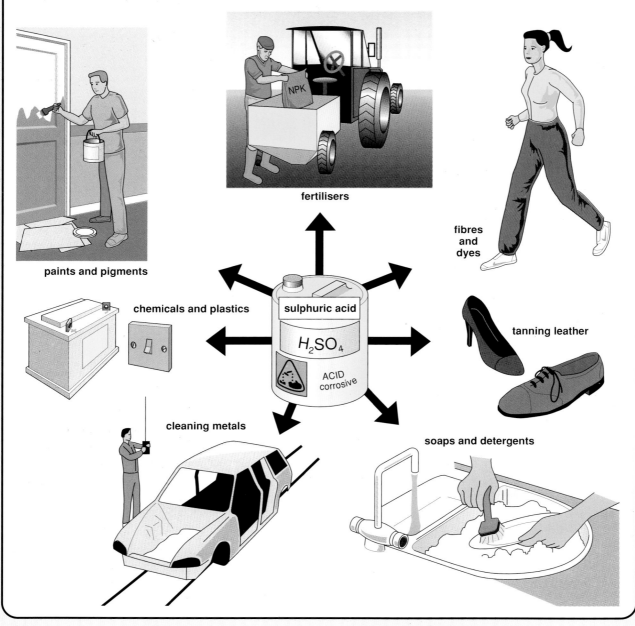

fertilisers

fibres
and
dyes

paints and pigments

chemicals and plastics

sulphuric acid

H_2SO_4

ACID
corrosive

tanning leather

cleaning metals

soaps and detergents

▷ Chemistry at work : Sulphuric acid, H_2SO_4

The Contact process

Sulphuric acid is made in the Contact process.
The raw materials are sulphur, air and water.
Look at the diagram below :

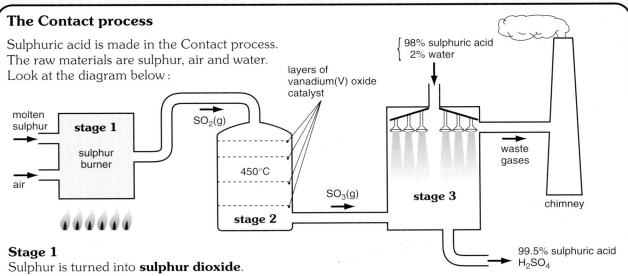

Stage 1
Sulphur is turned into **sulphur dioxide**.
We can import the sulphur on ships from Poland or
the USA.
It can also be extracted from impurities in
crude oil or natural gas. However North Sea gas
contains very little sulphur, so it can't be used.
The sulphur burns in air :

sulphur + oxygen ⟶ sulphur dioxide
$$S(l) \; + \; O_2(g) \; \longrightarrow \; SO_2(g)$$

Stage 2
The sulphur dioxide is turned into **sulphur trioxide**.

sulphur dioxide + oxygen ⇌ sulphur trioxide
$$2\,SO_2(g) \; + \; O_2(g) \; \rightleftharpoons \; 2\,SO_3(g)$$

Notice that the reaction is reversible. You can read
more about this type of reaction in Chapter 17.
A catalyst, vanadium(V) oxide, is used to speed up
the reaction.
Why do you think there are 4 layers of catalyst ?

Stage 3
In the final stage, sulphur trioxide is changed into
sulphuric acid.
The sulphur trioxide gets absorbed into a mixture of
98 % sulphuric acid and 2 % water. In effect, the
sulphur trioxide reacts with the water :

sulphur trioxide + water ⟶ sulphuric acid
$$SO_3(g) \; + \; H_2O(l) \; \longrightarrow \; H_2SO_4(l)$$

Economic and environmental aspects
- In Stage 2, 99.5 % of the sulphur dioxide gets
  converted into sulphur trioxide. Sulphur
  dioxide causes acid rain, so strict controls are
  needed on the waste gases.

- The reactions in each stage give out heat. As
  much energy as possible is conserved.

- If you used water to absorb the sulphur trioxide
  in Stage 3, a fine mist of sulphuric acid would
  be formed. This can't be condensed and
  would pollute the air.

▷ Chemistry at work : Neutralisation

Acid soil

If soil is too acidic, most crops will not grow well.
Farmers can spread powdered limestone
or lime on the soil to neutralise it.

Experiment 12.11   Neutralising soil
Add 50 cm^3 of distilled water to some
acidic soil. Stir it well, filter, then add a few drops
of universal indicator.
Add powdered limestone until you neutralise
the solution.
- How can you see when you have added enough ?

Acid rain

Most power stations burn fossil fuels (see page 158).
This gives off acidic sulphur dioxide gas
which causes acid rain (see page 178).
Power stations can use lime or limestone
to neutralise the gas before it leaves the chimneys.
Calcium sulphate is formed in the reaction.
It is sold to the building industry to make plaster.

Baking powder

Baking powder helps cake-mix to rise.
It contains sodium hydrogencarbonate (known as
bicarbonate of soda) and a weak acid.
When water is added the two react. The reaction
is like an acid plus a carbonate.
Do you remember which gas is made ? (see page 145.)

Baking powder helps a cake rise to the occasion !

acid + a hydrogencarbonate ⟶ a salt + water + carbon dioxide

The carbon dioxide gets trapped in the cake-mix.
Self-raising flour has baking powder already added.

Treating stings

Bee stings are acidic. You can ease the pain
by neutralising the acid with bicarbonate of soda
(sodium hydrogencarbonate).

Wasp stings are alkaline. You can neutralise them
with vinegar (ethanoic acid).

Summary

Acids form solutions which:

- turn blue litmus red
- have a pH less than 7
- react with an alkali (or base) to give a salt and water – this is called **neutralisation**.
- react with a carbonate to give a salt, water and carbon dioxide
- react with metals to give a salt and hydrogen (the metal must be above copper in the Reactivity Series).

Salts are compounds made when we replace the hydrogen in an acid by a metal.
Hydrochloric acid (HCl) makes salts called chlorides.
Sulphuric acid (H_2SO_4) gives sulphates.
Nitric acid (HNO_3) gives nitrates.
Examples of salts are sodium chloride (NaCl), copper sulphate ($CuSO_4$) and silver nitrate ($AgNO_3$).

▷ Questions

1. Copy and complete:

   Acidic solutions turn blue litmus . . . . .
   Their pH is always . . . . than 7.
   Here are their common reactions:

   acid + base (or alkali) ⟶ a salt + ...

   acid + carbonate ⟶ a salt + water
                          + ...

   acid + metal ⟶ a salt + ...

   When an acid and alkali react to 'cancel each other out', we call it a . . . . reaction.

   A salt is made when the . . . . in an acid is replaced by a . . . . .

Acid	Salt
hydrochloric acid ⟶	. . . .
. . . . acid ⟶	sulphates
nitric acid ⟶	. . . .

2. Copy and complete these word equations:

   a) sodium hydroxide + ... acid ⟶ sodium chloride + water
   b) copper oxide + sulphuric acid ⟶ . . . . + ...
   c) copper . . . . + hydrochloric acid ⟶ copper . . . . + water + carbon dioxide
   d) . . . . + sulphuric acid ⟶ magnesium sulphate + hydrogen
   e) sodium hydroxide + nitric acid ⟶ . . . . + ...

3. Joe tested some solutions with universal indicator paper.
   He wrote down their pHs:
       1, 5, 7, 14
   but forgot to write the names of the solutions.
   Can you help him by matching the pHs to the correct solutions?

Solution tested	pH
distilled water	
sulphuric acid	
sodium hydroxide	
vinegar	

4. Marie and Sakib want to make some crystals of copper sulphate.
   They have dilute sulphuric acid and black copper oxide powder.
   a) Describe how they can get copper sulphate crystals safely.
   b) How can they tell when the sulphuric acid has been neutralised?
   c) What type of substance is the black copper oxide powder – an alkali or a base?
   d) Write a word equation and a symbol equation for the reaction.

5. The table below shows the conditions some plants prefer:

Plant	pH
apple	5.0–6.5
potato	4.5–6.0
blackcurrant	6.0–8.0
mint	7.0–8.0
onion	6.0–7.0
strawberry	5.0–7.0
lettuce	6.0–7.0

a) Which plants grow well over the largest *range* of pH values?
b) Which plant can grow in the most acidic soil?
c) Describe how you can test the pH of a soil.
d) How can you neutralise an acidic soil?

6. Sulphuric acid is made in the Contact process.
a) What are the raw materials for the process?
b) Draw a flow diagram showing the steps in making sulphuric acid. Include word equations.
c) What is the catalyst used in the process?
d) In the last step, why don't we dissolve the sulphur trioxide in water?
e) Draw a spider diagram showing the uses of sulphuric acid.

7. Alex has 3 unknown salts – A, B and C. He does a flame test on each salt. These are his results:

Salt	Colour of flame
A	yellow
B	lilac
C	green/blue

a) Look back to page 151 and name the metal in each salt.
b) Alex dissolved each salt in dilute nitric acid. When he added silver nitrate solution to A, a pale yellow precipitate was formed. He did the same to B, but the precipitate was white.
C formed a white precipitate with barium nitrate solution.
Name salts A, B and C.

8. Look at the table below.
It shows the solubility of potassium nitrate at different temperatures.

Temperature (°C)	Solubility (g/100 g of water)
20	32
40	64
60	110
80	169
100	246

a) Draw a solubility curve for potassium nitrate. (see page 147.)
b) What pattern can you see from your graph?
c) What is the solubility of potassium nitrate at
    i) 50 °C   ii) 70 °C?
d) What does a 'saturated solution' mean?
e) How can you make a saturated solution of potassium nitrate? No solid should be present.

9. a) Vani has a solution which she thinks might be acidic. Describe 3 tests she could do to see if it is acidic or not.
b) Explain why water is needed before a substance can show its acidic properties.

10. Here is a list of soluble salts:

sodium nitrate – $NaNO_3$
potassium chloride – KCl
magnesium sulphate – $MgSO_4$
calcium chloride – $CaCl_2$
lead nitrate – $Pb(NO_3)_2$

a) Choose a pair of salts you could mix to make the insoluble salts:
    i) lead chloride   ii) calcium sulphate.
b) i) How would you collect a pure sample of each salt made in part a)?
    ii) Write a word equation for each reaction.
    iii) Write a symbol equation for each reaction. Include state symbols.
    iv) Write an ionic equation for each reaction.

11. Look through this chapter (and others if you have time) and design a poster showing some uses of salts.

Further questions on page 228.

chapter 13

▷ Hydrocarbons

Imagine you could vote in a 'Molecule of the Century' competition. A vote for a **hydrocarbon** would stand a good chance of winning!

So what is a 'hydrocarbon'? And why are they so important?

As the name suggests:

> **A hydrocarbon is a compound containing only hydrogen and carbon.**

One of the world's most important raw materials is **crude oil**. Crude oil is a *mixture* of hydrocarbons.

The hydrocarbons in crude oil are not only vital **fuels**. They are also the starting materials for many new products, such as **plastics**.

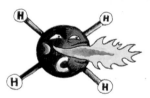

We get petrol from crude oil

The alkanes

There are lots of different hydrocarbons in crude oil. Most of them are called **alkanes**.

Natural gas, which is found with crude oil, is mainly methane. This is the smallest alkane.

The alkane molecules have a 'backbone' of carbon atoms. Their carbon atoms are surrounded by hydrogen atoms.

Look at the pictures of some alkanes below:

My name is methane –
If you want a fire,
Just light the gas
And turn me higher!

methane   ethane   propane   butane   pentane

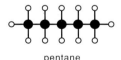

● = carbon
○ = hydrogen

Notice the bonds that join the atoms together: Carbons have 4 bonds. Hydrogens have 1 bond.

You can see the names and formulas of the first few alkanes in this table.

Notice that all their names end in **-ane**.

- Can you see a pattern in their formulas?
- Can you work out the formula of hexane?
- Can you draw a picture of hexane?

Name	Formula
methane	CH_4
ethane	C_2H_6
propane	C_3H_8
butane	C_4H_{10}
pentane	C_5H_{12}
hexane	

The general formula of an alkane is:

$$C_nH_{2n+2}$$

where *n* can be any number.

▷ Fossil fuels

Most of our common fuels are **fossil fuels**.
Can you name any?

Coal, crude oil (which gives us petrol), and
natural gas are all fossil fuels.

Coal is the odd one out as it is not a hydrocarbon.
It does contain carbon and hydrogen.
However, there are also other types of atoms,
such as oxygen, in some of its molecules.

Fossil fuels have taken millions of years to form.

Coal came from trees and ferns that died and
were buried beneath swamps.

Crude oil was formed from animals which lived in the sea.

The plants and animals got their energy from the Sun.

So when you burn a fuel you are using energy that
started off in the Sun!

Fern fossils are found in coal

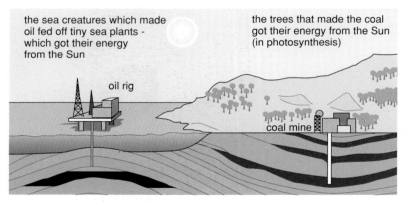

the sea creatures which made
oil fed off tiny sea plants -
which got their energy
from the Sun

the trees that made the coal
got their energy from the Sun
(in photosynthesis)

oil rig

coal mine

*Scientists predict our supplies of
crude oil could run out within your
life-time (in about 50 years time).
Coal could last another 300 years.*

Fossil fuels are called **non-renewable** fuels because once we
use up our supplies on Earth they will be gone forever.

The story of oil begins

Crude oil was made from the bodies of tiny sea
creatures that died about 150 million years ago.

These animals were buried under layers of sand
and silt on the sea bed. Their bodies did not
decay normally as the bacteria feeding on them
had little or no oxygen in these conditions.

As the pressure and temperature slowly
increased, they were changed into oil.

Natural gas is usually found with the crude oil.

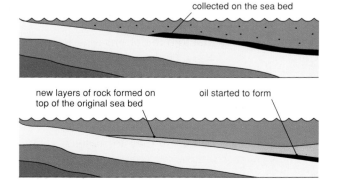

dead sea creatures
collected on the sea bed

new layers of rock formed on
top of the original sea bed

oil started to form

Finding oil

Oil supplies are scarce.
Oil companies, like BP and Shell, are looking for new oil all the time.
So how do they find their oil?

First of all scientists look for clues on the Earth's surface. Look at the diagram opposite:

Crude oil soaks into porous rock, just like water soaking into a sponge. The oil rises towards the surface but is usually stopped before it gets there by a layer of non-porous rock.

The oil is usually found under a dome shaped layer called a cap rock or anti-cline (see page 300).

Seismic survey

If an area looks good, scientists can find the structure of the rocks underground. They do this by a seismic survey.

Small explosions are set off on the surface.
These send out shock waves.
The waves that bounce back from each layer are picked up by sensors.

A computer helps to analyse these echoes. It then draws a map of the rocks beneath the surface.

If the layers are like the ones shown above, there might be oil. The scientists do not know for sure until they actually drill down. If rock containing oil is found, more wells are drilled. This helps the company see if it is worthwhile going into full production.
A mistake at this stage is very costly!

Transporting oil

There are two ways to move the oil from the oilfield to the refinery:
i) by pipeline or ii) by oil tanker.

Pipelines are often used when the oil is found reasonably close to the refinery. For example, North Sea oil is piped to Aberdeen in Scotland.

Giant ships called oil tankers take oil all over the world. However, accidents can happen at sea and the oil can be spilled.
The effects on wildlife are disastrous (see page 175).

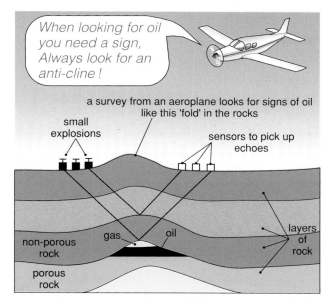

When looking for oil you need a sign, Always look for an anti-cline!

a survey from an aeroplane looks for signs of oil like this 'fold' in the rocks

small explosions

sensors to pick up echoes

non-porous rock

gas   oil

layers of rock

porous rock

A seismic survey

An exploration rig

Oil tankers can be 400 m long. The crew sometimes use bicycles to get around the ship.

▷ Distilling crude oil

At the refinery

When crude oil reaches the refinery it is a thick black, smelly liquid. It is not much use to anyone.

You learned on page 157 that crude oil contains a mixture of different hydrocarbons. At the refinery these are sorted out into groups of useful substances called **fractions**.

These fractions are separated by **fractional distillation**.

We can distil crude oil in the lab to help you understand what happens in the refinery.

An oil refinery at night

Demonstration 13.1 *Distillation of crude oil*

The apparatus is set up as shown in a fume-cupboard.

Heat the crude oil gently at first. Collect a few drops of the first liquid that collects. Keep heating and change the receiving tube. Now collect the liquid that distils up to 150 °C. Again change the tube and collect the liquid when you heat strongly.

Pour each fraction collected onto a watch glass.

Note its colour and how thick it is.

Try to light each fraction with a lighted splint. What happens?

* Why is the receiving tube kept in cold water?

* You need a fuel for a car. Why would you use the first fraction collected?

* Why would you use the last fraction to lubricate a car engine?

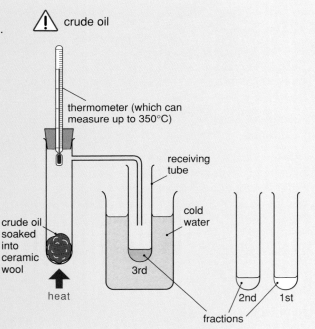

crude oil

thermometer (which can measure up to 350°C)

receiving tube

cold water

crude oil soaked into ceramic wool

3rd

heat

2nd   1st

fractions

Q. What do you call a hydrocarbon who tells rude jokes?

A. Crude oil!

There was a young girl called Eve,
Who boiled oil with a friend called Steve.
Small molecules flew
Up out from the brew
As they were the first ones to leave.

Looking for patterns

Fraction	Size of molecules	Colour	Thickness	How it burns
low boiling point (up to 80 °C)	small	colourless	runny	lights easily, (flammable) clean flame
medium boiling point (80–150 °C)	medium	yellow	thicker	harder to light, some smoke
high boiling point (above 150 °C)	large	dark orange	thick (viscous)	difficult to light, smoky flame

Look down each column in the table above:
What patterns can you see as the boiling point of
the fraction gets higher?

Explaining the distillation

If you have a plate of spaghetti, you find that the
short strands are easier to pull out than the longer
ones. This helps to explain the distillation of
crude oil, Instead of spaghetti, think of molecules!

As the oil is heated, the small molecules
boil off first. These gas molecules are then
condensed (turned back to liquid) in the
cold receiving tube.

Small hydrocarbons have lower boiling points
than large ones. They are easier to separate from
the mixture of molecules in crude oil.

As you carry on heating, the temperature of the
crude oil rises. The larger molecules are then
boiled off and are collected.

Remember:

*The long pieces of spaghetti get tangled up.
They are harder to separate out, just like the
long molecules in crude oil.*

> **Small hydrocarbons
> have lower boiling
> points than large
> ones.**

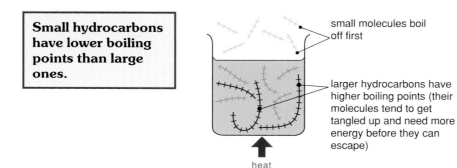

small molecules boil off first

larger hydrocarbons have
higher boiling points (their
molecules tend to get
tangled up and need more
energy before they can
escape)

heat

▷ Fractional distillation in industry

In an oil refinery the crude oil is separated into its fractions. This happens in huge **fractionating columns**.

Remember that a **fraction** is a group of hydrocarbons with similar boiling points.

Just like distillation in the lab, they use the different boiling points of the hydrocarbons to separate them. But there is a difference.

In Demonstration 13.1 we boiled off each fraction in turn. In industry, they boil up all the fractions together. Then they condense them at difference temperatures at the same time.
You can see this in the column shown below.

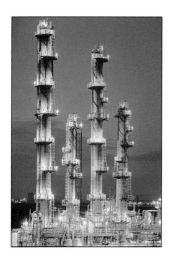

A fractionating column

low temperature

70 °C → petroleum gases

petrol (gasoline)

kerosine (paraffin)

diesel

lubricating oil

heavy fuel oil

crude oil is heated and enters as a gas

high temperature

360 °C → bitumen

small molecules
- low boiling point
- light in colour
- easy to light
- runny

large molecules
- high boiling point
- dark in colour
- hard to light
- thick (if still a liquid at room temperature -bitumen is a solid)

Explanation
The crude oil is heated up and evaporates. It enters the column as a gas.

The fractionating column is hot at the bottom and cooler at the top. This means that the larger hydrocarbons, with the high boiling points, turn back to liquids nearer the bottom.

At the high temperatures there, the smaller hydrocarbons stay as gases. They rise up the column. The different fractions now condense at different levels.

At the top of the column there are hydrocarbons with low boiling points. At 70 °C these have still not condensed. They come out of the top as gases.

Fraction	length of carbon chain
petroleum gases	C_1–C_4
petrol	C_4–C_{12}
kerosine	C_{11}–C_{15}
diesel	C_{15}–C_{19}
lubricating oil	C_{20}–C_{30}
fuel oil	C_{30}–C_{40}
bitumen	C_{50} and above

▷ Cracking

After distilling the crude oil, the oil companies find
that they have too many large hydrocarbons.
We just don't need that much of the heavy fractions.

Yet the smaller hydrocarbons, like petrol, are in
great demand. So scientists have found a way to
change the larger, less useful molecules into
smaller, more useful ones.

The reaction used is called **cracking**.

The big molecules are broken down by *heating*
them as they pass over a **catalyst**. A catalyst
helps to speed up a reaction (see page 198).

In the refinery this happens inside a **cracker**!

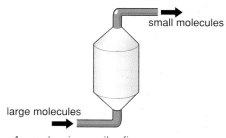

small molecules

large molecules

A cracker in an oil refinery

It's a cracker

Do-it-yourself cracker

Q. What do you call
two mad scientists
in an oil refinery?

A. Crackers!

Experiment 13.2   Cracking

In this experiment you can crack a large molecule
(paraffin) into smaller ones.

Set up your apparatus as shown:

⚠ *You must take the end of the delivery
tube out of the water before you stop heating.*
(You don't want cold water to be sucked back into
your hot tube!)

Start by heating the aluminium oxide strongly.
Then just move the flame onto the paraffin every
now and again. This is just to make sure that
some vapour is passing along the tube.
(Don't collect the first few bubbles that appear.
This is hot air inside the tube expanding.)

Collect two test-tubes of gas. The gas is **ethene**.

Test the ethene with a lighted splint.
What happens?

Test the other tube by adding a little bromine
water. Replace the bung quickly and shake.
What happens?

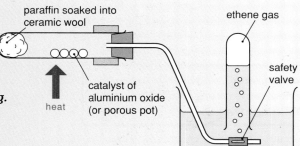

paraffin soaked into
ceramic wool

ethene gas

heat

catalyst of
aluminium oxide
(or porous pot)

safety
valve

Remember:

**Cracking is when we break down large
hydrocarbons into smaller, more useful
ones. This is done at high temperatures,
using a catalyst.**

▷ Making plastics

Whenever oil companies crack large molecules into smaller ones, **ethene** is made.

Ethene is a very useful little molecule. It is the starting material for many **plastics**.

Plastics were first made on a large scale in the 1930s. They are now a very important part of our modern world.

Look at the picture of a toddler's bedroom from around 1900: Nothing in it is made from plastics.

Polymers

Plastics are huge molecules. They are usually long chains, made from thousands of atoms. These long chain molecules are called **polymers**.

(**Poly** meaning *many* e.g. a polygon is a many sided shape.)

Polymers are made by joining together thousands of small, reactive molecules called **monomers**.

(**Mono** meaning *one* e.g. a monorail is a railway with only one track.)

It's rather like stringing beads together to make a necklace. Using real beads, your polymer necklace would be about half a kilometre long!

> **Lots of small, reactive molecules called monomers join together to make a polymer.**

What things would be made from plastics nowadays?

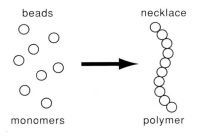

beads   necklace

monomers   polymer

You can also get the idea by using shapes:

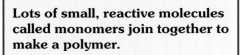

monomers

polymerisation

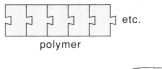

polymer   etc.

The reaction is called **polymerisation**.
The most common monomer is ethene.
When it joins together in a long chain it makes **poly(ethene)**. We know it better as polythene:

lots of ethenes ⟶ poly(ethene)

> **monomers ⟶ polymer**

PRETTY POLLY.

Poly-parrot?

▷ Ethene and the alkenes

You can see how ethene can form a polymer by looking more closely at its molecule. Its formula is C_2H_4.

Notice that ethene is a hydrocarbon. Like the alkane family (see page 157), it contains only hydrogen and carbon atoms. However, they are joined together differently.

Ethene belongs to a family of hydrocarbons called the **alkenes**. Look at the table:

Their names start off like the alkanes, but end in **-ene** instead of -ane.

Remember the alkanes have only single bonds joining their atoms together. The alkenes have **double bonds** between carbon atoms.

(If you want to know more about bonds, read Chapter 20.)

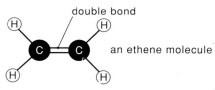

an ethene molecule

A double bond makes a molecule reactive.

Ethene even reacts with itself to make poly(ethene). (See the next page for details.)

Name	Formula	Picture of molecule
ethene	C_2H_4	
propene	C_3H_6	
butene	C_4H_8	

The table shows the first three members of the **alkene** family.
- Can you see a pattern in their formulas?
- Can you guess the names and formulas of the next two alkenes?
  (Look at the table of alkanes on page 157 for clues.)
- Can you draw a molecule of butene?
- Why is there no alkene with just one carbon atom?

Saturated and unsaturated molecules

You have probably seen margarines advertised as 'high in poly-unsaturates'. The molecules in margarine have lots of double bonds between carbon atoms.

Ethene and the other alkenes are *also* **unsaturated** molecules, with double bonds.

On the other hand, the alkanes are said to be **saturated**. They contain only single bonds.

You can test to see if a compound is unsaturated.

Compounds with double bonds turn yellow **bromine water** colourless.

Experiment 13.3   Testing margarine and butter
Do the test for double bonds on some margarine and then on some butter.
Which has more double bonds?

⚠ bromine water

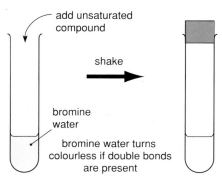

add unsaturated compound

shake

bromine water

bromine water turns colourless if double bonds are present

The test for an unsaturated compound

▷ Polymerisation

You can now look at polymerisation in more detail.
There are two types of reaction to make polymers.
These are **addition** reactions and **condensation**
reactions.

1. Addition reactions

The diagram of the shapes joining together
on page 164 is an example of addition.
Here is another with more detail added.

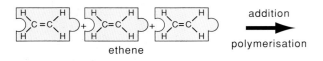

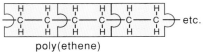

ethene   poly(ethene)

In addition reactions the monomers have at least
one double bond between carbon atoms.

The polymer is the only thing formed in the reaction.

The reaction of ethene to make poly(ethene) is the
best known example, as shown above.

The reaction can be shown like this:

$$n\,C_2H_4 \longrightarrow (C_2H_4)_n$$

where n = a large number.

Look at the diagram below:

The double bonds in ethene 'open up' and
neighbouring molecules join end to end.

I really feel I have to say
A life of crime just does not pay
While you are free – a monomer
We're chained up – a polymer.

This supermarket worker is making his own addition
polymer!
What are the monomers in his polymer?
What would you call the polymer? Poly(trolley)?

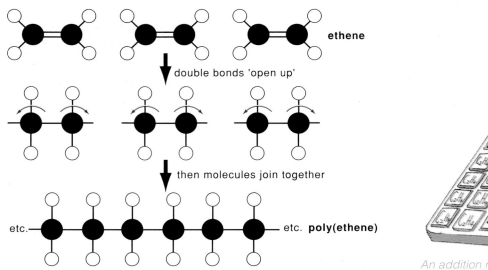

ethene

double bonds 'open up'

then molecules join together

etc. **poly(ethene)**

An addition reaction?

166

Other addition polymers

Some of the hydrogen atoms in ethene can be
swapped for different atoms. You can then get
a new polymer. Look at the examples below:

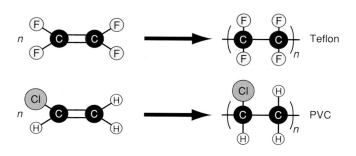

Teflon

PVC

Teflon is the non-stick lining on pans

2. Condensation reactions

This is the other type of polymerisation.
Nylon is an example of a polymer made in a
condensation reaction.

Nylon is very strong

Experiment 13.4   Making nylon

Put a thin layer of monomer A into the bottom of a very small beaker.
Carefully pour a layer of monomer B on top of this.
● What do you see happen?
Gently draw a thread out of the beaker using a pair of tweezers.
Wind it around a test-tube as shown.
Do not touch the nylon formed.

⚠ monomers

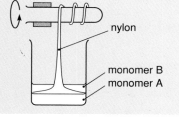

nylon

monomer B
monomer A

You see fumes given off as the two
different monomers react together.
The fumes are hydrogen chloride (HCl) gas.
A small molecule is always given off
in a condensation reaction.

The monomers have reactive parts at
both ends of their molecules.
They join together, end to end, to make a long chain.

A condensation reaction?

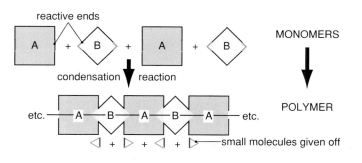

▷ Properties of plastics

Why are so many things made out of plastics?
They are certainly cheap to make.
However, lots of plastics do the job they are
designed for better than traditional materials.

What advantages do
a) PVC gutters have over iron ones?
b) melamine kitchen work surfaces have over
   wooden ones?
c) poly(propene) milk crates have over
   metal ones?

We can make plastics that do their jobs well
in all sorts of ways.
For example, poly(styrene) is the plastic used
to make yoghurt pots. But if some gas is blown
into it during moulding you get 'expanded' poly(styrene).
This is the plastic that crumbles very easily.
It is used to hold hot drinks and 'fast food'.
The gas trapped inside makes it an excellent
heat insulator.

What are the disadvantages of plastics in
house fires or in rubbish dumps?

*The driver of this car escaped without serious
burns thanks to Kevlar. Racing drivers wear fire-
proof suits made from this new polymer.*

Structure of plastics

Experiment 13.5   Heating plastics
Heat a sample of a thermoplastic and a thermoset
on a tin lid in a fume-cupboard.
● Which melts more easily?

When the thermoplastic softens, use a glass rod to
draw out a thread. You are remoulding your plastic.

● What eventually happens to your thermoset?

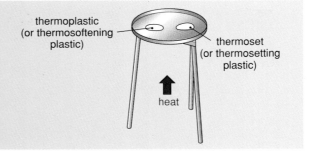

**Thermoplastics soften easily and can be
remoulded into new shapes. They are
sometimes called thermosoftening plastics.**

**Thermosets (or thermosetting plastics) do not
soften. If you heat them strongly enough, they
eventually break down and char. They are hard
and rigid.**

These different properties can be explained if you
look at the arrangement of the polymer chains:

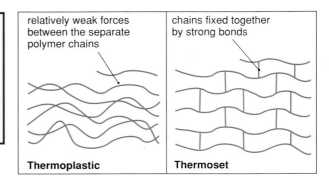

Summary

Crude oil contains a mixture of **hydrocarbons**. Hydrocarbons are compounds made of hydrogen and carbon only.

Crude oil is separated into groups of useful substances (fractions) by **fractional distillation**. This works because different hydrocarbons have different boiling points.

The small hydrocarbons
- have lower boiling points,
- are lighter in colour,
- are easier to light, burning with a cleaner flame,
- are thinner and more runny.

The large molecules from crude oil can be broken down or **cracked** into smaller, more useful molecules. This is done at high temperature, using a catalyst.

Small, reactive molecules, called **monomers**, can join together to make very large molecules called **polymers**.

▷ Questions

1. Copy out and complete :
   a) A hydrocarbon is a compound containing . . . . and carbon atoms only.
   b) Crude oil is a . . . . of hydrocarbons. In an oil . . . . , the crude oil is separated into its fractions by . . . . The heated oil enters the fractionating . . . . as a gas. The hydrocarbons have different . . . . points and condense at different temperatures. The smaller molecules, with the lower boiling points, are collected near the . . . . of the column.
   c) Large hydrocarbons can be cracked by heating them with a . . . . . The new molecules made are . . . . and more useful.
   d) When lots of small, reactive molecules join together, they make a . . . . . The small molecules you start with are called . . . . .

2. Carla distils some crude oil.
She collects 3 fractions in different test-tubes.
But at the end of her experiment, the tubes get mixed up.
Give 3 ways that Carla could find out which order they were collected in ?

3. a) Copy and complete this table :

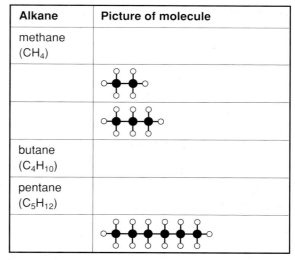

Alkane	Picture of molecule
methane (CH_4)	
butane (C_4H_{10})	
pentane (C_5H_{12})	

b) Petrol contains the alkane with 8 carbons. Can you guess its name ? Draw a picture of the molecule.

4. Imagine you are a small hydrocarbon molecule in crude oil.
Describe what happens to you from the time you are discovered by an oil company, to the time you end up heating beans on a camping stove.

5. Sketch this diagram of a fractionating column.

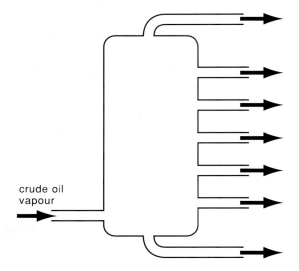

crude oil vapour

Fill in the missing fractions.
Say what each fraction is used for.

6. a) Finish off this equation:

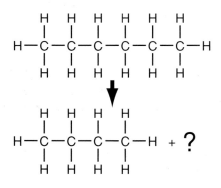

b) What is this type of reaction called?
c) What are the names of the 2 molecules made in the reaction?
d) What must you do to make this reaction happen?
e) Look at the molecules in the reaction: Write down the formula of each molecule in a chemical equation for the reaction.

7. Ethene is an **unsaturated hydrocarbon**.
a) What is a hydrocarbon?
b) What is an unsaturated molecule?
c) What is the formula of ethene?
d) Why is eth**ene** more reactive than eth**ane**?

8. a) What happens in a **polymerisation** reaction? Use the words *monomers* and *polymer* in your answer.
b) What are the **monomers** called that make
   i) poly(ethene)?
   ii) poly(styrene)?
   iii) poly(propene)?

9. a) How can you tell the difference between a **thermoplastic** and a **thermoset**?
b) How do their structures help to explain these differences?
c) What are the most important properties for the plastics used to make:
   i) a light switch?
   ii) a fizzy drinks bottle?
   iii) a pair of sandals for the beach?
   iv) a wind shield for a motor-bike?

10. Copy and complete this table:

Object	Traditional material	Plastic used
a) drain pipe	iron	
b) disposable cup	paper	
c) blouse	cotton	
d) disposable bag		poly(ethene)

What are the advantages of the plastic in each example?

11. Finish off this rhyme:

A young chemist was getting quite drastic,
In her efforts to find a new plastic.
The new molecule she sketched
Would spring back when it stretched
Like rubber it's described as . . . . .

12. a) Describe how crude oil was formed.

b) Imagine that you are a careers officer.
Draw a flow chart to show the steps from finding crude oil to getting it to an oil refinery.
Write down the career opportunities at each stage in your flow chart.

13. a) Complete this general formula for the alkanes:

$$C_nH_?$$

b) What is the formula of the alkane with 9 carbon atoms?
Look at the boiling points in this table:

Alkane	Number of carbon atoms	Boiling point (°C)
methane	1	−161
ethane	2	−88
propane	3	−42
butane	4	−0.5
pentane	5	
hexane	6	69

c) Draw a graph of their boiling points (up the side) against the number of carbon atoms (along the bottom).

d) What is the general pattern you see from your graph?

e) Use your graph to predict the boiling point of pentane.

14. a) Draw a 'spider' diagram like this to show the useful materials we get from crude oil.

Get your information from page 162 and page 172.

b) Why do some people think that using fuels from crude oil is a waste of our resources?

15. Look at this key to identify plastics:

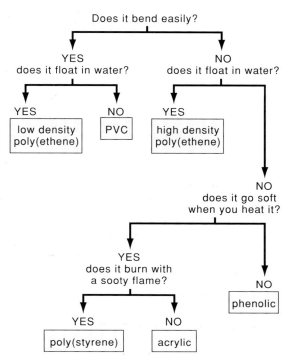

a) Which plastic bends easily and sinks in water?

b) Which plastic does **not** bend easily, float in water or go soft when you heat it?

c) Use the key to say as much as you can about acrylic.

d) Notice that in the key, it says that poly(styrene) does not float. However, it can be changed in its manufacture into a form which does float.
  i) What is this type of poly(styrene) called?
  ii) How is it made?
  iii) What are its useful properties?
  iv) What is it used for?

16. a) What are the two types of polymerisation reaction?

b) Describe how the two types of reaction are similar.

c) Describe how the two types of reaction are different.

Further questions on page 230.

WOLVERHAMPTON COLLEGE

A source of new materials

You have already seen some uses of the fractions
we get from crude oil (see page 162).
You can also get a light fraction called **naphtha**.
It is used to make many new products.

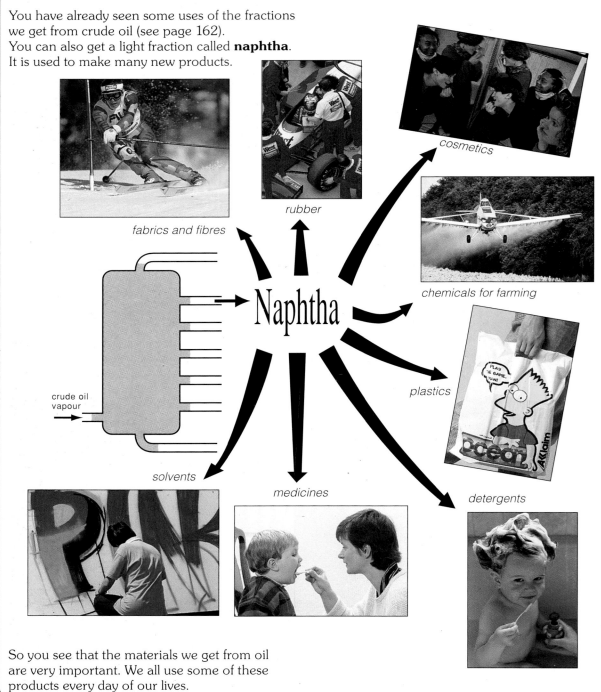

fabrics and fibres

rubber

cosmetics

chemicals for farming

crude oil
vapour

Naphtha

plastics

solvents

medicines

detergents

So you see that the materials we get from oil
are very important. We all use some of these
products *every* day of our lives.

All plastics are made by small molecules (monomers) reacting together to make very long molecules (polymers).
The plastic is always named after its monomer.
You just put poly- in front of the monomer's name.
Look at these examples:

Monomer	Polymer
ethene ——▶	poly(ethene)
styrene ——▶	poly(styrene)
vinyl chloride ——▶	poly(vinyl chloride)

As you can see, the names can get quite long!
So many plastics are known by their trade names.
Well-known examples are perspex and nylon.
(Nylon gets its name from two famous cities.
Can you guess which ones?)

Here are some common plastics and their uses:

Special plastics have been injected into the timbers of the Mary Rose to preserve them. The ship sank in 1545 and was raised to the surface in 1982.

poly(ethene)

poly(styrene)

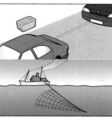

poly(vinyl chloride) PVC

poly(propene)

nylon

melamine

phenolic resins

You know that the world's crude oil will probably run out within your life-time.
Look at all the uses of materials we get from oil:
How would your life change without them?

Greater Manchester Council is thinking ahead.
It has patented a way of changing our rubbish into crude oil.
First of all, any glass or metal is removed.
Then they use high temperatures and pressures, just like when natural crude oil was made.

Rubbish has been turned into oil on a small scale. As oil becomes scarce, and its price rises, it may become economic on a large scale.

▷ Chemistry at work : Detergents

Many detergents are made from the products of crude oil.
Washing-up liquid is an example.

Detergents are substances which help the cleaning action
of water.

Water is good at dissolving many things.
However, it cannot dissolve oil or grease.
This is where detergents help.

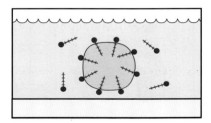

the 'head' of the
molecule is strongly
attracted to water

the 'tail' is a long hydrocarbon
chain which dissolves in grease

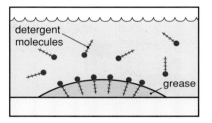

*The 'tails' of the detergent molecules
bury themselves into the grease*

*The 'heads' stick out and are pulled
towards the water molecules*

*The grease then floats off into the
water*

Experiment 13.6   Detergents are 'wetting agents'
Collect some water in a beaker.
Use a dropper to carefully put a drop of the water
on to a flat piece of cotton.

Now add a few drops of detergent to the water
in your beaker.
Again, place a drop on the cotton.

• What difference do you see?

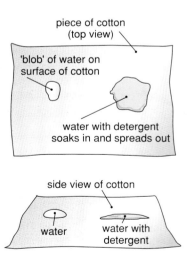

piece of cotton
(top view)

'blob' of water on
surface of cotton

water with detergent
soaks in and spreads out

Detergents help water to soak into clothes when
you wash them. They form a thin 'skin' on top
of the water. This breaks down the strong
forces of attraction between water molecules
at the surface. Detergents reduce the water's
surface tension.

side view of cotton

water   water with
detergent

The water can then spread out more easily.
That's why detergents are called **wetting agents**.

▷ Chemistry at work : Uses of detergents

Soapless detergents

Soaps are detergents. Traditionally, they are
made from animal fats and plant oils.
Using soap in areas with hard water causes
'scum' to form (see page 128). The white bits of
'scum' can stick to clothes when they are being
washed.

However, **soapless detergents** from crude oil
do not have this problem.

*Which plant oils do you think
this soap is made from ?*

Experiment 13.7   Hard water

Add a few drops of soap solution to half a test-tube of
hard water. Put a bung at the top and shake the tube.

● What happens ?

Now repeat the experiment but use a *soapless* detergent.
● What difference do you notice ?

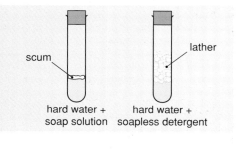

hard water +
soap solution

hard water +
soapless detergent

Soapless detergents do not make 'scum' in hard water.
No detergent is wasted reacting with the hardness,
so you save money as well.
About 80 % of all detergents made are
soapless detergents.

Treating oil spills

As you know from page 159, crude oil
is transported in giant oil tankers. If these ships
have an accident, the crude oil can escape. It floats
on top of the sea, forming an oil slick.
Soapless detergents are used to clean up the mess.
The detergent breaks up the slick. Then the oil
is spread out by the action of the waves.

*This oil tanker was
grounded on the rocks
near Shetland*

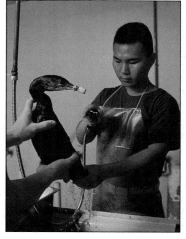

*Birds like this can be rescued
by cleaning the oil from their
feathers with detergents*

chapter 14

Energy Transfer

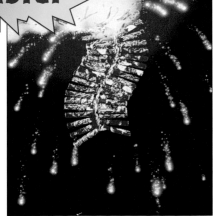

The chemical energy in these fireworks is transferred to heat, light and sound energy

We all need the energy we get from chemical reactions.
Energy heats our homes and powers industry.
Energy from the chemical reactions inside our bodies keeps us all alive.

Whenever chemicals react, we get a transfer of energy.
The energy usually ends up as heat. Sometimes we also get light energy or sound energy as well.
Can you think of a reaction which gives out heat, light and sound?

▷ Fuels

Fuels store chemical energy.
When we burn a fuel, its chemical energy is released.
We can use this energy to give us heat or light.

Food is the fuel for our bodies. We 'burn' sugar by reacting it with oxygen in our cells.
Luckily for us, the reactions in our bodies are carefully controlled.
We don't burst into flames! But fuels often do.

Some restaurants are run like petrol stations. Instead of buying petrol to fuel your car, you drive in and buy food to fuel your body

The fire triangle

Do you know which fuel we burn in gas fires and cookers?
Bunsen burners also use methane gas.
How do you light the gas from a Bunsen burner?
Which gas in the air is reacting with the methane as it burns?

> **You need 3 things to make a fire:**
> - **fuel**
> - **heat**
> - **oxygen.**

*Whenever you come across **heat**,*
*And **fuel** and **oxygen** meet.*
You're sure to get fire,
The flames will lick higher –
*The **fire triangle's** complete!*

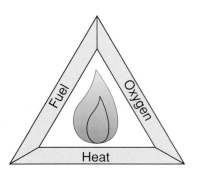

The fire triangle

If you remove one part of the fire triangle, the fire goes out.
How do you turn off a Bunsen burner?
Which part of the fire triangle are you removing?

▷ Combustion

As you know from the last chapter, the fuels
we get from crude oil are called hydrocarbons.
Petrol is a mixture of hydrocarbons.
Can you remember which 2 elements make up
a hydrocarbon? Petrol contains octane. Can you
guess how many carbon atoms there are in octane?

When we burn a fuel, the reaction is called **combustion**.
The fuel reacts with oxygen gas from the air and heat is given out.
But what is made in the reaction? You can find out
in the next experiment:

Combustion is a useful reaction

Experiment 14.1   *Products of combustion*

Set up the apparatus as shown:
Let it run until you see some changes in the U-tube
and in the limewater.

⚠ flammable liquids

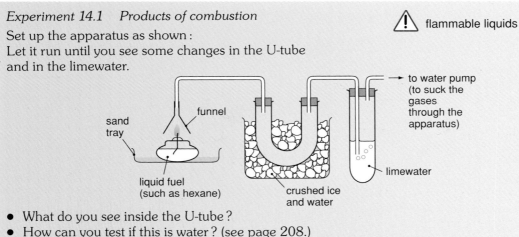

* What do you see inside the U-tube?
* How can you test if this is water? (see page 208.)
Try out your test if you collect enough liquid.
* What happens to the limewater?
* Which gas makes limewater go milky?

When hydrocarbons burn, they are **oxidised**.
We get carbon dioxide and water formed (***never*** hydrogen!):

> **hydrocarbon + oxygen ⟶ carbon dioxide + water**

Incomplete combustion

There is only a small amount of oxygen inside a car engine.
There is not enough to turn all the carbon in the hydrocarbons
into carbon dioxide. Some **carbon monoxide**, a toxic gas,
is also made.
Catalytic converters on exhausts can turn carbon monoxide into
carbon dioxide.
Sometimes fuels burn with a smoky flame. Incomplete
combustion means that **carbon** itself is given off as soot.

*Carbon monoxide is given off from car
exhausts. This gas stops your blood
carrying oxygen around your body.*

▷ Acid rain

> Burning fossil fuels makes **acid rain**.

Most fossil fuels contain sulphur as an impurity.
When we burn the fuel, the sulphur is oxidised.
It turns into **sulphur dioxide** (SO_2) gas.

Power stations burning coal or oil give off most sulphur dioxide.
This is the main cause of acid rain. The gas dissolves in rain-water, and reacts with oxygen in the air, to form sulphuric acid.

Coal-fired power stations give off sulphur dioxide gas. This causes acid rain.

Cars also make our rain acidic.
Car exhausts give off **nitrogen oxides**.
These make nitric acid when it rains.

Experiment 14.2   Effect of sulphur dioxide on plants

Set up the apparatus as shown :
The sodium compound gives off sulphur dioxide which is toxic.
Leave the seeds for a few days.

⚠ sodium metabisulphite

sodium meta-bisulphate added to make sulphur dioxide

cress seeds

cotton wool

- What effect does sulphur dioxide have on the growth of the seeds ?

Effects of acid rain

1. **Forests** – Trees are damaged and even killed.
Over half the forests in Germany are dead or dying.
2. **Fish** – Hundreds of lakes in Norway and Sweden now have no fish left in them at all.
Aluminium, which is normally 'locked' in the soil, dissolves in acid rain. It then gets washed into the lakes, where it poisons the fish.
3. **Buildings** – Acid rain attacks buildings and metal structures.
Limestone buildings are most badly affected.

What can be done ?

We can burn less fossil fuels by using energy more efficiently.
Or we could use alternative forms of energy. Do you know any 'cleaner' ways to produce electricity?
Would these bring their own problems for our environment?

We are now starting to remove sulphur from fossil fuels before we burn them. The sulphur can then be used to make sulphuric acid (see page 153).

We can also get rid of the acidic gases before they leave power stations. A mixture of limestone and water neutralises the sulphur dioxide (see page 154).

Acid rain damages buildings

*Nitrogen oxides are changed into harmless nitrogen gas by **catalytic converters** in car exhausts.*

▷ Greenhouse effect

The Earth's atmosphere acts like a greenhouse.
It lets rays from the Sun through to warm
the Earth. But gases, such as carbon dioxide and water vapour,
absorb some of the heat waves given off as the Earth cools down.

We are lucky to have these natural 'greenhouse gases'.
Without them, the Earth would be about 30 °C colder!
How do you think that would affect life on Earth?

However, we are making more and more of these gases.
Look back at Experiment 14.1:
When we burn a hydrocarbon, which gases are given off?
Whenever we burn a fuel we make carbon dioxide.
We are now burning up fossil fuels at an incredible rate.
This disturbs the natural balance of carbon dioxide (see page 276).

Although plants absorb carbon dioxide, we are cutting down
huge areas of forest every day. The trees are often just burned
to clear land for farming. This makes even more carbon dioxide.

More carbon dioxide, plus other 'greenhouse gases', such as
methane from cattle, could be making the Earth hotter.

Look at the graph opposite:

What is the general pattern?
But some scientists are not sure if these changes are just
part of the Earth's natural variations.
However, if temperatures go on rising, it will affect the Earth.
Again, scientists disagree on the changes and
how long they will take to happen.

Oceans could expand, causing a rise in sea levels.
The shape of the world map would change as low lands flood.
Climates could change around the world. However, scientists
are not sure exactly how different places will be affected.
An experiment on a global scale is not easy to predict,
even using computers.

What can be done?

As with acid rain, burning less fossil fuels will help.
But cleaning the gases given off will not reduce
the amount of carbon dioxide released into the air.
However, nitrogen oxides, which are also 'greenhouse gases',
can be removed from car exhausts by catalytic converters
(see page 178).

Planting trees to replace those cut down will help to restore
the Earth's natural balance (see Carbon Cycle, page 276).

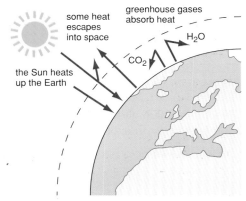

*Carbon dioxide and water vapour
are the main 'greenhouse gases'*

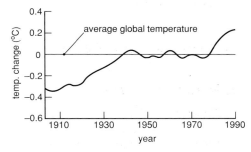

Average temperatures, 1900–1990.

*Like the glass in a greenhouse the atmosphere
lets light in but heat energy is trapped inside.*

▷ Exothermic and endothermic reactions

Exothermic reactions

We looked at the combustion of a fuel on page 177.
Think about what happens when we burn a fuel:
Is energy given out or taken in as the fuel burns?

Reactions which give out heat are called **exothermic**.
Combustion is an exothermic reaction.

Do you know any other reactions which are exothermic?

The charcoal (carbon) reacts with oxygen in this barbecue. Heat from the exothermic reaction cooks the food.

Experiment 14.3   Feeling hot!

Collect 25 cm^3 of copper sulphate solution in a small beaker.
Add a spatula of zinc powder. Stir it with a glass rod.
Carefully touch the outside of the beaker.

- What do you see happen?
- Does the beaker feel hot or cold?
- Does the reaction give out heat?
- Can you write a word or symbol equation for this reaction? (see page 82.)

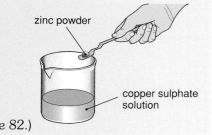

zinc powder

copper sulphate solution

The displacement reaction between zinc and
copper sulphate gives out heat.
It is an exothermic reaction.

> **Exothermic reactions give out heat energy.**

Endothermic reactions

Some reactions take in heat from
their surroundings.
These are called **endothermic** reactions.

Experiment 14.4   Feeling cold!

Add 3 spatulas of ammonium nitrate to 25 cm^3 of water
in a small beaker. Stir it with a glass rod.
Hold the beaker in the palm of your hand.

- What do you feel?
- Is heat energy given out to your hand? Or is energy
  being taken from your hand?

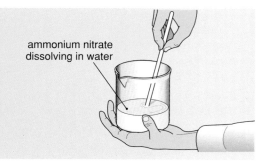

ammonium nitrate dissolving in water

When ammonium nitrate dissolves it takes in heat energy
from its surroundings. Its surroundings include the beaker,
the glass rod, the water, the air around it, and your hand!

> **Endothermic reactions take in heat energy.**

▷ What happens to the temperature?

You have seen how some reactions give out heat,
and others take in heat.
We know that when fuels burn, heat is given out.
What happens to the temperature near the burning fuel?
Does the temperature rise or fall in an exothermic reaction?

Think about the experiments on the previous page:
What do you think happens to the temperature in each one?
What can you use to check your ideas?
(Try this out if you have time.)

We find that:

> • in **exothermic** reactions, the **temperature goes up**,
> • in **endothermic** reactions, the **temperature goes down**.

Now let us look at some reactions to see if
they give out heat or take in heat:

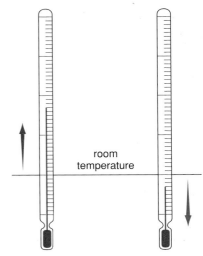

exothermic
(temperature rises)

endothermic
(temperature falls)

Experiment 14.5   Exothermic or Endothermic?
Use the apparatus as shown:
Work with each pair of substances in turn.
Record your results in a table.

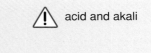 acid and akali

Reaction	temp. before mixing (°C)	temp. after mixing (°C)	Exothermic or Endothermic?
sodium hydroxide solution + dilute hydrochloric acid			
sodium hydrogencarbonate solution + citric acid			
copper sulphate solution + magnesium powder			
dilute sulphuric acid + magnesium ribbon			

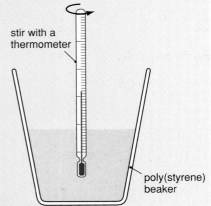

stir with a
thermometer

poly(styrene)
beaker

*Record the maximum or minimum
temperature during each reaction*

Look at your results:
• Did you find more exothermic or endothermic reactions?
• The first reaction is between an acid and an alkali.
  What do we call this **type** of reaction? (see page 141.)
• Which gas is given off in the second reaction in the table?
  (see page 154)
• Which **type** of reaction takes place between copper sulphate
  and magnesium? (see page 82.)
• Which gas is given off in the last reaction in the table?
  (see page 145.)

▷ Energy level diagrams

You have now seen some examples of exothermic and endothermic reactions.
Can you recall which gives out heat and which takes in heat? Look at the picture opposite:
It might help you to remember.

We can show the energy transfers in reactions on an **energy level diagram**.

These show us the energy stored in the reactants compared to the energy stored in the products.
Look at the examples below:
(Remember that reactants are the substances we start with and products are the new substances made in the reaction.)

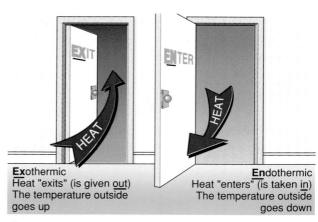

Exothermic
Heat "exits" (is given <u>out</u>)
The temperature outside goes up

Endothermic
Heat "enters" (is taken <u>in</u>)
The temperature outside goes down

Exothermic energy level diagram

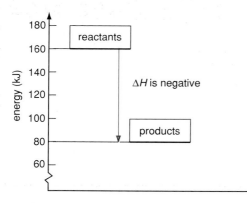

ΔH (we say 'delta H') is the symbol for the 'change in energy' in a reaction.
Look at the energy level diagram opposite:
It is for an exothermic reaction.
Notice that:
the products have **less energy** than the reactants.

ΔH **is negative for an exothermic reaction.**

The difference in energy is given out as heat.
Therefore, the temperature rises.

For example,

$$HCl + NaOH \longrightarrow NaCl + H_2O \qquad \Delta H = -58 \, kJ/mol$$

• Draw an energy level diagram to show this change.

Endothermic energy level diagram

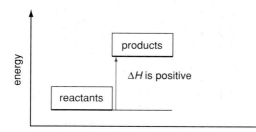

In endothermic reactions, the products have more energy than the reactants.

ΔH **is positive for an endothermic reaction.**

The extra energy needed to form the products is taken in from the surroundings.
Therefore, the temperature falls.

▷ Chemistry at work : Exothermic reactions

Fireworks

Have you ever wondered how we get
the stunning effects you see at a firework display?
There are plenty of combustion reactions, mainly
involving gunpowder.

Gunpowder was discovered about a thousand years ago
by the Chinese. Firecrackers were used in
religious festivals.
To get the fierce, exothermic reaction, you need a fuel and
a rapid supply of oxygen. The oxygen is provided
by an **oxidising agent**, such as potassium nitrate (KNO_3).

fuel + oxidising agent ⟶ gas products (+ heat)

Look at the diagram of the rocket:

Can you explain how it works?

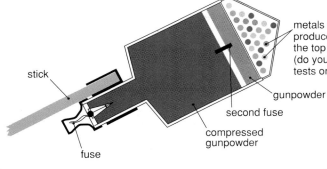

metals and their compounds
produce stars and sparks at
the top of the rocket's flight.
(do you remember your flame
tests on page 151?)

stick

gunpowder

second fuse

compressed
gunpowder

fuse

Explosives

What uses can you think of for explosives?
Most people think about military uses first,
such as bombs, missiles and hand grenades.

However, they have important peaceful uses
as well. For example, blasting tunnels,
clearing old buildings, underground mining
and quarrying.

Explosions, like those in fireworks, are combustion
reactions that make large volumes of hot gas from
solid or liquid reactants. The sudden increase in volume
results in a shock wave of incredible force – the explosion.

*These flats were demolished by
TNT (tri-nitrotoluene).
Dynamite was invented in 1867 by Alfred Nobel.
What else is he famous for?*

▷ Making and breaking bonds

We have already seen how atoms 'swap partners'
in chemical reactions.
This means that the bonds which join atoms
to each other must be broken.
New bonds must be made as the products form.

Do you think that energy is needed to break bonds?
Think of it as pulling apart 2 strong magnets.
You have to put in energy to separate them.
Therefore:

> **Breaking bonds requires energy. It is endothermic.**

What about making new bonds? That's like
the 2 magnets leaping across a gap because of their
attraction for each other.

> **Making new bonds gives out energy. It is exothermic.**

We can show these changes on an energy level diagram.
Let's look at the reaction between hydrogen (H_2) and
chlorine (Cl_2). They make hydrogen chloride (HCl).
The reaction needs energy to start it off:

$$H_2(g) + Cl_2(g) \longrightarrow 2\,HCl(g)$$

We must supply energy to break bonds!

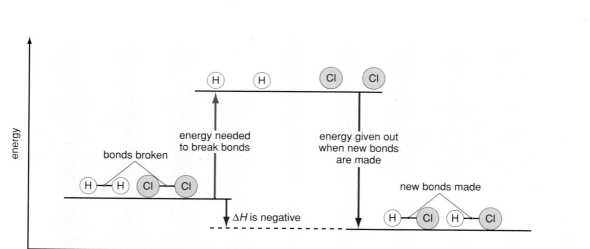

- Which involves more energy –
  breaking the original bonds (endothermic) or making the new bonds (exothermic)?
- Is the overall reaction exothermic or endothermic?

▷ Bond energy

We can work out the energy needed to
break different chemical bonds. This energy
is called the **bond energy**.

Look at the table of bond energies opposite:
Some bonds are stronger than others.
Which is the strongest bond shown in the table?

Notice that the units are **kJ/mol**. ΔH is also
measured in kJ/mol. This stands for
kilojoules per mole. It is the energy needed to
break a set number of bonds (a number which
chemists call 'the mole').
You can read about the quantity called the mole
on page 310.

Bond	Bond energy (kJ/mol)
H−H	436
Cl−Cl	242
H−Cl	431
C−H	413
C−C	347
C−O	335

Calculating ΔH

We can use the energy level diagrams and bond energies
to work out the energy change (ΔH) for a reaction.

Let's look at the reaction between hydrogen and
chlorine again. Look at its energy level diagram
on the previous page:
You can use this and the bond energies at
the top of this page to calculate ΔH:

How many H−H and Cl−Cl bonds are broken?
We can think of this as the energy needed to
start off the reaction.

Add up the bond energies:

$$+ [1 \times (\text{H–H})] + [1 \times (\text{Cl–Cl})]$$
$$= +(436 + 242)$$
$$= +678 \, \text{kJ/mol}$$

How many new HCl bonds are made?
Remember that making bonds is exothermic.
Energy is given out. This is given a negative sign.

$$- (2 \times \text{H–Cl})$$
$$= -(2 \times 431)$$
$$= -862 \, \text{kJ/mol}$$

Now we can work out the overall energy change (ΔH):

$$(+678) + (-862)$$
$$= -184 \, \text{kJ/mol}$$

So the reaction is exothermic.
More energy is given out making new bonds than
is taken in breaking the original bonds.

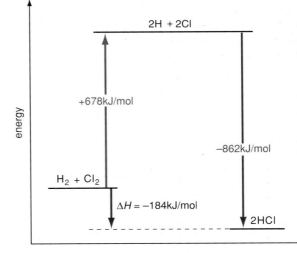

*The calculation can be shown on
an energy level diagram*

Bond energies are average values
for the bonds in different
molecules. Therefore these
calculations only give us a rough
value for ΔH.

▷ Chemistry at work : Putting out fires

Can you remember the fire triangle ? (see page 176.)
To put out a fire you need to remove one part of the triangle.

Removing the heat

When fire-fighters tackle a house fire they
often spray water on to the flames. This
cools down the fire.
Why do they spray those parts of the building
around the fire as well ?
What types of fire should you never use water on ?

Removing the fuel

Look at this gas-well fire :
The best way to put out a fire like this is to
cut off the flow of gas.
When new forests are planted, large channels
are left with no trees.
Why do you think this is a good idea ?

Removing the oxygen

Have you ever had a fire in your kitchen ?
People sometimes heat oils or fats above
their flash points. The flash point of a substance
is the temperature at which it ignites.
This happens in chip-pan fires.
If water is thrown on to burning oil or fat,
it makes the fire worse. The water turns to steam,
and sends burning oil flying into the air.
Look at the photo :
How does the damp tea-towel put out the fire ?
Why must you leave the pan covered by
the tea-towel for some time after the fire ?

Some fire extinguishers give off carbon dioxide gas.
They are good at putting out electrical fires.
They smother the fire, starving it of oxygen.
Why don't we use water on electrical fires ?

Can you think of a problem with using
a carbon dioxide extinguisher outdoors ?
Look at the photo opposite :
Fire crews at a plane crash spray foam onto the fire.
Carbon dioxide gas is trapped in the foam
so it stays on the fire.

List the things that you think are important
for an ideal fuel. Think about:
how much energy is given out, transport, storage, safety,
pollution, how easy it is to light, plus your own ideas.
Your teacher will tell you which fuels you can test.
Plan an investigation to see which fuel is best.
- How will you make it a fair test?
- How will you make it safe?

⚠ Make sure your teacher checks your plan before you start!

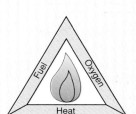

Summary

- Three things are needed for a fire – fuel, heat, and oxygen.
  If one part of this 'fire triangle' is removed, the fire goes out.
- The reaction of a fuel with oxygen is called **combustion**.
- When a hydrocarbon burns, it forms carbon dioxide and water.
- If a hydrocarbon burns in a limited supply of oxygen,
  it makes toxic carbon monoxide gas. Sometimes carbon (soot) is formed.
- Exothermic reactions give out heat. The temperature rises.
- Endothermic reactions take in heat. The temperature falls.

The fire triangle

▷ Questions

1. Copy and complete:
   a) The 3 things we need for a fire can be shown
      in the .... :

   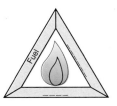

   b) When a hydrocarbon burns in plenty of
      oxygen, it gives carbon dioxide and ..... .
      This reaction is called .... (or oxidation).
      In a limited supply of oxygen, we also get
      toxic, carbon .... gas and possibily ..... .
   c) Exothermic reactions give out .... , and the
      temperature ..... .
      .... reactions take in heat, and the
      temperature .... .

2. Plan an investigation to see which of 3 liquid
   fuels gives off most heat per gram.
   Make sure that your plan is safe.

3. Zara and Lee want to test the products formed
   when a hydrocarbon burns.
   They set up the experiment below:

   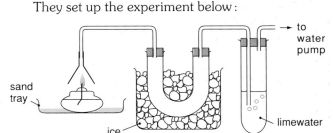

   a) Why do they put ice around the U-tube?
   b) How can they test that the liquid formed in
      the U-tube is water?
   c) The other product is carbon dioxide.
      What happens to the limewater?
   d) There is a small amount of carbon dioxide in
      the air. How can they show that the
      carbon dioxide they test for is not just the
      carbon dioxide in the air?
   e) Natural gas is a hydrocarbon called methane.
      Copy and complete the equations below:

   methane + oxygen $\longrightarrow$ .... + ...
   CH_4 + O_2 $\longrightarrow$ .... + ...

4. a) Petrol burns in a car engine.
Explain how carbon *monoxide* gas is
formed.
   b) Carbon monoxide bonds to the
haemoglobin in your blood. Explain how
this makes it toxic?
   c) Several holiday-makers die from carbon
monoxide poisoning each year. Poorly
ventilated gas heaters are often to blame.
Imagine that you are a travel agent. Write a
letter to the owner of some holiday homes
explaining the dangers.

5. Many power stations burn fossil fuels.
   a) Name 3 fossil fuels. (see page 158.)
   b) Which gas given off from power stations
can cause acid rain?
   c) What are the effects of acid rain?
   d) Make a list of the things we can do to
reduce the problem of acid rain.

6. Look at the diagram of a **catalytic converter**
below.

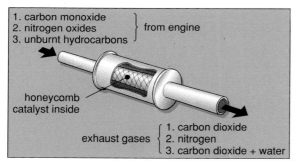

   a) Explain how a catalytic converter helps to
reduce acid rain.
   b) Does a catalytic converter help to reduce the
greenhouse effect?   Explain your answer.

7. Look at this table:

Reaction	Starting temp.(°C)	Final temp.(°C)
A + B	19	27
C + D	20	25
E + F	19	17

   a) Decide whether each reaction is exothermic
or endothermic? How can you tell?
   b) The volume of solution was the same in each
reaction. Which had the largest energy change?

8. When hydrochloric acid and sodium hydroxide
react in a beaker, the temperature rises:

$$HCl + NaOH \longrightarrow NaCl + H_2O$$
$$\Delta H = -58 \text{ kJ/mol}$$

   a) Is the reaction exothermic or endothermic?
Give 2 reasons for your answer from the
information above.
   b) Copy and complete this energy level diagram:

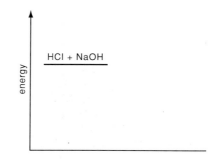

9. Hydrogen burns in air to form steam.

$$2 H_2 + O_2 \longrightarrow 2 H_2O$$

   a) Copy the equation above and put in the
state symbols.
   b) What is this type of reaction called?
   c) Draw an energy level diagram, like the one
on page 184, which shows the breaking and
making of bonds when hydrogen burns.
(H$_2$ has an H–H bond,
O$_2$ contains a double bond, O=O,
H$_2$O contains two O–H bonds.)
   d) Use the bond energies in this table to
calculate ΔH for the reaction:

Bond	Bond energy (kJ/mol)
H–H	436
O=O	498
O–H	464

   e) Why do you think that the bond energy of
the O=O bond is higher than the other 2
values in the table above?

10. Design a leaflet for your parents which
explains about the greenhouse effect.

Further questions on page 232.

Rates of Reaction

chapter 15

Some reactions are fast, and others are slow.
Can you think of a reaction which happens
very quickly?
Fast reactions, like dynamite exploding,
start and finish within a fraction of a second.
Slow reactions, like concrete setting, may take
days, weeks, or even years to finish.
Can you think of another slow reaction?

The chemicals in the base of a 'party-
popper' react in a fraction of a second

*This combustion reaction lasts a few
seconds*

The copper on this roof takes
years to react in the air

What is 'rate of reaction'?

The rate of a reaction tells us **how quickly**
a chemical reaction happens.

It is important for people in industry
to know how fast a reaction goes. They have to
know exactly how much of their product
they can make each hour, day or week.
In a shampoo factory, the rate might be
100 bottles per minute.

We can't work out the rate of a reaction
from its chemical equation. Equations can only
tell us how much product we can get. They don't
say how quickly it is made.

We can only find the rate by actually doing experiments.

During a reaction, we can measure how
much reactant is used up *in a certain time*.
On the other hand, we might choose to measure
how much product is formed in a certain time.

reactants

products

*You can see how we can measure the rate
of reactions on the next two pages*

189

▷ Measuring rates of reaction

Let's look at a reaction that we have met before –
calcium carbonate and acid:

calcium carbonate + hydrochloric acid ⟶ calcium chloride + water + carbon dioxide
$CaCO_3(s)$ + $2\,HCl(aq)$ ⟶ $CaCl_2(aq)$ + $H_2O(l)$ + $CO_2(g)$

reactants   products

How can we measure the rate of this reaction?
We can measure how quickly one of the reactants
is being used up. However, it is not easy to
measure the amount of calcium carbonate or
hydrochloric acid as the reaction is happening.

Let's think about measuring one of the products.
Look at the equation above:
Which one of the products is a gas?
It is much easier to measure **how much gas**
is being made as the reaction goes along.

Try one of the next experiments to measure
the rate of this reaction:

Experiment 15.1   Volumes of gas given off (1)

Set up the apparatus as shown:
Measure the volume of gas collected every 30 seconds.
Start your timing as soon as you put
the bung into the flask.
Put your results into a table like this:

Time (s)	Volume of gas (cm³)
0	0
30	

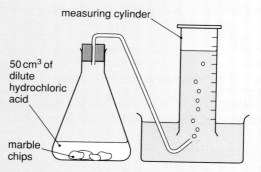

Plot a line graph of your results. Put time along the bottom axis
and volume of carbon dioxide gas up the side.

Experiment 15.2   Volumes of gas given off (2)

Set up the apparatus as shown:

Repeat the method above.
Take the bung out of the flask when
you have collected 100 cm³ of gas.

Record your results and plot a graph as above.

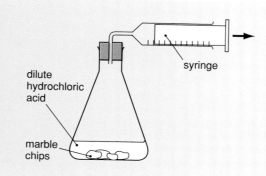

Experiment 15.3   Measuring the mass of gas given off

Set up the apparatus as shown:

Measure the mass every 30 seconds.
Record your results in a table like this:

⚠ acid

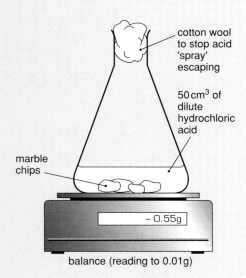

cotton wool
to stop acid
'spray'
escaping

50 cm³ of
dilute
hydrochloric
acid

marble
chips

– 0.55g

balance (reading to 0.01g)

Time (s)	Mass (g)	Loss in mass (g)
0		0
30		

Some balances have a **TARE** button. You can
press this as you start timing. The balance will now
give you the loss in mass directly.

Plot a line graph of your results.
(Put loss in mass up the side and time along the bottom.)
The loss in mass is the mass of gas given off.

Graphs and rates of reaction

Are your graphs shaped like the one shown here?
We can use graphs to measure the rate of a reaction
at any given time.
The slope (or gradient) tells us how quickly the reaction
was going at that time.

> **The steeper the slope, the faster the reaction.**

Look at the graph:

- When is the reaction fastest?

- How can you tell that the reaction is slowing down
  as time passes?

- How do you know when the reaction has stopped?

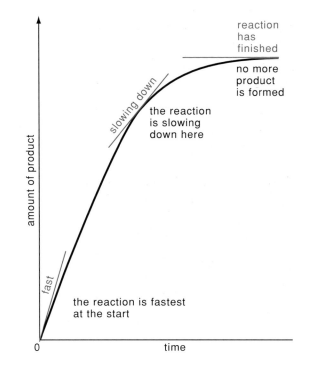

reaction
has
finished

no more
product
is formed

slowing down

the reaction
is slowing
down here

amount of product

fast

the reaction is fastest
at the start

0   time

▷ Effect of surface area

Have you ever tried to light a bonfire
or a camp fire? Which burns more quickly –
a block of wood or a pile of wood shavings?

We find that small pieces of solids, especially powders,
react faster than large pieces.

It's like frying two pans of chips.
One has potato cut into small, thin chips.
The other pan has bigger, thicker chips.
Which chips will be cooked first?
Which chips have the larger surface area?

Surface area is a measure of how much
surface is exposed. So for the same mass of potato,
small chips have a larger surface area than big chips.

*Lumps of coal burn slowly on a coal fire. However, coal
dust in the air down a mine can cause an explosion!*

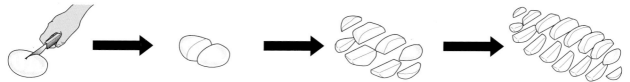

You increase the surface area of the potato each time you cut it smaller

Let's look at the effect of increasing surface area on
the rate of a reaction:

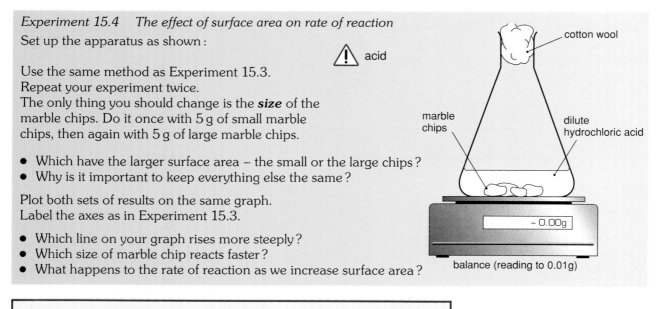

Experiment 15.4   The effect of surface area on rate of reaction

Set up the apparatus as shown:

⚠ acid

Use the same method as Experiment 15.3.
Repeat your experiment twice.
The only thing you should change is the **size** of the
marble chips. Do it once with 5 g of small marble
chips, then again with 5 g of large marble chips.

cotton wool

marble
chips

dilute
hydrochloric acid

- Which have the larger surface area – the small or the large chips?
- Why is it important to keep everything else the same?

Plot both sets of results on the same graph.
Label the axes as in Experiment 15.3.

- Which line on your graph rises more steeply?
- Which size of marble chip reacts faster?
- What happens to the rate of reaction as we increase surface area?

– 0.00g

balance (reading to 0.01g)

> **As we increase the surface area, we increase the rate of reaction.**

The collision theory

As you know, all substances are made up of particles.
The particles might be atoms, molecules or ions.
Before we can get a chemical reaction,
particles must crash together. They must collide.

This is called the **collision theory**.

Think about the rate of a reaction.
What do you think happens to the number of collisions
between particles if you speed up a reaction?

Particles must collide before they can react!

> **The more collisions between particles in a given time, the faster the reaction.**

Explaining the effect of surface area

Iron reacts with oxygen when you heat it in air.
What do you think it forms? (see page 46.)

Experiment 15.5   Sparklers!

Compare what happens when you heat:
1. an iron nail
2. iron wool
3. iron filings.
Hold the iron nail and iron wool in tongs as you heat them.
Gently sprinkle a few iron filings into a Bunsen flame
from the end of a spatula.

- Put the 3 types of iron in order of increasing surface area.
- What effect does increasing the surface area of the iron have on the rate of its reaction?

Think about burning iron filings.
Powders have a very large surface area.
There are lots of iron atoms exposed at its many surfaces.
The oxygen molecules in the air can attack
any of these iron atoms.
With iron filings, there are lots of collisions
in a given time. The reaction is very fast.
Compare this with heating the iron nail.

The iron nail has a small surface area. It only reacts slowly.

When a solid lump is cut into pieces,
Its rate of reaction always increases.
In the lump, most particles are locked up inside,
In order to react, they have to collide!
But powders have lots of particles exposed,
If cut fine enough, they might even explode!

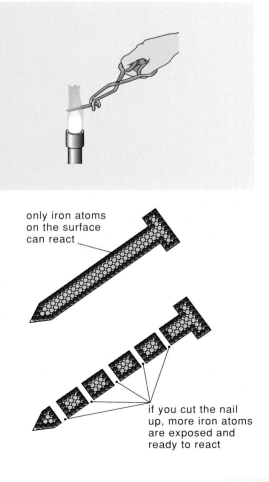

only iron atoms
on the surface
can react

if you cut the nail
up, more iron atoms
are exposed and
ready to react

▷ Effect of concentration

Look at these instructions from a washing powder:

The washing powder dissolves into the water in your washing machine, making a solution.
The washing powder contains substances which react with stains to remove them.

What happens to the concentration of the solution in your machine as you add more cups of powder?

If your washing is not badly stained, you can save money by adding less powder.
But what do you think happens if you use just 1 cup of powder on washing with difficult stains?
You will probably have to wash the clothes several times.
It is better to follow the instructions given on the packet and just wash them once!

As you add more cups of powder, you are increasing the concentration of the solution.

So what happens to the rate at which the washing powder reacts with stains, as you increase the concentration?

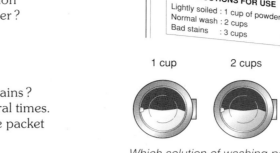

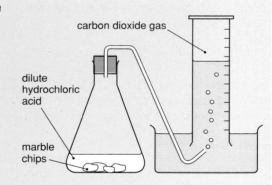

Which solution of washing powder is most concentrated?

Experiment 15.6   Effect of concentration on rate of reaction

In this experiment you will **vary the concentration** of the acid each time.
- What other factors must be kept the same?

Set up the apparatus as shown:
Time how long it takes to collect 20 cm³ of gas.
Record your results in a table like this:

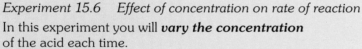

Acid (cm³)	Water (cm³)	Time to collect 20 cm³ of gas (s)
10	40	
20	30	
30	20	
40	10	
50	0	

less concentrated

↓

more concentrated

- Which test gave the fastest reaction?
- What happens to the rate of reaction as you increase the concentration of acid?

As we increase the concentration, the rate of reaction increases.

Explaining the effect of concentration

You already know about the collision theory from page 193.
We can use it to explain why
more concentrated solutions react more quickly.
Let's think about the reaction in the last experiment:

The acid particles can only react with the marble chips
when they collide.
Look at these diagrams:

acid
particles

marble
chip

- Which beaker has the
  faster reaction?
- Why?

If this is a IM solution of acid . . . . . . .this is a 2M solution. There are twice as many
acid particles **in the same volume of water**

The acid particles move randomly through the water.

As you increase the concentration of the acid, there are
more acid particles in the same volume.
Therefore there is a greater chance of acid particles
colliding, and reacting, with particles on the surface of
the marble. You increase the rate of the reaction.

It's a bit like dancing at a club. When a popular record
is played, lots more people crowd on to the dance floor.
The concentration of people on the dance floor increases.
There is now a lot more chance of bumping into
another dancer!

Gas reactions

Look at the syringes opposite:
If the end is sealed, how can you increase the pressure
of the gases inside the syringe?
By pressing the plunger in, you now have the
same number of gas particles in a smaller volume.
In other words, you have increased the concentration
of the gas.

Therefore:

> **In reactions between gases, increasing the pressure,
> increases the rate of reaction.**

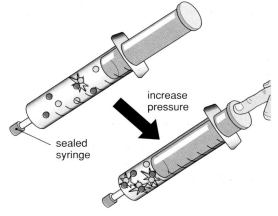

increase
pressure

sealed
syringe

*There are more collisions in a given time when
you increase the pressure of a gas*

▷ Effect of temperature

Why do we keep our food in a fridge?
Some of the substances in food react with
oxygen in the air.

Have you ever tasted milk that has gone off?
If you have, you will know the sour taste of acids!
Oils and fats in many foods turn 'rancid'
when left in air. They react and turn into acids.

The **low temperature** in your fridge **slows down**
the reactions that make food go off.

Let's look at an experiment to measure
the effect of temperature on rate of reaction:

*What happens to the rate of chemical reactions
inside a fridge?*

Experiment 15.7   The effect of temperature on rate of reaction

Mix equal volumes of sodium thiosulphate solution and
dilute hydrochloric acid in a flask.
● What do you see?

The solution goes cloudy because we get
a precipitate of sulphur as the solutions react.
We can time how quickly the solution gets cloudy
to measure the rate of reaction.
The diagram opposite shows you how to do this:

Warm 50 cm³ of sodium thiosulphate solution to
one of the temperatures in the table below.
Then place the flask on your cross.
Add 5 cm³ of hydrochloric acid and swirl.
Time how long it takes for the cross to disappear.

⚠ acid
sulphuric dioxide

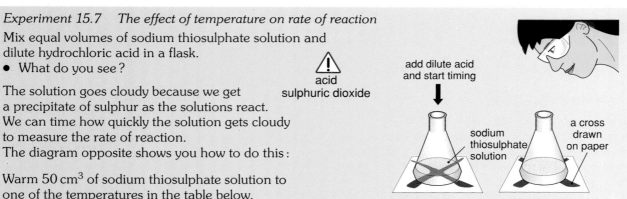

add dilute acid
and start timing

sodium
thiosulphate
solution

a cross
drawn
on paper

*Time how long it takes for the cross to
disappear*

Record your results in a table like this:

Temp. (°C)	Time for cross to disappear (s)
25	
35	
45	
55	

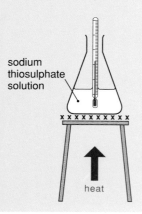

sodium
thiosulphate
solution

x x x x x x x x x x

heat

● How did you make this a fair test?
● At which temperature did the cross disappear most quickly?
● What is the pattern in your results?

From this experiment we find that:

> **As we increase the temperature, we increase the rate of reaction.**

Explaining the effect of temperature

What happens to the way particles move
when you heat them up?
The particles have more energy. They move around
more quickly.
As they travel faster, there are more collisions
in a certain time. Therefore, reactions get faster
as we raise the temperature.

But there is another reason why the rate increases.

Some colliding particles just bounce off each other.
They don't bang together hard enough to
start a reaction. They don't have enough energy.

However, at higher temperatures, the particles
are moving faster. They crash together harder.
Therefore, more collisions produce a reaction.

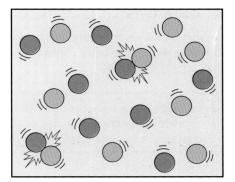

Reaction at 30 °C

> **So, raising the temperature:**
> **1. makes particles collide more often in a certain time, and**
> **2. makes it more likely that collisions result in a reaction.**

Because there are **more, effective collisions**
temperature has a large effect on rates of reaction.
If you raise the temperature by 10 °C, you
roughly double the rate of many reactions!

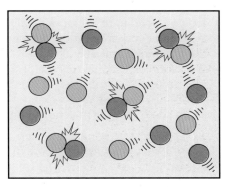

Reaction at 40 °C

Example

Here are some typical results:
Everything was kept the same in each experiment,
except the temperature.

Look at the graph:

Notice that you don't get any more of the product
at a higher temperature.
You get the **same amount**, but **quicker**

- Is the reaction faster at 30 °C or 40 °C?

- How can you tell which reaction is faster?

- If you did the same experiment at 50 °C,
  what would the line on the graph look like?

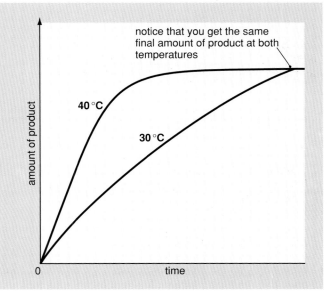

▷ Catalysts

You have already met catalysts on page 57.
Can you remember which type of metals (and their compounds) make good catalysts?

> **A catalyst is a substance which speeds up a chemical reaction. At the end of the reaction, the catalyst is chemically unchanged.**

The filler sets in a few minutes once the catalyst is mixed in

Have you ever seen a damaged car that has been repaired with filler?
Car repair kits use a catalyst to harden the filler quickly.
Look at the instructions from a repair kit:

- Do you need to use a lot of catalyst?
- Why must you prepare the surface *before* you mix the filler and catalyst?
- Why should you only mix the amount that you plan to use?

INSTRUCTIONS FOR USE:
1. Prepare the surface to be repaired. Make sure it is clean and dry.
2. Mix the filler and catayst as shown:

   filler
   catalyst
3. Apply the filler immediately.

You can see a catalyst in action in the next experiment:

Experiment 15.8 Breaking down hydrogen peroxide

Pour some hydrogen peroxide solution into a large test-tube.
- What do you see around the inside of the tube?
- Are the bubbles forming quickly?

The solution gives off oxygen gas as it breaks down.
Try testing for oxygen gas with a glowing splint.
What happens?

Now add a little manganese(IV) oxide, and test for oxygen again.
- What happens as soon as you add the manganese(IV) oxide?
- Did your glowing splint re-light this time?

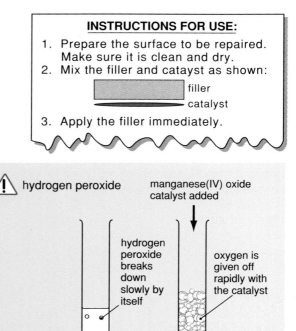
⚠ hydrogen peroxide

manganese(IV) oxide catalyst added

hydrogen peroxide breaks down slowly by itself

oxygen is given off rapidly with the catalyst

The manganese(IV) oxide is a catalyst for this reaction:

hydrogen peroxide $\xrightarrow[\text{MnO}_2(s)]{\text{manganese(IV) oxide}}$ water + oxygen

$$2\,H_2O_2(aq) \xrightarrow[\text{MnO}_2(s)]{} 2\,H_2O(l) + O_2(g)$$

We say that the manganese(IV) oxide *catalyses* the reaction.

Notice that the catalyst does not actually appear in the equation. We can write it above the arrow, showing it is there during the reaction.

- How can you get the manganese(IV) oxide back to use again after the reaction? (**Hint**: It is insoluble in water.)

198

How catalysts work

Do you remember the energy level diagrams from page 182? They show us the energy change when substances react together.

But before reactants can turn into products, they need enough energy to start off the reaction. On page 197 we said that sometimes particles with low energy can collide, but not react.

It's like lighting a gas cooker. We need to supply energy (from a spark or a match) before the gas starts to burn.

> **The energy needed to start a reaction is called its activation energy.**

Look at the energy level diagram:
Once an exothermic reaction starts, its provides the energy itself to keep the reaction going.

> **A catalyst lowers the activation energy.**

Catalysts make it easier for particles to react. You can think of it like a high-jump competition. If you lower the bar, a lot more people can jump over it.
With a catalyst, a lot more particles have enough energy to react.

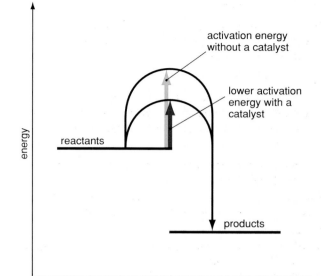

*Just use a twist
Of your catalyst
And reactions will shoot
Through an easier route!*

Investigation 15.9   Catalysts

Here are two problems to investigate:

1. Which metal oxides catalyse the breakdown of hydrogen peroxide?
2. Does the amount of catalyst affect the rate at which hydrogen peroxide breaks down?

- What do you predict will happen?
- How will you make it a fair and safe test?
- How will you judge how quickly the hydrogen peroxide breaks down?
  Check your plan with your teacher before you start.
- Was your prediction correct?

Investigation 15.10   Magnesium and acid

You have seen magnesium ribbon react with
dilute acid on pages 55 and 79.

Use your ideas from this chapter to investigate
the factors which affect the rate of this reaction.

- Choose which factor you will investigate.
- Predict and explain what you think will happen.
- Plan a fair and safe test.

Show your plan to your teacher before you start.

Summary

Chemical reactions are speeded up by increasing

- **surface area**
- **concentration (or pressure if gases are reacting)**
- **temperature**.

The **collision theory** explains why these factors
affect the rate or speed of a reaction. When particles
collide more often in a certain time, reactions speed up.
With higher temperatures, the collisions are also harder.
This means that more collisions produce a reaction.

Some reactions are also speeded up by a **catalyst**.
The catalyst itself is not chemically changed
at the end of the reaction.

▷ Questions

1. Copy and complete:
   a) Small pieces of solid, especially powders,
      have a .... surface area.
      The .... the surface area, the faster the
      reaction.
   b) The more concentrated a solution is, the ....
      it reacts. This is because there are more
      particles in the same ..... Therefore, the
      particles .... more often in a certain time.
   c) The .... the temperature, the faster the
      reaction. Hot particles have more energy, so
      they move around more ..... This means
      that they collide .... often. The collisions are
      also .... and more effective.
   d) A .... is a substance which speeds up a
      reaction, but is chemically .... itself at the
      end of the reaction.

2. *Explain* how the witch in the cartoon above
   makes her potions so quickly!

3. Imagine that the pupils in a school playground
   are reacting particles. A reaction happens each
   time the pupils bump into each other hard
   enough to say 'Ow!'.
   a) What happens to the pupils as the
      temperature goes up?
   b) Explain how a) affects the rate of their
      reaction.
   c) Think of 2 ways to increase the
      concentration of pupils in the playground.
   d) Explain how c) affects the rate of their
      reaction.

4. Hassan and Zoe want to measure the rate of reaction between zinc and dilute sulphuric acid.

They set up their apparatus as shown below:

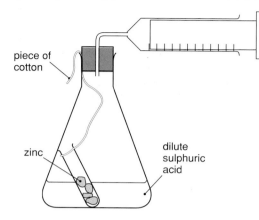

piece of cotton

zinc

dilute sulphuric acid

a) Why is the zinc in a test-tube?
b) How could they start the reaction?

Zoe read the volume of gas collected every minute. Hassan recorded the results, as shown below:

time (mins)	0	1	2	3	4	5	6	7	8
Volume of gas (cm³)	0	15	24	32	33	39	40	40	40

c) Plot Hassan's results on a graph.
   Put a circle around the point on your graph which seems to be a mistake. Now join the points with a 'line of best fit'.
d) During which minute was the reaction fastest?
e) How long did the reaction take to finish?
f) Name the gas given off in the experiment.
g) If you add a little copper sulphate, the gas is given off more quickly.
   Draw a dotted line on your graph to show what would happen.

5. a) What is a **catalyst**?
   b) Hydrogen peroxide decomposes to form water and oxygen gas. The reaction is catalysed by some transition metal oxides. You are given oxides of copper, manganese and nickel. Describe how you can test which is the best catalyst.
   c) How can you get the metal oxides back to use again when the reaction has finished?

6. A group of students are studying the effect of surface area on rate of reaction.
They use marble chips (calcium carbonate) reacting with dilute hydrochloric acid.

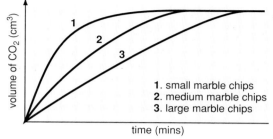

volume of CO₂ (cm³)

time (mins)

1. small marble chips
2. medium marble chips
3. large marble chips

a) What did the students investigating the reaction have to do to make it a **fair test**?
b) Which size of marble chips has the largest surface area (given the same mass of each)?
c) Which marble chips reacted fastest? How can you tell?
d) The students doing the experiments also tried reacting the same mass of **powdered** calcium carbonate with the acid. What would their results look like on the graph above?

7. The reaction in question 6 can also be followed by recording the mass of a flask containing the reactants.
a) Why is there a gradual loss in mass?
b) Draw the apparatus you would use to do this experiment. Why do you use cotton wool in the mouth of the flask?
   Here are some results obtained at 20 °C:

Time (mins)	Mass of flask and its contents (g)
0	80.00
1	78.50
2	77.50
3	76.95
4	76.60
5	76.41
6	76.33
7	76.30
8	76.30

c) Draw a graph of mass against time.
d) Draw a dotted line on your graph showing the reaction at 30 °C.

Further questions on page 234.

chapter 16

Enzymes

Have you ever seen adverts on TV for
'biological' washing powders?
These contain **enzymes** which break down stains.

> **Enzymes are *biological catalysts*.**
> **An enzyme is a large protein molecule.**

Enzymes help reactions take place at the
quite low temperatures inside living things.

All plants and animals, including ourselves, depend on
enzymes to stay alive. Each enzyme catalyses
a particular chemical reaction.
For example, an enzyme called amylase is in our saliva.
It starts to break down starchy foods in our mouths.

On page 198 we saw the breakdown of hydrogen peroxide
using a catalyst. Hydrogen peroxide is a poison.
It can build up inside living things.
However, we have an enzyme in many of our cells
which can break down the poison.

You can watch the reaction in the next experiment:

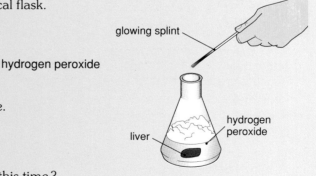

Enzymes help to break down our food

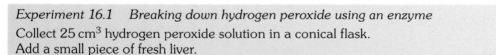

Experiment 16.1   Breaking down hydrogen peroxide using an enzyme

Collect 25 cm³ hydrogen peroxide solution in a conical flask.
Add a small piece of fresh liver.
- What happens?

Test the gas given off with a glowing splint.
- What happens? Which gas is given off?   ⚠ hydrogen peroxide

Some plants can also break down hydrogen peroxide.

Chop up a piece of potato or celery into small bits.
Add them to 25 cm³ hydrogen peroxide solution.
- What happens?
- Is the hydrogen peroxide broken down as quickly this time?

glowing splint

liver

hydrogen
peroxide

An enzyme in the liver can break down hydrogen peroxide
very quickly. Like all enzymes, it is very efficient.
Each enzyme molecule can deal with thousands of
reacting molecules *every second*!

$$\text{hydrogen peroxide} \xrightarrow{\text{enzyme in liver}} \text{water } + \text{ oxygen}$$

How enzymes work

Enzymes are large molecules.
Each different enzyme has its own *special shape*.
The reactants fit into the enzyme, like a lock and key.
The reactant slots into the enzyme at its **active site**.
Look at the diagram below:

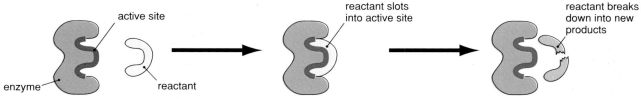

Other enzymes can build up big molecules from small ones.

Effect of temperature on enzymes

Look at this box of biological washing powder:
At which temperature does it work well?
The enzymes in the powder don't work if you
use water that is too hot.
Try this experiment to see how temperature affects enzymes:

> **Experiment 16.2   Heating enzymes**
> You can compare how well the enzymes in
> fresh liver and boiled liver work.   ⚠ hydrogen peroxide
> See how quickly they break down hydrogen peroxide.
> Repeat Experiment 16.1. Then try it again using
> liver you have boiled in water for 5 minutes.
> ● How did you make it a fair test?
> ● What difference do you notice between fresh liver and boiled liver?

Enzymes don't work at high temperatures.

As the temperature rises, what do you think happens
to the way an enzyme molecule shakes about?

If the enzyme gets too hot, it changes shape.
So the reactants will no longer fit snugly into
the enzyme's active site. It can't catalyse the reaction.
We say that the enzyme is **denatured**.

Look at the graph opposite:
● What do we call the temperature at which an enzyme works best?
● What is your body temperature? Why do you think that
   most enzymes work best at around 40 °C?

You can find out how we use enzymes on the next 3 pages.

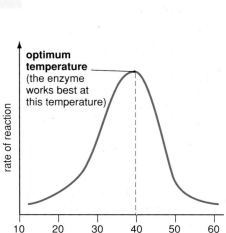

Changes in pH also denature enzymes

▷ Fermentation

People have used enzymes to make new products for thousands of years. Alcoholic drinks and bread are both made using the enzymes in **yeast**.

Making alcohol (ethanol)

Yeast is a type of fungus. Like all living things, it contains enzymes. Yeast feeds on sugars, turning them into alcohol.
The reaction is called **fermentation**.
You can ferment a sugar (glucose) in the next experiment:

Experiment 16.3   Fermentation

Set up the apparatus as shown:
Put it somewhere warm.
(Near a radiator is a good place.)
Leave it for 10 minutes to start reacting.
● What happens inside the flask?
You can now leave your experiment until the next lesson.
● What has happened to the limewater?
● Which gas is given off during fermentation?

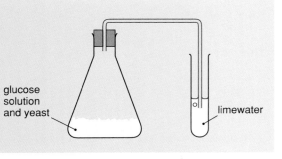

glucose solution and yeast

limewater

The enzymes in yeast break down the sugar, **glucose**, into **ethanol** (which we know as alcohol). Carbon dioxide is also given off.

glucose $\xrightarrow{\text{fermentation}}$ ethanol + carbon dioxide
(sugar)   (alcohol)

$C_6H_{12}O_6 \xrightarrow{\substack{\text{enzymes in} \\ \text{yeast}}} 2\,C_2H_5OH + 2\,CO_2$

The amount of ethanol in the fermenting mixture cannot rise above about 18 %. At this level, the ethanol poisons the yeast.
We have to **distil** the mixture to get purer ethanol.

Can you remember how to distil a mixture of liquids?
You can distil the ethanol from your fermented mixture using the method on page 19.

Many people brew their own wine or beer. The air-lock at the top of the flask lets CO_2 gas escape, but won't let bacteria from the air in. Why is this important?

There was an unfortunate beast.
Who fermented some sugar with yeast.
When he swallowed the brew
His stomach, it grew
'Til BANG! CO_2 was released.

Making bread

Have you ever wondered how the tiny holes get inside bread?
By 4000 BC, the Egyptians had found out that yeast makes bread rise.

The yeast feeds on sugar, as in brewing.
Which gas is given off in fermentation?
The carbon dioxide gas gets trapped in the dough.
This makes the bread rise.

Look at this recipe for making bread:

Can you see the holes where carbon dioxide gas was trapped in the dough?

Home-made bread

1. Mix dried yeast with some sugar in warm water.
2. When it has a froth, add it to flour with a little salt.
3. Mix and knead the dough.
4. Leave the mixture in a warm place for at least an hour.
   The dough should rise to about twice its volume.
5. Bake in a hot oven at 200 °C.

- Why must you add sugar to the yeast in step 1?
- What causes the froth in step 2?
- Why do you leave the mixture in a warm place
  for at least an hour before it goes into the hot oven?
  (Think about the effect of temperature on enzymes.)
- What do you think happens to the size of the gas bubbles
  in the bread as it is baked?
  (Think about the effect of temperature on gases.)

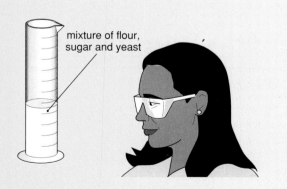

This baker is kneading dough. She will then leave it to rise, before baking it.

Experiment 16.4   Rising dough!

Put 20 g of flour in a beaker.
Add 1 g of sugar. Slowly pour in
25 cm^3 of yeast solution, stirring as you add it.

You should get a smooth paste.
Pour the paste into a large measuring cylinder,
without letting it touch the sides.

Record the volume of your mixture every 2 minutes.
Stop after 30 minutes.

mixture of flour, sugar and yeast

Time (mins)	Volume of mixture (cm^3)

Plot your results as a line graph.
(Put volume of mixture up the side and time along the bottom.)

- Explain the pattern you see in your graph.

▷ Chemistry at work : Dairy products

For thousands of years, people have made **cheese** and **yoghurt** from milk. However, they did not know about enzymes and how they helped!

Milk contains a sugar called lactose. Natural bacteria in the milk turn this into *lactic acid*. It is the first step in making cheese or yoghurt. The lactic acid makes the milk taste sour and it helps to preserve it.

Nowadays cheese and yoghurt makers use pasteurised milk. This has been heated to kill any bacteria. So they add their own bacteria to start off the process.

Enzymes in the bacteria break down lactose into two simpler sugars. Then other enzymes convert the sugars into lactic acid.

It is thought that yoghurt was first made in the Middle East

Cheese

After the milk has gone sour, cheese makers add rennet. We get this from the stomachs of calves. The enzymes in it clot their mothers' milk. But now you can buy 'vegetarian' cheese. The enzymes used for clotting this cheese come from fungi (yeast).

The soggy lumps formed contain **curds** (the solid) and **whey** (the liquid). The curds are pressed into blocks and left to mature. In this final stage, other enzymes work on proteins and fats to give the cheese its taste and texture.
Cheeses, like cheddar, are left up to 9 months to mature. However, new enzymes can do the job in half the time.

The holes in this cheese were made by bacteria giving off carbon dioxide

Uses of whey

For every kilogram of cheese we make, we get 9 litres of liquid whey. This has its uses (besides a snack for Little Miss Muffet!):

whey

enzymes held on plastic beads

fuel   alcoholic drinks   fermented by   **ethanol** ◀ **WHEY** ▶ **sugary syrup**   enzymes   cakes and sweets
enzymes in yeasts   from fungus

Investigation 16.5   Factors affecting enzymes

How can we make enzyme reactions faster or slower?
Choose one of the reactions in this chapter to investigate.
Which factor will you look at?
How will you judge the rate of reaction?
Plan a fair and safe test. Show it to your teacher before you start.

Investigation 16.6   Biological washing powder

Look at the box of biological washing powder
on page 203.
Plan a fair test to see if temperature affects
how well a powder containing enzymes works.
Show the plan to your teacher before you start.

Summary

- **Enzymes** are *biological catalysts*.
- They are large protein molecules.
- They catalyse specific reactions.
- Parts of their molecules have special shapes.
  Reacting molecules slot into these **'active sites'**.
  Then the reaction takes place very quickly,
  at a relatively low temperature.
- Enzymes change their shape if you heat
  them too strongly. They no longer work,
  and we say that they are **denatured**.
  Changing the pH also denatures enzymes.

> **Remember!**
> **Enzymes are molecules found in living things.**
> **They are not living things themselves, so they cannot be killed!**

▷ Questions

1. Copy and complete:
   Enzymes are called biological . . . . .
   These large . . . . molecules have special areas
   called . . . . sites. Reactants . . . . into the enzyme,
   and react very quickly.
   Each enzyme has a . . . . shape to fit certain
   molecules.
   If the temperature gets too . . . . , the enzyme
   molecule changes shape. It is . . . . .
   Adding acid or . . . . can also stop enzymes
   working.

2. Each enzyme has an optimum temperature and
   an optimum pH.
   a) What does this mean?
   b) We store food in a fridge or freezer. What
      effect does this have on the enzyme reactions
      in bacteria?
   c) Why do enzymes in your stomach work well
      at a pH of less than 7? (see page 140.)

3. We break down starch in our food into glucose.
   The breakdown starts in our mouths, with the
   enzyme, amylase.
   Gina did an experiment to see how temperature
   affected the amylase. She added amylase to
   starch solutions at different temperatures. Then
   she tested the solutions for starch every minute.
   (Iodine solution turns blue/black in starch.) She
   recorded the time for the starch to break down
   at each temperature.

Temperature (°C)	30	35	40	45	50	55
Time to break down starch (mins)	10	5	2	7	15	30

   a) How could Gina tell when all the starch had
      been broken down?
   b) Plot Gina's results as a line graph.
   c) What pattern can you see in Gina's results?
   d) *Explain* Gina's results.

Further questions on page 236.

chapter 17

Reversible  Reactions

Have you ever seen a toothbrush that
changes colour as you use it?
The plastic contains substances which change
colour as they get warm.
What happens when the toothbrush cools down again?

Look at the picture opposite:
Why do you think that the brush changes
colour at both ends?

> **Changes which can go backwards or forwards
> are called reversible.**

Some chemical reactions are reversible.
The products can react to give us back the
reactants that we started with.
Let's look at an example:

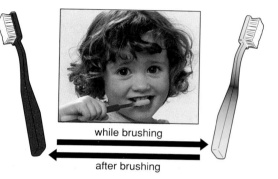

while brushing

after brushing

Experiment 17.1   Changing copper sulphate
Gently heat some blue (hydrated) copper sulphate crystals
as shown:
Stop when the blue crystals have changed.

- What happens? What do you notice at
  the mouth of the test-tube?

Let the test-tube cool down.
Now add a few drops of water from a dropper.
- What happens?
- How can you get the white powder back again?

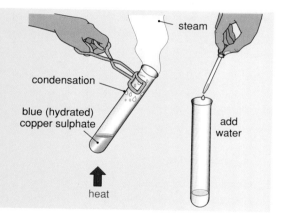

steam

condensation

blue (hydrated)
copper sulphate

add
water

heat

When you heat blue (hydrated) copper sulphate, it loses
the water which is bonded in its crystals.
You get a white powder called anhydrous copper sulphate.
If you add water, the blue (hydrated) copper sulphate
is formed again.

Reversible reactions are shown by arrows pointing in both directions:

hydrated copper sulphate $\rightleftharpoons$ anhydrous copper sulphate + water
   (blue crystals)   (white powder)

$$CuSO_4.5H_2O \quad \rightleftharpoons \quad CuSO_4 \quad + \quad 5H_2O$$

You can use the backward reaction to test for water.
Anhydrous copper sulphate turns blue
if water is present.
If the water is **pure** it should boil at 100 °C.

*Does this liquid contain water?
Anhydrous copper sulphate
can tell you! What happens if
water is present?
The other test for water is:
blue cobalt chloride turns pink*

More reversible changes

Indicators changing colour are also examples of
reversible changes.
They are one colour in acid, and another colour in alkali.
Can you remember the colour of litmus
in acid and in alkali?

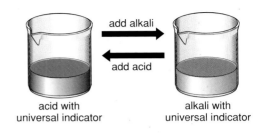

acid with
universal indicator

alkali with
universal indicator

Look back to experiment 12.1 on page 141.
You were trying to neutralise an acidic solution
with alkali. Which indicator did you use?
Why don't you need to start all over again
if you add too much alkali?

Experiment 17.2 *'Changing colour'*

⚠ acid and alkali

Phenolphthalein indicator is colourless in acid,
and pink-purple in alkali.

Add some phenolphthalein to a beaker of water.
Rinse another beaker with sodium hydroxide solution.
The second beaker looks empty, but it now has
drops of alkali in it.
Pour the water from the first beaker into it.

● What happens? Why?

● A third beaker has a little dilute acid in it.
Pour your solution into this beaker.

● What happens? Why?

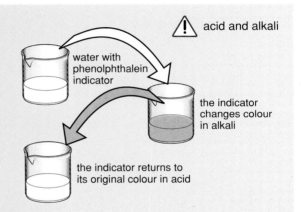

water with
phenolphthalein
indicator

the indicator
changes colour
in alkali

the indicator returns to
its original colour in acid

Do you remember the diffusion experiment on page 9?
When ammonia and hydrogen chloride gases meet
they react. They form a white cloud of ammonium chloride.

You can reverse this reaction in the next experiment:

Experiment 17.3   *Heating ammonium chloride – a reversible reaction*
Gently warm some ammonium chloride in a boiling tube.

● What do you see on the cool part of the tube, near the top?
● How can you explain what happens in the tube?

⚠
ammonium chloride   heat

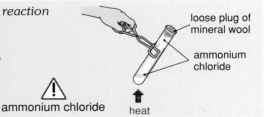

loose plug of
mineral wool

ammonium
chloride

Ammonium chloride solid is broken down by heat, forming
ammonia and hydrogen chloride gases.
At lower temperatures, the ammonia and hydrogen chloride
react to re-form the ammonium chloride.

ammonium chloride ⇌ ammonia + hydrogen chloride

$$NH_4Cl(s) \rightleftharpoons NH_3(g) + HCl(g)$$

▷ Dynamic equilibrium

Many reactions are 'one-way only'.
The starting materials react to form the products.
The products can't easily be turned back
into the starting materials again.
Imagine trying to turn a cake back into
flour, sugar, butter and eggs!

However, sometimes products can re-form reactants.
You have seen some reversible reactions
on the last 2 pages.

If you don't let any reactants or products escape,
both forward and backward reactions can happen
at the same time. Reactants make products,
and, at the same time, products make reactants.

Eventually both the forward and backward reactions
will be going *at the same rate*.
When this happens it is called **dynamic equilibrium**.

Do you know what the word 'dynamic' means?
You might have read about dynamic footballers,
or dynamic pop-stars. People who have lots of
energy and are always on the move!

'Dynamic' refers to movement. In dynamic equilibrium
there is constant movement.
Reactants are changing to products. Products are changing
to reactants. Eventually, we reach a point of equilibrium.

> **At the point of equilibrium, the rate of the forward
> reaction and backward reaction is the same.**

What do you think happens to the amount of reactants and
products at that point?
When **equilibrium** is reached, the amount of each
substance *stays the same*. There *appears* to be no change.

Look at the cartoon opposite:
It helps to explain dynamic equilibrium.

*Both back and forth, and to and fro,
The equilibrium does go.
Forwards and backwards, at the same rate,
The system reaches a steady state!*

*If you look from the side, the man stays in the
same position. He is running up at the same rate
as the escalator moves down.*

The position of equilibrium

Dynamic equilibrium is not like a balancing see-saw.
There does not have to be equal amounts of
reactants and products in the equilibrium mixture.

Look at the cartoon opposite:

The man can appear to be still near the top or
near the bottom. He doesn't have to be half-way up
the escalator. As long as he is climbing at the same
rate as the steps are going down, he is in
dynamic equilibrium.

Therefore, the position of equilibrium can lie
in favour of the reactants or the products.
It can lie to the left or to the right, as you look at
the equation.

You have seen a reaction at equilibrium before on
page 105.

$$H_2O(l) \rightleftharpoons H^+(aq) + OH^-(aq)$$

left-hand   right-hand
side   side

There are only a few H^+ and OH^- ions in water.
Which side of the equation does the equilibrium lie?
Look at the arrows ($\rightleftharpoons$) showing a
reversible reaction *at equilibrium*.
Notice that they are slightly different from the ones
shown earlier for reversible reactions ($\rightleftharpoons$).

Look at the pictures below:
They might help you to understand how the
position of equilibrium can lie to the left or
to the right.

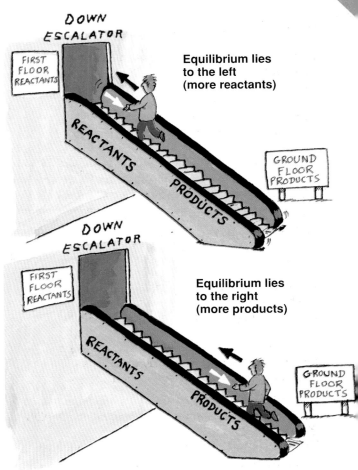

**Equilibrium lies
to the left
(more reactants)**

**Equilibrium lies
to the right
(more products)**

*The man running up the 'down-escalator' can appear to be
still on any part of the staircase*

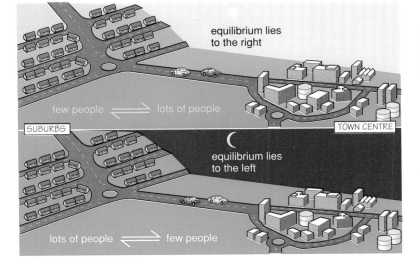

equilibrium lies
to the right

few people $\rightleftharpoons$ lots of people

SUBURBS   TOWN CENTRE

equilibrium lies
to the left

lots of people $\rightleftharpoons$ few people

*Just after rush hour there are more
people in the town centre than in the
suburbs. Some people go home early
but these are replaced in the town
centre by shoppers.*

*At night, most people have gone
home. Some night-workers arrive in
the town centre, but these are
replaced in the suburbs by people
leaving work late.*

▷ Affecting the position of equilibrium

We can change the position of equilibrium
by altering conditions.
For example, we can change concentrations of reactants
or products. Temperature also affects the
equilibrium mixture.
If the reaction has gases in it, then changing the
pressure might affect the equilibrium as well.

*The French chemist, Le Chatelier (1850–1936),
did much of the early work on equilibrium
mixtures*

> **The position of equilibrium shifts to try to cancel out
> any changes you introduce. (Le Chatelier's Principle.)**

Changing concentrations

For example, you might increase the concentration
of a reactant. This will make the forward reaction
go faster for a while, until we reach equilibrium again.

In effect, we have added more to the left-hand side,
so the equilibrium shifts to the right,
as if to remove it.

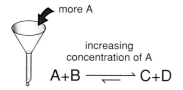

more A

increasing
concentration of A

$$A + B \rightleftharpoons C + D$$

equilibrium moves to right to
reduce the concentration of A

Changing temperature

Can you think what happens if you *increase* the
temperature of an equilibrium mixture?
The position of equilibrium shifts to
reduce the temperature.

Look at the reaction below:
It is used in industry to make ammonia (NH_3)
in the Haber process. (see pages 216 and 219.)

$$N_2(g) \; + \; 3H_2(g) \; \rightleftharpoons \; 2NH_3(g) \quad \Delta H \; = \; -92 \, kJ/mol$$

The forward reaction is exothermic, giving out heat.
The backward reaction is endothermic. It takes in heat.
So if you increase the temperature, the backward reaction
is favoured, as this will lower the temperature.
Therefore, at high temperatures, the equilibrium mixture
will have more N_2 and H_2 than before (see page 217).

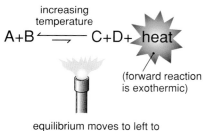

increasing
temperature

$$A + B \rightleftharpoons C + D + \text{heat}$$

(forward reaction
is exothermic)

equilibrium moves to left to
get rid of the extra heat

Changing pressure

Changing the pressure can also affect a mixture at equilibrium.
However, there must be different numbers
of gas molecules on either side of the equation.
If you increase the pressure, the equilibrium shifts to
try to reduce it again.
Moving to the side with the least number of gas molecules
will lower the pressure.

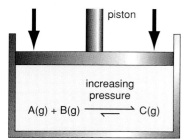

piston

increasing
pressure

$$A(g) + B(g) \rightleftharpoons C(g)$$

equilibrium moves to the side with
the least number of gas molecules
to reduce the pressure

You can change the position of equilibrium in
the next experiment:

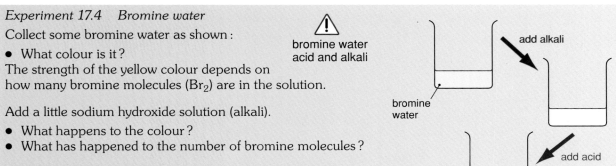

Experiment 17.4   Bromine water

Collect some bromine water as shown:
- What colour is it?

The strength of the yellow colour depends on
how many bromine molecules (Br_2) are in the solution.

Add a little sodium hydroxide solution (alkali).
- What happens to the colour?
- What has happened to the number of bromine molecules?

Now add dilute hydrochloric acid.
- What change do you see now?
- What has happened to the number of bromine molecules?

⚠ bromine water
acid and alkali

add alkali

bromine
water

add acid

Bromine water is an equilibrium mixture:

$$Br_2(aq) \; + \; H_2O(l) \; \rightleftharpoons \; Br^-(aq) \; + \; OBr^-(aq) \; + \; H^+(aq)$$
yellow   colourless

When you add alkali (OH^-), H^+ ions are removed.
(Remember neutralisation on page 146:
$$H^+ \; + \; OH^- \longrightarrow H_2O.)$$
The equilibrium moves to the right to try to
replace the H^+ ions. This means that more
Br_2 and H_2O must react, and the yellow colour fades.

When you add acid, H^+ ions are added to the mixture.
The equilibrium shifts to the left to get rid of them.
This makes more Br_2 molecules, and the yellow
colour gets deeper again.

"Which way will the balance lie?"
Le Chatelier did cry.
"It will move to cancel out
Whichever change you bring about!"

Now try this experiment:

Experiment 17.5   Chromate in equilibrium with dichromate

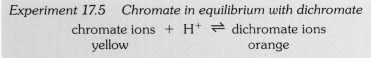

chromate ions + H^+ ⇌ dichromate ions
yellow   orange

Add a little dilute sulphuric acid to
some potassium chromate(VI) solution.
- Which colour change do you see?
- What has happened to the number of chromate and
  dichromate ions in the beaker?
- How could you get back more chromate ions?

Try adding some sodium hydroxide solution (alkali). What happens?
- Can you explain the changes in this experiment?

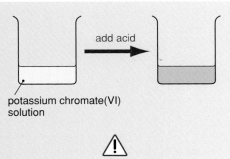

add acid

potassium chromate(VI)
solution

⚠ potassium chromate(VI)
acid and alkali

▷ Strong and weak acids

We have looked at acids before in Chapter 12.
You know that all acids contain hydrogen (page 143) and that
$H^+(aq)$ ions are in all acidic solutions (page 146).

However, some acids are better at producing
$H^+(aq)$ ions than others. These are called **strong acids**.

Imagine you start with the same number of acid molecules,
in the same volume of water. A strong acid will give more
$H^+(aq)$ ions than a weak acid.

Hydrochloric acid is a strong acid.
Ethanoic acid is a weak acid.

You will see some differences between strong and weak acids
in the next experiment:

A car battery contains
sulphuric acid – a strong acid

Oranges contain
citric acid – a weak acid

Experiment 17.6   Testing a strong and weak acid

Try the tests below using solutions of hydrochloric acid and
ethanoic acid.
- Why must both acids have the same concentration?

Test 1   Add universal indicator solution to both acids.
- What are their pHs?

Test 2   Add the same amount of magnesium ribbon to both acids.
- What difference do you notice?

Test 3   Add a spatula of sodium carbonate to both acids.
- What difference do you notice?

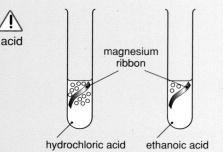

acid

magnesium ribbon

hydrochloric acid   ethanoic acid

Strong acids split up (dissociate) almost completely in water.
For example:

$$HCl(g) \xrightarrow{\text{water}} H^+(aq) + Cl^-(aq)$$

hydrochloric acid

However, weak acids reach **dynamic equilibrium**.
The acid molecules split up, just like a strong acid.
But at the same time, the H^+ ions and negative ions that are made
join up again. They form the original acid molecules.
For ethanoic acid:

$$CH_3COOH(aq) \rightleftharpoons CH_3COO^-(aq) + H^+(aq)$$

Equilibrium is reached when the molecules split up at the
same rate as the ions join back together again.

The weaker the acid, the further the position of equilibrium lies
to the left. There will be more molecules
in the solution, and fewer $H^+(aq)$ ions – the ions that
cause acidic properties.

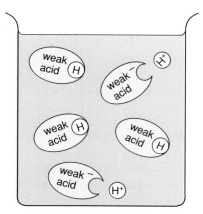

Solutions of weak acids contain
'undissociated' molecules in equilibrium
with H^+ ions and negative ions

Summary

- Many reactions are 'one-way' only.
  Reactants form products. The products formed cannot turn back into the reactants again.
- Some reactions are **reversible**.
  Reactants form products. However, in different conditions, the products can also react together to form the reactants again.
- If nothing is allowed to escape, a reversible reaction can reach a position of **equilibrium**.
  The amount of reactants and products stays the same.
- At this point, the reaction is in **dynamic** equilibrium.
  The forward reaction and the backward reaction are going at the same rate.
- The position of equilibrium can be altered by changing the conditions. The position of equilibrium always shifts to try to cancel out the change introduced.
  (Adding a **catalyst** does not affect the composition of an equilibrium mixture. However, it does speed up the rate at which equilibrium is reached.
  So a catalyst cannot increase yield – you get the same amount of product, but faster!)

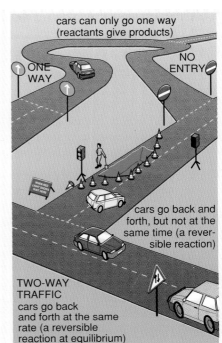

cars can only go one way
(reactants give products)

ONE WAY

NO ENTRY

cars go back and forth, but not at the same time (a reversible reaction)

TWO-WAY TRAFFIC
cars go back and forth at the same rate (a reversible reaction at equilibrium)

▷ Questions

1. Copy and complete:
   Reactions which can go forwards or backwards are called . . . . .
   An . . . . mixture contains constant amounts of reactants and products.
   When the rate of the forward reaction equals the rate of the backward reaction, we call it . . . . equilibrium.
   We can change the position of equilibrium by altering concentrations or . . . . . (Pressure affects equilibria if there is an imbalance of . . . . molecules.)
   A . . . . does not affect the position of equilibrium, but equilibrium is reached more quickly.

2. Hydrated copper sulphate is made up of blue crystals.
   a) Explain what happens if you heat the blue crystals.
   b) How can you get hydrated copper sulphate back again?
   c) Write an equation showing this reversible reaction.

3. Here is an example of dynamic equilibrium:
   $$ICl(l) + Cl_2(g) \rightleftharpoons ICl_3(s)$$
   | brown | yellow/ | yellow |
   | liquid | green gas | solid |

   The equilibrium can be set up in a glass U-tube.

   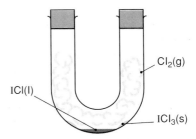

   $Cl_2(g)$

   $ICl(l)$

   $ICl_3(s)$

   a) The equilibrium mixture contains the 3 states of matter. What does this statement mean?
   b) The pressure inside the U-tube is increased. What happens to the equilibrium mixture? Explain your answer.
   c) What would happen to the equilibrium mixture if the chlorine gas was allowed to escape?
   Explain your answer.

   Further questions on page 236.

▷ Chemistry at work : The Haber process

The Haber process is used in industry
to make ammonia (NH_3).

Ammonia is a very important chemical.
It is used to make fertilisers,
such as ammonium nitrate (see page 223).
Ammonia is also used to make nitric acid,
which we use to produce explosives (see page 221).

These uses meant that it was important to discover
how to make ammonia on a large scale.

The story starts just before the First World War in Germany.
In preparation for war, the Germans realised
that they would need to make their own
fertilisers and explosives. Both were made from
nitrogen compounds imported from South America.
The supplies of nitrogen compounds – from bird droppings
in Peru and sodium nitrate from Chile – had nearly
run out. When war started, they wouldn't be able to
ship them back to Germany anyway.
So scientists raced to find a way to turn
nitrogen gas in the air into useful nitrogen compounds.

Fritz Haber was a lecturer in a technical college in Germany.
In 1909 he managed to make an equilibrium mixture
containing nitrogen, hydrogen and ammonia.

$$N_2(g) \ + \ 3H_2(g) \ \rightleftharpoons \ 2NH_3(g)$$

Haber's apparatus is shown opposite :
He had shown that it was possible to turn nitrogen
into ammonia. However, with this equipment
he could only make about 100 g of ammonia !

The German chemical company BASF then invested
over a million pounds to 'scale up' the process.
The process needed high pressures. The first
reaction vessel blew up under the strain !

It was a chemical engineer called Carl Bosch
who eventually solved the problem.
He devised a double-walled steel vessel
which could work safely at 300 times atmospheric pressure.

Over 6500 experiments were carried out to find
the best catalyst. An *iron catalyst* worked well.
It was improved further by adding traces of other
metal oxides.

*Fritz Haber (1868–1934) got the Nobel Prize
for Chemistry in 1918 for making ammonia
from nitrogen and hydrogen*

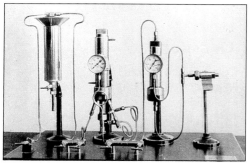

Haber's apparatus

*Carl Bosch (1874–1940) was awarded the
Nobel Prize for Chemistry in 1931 for his work
on high-pressure reactions*

In 1913, the first ammonia factory was making
about 30 tonnes a day.
Without this supply, the First World War
might have ended much sooner.

However, the Haber process is still used today to make
millions of tonnes of ammonia. About 85 % of this ammonia
goes on to make fertilisers to help feed the world!

This is an example of both the good and bad effects of
the chemical industry.

Conditions chosen for the Haber process

Look at the reaction below:

$$N_2(g) + 3H_2(g) \underset{\text{catalyst}}{\overset{\text{iron}}{\rightleftharpoons}} 2NH_3(g) \qquad \Delta H = -92\,\text{kJ/mol}$$

People running the process must choose
the conditions carefully. They want to make
as much ammonia as possible, as quickly as possible.

Look at the graphs opposite:

- What happens to the amount of ammonia in the
  equilibrium mixture when you
  - raise the pressure?
  - raise the temperature?

You can get high yields of ammonia by using high pressure
and a low temperature.

The conditions chosen for the Haber process are

- **a pressure between 150 and 300 atmospheres**
- **a temperature between 400 and 450 °C.**

- Why do you think that we don't use even higher pressures?
  Think about the safety problems that Bosch faced.
  What about the costs involved?

- Why aren't lower temperatures used?
  Think about your work on rates of reaction.
  It's no use getting a very high yield of ammonia
  if you have to wait days to get it!

The equilibrium mixture contains only about 15 % ammonia.
It is constantly drawn off by cooling it down into a liquid.

The unused gases are re-cycled.
You can see a flow chart for the Haber process on page 219.

> **The catalyst speeds up the rate
> at which we reach equilibrium.
> However, it does not increase
> the yield of ammonia.**

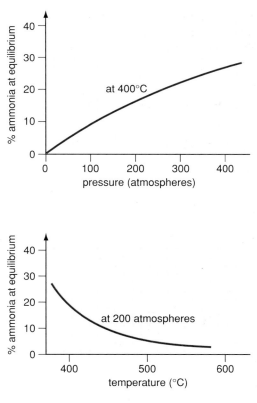

chapter 18

Products from air

Have you ever seen a farmer or a gardener speading
fertiliser on their soil?
Farmers add millions of tonnes of fertilisers to
the soil each year.

Most fertilisers, such as ammonium nitrate, contain
nitrogen. Its chemical formula is NH_4NO_3.
Plants need nitrogen to grow. They use it
to make proteins.

Look at the way nitrogen is re-cycled in nature:

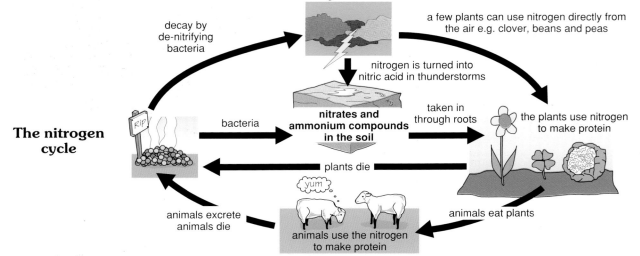

The nitrogen cycle

nitrogen in the air

decay by de-nitrifying bacteria

a few plants can use nitrogen directly from the air e.g. clover, beans and peas

nitrogen is turned into nitric acid in thunderstorms

bacteria

nitrates and ammonium compounds in the soil

taken in through roots

the plants use nitrogen to make protein

plants die

RIP

animals excrete animals die

animals use the nitrogen to make protein

yum

animals eat plants

We disturb the **nitrogen cycle** by farming crops.
The crops take nitrogen from the soil as they grow.
Then the farmer harvests the crop. The plants are
cut down and taken away. Therefore, they are
never allowed to rot back into the soil.
Nitrogen is removed, but not replaced.

The natural cycle can replace some nitrogen.
Look at the cycle above:
How can nitrogen get back into the soil?
These sources cannot supply enough nitrogen for
next year's crop. So farmers need fertilisers.

Almost 80% of the air is nitrogen gas. So you might
think that plants have plenty of nitrogen available.
However, only a few types of plant can use nitrogen
directly from the air. These include peas, beans and clover.

Most plants need nitrogen in a soluble form in the soil.
Then they can absorb it through their roots.

*Crops are harvested. They don't have
a chance to replace the nitrogen they
have taken from the soil by decaying
naturally*

▷ Fixing nitrogen

We have a very cheap supply of nitrogen – the air.
But how can we turn it into a form that
plants can use?

Turning nitrogen from the air into nitrogen compounds
that plants can use is called **'fixing'** nitrogen.
Chemists have found a way to 'fix' nitrogen.

The first step is to change *nitrogen gas into ammonia*.
Look at the next section to find out how
this is done.

The Haber process

A German chemist called Fritz Haber discovered
how to make ammonia from nitrogen gas in 1909.

nitrogen + hydrogen ⇌ ammonia

$$N_2(g) + 3H_2(g) \rightleftharpoons 2NH_3(g)$$

The same reaction is used today to make
millions of tonnes of ammonia.
You can read more about the Haber process on page 217.
Look at the flow diagram of the process below:

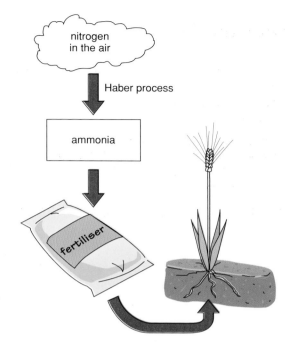

Nitrogen fixation

The Haber process

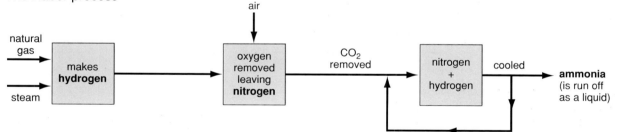

Notice from the equation above that the reaction is reversible.
At the same time as ammonia is made,
it splits up into nitrogen and hydrogen again.
However, any un-reacted nitrogen and hydrogen are
re-cycled and used again.

Energy from the process is also re-cycled to save money.
Many reactions in the process are exothermic. The energy
they give out is used to heat reaction vessels and
to make steam. As well as making hydrogen,
the steam powers compressors. These produce
the high pressures needed in the process.

> **Facts about the Haber process**
> *Raw materials*
> Air (for nitrogen)
> Natural gas (to make hydrogen)
> Steam (to make hydrogen and to
> generate high pressures)
> *Conditions*
> Temperature: about 450 °C
> Pressure: about 200 atmospheres
> Catalyst: mainly iron

▷ Ammonia

Remember that we make ammonia in the Haber process.
The ammonia can be used as a fertiliser itself.
However, most is changed into compounds of ammonia.
These compounds have advantages over ammonia
as fertilisers (see page 222).

You might have come across ammonia before.
Have you ever smelt a bottle of smelling salts?
If you have, you will certainly remember
the sharp, unpleasant smell of ammonia gas.

In the next two experiments you can make and test
some ammonia gas.

This farmer is injecting ammonia into a field. Look at the properties of ammonia on the next page. What are the disadvantages of using ammonia directly as a fertiliser?

Experiment 18.1   Making ammonia in the lab

Set up the apparatus as shown in a fume-cupboard:

Heat the mixture and collect a test-tube of
ammonia gas.

You can tell when the tubes are full by holding
a damp piece of red litmus paper near
the mouth of the test-tube. The red litmus
changes blue when the test-tube is full.

Put a bung in the test-tube when it is full
of ammonia.

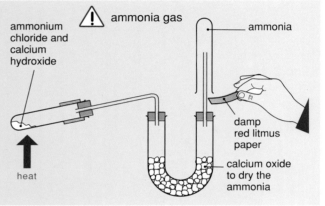

ammonium chloride and calcium hydroxide

ammonia gas

ammonia

damp red litmus paper

calcium oxide to dry the ammonia

heat

You can now test some properties of ammonia gas:

Experiment 18.2   Does ammonia dissolve in water?

Hold a stoppered test-tube of ammonia under
some water in a beaker.
Take out the bung, with the mouth of the tube
under the surface.
Shake it gently from side to side.
Compare this to a test-tube full of air.

- What happens to the level of the water in the test-tube
  full of ammonia?
- What does this test tell you about how soluble ammonia
  is in water?

Your teacher might show you the Fountain experiment
which shows how soluble ammonia is.

ammonia gas

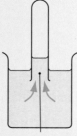

water replaces the ammonia which dissolves in the water

Properties of ammonia

From the last two experiments we can work out
a lot about ammonia gas.
Has it got any colour?
Look at the way we collected it:
Do you think it is more dense or less dense than air?
We used litmus paper to see when the test-tube
was full of ammonia. How could we tell?
What does this tell you about ammonia gas?
Litmus is used as the test for ammonia gas.

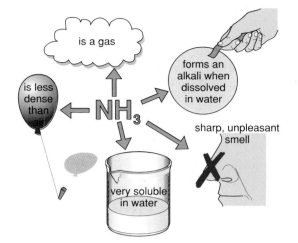

> **Ammonia is the only common *alkaline gas*.
> It turns damp red litmus paper blue.**

Ammonia into nitric acid

About 10% of the ammonia made in the Haber process
is turned into nitric acid.
You will see how the nitric acid can react with
ammonia to make fertiliser on page 223.
Look at the flow diagram below:

*Can you remember how ammonia reacts with
hydrogen chloride gas?* *(see page 9.)*

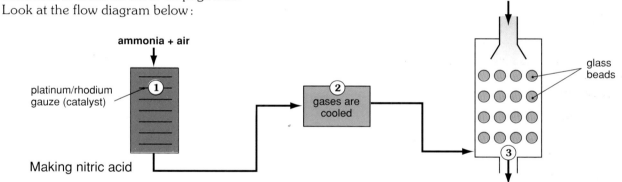

Making nitric acid

1. In the first stage ammonia reacts with oxygen.
   The ammonia is *oxidised*.
   This reaction will not happen without a catalyst.
   Platinum, mixed with rhodium, is used at 900 °C,

$$\text{ammonia} + \text{oxygen} \xrightarrow{\text{platinum/rhodium}} \text{nitrogen monoxide} + \text{water}$$

2. Then the nitrogen monoxide is mixed with air.
   It changes into nitrogen dioxide:

$$\text{nitrogen monoxide} + \text{oxygen} \longrightarrow \text{nitrogen dioxide}$$

3. Finally, the nitrogen dioxide and more oxygen react
   with water to make **nitric acid, HNO_3**.

$$\text{nitrogen dioxide} + \text{oxygen} + \text{water} \longrightarrow \text{nitric acid}$$

▷ Making fertilisers

As you know from page 220, ammonia can be used as a liquid fertiliser itself. However, it has some disadvantages. As a liquid, it has to be injected into the soil. It is much easier to spread solid pellets of fertiliser on a field. Ammonia makes the soil alkaline. You also lose some nitrogen as ammonia gas evaporates from the soil.

We can make solid fertilisers by reacting ammonia (an alkali) with **an acid**.
Remember that a salt forms when an acid and an alkali react together (see page 142).
Can you remember what this type of reaction is called?

You can make your own fertiliser in the next experiment:

Solid fertilisers are made into pellets so that we can spread them easily

---

Experiment 18.3   Making ammonium sulphate fertiliser

Collect 25 cm³ of ammonia solution in a small conical flask.
Add dilute sulphuric acid, 1 cm³ at a time, from a burette.
After adding each cm³ of acid, swirl your flask.
Dip a glass rod into the solution. Then test a drop of the solution on a piece of blue litmus paper.

⚠ acid and alkali

Keep adding acid until the litmus just turns pink.
● How much sulphuric acid did you need to neutralise the ammonia solution?

Then pour the solution into an evaporating dish.
Heat it on a water bath until about half of the solution has evaporated off.
Leave the rest of the solution to evaporate off slowly.

● What do your crystals of fertiliser look like?
● What is the fertiliser's chemical name?

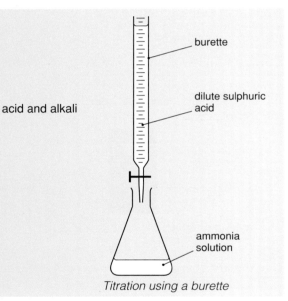

Titration using a burette

The sulphuric acid neutralises the ammonia solution.
The salt that we make is called **ammonium sulphate**:

ammonia + sulphuric acid ⟶ ammonium sulphate
$2\,NH_3(aq)$ + $H_2SO_4(aq)$ ⟶ $(NH_4)_2SO_4(aq)$

Notice that compounds of ammon**ia** are called ammon**ium** salts.

Investigation 18.4   Testing your own fertiliser

Plan an investigation to see if your ammonium sulphate affects the growth of a seedling.
Ask your teacher to check your plan before you start.

Ammonium nitrate fertiliser

Ammonium nitrate is a very important fertiliser.
Do you know which acid reacts with ammonia
to make ammonium nitrate?

On page 221, we saw how ammonia is turned into
nitric acid. Most of this nitric acid is used to
make ammonium nitrate fertiliser.
Look at the diagram below:

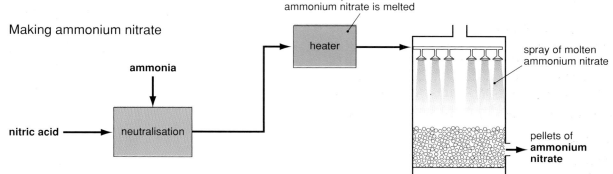

Making ammonium nitrate

water is evaporated off and
ammonium nitrate is melted

heater

ammonia

nitric acid — neutralisation

spray of molten
ammonium nitrate

pellets of
**ammonium
nitrate**

air blown in

Which fertiliser contains most nitrogen?

Ammonium nitrate and ammonium sulphate are
common 'nitrogen' fertilisers. Urea is also used
in poorer countries.

But which of these contains most nitrogen?
Can you remember how to calculate
relative formula masses (see page 35).
Look at the examples below:

Ammonium sulphate, $(NH_4)_2SO_4$	Ammonium nitrate, NH_4NO_3	Urea, $CO(NH_2)_2$
$2 \times N = 2 \times 14 = \quad 28$ $8 \times H = 8 \times 1 = \quad 8$ $1 \times S = 1 \times 32 = \quad 32$ $4 \times O = 4 \times 16 = \underline{+\ 64}$ Formula mass $= \quad 132$	$2 \times N = 2 \times 14 = \quad 28$ $4 \times H = 4 \times 1 = \quad 4$ $3 \times O = 3 \times 16 = \underline{+\ 48}$ Formula mass $= \quad 80$	$1 \times C = 1 \times 12 = \quad 12$ $1 \times O = 1 \times 16 = \quad 16$ $2 \times N = 2 \times 14 = \quad 28$ $4 \times H = 4 \times 1 = \underline{+\ 4}$ Formula mass $= \quad 60$
Fraction of N $= \dfrac{28}{132}$	Fraction of N $= \dfrac{28}{80}$	Fraction of N $= \dfrac{28}{60}$
% of N $= \dfrac{28}{132} \times 100 = 21.2\%$	% of N $= \dfrac{28}{80} \times 100 = 35\%$	% of N $= \dfrac{28}{60} \times 100 = 46.7\%$

So urea has the highest percentage of nitrogen.
Urea is found in manure. It is not as soluble as
ammonium fertilisers so it takes longer to release
its nitrogen. On the other hand, it is not
washed out of the soil (**leached**) so easily.
The leaching of fertiliser causes pollution problems (see page 226).

▷ Nitrogen, phosphorus and potassium – N, P and K

Plants also need other elements, besides nitrogen,
for healthy growth.
Phosphorus (P) and **potassium (K)**, like nitrogen,
are often added to the soil in fertilisers.

Look at the diagram of the plants opposite :
Each one has missed out on one of the 3 essential elements.

- What happens if a plant does not have enough :
  - nitrogen ?
  - phosphorus ?
  - potassium ?

Farmers can buy fertilisers which provide nitrogen,
phosphorus and potassium. Nobody has ever made
a compound of these 3 elements that plants can use.
Therefore, the bags of fertiliser contain mixtures
of compounds.

You can find out about your soil with a special
soil-testing kit. It tells you which element(s)
your soil needs.
You can then buy a fertiliser to suit your soil.

Look at the bags of fertiliser below :
The percentage of nitrogen is the first number,
followed by phosphorus, then potassium.
These numbers are called the **N : P : K** value of the fertiliser.

nitrogen is needed for the proteins in leaves and stalks

phosphorus speeds up the growth of roots, and the ripening of fruit

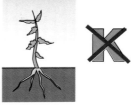

potassium protects plants against disease and frost damage. It promotes seed growth

There was a young man from Leeds
Who swallowed a packet of seeds
With N, P and K
And pesticide spray
He's now fully covered in weeds !

20 : 8 : 14   14 :14 : 14   10 : 25 : 15

A   B   C

- Which fertiliser would you use :
  - if your soil needed topping up with all 3 elements ?
  - if your soil was very low in phosphorus ?

Investigation 18.5   Fertilisers

Plan an investigation to answer **one** of these problems :
- How does the amount of fertiliser affect plant growth ?
- What effect do nitrogen, phosphorus and potassium
  have on plant growth ?
- Which mixture of nitrogen, phosphorus and potassium
  is best ?

Make sure that you plan a fair test. Is it safe ?
Check your plan with your teacher before you start.

Here are some compounds that
you could use as fertilisers :
- ammonium nitrate, NH_4NO_3
- calcium phosphate, $Ca_3(PO_4)_2$
- potassium chloride, KCl.

Test if any of these affect
the pH of the soil.
Will this affect your test ?

▷ A fertiliser factory

There is a large fertiliser factory at Billingham
on Teesside. On this page we can see why this
is a good place to have the factory.

The factory can make its own ammonia and nitric acid.
These react with each other to make **ammonium nitrate**, NH_4NO_3.
Which essential element does this give to plants?

*You can see how large the site at
Billingham is*

There is also a sulphuric acid plant on the site.
The sulphuric acid is used to make phosphoric acid from
phosphate rock.
The phosphoric acid reacts with more ammonia to make
ammonium phosphate fertiliser, $(NH_4)_3PO_4$.

Look at the formula of ammonium phosphate above:
Which *two* essential elements does it provide?

Potassium is put into fertilisers as **potassium chloride**, KCl,
or **potassium nitrate**, KNO_3.
Which potassium compound provides *two* essential elements?

Look at the map:

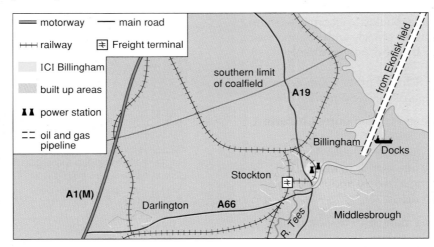

So why build the factory at Billingham?
It is near the North Sea. This is important for a supply of
natural gas. Remember that natural gas is a raw material for
the Haber process (see page 219).
Which river is nearby? Plenty of water is needed
to make steam. What is steam used for when making ammonia?

Is the factory near a port to bring in phosphate rock and
sulphur (to make sulphuric acid) from other countries?
The company can also export their fertilisers from a port.
Why are good road and rail links important?
What would be your concerns if a large fertiliser factory
was built near your home?

*You need good transport systems to
distribute your product*

▷ The trouble with fertilisers . . .

As you know from page 218,
most plants take up nutrients through
their roots. So fertilisers have to be
soluble in water.

Sometimes too much fertiliser is added to the soil.
Sometimes it is added at the wrong time
of year. (Why do you think that spring
is the best time?)
This can cause pollution in rivers.

Some fertiliser is washed down through
the soil by rain. It is **leached** out of the soil.
The dissolved fertiliser drains from the fields
into rivers.

Tiny plants, called algae, thrive on the fertiliser.
They start to cover the surface of the water.
This cuts off light to other living things
in the river.

When the algae die, bacteria decompose them.
The bacteria multiply quickly with so much food.
They use up much of the oxygen dissolved
in the water.
This means that fish and other water animals
cannot get enough oxygen. Soon they die.

This chain of events is called **eutrophication**.

Nitrate fertilisers are very soluble. They are
finding their way into our drinking water.
People are starting to worry about
a possible health risk.

In this country, as many as 5 million people
are at times drinking more than the
recommended amount of nitrate.

There is concern about stomach cancer
and 'blue baby' disease (when a new-born baby's
blood is starved of oxygen).

However, others argue that there is no evidence.
Links between the levels of nitrate in our water
and disease have not been proved.
But everyone agrees that it is wise to limit
the amount of nitrate we drink.

Fertiliser is 'leached from the soil'

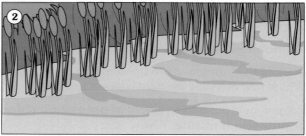

Algae thrive

Bacteria decompose the algae and use up the
dissolved oxygen. Fish die without oxygen.

Plants in this polluted river are thriving on fertilisers
leached from fields

Summary

Farmers add fertiliser to their soil to provide nutrients.
Nitrogen, phosphorus and potassium are all
needed for healthy plant growth.
Nitrogen fertilisers are made from ammonia (NH_3).
Ammonia is made in industry by the Haber process :

$$\text{nitrogen} \; + \; \text{hydrogen} \; \rightleftharpoons \; \text{ammonia}$$
$$N_2(g) \; + \; 3H_2(g) \; \rightleftharpoons \; 2NH_3(g)$$

Ammonia is an alkali. It reacts with acids,
making the salts we use as fertilisers. For example,

$$\text{ammonia} \; + \; \text{nitric acid} \; \longrightarrow \; \text{ammonium nitrate}$$
$$NH_3(aq) \; + \; HNO_3(aq) \; \longrightarrow \; NH_4NO_3(aq)$$

Fertilisers can be washed out (leached) from the soil.
They get into rivers and lakes causing eutrophication
(see page 226).

▷ Questions

1. Copy and complete :
Farmers add 3 essential nutrients to their soil :
.... (N), ... (P) and .... (K).
Ammonia is made by the .... process. Nitrogen
and .... are reacted together to make the
ammonia.
Ammonia reacts with .... to make salts.
For example,
ammonia + ... acid ⟶ ammonium nitrate
Fertilisers can be washed out, or l_____,
from the soil. Then they can cause
e_____ in rivers and lakes.

2. a) Draw a flow diagram of the nitrogen cycle.
b) Farmers add nitrogen fertilisers to their soil.
Explain why they have to do this when there
is so much nitrogen in the air.
c) In olden days farmers used to 'rotate' their
crops.
One of their fields was left without a crop
every few years. Clover was grown in the
field. This was ploughed into the soil before
seeds were planted the following year. Why
was this a good idea ?

3. Ammonia is made in industry by the Haber
process.
a) Write the word and symbol equation for
making ammonia.
b) What are the raw materials for the nitrogen
and hydrogen used in the process ?
c) What is the catalyst used ?
d) What temperature and pressure are chosen
for the process ?
e) Look back to page 217.
Explain why the conditions in d) are used.

4. Describe how we make nitric acid in industry.
Include a flow diagram of the process.

5. What factors would you look for in siting a
fertiliser factory ?

6. Rivers and lakes can be polluted by fertilisers.
Design a leaflet for farmers explaining the
problem.
Suggest how they might help reduce the
problem.

Further questions on page 237.

▷ Acids and Alkalis

1. This question is about acids and alkalis.

a) Copy and complete the following table. [3]

Colour for universal indicator	pH of solution
red	
	11
green	

b) The reaction between an acid and an alkali can be summarised as:

acid + alkali ⟶ salt + water.

i) Name this type of reaction. [1]
ii) Name the salt that would be formed by reacting dilute hydrochloric acid with potassium hydroxide solution. [1]
iii) Name the acid and alkali needed to produce the salt sodium nitrate. [2]

(WJEC)

2. a) Clare made sodium chloride solution by adding sodium hydroxide solution, an alkali, to hydrochloric acid.

i) What name is given to substances, such as sodium chloride, formed from the reaction of an acid with an alkali? [1]
ii) Name the process taking place in this reaction. [1]
iii) What should Clare use to find out when she has added enough sodium hydroxide solution to react with all the hydrochloric acid? [1]
iv) Describe how she should use this to make sure she added the correct amount of sodium hydroxide. [2]

b) Sodium chloride can be separated from its solution by evaporation. Draw a labelled diagram to show how this is done. [3]

c) Milk of Magnesia can cure indigestion. Explain how Milk of Magnesia works. [2]

(ULEAC)

3. Zinc sulphate crystals can be made in a laboratory.
This question is about making the crystals.
25 cm³ of dilute sulphuric acid are first added to lumps of zinc.

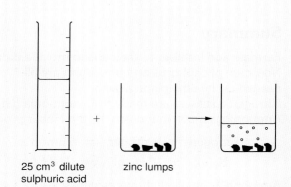

25 cm³ dilute sulphuric acid   zinc lumps

The zinc and acid stop bubbling after two hours.

a) After two hours the reaction has finished. All the acid has reacted. Some of the zinc has changed into zinc sulphate solution. There are still some lumps of zinc left. How can you separate the lumps from the solution? Use a diagram if it helps you to explain. [1]

b) The next thing to do is to get crystals from the solution. Describe how you could do this. Draw a diagram if it helps you to explain. [1]

(MEG)

4. An acid and an alkali react together to form a salt. These reactions are always exothermic.

a) i) What name is given to the reaction between an acid and an alkali? [1]
ii) What substance, other than a salt, is always formed when an acid reacts with an alkali? [1]

b) Copy and complete the following table to show the salt formed on mixing the alkali and the acid.

Alkali	Acid	Salt
....	nitric acid	sodium nitrate
barium hydroxide	hydrochloric acid	....
....	....	potassium sulphate

[4]

c) Describe how you could prepare a solution of magnesium chloride starting with dilute hydrochloric acid. Include in your answer what you would do, what you would **see** and how you would make sure that all the hydrochloric acid had been used up. [5]

(ULEAC)

5. a) Copy and complete the table below : [1]

Chemicals reacted	Two products formed
zinc + sulphuric acid	zinc sulphate + hydrogen
zinc oxide + hydrochloric acid	(i) + (ii)

b) Describe, with the aid of labelled diagrams and written work, how you would make **one** of the salts named in part a) above. [4]

c) Write equations for the following reactions:
   i)   When magnesium metal is reacted with very dilute nitric acid the products are magnesium nitrate and hydrogen gas. [2]
   ii) When copper(II) oxide is reacted with dilute sulphuric acid the products are copper(II) sulphate and water. [2]
                                        (WJEC)

6. Sodium carbonate reacts with acids.
   a) Complete the word equation

sodium   + hydrochloric ⟶ sodium   + ... + water
carbonate   acid   chloride
                                                    [1]

   b) Name the salt produced if sodium carbonate reacts with dilute nitric acid. [1]   (NEAB)

7. Complete the following word equations
   a) zinc + sulphuric acid ⟶ .... + ...   [1]
   b) sodium   + nitric ⟶
      hydroxide   acid   .... + ...   [1]
   c) magnesium + hydrochloric ⟶
      carbonate   acid   ..... + ... + water
                                        [1]   (NEAB)

8. A student made a sample of zinc sulphate crystals.
   She added excess zinc metal to acid and warmed the mixture. When the reaction was finished, she filtered the mixture. She left the solution to allow crystals to form.
   a) Name the acid she used. [1]
   b) Name the gas formed by the reaction. [1]
   c) i)   Why did she use excess zinc metal? [1]
      ii) Why did she warm the mixture? [1]
      iii) Why did she filter the mixture? [1]
                                        (ULEAC)

9. The diagrams show what happens when an acid is added to an alkali.

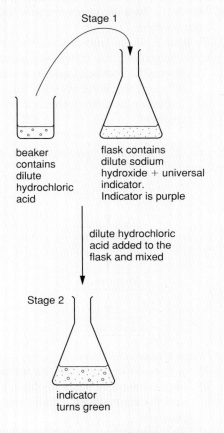

Stage 1

beaker contains dilute hydrochloric acid

flask contains dilute sodium hydroxide + universal indicator.
Indicator is purple

dilute hydrochloric acid added to the flask and mixed

Stage 2

indicator turns green

a) What is present in the flask at stage 2, besides universal indicator and water? [1]
b) Write an ionic equation to show how water is formed in this reaction and state the sources of the ions. [3]   (NEAB)

10. a) Give the symbol for the ion which is produced when :
   i)   any acid
   ii) any alkali
   dissolves in water. [2]
   b) Copy and complete the following word equation.

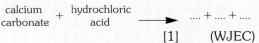

calcium   + hydrochloric ⟶   .... + ... + ...
carbonate   acid
                                        [1]   (WJEC)

▷ Products from oil

11. Crude oil is a mixture of hydrocarbons.
  a) Name the **two** elements found in every hydrocarbon. [2]
  b) To turn crude oil into useful products, it has to be separated into different fractions.
  i) Name the method used to separate different fractions in crude oil. [1]
  ii) Explain how this method of separation works. [2] (MEG)

12. Crude oil is used as a raw material to make polymers:

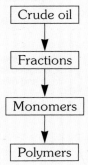

  a) Name the process used to
  i) separate the crude oil into fractions [1]
  ii) break down the fractions from crude oil into the monomers, ethene and propene. [1]
  b) i) To which group of compounds do ethene and propene belong? [1]
  ii) What would you see if a few drops of bromine water were shaken in a test tube containing ethene? [2]
  c) i) Name one addition polymer. [1]
  ii) Name a polymer used to make fibres for clothes. [1] (NEAB)

13. The demand for the fractions containing smaller hydrocarbons, eg petrol, is higher than for those containing larger hydrocarbons. Smaller hydrocarbons are produced from larger ones by the process called cracking.
  a) State **two** conditions which are required for the cracking of large hydrocarbons. [2]
  b) Octane and ethene may be made from decane, $C_{10}H_{22}$, by cracking. Write a balanced symbol equation for this reaction. [1] (MEG)

14. The diagram below represents a fractionating column used at an oil refinery. The points numbered 1 to 4 show the levels and temperatures at which different fractions are collected.

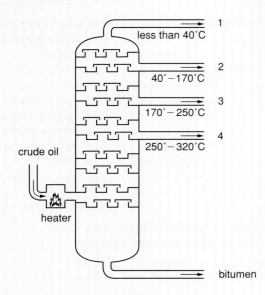

At which points would butane (boiling point 0°C) and octane (boiling point 126°C) be collected?

	Butane collected at point	Octane collected at point
A	1	2
B	2	1
C	2	3
D	3	2
E	1	4

[1] (MEG)

15. These four processes are used in the oil industry to manufacture ethene.
  1. cracking   2. drilling
  3. fractional distilling   4. polymerising
  In what order are three of them used?
  A 1 3 4
  B 2 1 3
  C 2 3 1
  D 3 1 4   [1] (SEG)

16. The equation below shows the cracking of a hydrocarbon compound into two different compounds, A and B.

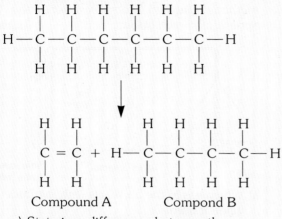

Compound A   Compond B

a) State **two** differences between the structures of compounds A and B. [2]

b) Why is compound A useful in industry? [1]
(NEAB)

17. a) Crude oil is a mixture of hydrocarbons. Crude oil is first separated into fractions by fractional distillation. Some of the fractions are used as fuels. The heavier fractions can be split up into smaller molecules by catalytic cracking.
One molecule of decane can be cracked to produce one molecule of ethene and one molecule of octane. This is done by passing decane over a powdered aluminium oxide catalyst at 500°C.

i) Balance the equation:
Decane $\longrightarrow$ ethene + octane
$C_{10}H_{22} \longrightarrow C_2H_4 + ...$ [1]

ii) Suggest why the decane **MUST** be heated before cracking can occur. [1]

b) Ethene is used in the manufacture of the plastic poly(ethene). Ethene is heated under high pressure in the presence of a catalyst. Many ethene molecules join together to form a giant molecule of poly(ethene). The diagram below shows what happens in the reaction:

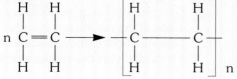

i) What is the name of this type of reaction? [1]

ii) Describe how the ethene molecules join together to form poly(ethene). [3]

iii) The poly(ethene) was heated and moulded into the shape of a bucket. The design of the bucket was changed. All the buckets were heated and then remoulded.
What type of plastic is poly(ethene)? Explain your answer. [2] (ULEAC)

18. Polythene is a thermosoftening plastic. Melamine is a thermosetting plastic.

a) What is meant by the terms
i) **thermosoftening?**
ii) **thermosetting?** [2]

b) i) Write down a use for a thermosetting plastic. [1]

ii) Explain why a thermosetting plastic is used for this job, rather than a thermosoftening plastic. [1]

c) Use your knowledge of the structures of these two types of plastic to explain why they behave differently when heated. [2]
(MEG)

19. The table below shows three of the substances which can be obtained from crude petroleum.

Name of substance	Formula	Structural formula	Use
methane	CH_4	H | $H-C-H$ | H	fuel
a)	C_3H_8	b)	c)
ethene	C_2H_4	d)	e)

Complete the table. [5]

f) What feature of an ethene molecule tells you that it is unsaturated? [1] (NEAB)

▷ Energy transfer

20. The diagram below shows a bunsen burner.

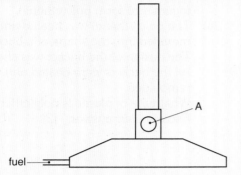

Use words from the list to complete the passage about the Bunsen burner. You may use each word once, more than once or not at all.

air	methane
argon	mechanical energy
carbon dioxide	nitrogen
chemical	physical
electrical energy	potential energy
heat	oxygen
kinetic energy	water vapour

In the Bunsen burner the fuel is mixed with a) which enters through the hole labelled A. When the fuel burns it reacts with the gas called b) and energy is given out as c). The fuel used in the Bunsen burner contains carbon and hydrogen which are changed during burning into d) and e). Burning is an example of a f) change because new substances are formed.   [6]   (NEAB)

21. The word equation for the burning of octane is:

octane + oxygen ⟶ carbon dioxide + water

a) Is the burning of octane an endothermic or an exothermic reaction?   [1]
b) Copy the equation above and underline the **products** of the reaction.   [1]
c) By looking at the above equation, work out the elements that **must** be present in octane.   [1]
d) Octane is one chemical present in petrol, which is used as a fuel. What is meant by a fuel?   [1]   (WJEC)

22. Methane CH_4 contains the elements carbon and hydrogen only. A student wanted to find out which new substances are produced when methane is burned. The student set up the apparatus shown below.

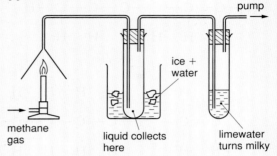

a) Which gas in the air reacts with methane when it burns?   [1]
b) Name the liquid collected.   [1]
c) Name the gas which turns limewater milky.   [1]
d) When methane burns an exothermic reaction takes place. What is meant by an exothermic reaction?   [2]   (NEAB)

23. a) What piece of apparatus is needed to show that a reaction is exothermic?   [1]
b) How could you show that the reaction between barium hydroxide solution and dilute hydrochloric acid is exothermic?   [4]   (ULEAC)

24. Orimulsion is a **fossil fuel**.
It is a mixture of tar and water.
Orimulsion is much cheaper than coal.
When Orimulsion burns it gives out energy.
There is a lot of sulphur in Orimulsion.
a) i) Fossil fuels store energy. Where did this stored energy **first** come from?   [1]
   ii) Will supplies of Orimulsion ever run out? Explain your answer in detail.   [3]
b) Several gases are made when Orimulsion burns. Carbon dioxide and sulphur dioxide are two of the gases.
   i) Explain how the sulphur dioxide is made.   [1]
   ii) Describe how sulphur dioxide can have a bad effect on the environment.   [2]
   iii) Describe how carbon dioxide can have a bad effect on the environment.   [2]
   (MEG)

25. The symbol equation below shows the reaction when methane burns in oxygen.

$$CH_4 + 2O_2 \longrightarrow CO_2 + 2H_2O$$

An energy level diagram for this reaction is shown below.

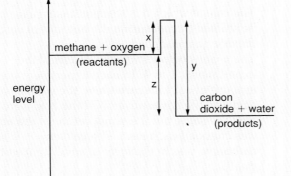

a) Which chemical bonds are broken and which are formed during this reaction? [4]

b) Explain the significance of x, y and z on the energy level diagram in terms of the energy transfers which occur when these chemical bonds are broken and formed. [6]

(NEAB)

26. Hydrogen (H_2) and chlorine (Cl_2) react together to make hydrogen chloride (HCl). The reaction is highly exothermic.

The equation for the reaction can be written as

$$H-H + Cl-Cl \longrightarrow H-Cl + H-Cl$$

a) During the reaction some bonds are made and others are broken.

i) Copy the equation below and put a ring around the bond(s) which is(are) broken. [1]

$$H-H + Cl-Cl \longrightarrow H-Cl + H-Cl$$

ii) Copy the equation below and put a ring around the bond(s) which is(are) made. [1]

$$H-H + Cl-Cl \longrightarrow H-Cl + H-Cl$$

iii) What energy change (transfer) takes place when bonds are broken? [1]

iv) What energy change (transfer) takes place when bonds are made? [1]

v) How does the difference in the energy involved in breaking and making bonds explain why the reaction between hydrogen and chlorine is exothermic? [1] (MEG)

27. **HYDROGEN
FUEL OF THE FUTURE**

It has been suggested that hydrogen could be used as a fuel instead of the fossil fuels that are used at present. The equation below shows how hydrogen burns in air.

$$2H_2 + O_2 \longrightarrow 2H_2O + heat$$

The hydrogen would be made from water using energy obtained from renewable sources such as wind or solar power. The water splitting reaction requires a lot of energy. You will find information about hydrogen on page 119.

a) Hydrogen was successfully used as a fuel for a Soviet airliner in 1988.
Why would hydrogen be a good fuel for use in an aeroplane? [2]

b) The water splitting reaction is shown in the equation below.

$$2H_2O \longrightarrow 2H_2 + O_2$$

$$\underset{H \quad H}{\overset{O}{\bigwedge}} + \underset{H \quad H}{\overset{O}{\bigwedge}} \longrightarrow \overset{H-H}{\underset{H-H}{}} + O=O$$

Use information from the table on page 188 to help you answer this question.

i) Calculate the energy needed to split the water molecules in the equation into H and O atoms.

$$2H_2O \longrightarrow 4H + 2O \qquad [2]$$

ii) Calculate the energy change when the H and O atoms join to form H_2 and O_2 molecules.

$$4H + 2O \longrightarrow 2H_2 + O_2 \qquad [2]$$

iii) Is the overall reaction:

$$2H_2O \longrightarrow 2H_2 + O_2$$

exothermic or endothermic? Use your answers to i) and ii) to explain your choice. [4] (NEAB)

▷ Rates of reaction

28. John is investigating the reaction between zinc and hydrochloric acid using the apparatus below. He adds pieces of zinc to the acid and bubbles of hydrogen gas are produced.

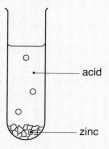

a) Complete the word equation for this reaction:

.... + ... ⟶ zinc chloride + ...   [2]

b) Suggest **four** ways that John could use to increase the rate of reaction.   [4]

c) Complete the following sentence.
During the experiment the test tube became warm because an .... chemical reaction was taking place. [1]   (ULEAC)

29. An investigation was carried out to see how the rate of decomposition of hydrogen peroxide could be changed.

Hydrogen peroxide ⟶ oxygen + water

Powdered manganese(IV) oxide was added to the hydrogen peroxide.

a) i) What effect does the manganese(IV) oxide have on the chemical reaction?   [1]

ii) What name is given to this type of chemical?   [1]

b) What happens to the rate of reaction if:

i) the concentration of the hydrogen peroxide is increased;   [1]

ii) lumps of manganese(IV) oxide are used instead of powder?   [1]   (SEG)

30. Calcium carbonate reacts with dilute hydrochloric acid as shown in the equation below.

$$CaCO_3(s) + 2HCl(aq) \longrightarrow$$
$$CaCl_2(aq) + H_2O(l) + CO_2(g)$$

The rate at which this reaction takes place can be studied by measuring the amount of carbon dioxide gas produced.

The graphs below show the results of four experiments, 1 to 4. In each experiment the amount of calcium carbonate, the volume of acid and the concentration of the acid were kept the same but the temperature of the acid was changed each time. The calcium carbonate was in the form of small lumps of marble.

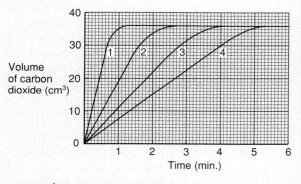

a) Apart from altering the temperature, suggest **two** ways in which the reaction of calcium carbonate and hydrochloric acid could be speeded up.   [2]

b) Which graph, 1 to 4, shows the results of the experiment in which the acid had the highest temperature? Explain fully how you know.   [2]

c) i) In experiment 2, how does the rate of reaction after one minute compare with the rate of reaction after two minutes?   [1]

ii) Explain, as fully as you can, why the reaction rate changes during experiment 2.   [2]   (NEAB)

31. Some students have studied the reaction between some metals and dilute hydrochloric acid. The metals react with the acid until they cannot be seen.
Bubbles of gas are produced during **all** the reactions.
The students know that

a metal + an acid $\longrightarrow$ a salt + hydrogen

a) Write a word equation for the reaction of zinc with dilute hydrochloric acid. [2]
b) Magnesium reacts with dilute hydrochloric acid to produce magnesium chloride and hydrogen.
Write a balanced symbolic equation for this reaction. [2]
c) They carried out an investigation to discover whether the concentration of acid used had any effect on the time taken for the magnesium to react completely. Equal volumes of acid and equal lengths of magnesium ribbon were used in each test. The table shows a set of results.

concentration of acid/ moles per dm³	time taken for magnesium to react completely/seconds
2.0	13
1.5	22
1.2	30
0.8	70
0.6	145
0.5	250

i) Plot the points on a graph to show the time taken for the reaction to finish when different concentrations of acid are used (reaction time up the side, concentration of acid along the bottom). [2]
ii) Finish the graph by drawing the best curve. [1]
iii) Use your graph to help you to describe how increasing the concentration of acid affects the rate of reaction. [1]
iv) Use your graph to predict the time taken for the reaction if the concentration of acid was 1.0 moles per dm³. [1]

v) Write down **two** other factors which could change the rate of this reaction. In each case state how the rate would change. [2]
vi) Use the idea of particles to explain the effect of changing concentration on the rate of reaction. [2]
d) One student asked if the class could repeat their experiment using potassium instead of magnesium. The teacher said 'Definitely not!'
Use your knowledge of the reactivity series to explain why the teacher was very wise to say this. [2] (MEG)

32. The table below gives the results from the reaction of excess marble chips (calcium carbonate) with (A) 20 cm³ of dilute hydrochloric acid, (B) 10 cm³ of the dilute hydrochloric acid + 10 cm³ of water.

Time in minutes	Total mass of carbon dioxide produced in grams	
	(A) 20 cm³ dilute HCl	(B) 10 cm³ of dilute HCl + 10 cm³ of H₂O
0	0.00	0.00
1	0.54	0.27
2	0.71	0.35
3	0.78	0.38
4	0.80	0.40
5	0.80	0.40

a) Plot the two curves on a graph (time along the bottom). Label the first curve (A) and the second curve (B). [3]
b) **Sketch, on the same grid**, the curve you might have expected for reaction (A) if it had been carried out at a higher temperature. Label this curve (C). [1]
c) **Sketch, on the same grid**, the curve you might have expected for reaction (B) if the marble chips had been ground to a powder. Label this curve (D). [1]
d) Explain your answer to part c). [1]
(WJEC)

▷ Enzymes

33. Yeast releases energy from sugars. This process is called fermentation.

a) Name **two** chemical substances formed during the fermentation process. [2]

b) Yeast works best within a certain temperature range.
Suggest the "best" temperature (°C) for yeast to work. [1]

c) The flow diagram shows how bread is made.

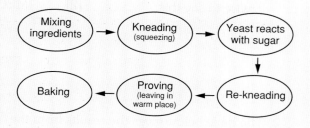

i) How does the dough change during "proving"? [1]

ii) What effect does "baking" have on the yeast? [1]   (SEG)

34. Ethanol (C_2H_6O) can be made by the fermentation of glucose ($C_6H_{12}O_6$). Carbon dioxide (CO_2) is also formed.

a) Write a balanced equation for the fermentation of glucose. [1]

b) Yeast must be added to glucose solution in order for the fermentation to occur.
Explain why yeast is needed. [1]

c) If the temperature during fermentation is increased to 70°C the reaction slows down and then stops completely. Explain why this happens. [1]

d) An increase in temperature from 25°C to 35°C will increase this rate of reaction. Explain this using the idea of collisions between particles. [2]   (MEG)

▷ Reversible reactions

35. Ethanol (C_2H_6O) is manufactured from ethene (C_2H_4) and steam (H_2O).
The equation for the reaction is
$$C_2H_4 + H_2O \rightleftharpoons C_2H_6O.$$

a) The sign $\rightleftharpoons$ indicates that this is a reversible reaction.
What is meant by a reversible reaction? [2]

b) The graph shows how the conversion of ethene into ethanol, at three different temperatures, will change as the pressure changes.

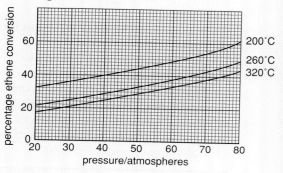

i)   How does the conversion of ethene into ethanol change as the pressure increases? [1]

ii) How does the conversion of ethene into ethanol change as the temperature increases? [1]

iii) What is the percentage conversion of ethene at 260°C and 55 atmospheres pressure? [1]

iv) A catalyst is used in this reaction. Why is a catalyst used? [1]
What effect does a catalyst have on the percentage conversion of ethene? [1]   (MEG)

36. In the manufacture of nitric acid, ammonia is oxidised to nitrogen monoxide.
$$4NH_3(g) + 5O_2(g) \rightleftharpoons 4NO(g) + 6H_2O(g)$$
The reaction is exothermic.
In industry a mixture of dry ammonia and air at about 7 atmospheres pressure is passed over a platinum catalyst at 900°C.
Explain how changing the conditions used could affect the **yield** of nitrogen monoxide. [6]   (SEG)

▷ Products from air

37. Ammonia and nitric acid are both important chemicals. Nitric acid is made from ammonia.

a) The word equations below show how nitric acid is made.

1. nitrogen + hydrogen ⟶ ammonia
2. ammonia + oxygen ⟶ nitrogen monoxide + water
3. nitrogen monoxide + oxygen ⟶ nitrogen dioxide
4. nitrogen dioxide + water ⟶ nitric acid

Use the word equations to help you answer these questions.

  i) From which **two elements** is ammonia made? [1]

  ii) Name **two** of the raw materials needed to make nitric acid. [2]

b) A large amount of nitric acid is reacted with ammonia to make a fertiliser.

nitric acid + ammonia ⟶ fertiliser

  i) The reaction is a neutralisation reaction.
What type of chemical must ammonia be? [1]

  ii) Complete the chemical name for the fertiliser made from ammonia and nitric acid.
ammonium .... [1]

  iii) The reaction of nitric acid with ammonia is exothermic.
Name the piece of equipment you could put into the solution to prove that the reaction is exothermic. [1]
(NEAB)

38. State one problem caused by farmers using too much fertiliser. [1] (NEAB)

39. Ammonia is manufactured by the Haber process, in which nitrogen and hydrogen react according to the equation shown below.

$$N_2 + 3H_2 \rightleftharpoons 2NH_3$$

a) What is meant by the symbol ⇌ ? [1]

b) Name **one** compound manufactured on a large scale from ammonia. [1]

c) Why is iron used in the Haber process and what effect does it have? [2]

d) The table below shows the percentage of ammonia present at equilibrium when nitrogen and hydrogen react at different temperatures and different pressures.

Pressure (atmosphere)	Ammonia present at equilibrium (%)				
	Temperature (°C)				
	100	200	300	400	500
10	88.2	50.7	14.7	3.9	1.2
25	91.7	63.6	27.4	8.7	2.9
50	94.5	74.0	39.5	15.3	5.6
100	96.7	81.7	52.5	25.2	10.6
200	98.4	89.0	66.7	38.8	18.3
400	99.4	94.6	79.7	55.4	31.9
1000	99.9	98.3	92.6	79.8	57.5

  i) What is meant by the statement that a reaction has reached equilibrium? [1]

  ii) What will be present in the equilibrium mixture with the ammonia? [1]

  iii) Use the table to say how the **percentage of ammonia** present at equilibrium is affected by:
increasing the temperature;
increasing the pressure [2]

e) How will the **rate of reaction** of nitrogen with hydrogen be affected by increasing the temperature? [1]

f) The maximum yield of ammonia shown in the table occurs at 1000 atmospheres pressure and 100°C. Why are these conditions **not** used commercially? [2]
(ULEAC)

chapter 19

Ionic compounds

This section explains the properties of materials.
To understand the ideas, you need to know about
the structure of atoms (see Chapter 3).

When we look at the Periodic Table, we find a group
of elements with almost no reactions at all.
Can you remember the name of this group?
What can you say about the arrangement of electrons
in their atoms?

We have seen on page 66 that the atoms of these
very stable noble gases all have **full outer shells of electrons**.
All other atoms would also like to have full outer shells.

In this chapter we will see how metals and non-metals
bond together in compounds.

*Metals, like sodium, react with
non-metals, like chlorine. The
compound formed is made of
ions.*

▷ Ionic bonding

Let's look at sodium chloride as an example:

> **Ionic bonds** form between *metals and non-metals*.

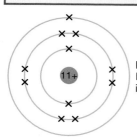

Na atom.
It has 1 electron
in its outer shell

Cl atom.
It has 7 electrons
in its outer shell

A sodium atom has 11 electrons (2,8,1)   *A chlorine atom has 17 electrons (2,8,7)*

Both atoms want to be stable by having full outer shells.
They will always take the easiest way to
fill their outer shell with electrons.

Notice that sodium has just 1 electron in its outer shell.
How do you think it could get a full outer shell?
Would it be easier for sodium to lose just 1 electron,
or to gain 7 electrons?

Look at the chlorine atom above:
It has 7 electrons in its outer shell.
How do you think it could get a full outer shell?
Would it be easier for chlorine to lose 7 electrons,
or to gain just 1 more electron?

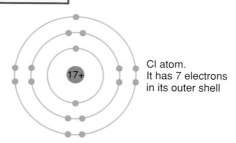

Metal atoms give electrons to non-metal atoms

When sodium reacts, it **loses** its 1 outer electron.
This leaves a full shell.
Where do you think sodium's electron goes to?

Chlorine accepts the electron from sodium.
It **gains** the 1 electron it needs to fill its
outer shell.
Look at the diagram below:

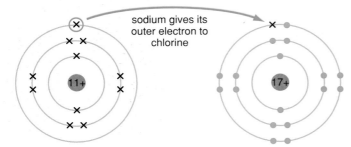

sodium gives its
outer electron to
chlorine

Remember that all atoms are neutral.
They have an equal number of positive protons
and negative electrons. So the charges cancel out.

However, after sodium has given an electron to chlorine,
the electrons and protons in both atoms no longer balance.

Let's add up the charges:

sodium 10 electrons = 10−   **chlorine** 18 electrons = 18−
       11 protons = 11+   17 protons = 17+
                  1+   1−

The atoms, which we now call **ions**, become charged: Na^+ and Cl^-.
You can show the ions like this:

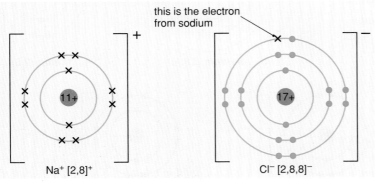

this is the electron
from sodium

Na^+ [2,8]$^+$ Cl^- [2,8,8]$^-$

As you know, opposite charges attract.
Therefore, the Na^+ ions and Cl^- ions are strongly attracted
to each other. This attraction sticks the ions together,
and is called an **ionic bond**.
Millions of ions bond together to form crystals.
You can see a diagram of this on page 243.

Opposites attract!

▶ More ionic compounds

We have looked at sodium chloride as an example of an ionic compound.
When sodium and chlorine react together, each sodium atom gives 1 electron to each chlorine atom.
The atoms 'satisfy' each other – one-to-one.
So the formula of sodium chloride is NaCl.

Magnesium is in Group 2 of the Periodic Table. Therefore, we know that it has 2 electrons in its outer shell.
How could it get a full outer shell?
What do you think happens if we react magnesium, instead of sodium, with chlorine?
Look at the diagram below:

When metal meets non-metal, the sparks they do fly.
"Give me electrons!" non-metals do cry.
"You've got a deal!" the metal responds,
Then ions attract to form their bonds.

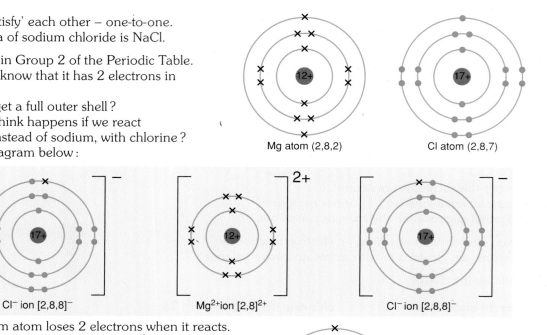

Mg atom (2,8,2)   Cl atom (2,8,7)

Cl⁻ ion [2,8,8]⁻   Mg²⁺ion [2,8]²⁺   Cl⁻ ion [2,8,8]⁻

The magnesium atom loses 2 electrons when it reacts.
Therefore, its ion has a 2+ charge, Mg^{2+}.

You can see that each magnesium atom can 'satisfy' 2 chlorine atoms.
So the formula of magnesium chloride is **MgCl$_2$**.

Now let's look at sodium reacting with oxygen:
An oxygen atom has 6 electrons in its outer shell.
How can it get a full outer shell?
Look at the diagram below:

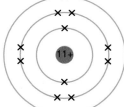

Na atom (2,8,1)

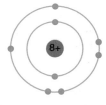

O atom (2,6)

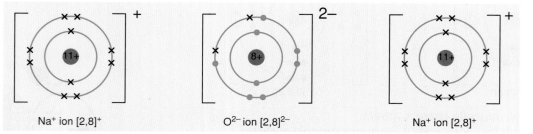

Na⁺ ion [2,8]⁺   O²⁻ ion [2,8]²⁻   Na⁺ ion [2,8]⁺

The oxygen atom gains 2 electrons, each with a negative charge.
Therefore its ion has a 2− charge, O^{2-}.
It takes 2 sodium atoms to 'satisfy' 1 oxygen atom.
So the formula of sodium oxide is **Na$_2$O**.

Working out the formula

You have now seen how 3 ionic compounds are formed.
Look at the ions which make up each compound:

Ionic compound	Formula	Ions present
sodium chloride	NaCl	1 Na$^+$, 1 Cl$^-$
magnesium chloride	MgCl$_2$	1 Mg^{2+}, 2 Cl$^-$
sodium oxide	Na$_2$O	2 Na$^+$, 1 O^{2-}

Now add up the charges on the ions in each compound.
What do you notice? Do they balance out?

Ionic compounds are **neutral**.
The charges on their ions cancel each other out.
Knowing this, and the charge on the ions,
we can work out the formula of any ionic compound.

Example

Magnesium oxide
Magnesium ions have a 2+ charge, Mg^{2+}.
Oxide ions have a 2− charge, O^{2-}.
The charge on 1 magnesium ion balances out
the charge on 1 oxide ion.
$(2+) + (2-) = 0$
Therefore, they bond one Mg^{2+} with one O^{2-}.
The formula is **MgO**.

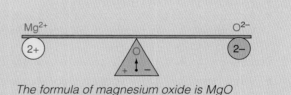

The formula of magnesium oxide is MgO

Example

Aluminium oxide is a little more difficult.
Aluminium ions have a 3+ charge, Al^{3+}.
Oxide ions have a 2− charge, O^{2-}.
So how many aluminium ions and oxide ions
combine to balance each other out?
2 Al^{3+} ions will cancel out 3 O^{2-} ions.
$2 \times (3+) = 6+$ and $3 \times (2-) = 6-$
$$(6+) + (6-) = 0$$
Therefore the formula is **Al$_2$O$_3$**.

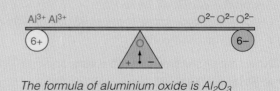

The formula of aluminium oxide is Al$_2$O$_3$

Notice that the metal always comes in front
of the non-metal in the formula.
See if you can copy and complete the table below:

	chloride, Cl$^-$	bromide, Br$^-$	oxide, O^{2-}
sodium, Na$^+$	NaCl		Na$_2$O
magnesium, Mg^{2+}	MgCl$_2$		
aluminium, Al^{3+}			Al$_2$O$_3$

▷ Properties of ionic compounds

You now have seen how metals bond with non-metals.
Metals give electrons to non-metals. This means that:

> **Metals always form positive ions, and
> non-metals form negative ions.**

Look at the photo of two ionic compounds:
Can you see any similarities?
You can test an ionic compound
in the next experiment:

Here are crystals of two ionic compounds

Experiment 19.1   Testing ionic compounds

1. Spread a few grains of sodium chloride on a microscope slide.
   Focus your microscope on the grains.

   * What shape are the grains?
   * Are the angles at the surface of the grains similar?
     We call solids with regular angles **crystals**.

2. Heat some sodium chloride crystals strongly in a test-tube.

   * What happens? Does sodium chloride have a **high melting point**?

3. Add 2 spatulas of sodium chloride to half a beaker of water.
   Stir it with a glass rod.

   * What happens? Is sodium chloride **soluble in water**?

4. Set up the circuit as shown:
   Dip the electrodes into some solid sodium chloride.

   * Does the solid conduct?

   Now half-fill the beaker with water, and stir.

   * Does the bulb light up now?
   * Does the **solution conduct electricity**?

⚠ chlorine gas

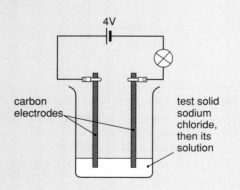

carbon electrodes

test solid sodium chloride, then its solution

4V

Here is a list of the properties of ionic compounds.

Ionic compounds:

* are made of crystals (which can be split along certain angles)

* have high melting points

* are often soluble in water

* conduct electricity when molten or dissolved in water,
  but not when solid. (Page 97 explains why.)

*We transferred electrons and
lost our hearts,
'Til electrolysis do us part.*

*(Let's hope it doesn't rain – or the
marriage could soon be dissolved!)*

▷ Giant ionic structure

Scientists need to know how the ions are arranged
in ionic compounds. This helps to explain how
ionic compounds behave.
We can get information by firing X-rays
at a crystal. The X-rays make a pattern as they pass
through the crystal. The pattern gives us clues
about the arrangement of the ions.

*Dorothy Hodgkin used
X-rays to help show the
structure of materials*

Scientists have found that the ions form **giant structures**.
Millions of positive and negative ions are
fixed in position.

Look at the diagram below:

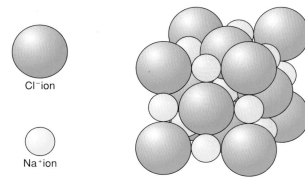

Cl⁻ ion

Na⁺ ion

*Part of the giant
ionic structure of
sodium chloride*

Can you see that the ions are arranged in a regular pattern?
This explains the regular angles of ionic crystals.

Why do you think that ionic compounds have
high melting points?
Remember that opposite charges attract, forming
strong ionic bonds.
Imagine trying to separate all the ions in the
giant structure above! It takes a lot of energy to
overcome all that electrostatic attraction.

the oxygen end of a water molecule
is slightly negative compared to the
hydrogen end

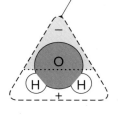

Many ionic compounds dissolve in water.
To explain this we need to look at
a water molecule in more detail:
The electrons in H_2O are not evenly spread.
One end of the molecule is slightly negative
compared to the other end.

Look at the diagram opposite:

The water molecules are attracted to
the ions and pull them from the giant structure.
The compound dissolves. Its ions are then free to move around.
(The electrolysis of ionic compounds is explained in Chapter 9.)

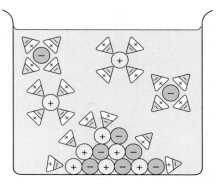

An ionic compound dissolving in water

▷ Chemistry at work : Ionic compounds – halides

We have already met lots of important ionic compounds
in this book.
For example, Chapter 10 is about salt (sodium chloride).
Look back at some of its uses.
Here are some other useful ionic compounds of the
halogens – the **halides**.

Sodium fluoride

If you eat sweet, sticky food, it can rot your teeth.
Bacteria in your mouth feed on the sugar,
making acid as they do so. This acid causes
tooth decay.
Fluoride ions help to prevent tooth decay.
As children grow, the fluoride forms part of the
calcium compounds in their teeth.
This makes it more difficult for acid to attack teeth.

Some water authorities add fluoride to their water supplies.
This greatly reduces the number of fillings children have.
However, too much fluoride can actually harm teeth.
In fact, higher doses are toxic (poisonous) !
This has led to many arguments about fluoride in water.
What do you think about adding fluoride to our water supplies ?

Sugary foods cause tooth decay

Silver halides

These are used on photographic film and paper.
Silver halides are affected by light.
Do you remember the tests for halides on p150 ?
Try the experiment below :

Experiment 19.2   Effect of light on silver halides

Add silver nitrate solution to two test tubes,
each containing sodium chloride. What happens ?
The white precipitate is silver chloride.
Do the same with two test tubes of sodium bromide,
then sodium iodide.
Place a test tube of each silver halide in a dark
cupboard for 5 minutes.
Leave the other 3 silver halides in the light.
● Describe the differences you see.

Developing a photograph

The silver halides are reduced to silver in sunlight.
This explains their use in photography.

Henri Becquerel discovered radioactivity in
1896. He noticed that a sample of uranium
salt 'fogged' a photographic plate left inside
a drawer.

Summary

When metals react with non-metals they form **ionic** compounds.
Metals give electrons to non-metals.
This makes **positive metal** ions, and **negative non-metal** ions.
The oppositely charged ions are attracted to each other
by strong electrostatic forces. This is called **ionic bonding**.
The ions are arranged in huge networks, called **giant ionic structures**.
Ionic compounds:
- are made of crystals
- have high melting points
- are often soluble in water
- conduct electricity when molten or dissolved in water
  (when free ions are present), but not when solid.

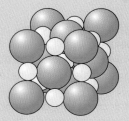

▷ **Questions**

1. Copy and complete:
   .... compounds are made from metals and non-metals.
   Metals always form .... charged ions, and non-metals form .... charged ions.
   These ions are arranged in .... ionic structures.
   Their crystals have .... melting points and many will .... in water.
   They conduct .... when molten or when in solution, but not when they are .....

2. Which of these substances have ionic bonds?

   ammonia, NH_3

   water, H_2O

   copper oxide, CuO

   zinc chloride, $ZnCl_2$

   lead bromide, $PbBr_2$

   potassium fluoride, KF

   methane, CH_4

   How did you decide?

3. Explain, using diagrams to help, how the atoms in a) and b) below, transfer electrons to form ions.
   (Remember that the 1st shell can hold 2 electrons, the 2nd shell 8 electrons, and the 3rd shell also holds 8 electrons.)

   a) Lithium, Li (which has 3 electrons) and fluorine, F (which has 9 electrons).

   b) Potassium, K (which has 19 electrons) and chlorine, Cl (which has 17 electrons).

4. Here are 3 metal ions:
   lithium, Li^+ calcium, Ca^{2+},   iron(III), Fe^{3+}
   Here are 3 non-metal ions:
   fluoride, F^- iodide, I^-,   sulphide, S^{2-}
   Draw a table, like the one on page 241, to show the formulas of the compounds between these metals and non-metals.

5. Look at the Periodic Table on page 344:
   a) What is the link between the group a **_metal_** is in and the charge on its ions? You can use sodium, magnesium and aluminium as examples.
   b) Try to find a simple mathematical equation that tells you the link between the charge on a **_non-metal_** ion and its group number. You can use oxygen and fluorine as examples.
   c) Carbon (which has 6 electrons) never forms ions. Why not?
      If it did, what do you think its charge would be?
   d) Hydrogen (which only has 1 electron) can form both H^+ ions and H^- ions. Try to explain this.
   e) Why do some people say that hydrogen should be above lithium, Li, in the Periodic Table, and others argue that it should be above fluorine, F?

6. Explain, using diagrams to help, how these atoms transfer electrons to form ions:
   a) Magnesium, Mg (which has 12 electrons) and fluorine, F (which has 9 electrons).
   b) Magnesium, Mg (which has 12 electrons) and oxygen, O (which has 8 electrons).

Further questions on page 264.

chapter 20

Covalent bonding

In the last chapter we saw how metals bond with non-metals.
Remember that metal atoms need to lose electrons, and non-metals want to gain electrons.

But think of all those hydrocarbons in Chapter 13!
Like many compounds, they are formed from **just non-metals**.
Which non-metals do they contain?

Both carbon and hydrogen atoms want to gain electrons.
So how do their atoms bond to each other?
How can they both gain electrons to get full outer shells?
It can't be like ionic bonding because there is no metal atom to give away electrons.

Two non-metal atoms can both **gain electrons by sharing!**
If their outer shells overlap, they share some of each other's electrons. This 'satisfies' both atoms.

Methane is an important fuel. Its formula is CH_4. The carbon and hydrogen atoms are joined to each other by covalent bonds.

> **Shared electrons form covalent bonds between non-metal atoms.**

Let's look at the smallest hydrocarbon, methane.
It's formula is CH_4.

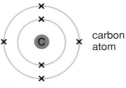

carbon atom

hydrogen atom

Carbon has 4 electrons in its outer shell.
It needs to gain 4 electrons to get a full outer shell.
(Remember that the 2nd shell can hold 8 electrons.)

Hydrogen has just 1 electron.
If it can gain 1 more electron, it will fill its shell.
(The 1st shell is filled by just 2 electrons.)

1 carbon atom and 4 hydrogen atoms overlap like this:

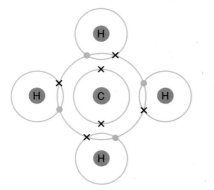

Count the electrons in the outer shell of each carbon and hydrogen atom in methane.
Are they all full?
Can you see that the carbon now has 8 electrons in its outer shell?
How many electrons does each hydrogen have?
Is hydrogen stable with this arrangement?

In Chapter 13 we showed covalent bonds like this:

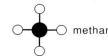

● = carbon
○ = hydrogen

methane, CH₄

This 'ball and stick' diagram shows the 4 single covalent bonds between C and H atoms

Let's look at another example of covalent bonding.
Chlorine gas does not exist as single atoms.
Remember that a chlorine atom has 7 electrons in its outer shell. It needs 1 more electron to fill it.
How can it manage to do this?

Like many gases, it is di-atomic. Two chlorine atoms bond together to make a Cl₂ molecule.
Look at the diagrams below of the Cl₂ molecule:

Chlorine atoms share a pair of electrons in a covalent bond

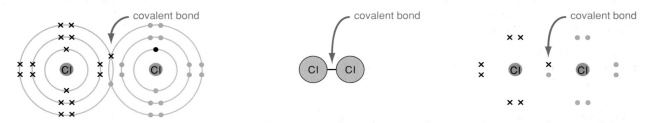

Three ways to show the covalent bond in Cl₂. The right-hand one is a 'dot and cross' diagram (showing the outer electrons only).

Count the electrons in the outer shell of each chlorine atom.
Do they both have 8 electrons? Are they both 'satisfied'?

Double bonds

Do you recall the molecule ethene from Chapter 13?
Its formula is C₂H₄. We said that its carbon atoms are joined by a 'double bond'.
Can you remember how it forms poly(ethene)? (See page 166.)

Oxygen is another molecule which contains a double bond. Look at the diagram below:

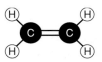

Ethene has a double covalent bond between its carbon atoms

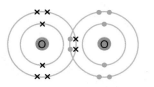

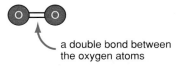

a double bond between the oxygen atoms

How many electrons are in the area of overlap?
How many electrons are in the single covalent bonds in CH₄ and Cl₂?
Each **pair of electrons** in the overlapping shells is a covalent bond.
Can you see why we call the bond between 2 oxygen atoms a **double** bond?

▷ Giant covalent structures

The great variety of life on Earth depends on
carbon's ability to form covalent bonds with itself.
As the element, carbon atoms can bond to
millions of other carbon atoms in both
diamond and graphite.

Carbon in the form of diamond

Do you know the hardest substance on Earth?
Look at the photo opposite:
Diamond's hardness makes it a very useful material.
You can read more about its uses on page 250.

Diamond is made from only carbon atoms.
Think back to the previous page.
How many covalent bonds can each carbon atom form?
Look at the diagram below:

*Some drills are tipped with diamonds. This
one cuts through rock when drilling for oil.*

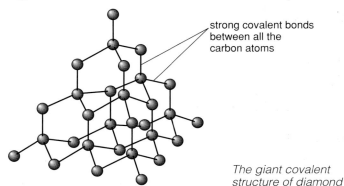

strong covalent bonds
between all the
carbon atoms

*The giant covalent
structure of diamond*

Each atom forms 4 strong covalent bonds with
its neighbours.
The atoms are arranged in a **giant covalent structure**.
Does diamond have a high or a low melting point?
Can you explain why?

Another substance with a giant covalent structure
is sand.
Its chemical name is silicon dioxide (SiO_2).
It melts at over 1500 °C.

Substances with giant covalent structures
are **not soluble in water**.
Their particles have no charge (unlike ionic compounds).
So water molecules are not attracted to them.

They **don't conduct electricity** in any state.
There are no free ions or electrons to carry the charge.
(Graphite is an exception; see the next page.)

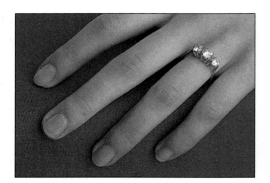

*Although diamond is very hard, it can be
split in certain directions (cleaved) to make
jewellery*

Carbon in the form of graphite

Another form of carbon is graphite.
Diamond and graphite are **allotropes** of carbon.
Allotropes are different forms of the same element
(in the same state).
The carbon atoms in graphite are also held together
in a giant covalent structure.

However, some of its properties are very different from
a typical giant covalent substance, such as diamond or sand.

If you touch a lump of graphite, it feels smooth
and slippery.
Your pencil contains graphite. As you move it across
your paper it flakes off, leaving a trail of carbon atoms.
Look at the diagram below:

Graphite (mixed with clay) is used in
pencil 'leads'

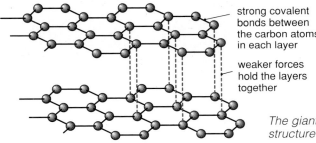

strong covalent
bonds between
the carbon atoms
in each layer

weaker forces
hold the layers
together

*The giant covalent
structure of graphite*

How many carbon atoms are joined to each other
by strong covalent bonds?
Why is this strange?
The 4th electron from each carbon atom is found
in the gap between the layers. These electrons
hold the layers together by a weak force.
The layers can slide over each other easily.
Does this explain its use in pencils?

Do you know the only non-metal element that conducts
electricity well? Think of the electrodes we use for
electrolysis in Chapter 9.
Electrons hold the layers together in graphite.
However, they are only held loosely to the carbon atoms.
They can drift along between the layers in graphite,
making it a conductor.
Do you think that graphite conducts better along its layers
or across them?

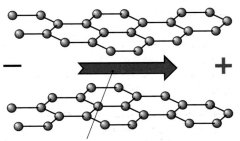

electrons can move along between
the layers in graphite

Graphite does not melt when you heat it.
At over 3000 °C it turns straight into a gas.
We say it **sublimes**. This is called **sublimation**.
Why does it take a lot of energy for graphite to sublime?

Uses of diamond

Jewellery

We all know about the use of diamonds in jewellery.
If you have ever looked in a jeweller's shop,
you will know how expensive they are.

Diamonds have ideal properties for gemstones.
A well-cut diamond reflects light better than
any other gem (it has 'brilliance').
It also disperses white light into
the colours of the spectrum (it has 'fire').

A diamond brooch

Cutting tools

Diamond is the hardest of all substances.
It is used on the edges of drills for oil wells.
(Look back to the photo on page 248.)
It also lines circular saws used to cut metal,
stone and other hard materials.

A new process can now fuse together tiny
diamonds. So instead of metal coated in diamonds,
you can now use a solid diamond tool on a lathe.
This can cut and shape the hardest materials.

Diamond coated surgical instruments are used
for delicate operations, like those on the eye.

An engraver using a diamond-tipped 'pen' to produce a design on glass

Another use

Which types of materials are the best conductors of heat?
Most people would say that metals are.
However, diamond is a better thermal conductor!
On the other hand, it is a poor electrical conductor.
This leads to its use in electronics to get rid
of heat produced in circuits.

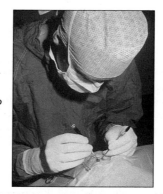

This surgeon is operating on an eye using diamond coated instruments

Uses of graphite

Pencils

We have already talked about graphite's use in pencils
on page 249. It is mixed with clay to make it harder.
You know that there are different grades of pencil,
such as H, HB, or 2B. Do you know which makes
the darkest lines on paper? How do you think the
amount of clay varies in each type of pencil?
Which type do you think needs sharpening most often?

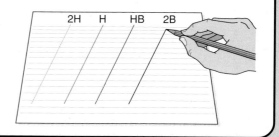

▷ Chemistry at work : Carbon

Lubricant

Graphite feels very slippery. It can be used as a powder
to lubricate metal parts on machinery.
When would you need to use solid graphite rather than oil?
Remember that graphite only turns to a gas at over 3000 °C!

In some lubricants, graphite is added to oil to
improve its properties.

*The layers of carbon
atoms slide over
each other easily,
making graphite a
good lubricant*

Graphite into diamond!

The diamonds used in cutting and grinding tools
are called **industrial diamonds**.
They are not mined from the ground, like gemstone diamonds.
They are made in factories from graphite.

Graphite is squeezed in a press and heated.
A metal is used as a solvent and a catalyst.
The temperature is about 1400 °C in the press,
and the pressure is 60 000 times normal air pressure!
The diamonds are made in a few minutes.
Under these conditions, anything containing carbon,
even wood, changes into diamonds!
The diamonds made are small and unattractive.
Manufacturers can vary the sizes to suit the use
by changing conditions.

*Industrial diamonds are small and
unattractive. However, scientists in the
USA have developed a new technique.
They recently made a diamond over
25 cm long!*

Bucky-balls

In 1985, a new form of carbon was discovered.
Its molecules are made from 60 carbon atoms
joined together. The atoms fold around and
make a ball-shaped molecule.

Look at the photo opposite:
The new molecule looks just like a football!
The carbon atoms form pentagons and hexagons,
like the panels on a football.

Its full name is buckminster-fullerene.
Scientists named it after an architect, Buckminster Fuller.
In 1967, he designed a bucky-ball shaped building
in Montreal.
The new molecule has excited a lot of interest. Others
have been discovered. One is shaped like a rugby ball
and others are shaped like tubes.
Scientists are now investigating their properties and
suggesting uses for them in the future.

▷ Simple molecular structures

You already know that covalent bonds are strong.
So have you ever wondered why lots of substances
with covalent bonds are easy to melt or boil?

Let's take methane, CH_4, as an example:
It has a very low boiling point.
It boils at $-161°C$!
(Compare this with the values given for the
giant covalent structures in the table opposite.)

By the time you get to room temperature
(about 20 °C), methane is already a gas.
And yet it has strong covalent bonds holding
its atoms together, just like diamond.
So why is it so easy to boil methane?

To answer this question, you must realise that
no covalent bonds are broken when methane boils.
When it boils, single CH_4 molecules move apart.
They separate from each other but they are still CH_4 molecules.

Compare this with the giant covalent structures of diamond,
silicon or sand. To boil these, we have to break apart
the whole giant structure. Millions of covalent bonds
do have to break in these examples.

> Substances, with **low** melting points and boiling points
> have **simple molecular structures.**

They have strong covalent bonds joining their atoms
within each molecule. However, they only have weak
forces between individual molecules.
We say that they have **weak inter-molecular bonds**.

*With 2 non-metals, each atom wants more
Both need electrons to make up the score.
A deal is struck, "Our electrons we'll share."
Covalent bonds formed by electron pairs.*

Giant Covalent Structure		Simple Molecular Structure	
Substance	**Boiling pt. (°C)**	**Substance**	**Boiling pt. (°C)**
diamond	4830	methane	−161
silicon	2355	water	100
sand (silica)	2230	chlorine	−35

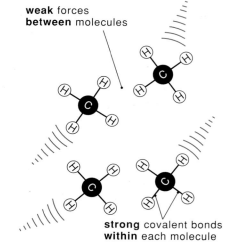

weak forces
between molecules

strong covalent bonds
within each molecule

Methane has a simple molecular structure

Experiment 20.1 Heating iodine

Use tweezers to put a few iodine crystals in a flask. Replace the bung.
Hold the base in your hands for a few minutes, as shown:
Look carefully through the flask, against a white background.

⚠ iodine

- What can you see?
- Do you think it is easy or hard to separate iodine molecules
  from each other? Do you think it has a giant structure?
- Iodine turns straight from a solid into a gas.
  What is this type of change called? (See the bottom of page 249.)

Iodine, I_2, has a simple molecular structure. Weak forces hold
its molecules in place in its crystals.

Experiment 20.2   Heating sulphur

Collect 2 spatulas of powdered sulphur in a test-tube.
Warm it slowly and gently over a Bunsen flame
in a fume-cupboard.
● What happens? Describe the changes you see as it melts.

⚠ sulphur dioxide gas
can be formed

When it has melted, heat the sulphur more strongly.
Keep the flame away from the mouth of the test-tube.
It could ignite any sulphur vapour escaping.
● How does the sulphur change?

When the liquid is about to boil, remove the mineral wool plug.
Pour it quickly into a beaker of cold water.
● What happens?

Get the solid formed out of the beaker.
Pull at it gently.
● What happens? Is the solid stretchy?

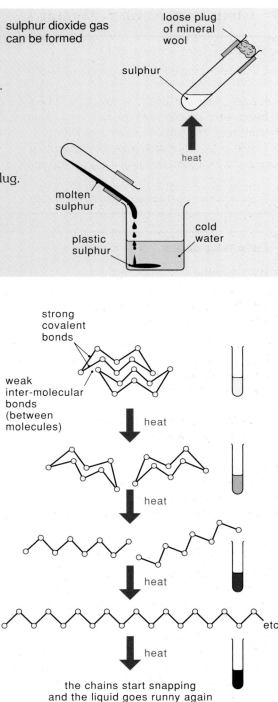

loose plug
of mineral
wool

sulphur

heat

molten
sulphur

plastic
sulphur

cold
water

1. Sulphur exists as S_8 molecules at room temperature.
   These crown-shaped molecules are packed neatly
   together to form crystals.

   strong
   covalent
   bonds

   weak
   inter-molecular
   bonds
   (between
   molecules)

2. It melts at 115 °C. This low melting point tells us
   that sulphur has a simple molecular structure.
   There are relatively weak forces **between** its molecules.

   heat

3. As the molten sulphur is heated more strongly,
   the rings of 8 sulphur atoms open up.
   They then join together to make long chains.

   heat

4. Near its boiling point the long chains start to
   break up. They escape from the liquid as a gas.

   etc

   heat

5. If you pour the molten sulphur into cold water,
   plastic sulphur is made. The sulphur does not
   have time to change back into its S_8 molecules.
   It is 'frozen' in a long chain structure, like rubber.
   Eventually the plastic sulphur goes hard.
   It changes back slowly into S_8 molecules again.

   the chains start snapping
   and the liquid goes runny again

   cold water

   plastic sulphur

▷ Chemistry at work : Water

The formula of water is **H₂O**.
The hydrogen and oxygen atoms are joined
by *covalent* bonds.

It has a simple molecular structure. The forces
between its molecules are not very strong.
(Although the forces are stronger than you
would expect for such a small molecule.)

Water freezes at 0 °C and boils at 100 °C.
Fortunately for us, this means that water
is a liquid at most temperatures on Earth.

I'm a molecule of
H₂O. Can you draw
my electrons to
show my covalent
bonds?

O has 8 electrons
H has 1 electron

Drinking water

Over two-thirds of your body is
made up of water.
The reactions that keep us alive
happen in solution.
So we need to drink plenty of
water each day.
Although over 70 % of the Earth's
surface is covered by water, only
about 1 % is fresh water.
Fresh water is treated to make it
safe to drink.
Look at the diagram :

*Over two-thirds of the
mass of your body
is made up of water !*

reservoir

clear water
tank

filtration

sedimentation
tank

storage reservoir

Addition of chlorine
to kill bacteria

mains
supply

Treating waste water

Have you ever wondered
what happens to all the water
that goes down our drains ?
First of all, it goes into
pipes called sewers.
Then it has to be treated
before it can be put back
into rivers.
Look at the diagram :

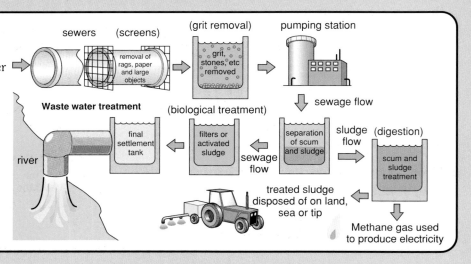

sewers   (screens)   (grit removal)   pumping station

removal of
rags, paper
and large
objects

grit,
stones, etc
removed

sewage flow

Waste water treatment   (biological treatment)

final
settlement
tank

filters or
activated
sludge

separation
of scum
and sludge

sludge
flow   (digestion)

river

sewage
flow

scum and
sludge
treatment

treated sludge
disposed of on land,
sea or tip

Methane gas used
to produce electricity

254

Summary

Non-metal atoms are bonded to each other by **covalent bonds**.
A covalent bond is a shared pair of electrons.
Covalent substances can have either:
- a **giant covalent structure**, or
- a **simple molecular structure**.

Giant covalent structures are huge 3-dimensional networks of atoms.
Millions of atoms are all joined by strong covalent bonds.
This means that they have high melting points and boiling points.
Simple molecular substances are made of small molecules.
The atoms in each molecule are joined together by
strong covalent bonds. However, there are only *weak* forces
of attraction *between* molecules.
Neither structure conducts electricity (except for graphite).

▷ **Questions**

1. Copy and complete:
   Non-metal atoms bond to each other by . . . .
   electrons. These are called . . . . bonds.
   Covalently bonded substances with high . . . .
   points and high boiling points, have . . . .
   structures.

   On the other hand, substances with low melting
   points and low boiling points have . . . . molecular
   structures. These have strong covalent bonds
   within each . . . . , but weak forces . . . . molecules.

   No covalently bonded substances conduct
   electricity, except . . . . .

2. Look at the table below:
   Substances A, B, C and D all have covalent
   bonds.

Substance	Melting point (°C)	Boiling point (°C)
A	−125	−90
B	5	170
C	2200	3900
D	55	325

   a) Which substance has a giant covalent
      structure?
   b) Which type of structure do the other
      substances have?
   c) Which substance is a gas at room
      temperature (about 20 °C)?
   d) Which substance is a liquid at room
      temperature?

3. Fluorine forms di-atomic molecules, F_2.
   (Fluorine atoms have 9 electrons.)
   Draw a diagram to show the bonding in an F_2
   molecule.

4. Water is a covalent molecule. Its formula is
   H_2O.
   (Hydrogen atoms have 1 electron.)
   (Oxygen atoms have 8 electrons.)
   a) Draw a diagram to show the bonding in an
      H_2O molecule.
   b) How can you tell that water has a simple
      molecular structure?

5. Carbon exists as diamond and graphite.
   a) What do we call different forms of the same
      element?
   b) Diamond and graphite have very different
      properties and uses.
   Use their structures to explain these
   differences.

6. Alan heated some sulphur in a test-tube inside a
   fume-cupboard. He heated it until it was almost
   boiling.
   a) Describe the changes Alan would *see* in the
      test-tube.
   b) Explain these changes.
   c) Why did he do his experiment in a fume-
      cupboard?

Further questions on page 266.

chapter 21

Metals and structures

▷ Metals

Think of some of the things around your home
that are made of metal.
Did you include all the wiring, any radiators,
your hot-water tank, or your cutlery and pans?
Do you know which metals these things are made from?
Which properties make metals good for these uses?

In the last two chapters we have looked at
ionic and covalent bonding. But the atoms in a metal
are held together in a different way.

▷ Metallic bonding

Do you remember all the properties of metals? (see page 45.)
Any ideas we have about the bonding and structure
of metals must be able to explain their properties.
In general, metals:

- have high melting and boiling points
- conduct electricity and heat
- are hard and dense
- can be hammered into shapes (they are malleable)
- can be drawn out into wires (they are ductile).

We believe that metal atoms (or ions)
are held together by a **'sea' of electrons**.
Look at the diagram below:

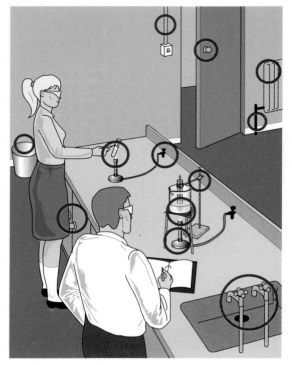

Metals are very useful materials

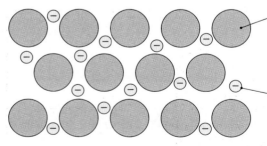

metal atoms (some
people describe them
as positive ions
because they donate
electrons into the 'sea'
of electrons)

'sea' of electrons
holds the metal
atoms together

Each metal atom gives up one or more of its electrons
into the 'sea' or 'cloud' of electrons.
The electrons can drift about in the metal.
These free electrons explain how electricity
can pass through solid metals.
What happens when one end of the metal is made positive
and the other end negative?

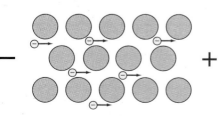

*Electrons move towards the positive charge.
These free electrons can also transfer heat
through metals quickly.*

▷ Structure of metals

As you know, most metals are dense.
This suggests that their atoms must be
packed closely together.
They also have high melting points.
This suggests that their atoms are arranged in
giant structures.

In metal structures, the gaps are few,
A 'sea' of electrons acts as a glue !
Lining up, row upon row,
On top of each other, the atoms do go.

Experiment 21.1   Close-packed structures

Arrange 4 pieces of wood in a square. You could use
4 books with a square hole between them.
The size of the square depends upon the size and
number of model metal atoms you can use.
Your model atoms must all be the same size,
just like a metal element.
(You can use marbles, table-tennis balls,
polystyrene spheres, etc.)

Fill the bottom of the square with model atoms.
Make sure that there are no gaps.
Now sit the second layer on top. Again, there
should be no gaps.

Now make a third layer. The atoms can sit in two possible positions,
1) directly above the centres of the atoms in the first row, or
2) with their centres not in line with the first row.

Try to make both structures.

Both of these giant, close-packed structures are shown below :

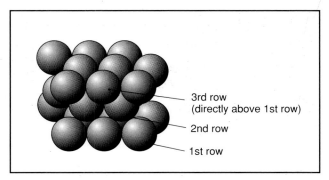

4th row
(directly above 1st row)

3rd row

2nd row

1st row

3rd row
(directly above 1st row)

2nd row

1st row

For example, gold or copper

For example, zinc or nickel

Do these explain why metals with these structures
are dense and have high melting points ?
Do you know any metals which don't have these properties ?
(See page 45.)

▷ Alloys

Have you ever travelled in an aeroplane?
Did you know that the aeroplane was made mainly
from aluminium?
Why do you think aluminium is chosen for this job?

Notice that aeroplanes are made **mainly** from aluminium.
If they were made from pure aluminium,
their wings would soon snap off!
Pure aluminium is not strong enough to cope with
the great stress put on wings during flight.

So how can we combine the low density of aluminium
with the strength an aeroplane needs?
Alloys give us the answer.

Aeroplanes are made from an aluminium alloy

An alloy is a mixture of metals.

If small amounts of another metal are added to aluminium,
it becomes a lot stronger.
The metals are mixed together when they are molten.
(Notice that metals never **react** with each other.
They form a mixture, not a new compound.)

You can see how alloying affects the structure
of a metal in the next experiment:

Experiment 21.2   Bubble bath!
Using the apparatus shown, make rows of
small bubbles in the dish. The plunger should be
pushed in slowly and steadily. This will make
sure that the bubbles are the same size.

The bubbles represent the atoms in a metal.
Remember their close-packed structures?
Fill the dish with bubbles.

- Do the bubbles line up in rows?
- What happens when a bubble bursts? Can you see
  how easily the rows of bubbles slide past each other?

Now inject a larger bubble into the middle of the dish.
This is like adding an atom of a different metal.
In other words, you have made an alloy!

- Can you see how this disturbs the regular pattern of bubbles?

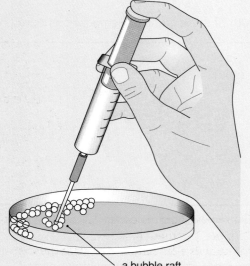

a bubble raft
(a petri dish containing a solution of
washing-up liquid)

Explaining the properties of alloys

Your observations from the last experiment will help you to understand alloys.

Look at the diagram below:

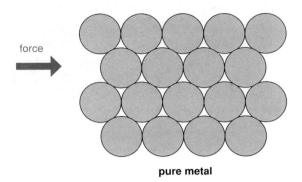

force

pure metal

layers slide over each other easily in a pure metal

In a pure metal, the atoms are all the same size.
Layers can slide over each other easily.
This happens when metals are hit with a hammer.
What do we call this property?
It also happens when a metal is stretched.
What do we call this property?

However, look what happens when we add some atoms of a different size:

*How do you think this copper blade was made?
Why didn't it smash?*

force

a different sized atom disrupts the regular pattern

the atoms can't slip past each other as easily in an alloy

alloy

The layers of atoms can't slide over each other as easily now.
They get 'jammed' in place.
The alloy is a lot harder and stronger than the original metal.

You can read about some uses of alloys on the next two pages.

▷ Chemistry at work : Alloys

You know that alloys are mixtures of metals.
The blend of metals has different properties to the original metals. We saw how alloying aluminium greatly increases its strength so it can be used to make aeroplanes. The alloy is called duralumin.
It has about 4 % copper and a little magnesium added to the aluminium.

We have also looked at the uses
of our most important alloy, steel, on page 92.
Some other useful alloys are described below.

Concorde is made from a special titanium alloy.

Coins

Are you carrying any coins today ? Have you any copper or, better still, silver coins ?
If you have some 'loose change', your coins will contain copper, but certainly not silver.
Silver would make the coins too expensive to make !

The table opposite shows you the mixture of metals used in each coin :

Why do you think these alloys are chosen ?
Coins must not corrode or wear down easily.
They must also be malleable enough to be stamped with complex patterns.

Coin	Metals in alloy
1p, 2p	copper (97 %), zinc (2.5 %), tin (0.5 %)
5p, 10p, 50p	copper (75 %), nickel (25 %)
20p	copper (84 %), nickel (16 %)
£1	copper (70 %), zinc (24.5 %), nickel (5.5 %)

Artificial joints

The joints in our bodies take a lot of wear and tear.
The 'ball-and-socket' type joints in the hip and shoulder have to work especially hard. Sometimes the joints are attacked by arthritis. This is a very painful and crippling disease.

Look at the photo opposite :
Now people can be fitted with replacement joints.
These are made of plastic and alloys.
What properties must an alloy used inside your body have ?

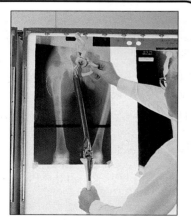

This hip joint is made from an alloy of titanium

▷ Chemistry at work : Alloys

Jewellery

Pure gold, as well as being very expensive, is a soft metal.
Just think of the wear and tear on a gold wedding ring. The metal is made more hard-wearing by alloying it with copper.

Have you got anything made from gold?
If you have, do you know what 'carat' gold it is?
This tells you how much copper is added to the gold.
The higher the carat, the less copper.
24-carat gold is pure gold. On the other hand, 9-carat gold is about two-thirds copper and one-third gold.

Brass

Have you ever heard a brass band or a pop group with a brass section?
Brass is a mixture of copper and zinc.
Musical instruments made of brass make a pleasing, sonorous sound.
It can also be stamped or pressed into the intricate shapes of the instruments.

Brass has other useful properties as well.
It is much stronger than copper or zinc.

Brass has a lower melting point than either metal. This makes it easier to cast into shapes.

Solder

Have you ever used a soldering iron?
Solder is used to join up parts of electrical circuits.

This alloy is made from lead and tin.
It has a low melting point for a metal.
Why is this important?
The solder is made into thick wire. It melts when held against a hot soldering iron.

Other alloys melt at even lower temperatures (about 70 °C).
These are used in automatic fire sprinklers.

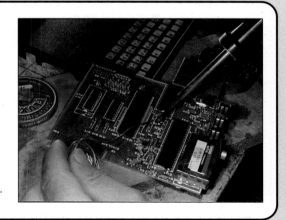

261

Summary

Metal atoms are bonded together by a 'sea' of electrons.
The electrons are free to drift between the atoms.
They move in one direction when an electric current flows.
Metal atoms are arranged in **giant structures**.
This explains why most metals have high melting points.
The atoms are usually *packed closely* together
in these giant structures.
This is why most metals have a high density.

Mixtures of metals are called **alloys**.
An alloy is stronger than the metals used to make it.

Metal atoms are usually 'close-packed'

Summary of structure and bonding

In this section, we have now seen how atoms bond together.
We have also looked at how the atoms, ions or molecules are arranged
in structures.
The bonding and structure of a substance explain its properties.

Here is a summary of the last 3 chapters so that you can compare
the different types of structure and bonding:

Bonding	ionic (between metals and non-metals)	covalent (between non-metals)		metallic (between metals)
Structures	giant ionic	giant covalent	simple molecular	giant metallic
Melting point	high	high	low	high
Conduct electricity ?	not when solid, but they do when molten or dissolved in water (when ions are free)	no	no	yes (has free electrons)
Example	sodium chloride	diamond	water	zinc

▷ Questions

1. Copy and complete:
A '....' or 'cloud' of electrons join metal atoms together in .... structures. Metals can .... electricity because these .... are free to drift through the structure.
Most metals have .... melting points because it takes a lot of energy to break down their .... structures.
Most metals are .... because there is not much space between their '....-packed' atoms.

2. Copy and complete:
There are 3 types of bonding – ionic, ... and .....

.... bonds form between metals and non-metals. The ions are arranged in .... structures, which have high melting points. Sodium chloride is an example. It does not conduct electricity when ...., as its ions are fixed in position. However, when molten or .... in water, the .... become free to move. It is electrolysed as it conducts.

Covalent bonds form between non-.... atoms. These substances can have either a .... structure, like diamond (with a .... melting point), or be made up of simple ...., like water (with a .... melting point). Neither type of structure conducts electricity. The only exception is .....

Substances with giant .... structures are the only ones that conduct electricity when solid.

3. a) Make a list of the general properties of metals.
   b) Write down any metals you know that don't have the usual metallic properties. You can find some help on page 45.
   c) Which property do *all* metals have in common?

4. a) Describe how you can show the structure of a metal using a set of plastic balls.
   b) How can you arrange the balls to show 2 different structures?

5. Anne has been given samples of aluminium, copper and an alloy of the two metals. She has rods, wires and blocks of the 3 metals.
   a) How would you make an alloy of aluminium and copper?
   b) Design a series of tests so that Anne can find out which of the 3 metals:
      i) is hardest
      ii) is most difficult to snap (has the greatest tensile strength)
      iii) resists corrosion best.
   Say how you made each one a *fair test*.
   c) What results would you expect for the hardness and tensile strength tests? Explain why.

6. Look at this table:

Substance	Melting point (°C)	Conducts electricity	
		when solid	when molten
A	1500	✓	✓
B	115	✗	✗
C	−0.5	✗	✗
D	660	✗	✓

Explain your answers to each question below:
   a) Which substance is made up of ions arranged in a giant structure?
   b) Which is a metal?
   c) Which substances are made up of relatively small individual molecules?
   d) Which is a non-metal *solid* with a simple molecular structure?
   e) Which substance is broken down as it conducts electricity?

7. Sodium, magnesium and aluminium are in Groups 1,2 and 3 of the Periodic Table. Sodium has 11 electrons, magnesium has 12 and aluminium has 13 electrons.
   a) Draw each atom showing the arrangement of electrons.
   b) The metal elements have metallic bonding. How many electrons do you think the atoms of each metal in a) donate into the 'sea' of electrons?
   c) Aluminium is the best conductor of electricity. Sodium is the worst. Can you explain this?

Further questions on page 269.

▷ Ionic compounds

1. Look at this information about sodium and chlorine :

$^{23}_{11}$Na sodium $^{35}_{17}$Cl chlorine

a) i) How many protons does an atom of sodium have ? [1]
ii) How many electrons does an atom of chlorine have ? [1]
iii) As well as electrons and protons, most atoms contain a third kind of particle. What is its name ? [1]

b) When sodium forms compounds it usually does so as a positive ion with one unit of charge.
i) What change in electron structure occurs when a sodium atom becomes a sodium ion ? [1]
ii) What change, if any, occurs in the nucleus when the ion is formed ? [1]

c) When chlorine forms an ionic compound it gains one electron. What symbol is used to represent the chloride ion formed in this way ? [1]

d) Explain why the formula for the compound formed when sodium and chlorine react is NaCl and **not** $NaCl_2$. [2]

e) What does the information given below tell you about the **structure** of each substance ?
Chlorine melts at $-101°C$.
Sodium chloride melts at $801°C$. [4]
(SEG)

2. When lithium reacts with fluorine, lithium fluoride, LiF, is formed. It is made up of positive and negative ions.
a) How are the positive lithium ions formed from lithium atoms ? [1]
b) How are the negative fluoride ions formed from fluorine atoms ? [1]
c) **Explain** how the ions are held together in lithium fluoride. [1]
d) Name this type of bonding. [1]
e) Explain why the bonding in lithium fluoride, LiF, produces a high melting point solid. [2]
(WJEC)

3. Atoms can form ions with a single negative charge. To do this the atom must
A   gain a proton
B   gain an electron
C   lose a proton
D   lose an electron [1]   (SEG)

4. The elements of Group 1 form ions with a single positive charge eg Na^+. The elements from Group 2 form ions with a double positive charge eg Ca^{2+}. Explain this in terms of their electronic structure. [2]   (MEG)

5. Use the Periodic Table on page 344 to help you answer this question.
a) An atom of the element with atomic number 9 has a mass number 19.
i) State the number of neutrons and protons in the nucleus of the atom.
ii) State the number of electrons in an atom of the element.
iii) Describe, with the aid of diagrams, the formation of ions in the reaction of the element with sodium.
iv) Give the chemical name of the compound formed when the element reacts with sodium. [7]
b) Explain why solid sodium chloride does not conduct electricity, but aqueous sodium chloride does. [3]   (ULEAC)

6. The diagrams below show the electronic structure of an atom of calcium and an atom of oxygen.

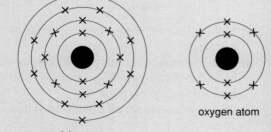

calcium atom   oxygen atom

a) Describe, as fully as you can, the ions that are formed when atoms of these elements react. [2]
b) Calcium oxide is an insoluble ionic compound. Why do ionic compounds have high melting points ? [2]

c) What must be done to the solid calcium oxide to make it conduct electricity? Suggest a reason for your answer. [2]
(NEAB)

7. The Periodic Table on page 344 may help you answer parts a), i) and ii) of this question. The diagram below shows the structure of sodium chloride.

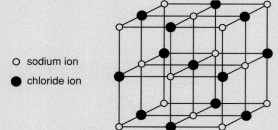

○ sodium ion
● chloride ion

a) i) How does the structure of a sodium ion differ from the structure of a sodium atom? [1]

ii) How does the structure of a chloride ion differ from the structure of a chlorine atom? [1]

iii) What type of chemical bond is present in sodium chloride? [1]

b) Use the diagram of sodium chloride to help you to explain why:

i) sodium chloride crystals can be cube shaped; [1]

ii) solid sodium chloride has a high melting point; [2]

iii) solid sodium chloride is an electrical insulator; [2]

iv) molten sodium chloride will undergo electrolysis. [2] (SEG)

8. Using the list of ions on page 343 write the formula of:
a) iron(II) sulphate;
b) iron(III) oxide. [2] (WJEC)

9. Sodium (Na) and chlorine (Cl_2) react together to form sodium chloride (NaCl).
a) Write a symbol equation for this reaction. [1]
b) Sodium chloride contains sodium ions (Na^+). Write an equation to show the formation of a sodium ion from a sodium atom.
Use the symbol e^- to represent an electron. [1] (MEG)

10. Magnesium oxide is a compound made up of magnesium ions and oxide ions.

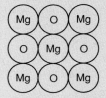

a) What is the charge on each magnesium ion? [1]
b) Explain how the magnesium ions get this charge. [2] (NEAB)

11. The element magnesium (atomic number 12) reacts with chlorine (atomic number 17) to form the compound magnesium chloride, $MgCl_2$.
a) Give the meaning of each of the following words
i) element   ii) compound [2]
b) The diagrams below show the electron shells in a magnesium atom and in a chlorine atom.
Copy and complete the diagrams to show the arrangement of electrons.

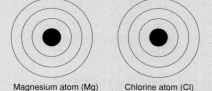

Magnesium atom (Mg)   Chlorine atom (Cl) [2]

c) What happens to these electron arrangements when magnesium reacts with chlorine to form magnesium chloride, $MgCl_2$? [4]
d) The compound magnesium chloride has **ionic bonding**. Explain what this means. [2] (SEG)

12. The table shows the properties of two substances.

Substance	Does it dissolve in water	Melting point °C	Does it smell	What colour is it?	Does it conduct electricity when …	
					solid?	melted?
A	yes	1000	no	white	no	yes
B	no	125	yes	yellow	no	no

a) Which of these substances has a giant ionic structure? [1]
b) Give **two** reasons for your choice? [2]
(NEAB)

Further questions on Structure and Bonding

13. The diagrams below show the arrangements of electrons in the *inner* energy levels (shells) of potassium and chlorine atoms.

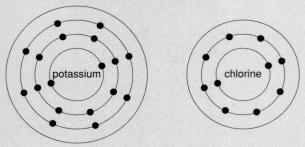

a) Use the Periodic Table on page 344 to help you answer this part of the question.
Copy and complete both the diagrams by adding the correct number of electrons in the outer energy level of each atom. [2]

b) Describe what happens when potassium atoms and chlorine atoms react to form potassium ions and chloride ions. [2]

c) Use the table on page 343 to help you answer this part of the question.
   i) Write the symbols for the ions of potassium, magnesium and chloride. [2]
   ii) Use your answers to write the formulas of potassium chloride and magnesium chloride. [2] (NEAB)

14. The diagram represents the arrangement of electrons in a magnesium atom.

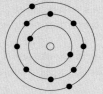

a) Copy and complete the table. [2]

	number of			electron arrangement
	protons	neutrons	electrons	
magnesium-24				2,8,2
oxygen-16		8	8	

b) Magnesium oxide contains ionic bonding. Explain fully, in terms of transfer of electrons and the formation of ions, the changes which occur when magnesium oxide is formed from magnesium and oxygen atoms [4] (MEG)

▷ Covalent bonding

15. Use the Periodic Table on page 344 to help you answer this question.
Explain, with the aid of diagrams, how covalent bonds are formed between carbon and hydrogen in methane, CH_4.
Indicate which noble gas electron configuration is achieved by the atoms. [3] (ULEAC)

16. Chlorine will combine with the non-metal element, carbon, to form this molecular compound.

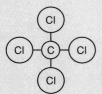

a) What is the type of bond in this molecule? [1]
b) Explain how these bonds are formed. (You may use a diagram.) [2] (NEAB)

17. Which of the substances A, B, C or D consists of small molecules?

Substance	Melting Point	Electrical conductivity of solid	Electrical conductivity of solution in water
A	high	nil	good
B	high	good	insoluble
C	low	good	insoluble
D	low	nil	nil

[1] (SEG)

18. The diagram represents an atom of fluorine. Only the outer electrons are shown.

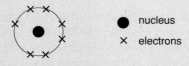

● nucleus
× electrons

The atoms in a fluorine molecule, F_2, are covalently bonded.
Draw a diagram to show the arrangement of electrons in a fluorine molecule. [2] (MEG)

19. One oxygen atom will bond to two hydrogen atoms to form a water molecule, H_2O. One nitrogen atom will bond to three hydrogen atoms to form ammonia, NH_3. Explain, with the help of diagrams showing the arrangement of electrons, why oxygen and nitrogen bond to different numbers of hydrogen atoms. [4] (MEG)

20. Hydrogen reacts with chlorine according to the equation:
$$H_2(g) + Cl_2(g) \longrightarrow 2HCl(g)$$
a) Name the type of bond present in hydrogen chloride. [1]
b) How is this type of bond formed? [1]
c) State **two** physical properties of hydrogen chloride which result from this type of bonding. [2]
d) Draw a diagram of the bonding in hydrogen chloride showing how all the electrons in each atom are arranged. [3]
(ULEAC)

21. a) Draw a dot and cross diagram to show the electronic structure of a molecule of chlorine(I) oxide, Cl_2O. Show only the electrons in the outermost shell (highest energy level), and use DOT for electrons from the oxygen atom and CROSS for electrons from the chlorine atoms. [2]
b) Explain, in terms of the forces present, why chlorine(I) oxide has a low melting point. [2]
(ULEAC)

22. The hydrogen halides (hydrogen fluoride, hydrogen chloride, hydrogen bromide and hydrogen iodide) are important chemicals. The diagram below represents a molecule of hydrogen chloride.

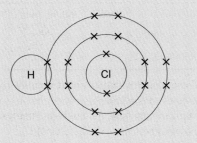

a) What type of particles are represented by the crosses (X)? [1]
b) What type of chemical bond holds the atoms in this molecule together? [1]
c) Would you expect hydrogen chloride to be a gas, a liquid or a solid, at room temperature and pressure? Explain your answer. [3]
(NEAB)

23. a) Silicon and carbon are both in Group 4 of the Periodic Table. They form the oxides, silicon dioxide (SiO_2) and carbon dioxide (CO_2). The properties of these two oxides are shown in the table below:

Property	Carbon dioxide	Silicon dioxide
Melting point	sublimes at $-78°C$	1610°C
Boiling point	sublimes at $-78°C$	2230°C
Electrical conductivity	poor	poor

Give the structures and bonding of carbon dioxide and silicon dioxide. Explain your answers. [4]
b) Draw a diagram to show the arrangement of outer electrons in a molecule of silicon chloride. (Atomic numbers: silicon = 14, chlorine = 17.) [4] (ULEAC)

24. Explain, as fully as you can, why a water molecule contains two hydrogen atoms but a hydrogen chloride molecule contains only one.

H—O—H   H—Cl

(You may use a diagram in your answer if you wish.) [3] (NEAB)

25. Fluorine forms a **gaseous** compound with oxygen, with the formula F_2O.
a) Explain how these two elements bond to form F_2O and name the type of bonding used. [3]
b) **Explain** why the oxide of fluorine, F_2O, is a gas. [2] (WJEC)

Further questions on Structure and Bonding

26. Pentane (C_5H_{12}) occurs in petrol (gasoline), and has the structure represented by the diagram:

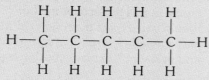

a) Which is the **most** volatile, heptane (C_7H_{16}), hexane (C_6H_{14}), or pentane? [1]

b) Name the type of bonding that occurs in pentane. [1]

c) Describe, in terms of electrons, how a hydrogen atom is joined to a carbon atom in **one** of the bonds in pentane. [2]

(WJEC)

27. Name these allotropes of the element carbon.

a)

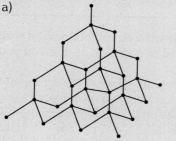

 b)

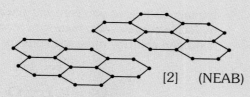

[2] (NEAB)

28. Both diamond and graphite

A are electrical conductors

B are lubricants

C form the same products when burnt

D have the same hardness [1] (SEG)

29. You can use graphite to lubricate machines because its structure

A allows it to melt at low temperatures

B consists of layers that slide over one another

C consists of small, round atoms loosely bonded to each other

D contains atoms that are strongly bonded to four other carbon atoms [1] (SEG)

30. Carbon can exist in two forms, graphite and diamond. Explain why graphite can conduct electricity but diamond cannot. [2]

(ULEAC)

31. Graphite is mixed with clay to make pencil leads.

a) i) Name the element of which graphite is one form. [1]

ii) Name one other crystalline form of this element. [1]

b) Sketch a diagram to show the arrangement of atoms in graphite. [2]

c) Suggest why this crystal structure of graphite enables it to leave a mark when a pencil is drawn across a sheet of paper. [1]

(ULEAC)

32. Ethanol (C_2H_5OH) is an addictive drug usually called alcohol.

Ethanol contains a single oxygen atom joined to a hydrogen atom by the same bonding as in water. A molecule of ethanol is shown below.

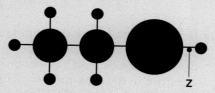

a) Copy the diagram of ethanol and draw an arrow labelled '**Y**' to show the oxygen atom. [1]

b) What type of chemical bond is shown at **Z**? [1]

c) Is ethanol an element or a compound? Give a reason for your answer. [1] (SEG)

33. The table below shows data on carbon, silicon and silicon carbide (a compound of silicon and carbon).

Substance	Group	Melting point (°C)	Hardness
carbon (diamond)	4	3550	very hard
silicon	4	1410	hard
silicon carbide	—	2700	very hard

a) Use the information in the table to help you suggest a suitable use for silicon carbide. [1]

b) Explain why silicon carbide has a very high melting point. [2] (ULEAC)

▶ Metals and Structures

34. Read the following account, taken from the *Express & Star*, and answer the questions which follow.

Warning on fake gold

Trading standards chiefs in Wolverhampton today warned Christmas shoppers to beware of fake gold chains and jewellery.

They advised people to avoid unlicenced street traders selling from suitcases who have been operating in the town centre.

Police officers caught "traders" selling jewellery described as 18 carat gold.

The fake gold was a mixture of nickel, copper and zinc with no trace of gold.

---

a) What is the name given to a mixture of metals? [1]

b) Use pages 342 and 343 to help you to complete the table. [3]

Name	Atomic number	Symbol	Density (g/cm³)	Melting point (°C)
nickel	28	Ni	8.9	1450
copper	29	Cu	i)	1084
zinc	30	Zn	7.1	ii)
gold	iii)	Au	19.3	1064

c) State why the fake gold chain would feel 'lighter' than a similar one made of real gold. [1]

d) i) Describe an experiment to show that fake gold conducts electricity. State what apparatus you would need, what you would do and what you would see. [3]

   ii) Why do metals conduct electricity? [2]

e) Explain why the experiment described in part d) would
   i) prove that the chain was **not** made of plastic. [1]
   ii) **not** prove that the chain was made of gold. [1] (NEAB)

35. Copper metal is used for making electric wire, coins, pipes and saucepans.
For each of the above uses give a **different** reason why copper is chosen. The first is done for you.

Use of copper	Reason for choosing copper
Electric wires	Good conductor of electricity
Coins	a)
Pipes	b)
Saucepans	c)

[3] (NI)

36. a) Describe the structure and bonding in metals. [3]

   b) Explain why metals such as nickel and platinum are good conductors of electricity. [2] (NEAB)

37. The table gives some data about metals and metal alloys. Use the data throughout this question.

metal or alloy	density g per cm³	melting point/°C	electrical resistivity/Ωm	tensile strength/MPa
aluminium	2.7	934	2.6	80
iron	7.8	1810	10	300
steel	7.8	1700	15	460
aluminium alloy	2.8	800	5	600
titanium	4.5	1950	53	620

a) The diagram shows the arrangement of particles in a layer in aluminium.

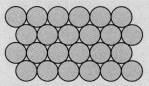

Draw a diagram to show a possible arrangement of particles in an aluminium alloy. [2]

b) i) The low electrical resistivity of aluminium means that aluminium is a very good electrical conductor. Explain how the structure of aluminium enables it to conduct electricity. [2]

   ii) Discuss the properties that should be considered by an engineer when choosing a material for overhead power cables. [5] (MEG)

Further questions on Structure and Bonding

38. a) The table gives some information about three materials.

Material	Reaction with oxygen	Reaction with acidic solution	Cost (£ per tonne)	Melting point (°C)	Density (g/cm³)	Tensile Strength (MN/m)
Carbon steel	forms porous oxide layer on surface, flakes off	dissolves slowly	500	1539	7.86	250–400
Stainless steel	non-porous layer of chromium oxide on surface, re-forms if scratched	does not dissolve	2000	1440	7.8–8.0	500–1000
Aluminium	non-porous layer of aluminium oxide, re-forms if scratched	dissolves very slowly	1300	659	2.70	140–400

Discuss the relative merits of using carbon steel, stainless steel and aluminium for making
 i) car bodies and
 ii) exhaust pipes. [6]

b) An alloy can be made from two metals. In very many cases the atoms of the two metals differ in size. In these cases the alloy is harder than the pure metals it contains. Explain why this is so. [3] (ULEAC)

39. a) By reference to their structure, explain how the particles in a piece of metal are held together and how the shape of the metal can be changed without it breaking. (You may use a diagram in your answer.) [5]

b) Explain why metals are good conductors of electricity and suggest why this conductivity increases across the Periodic Table from sodium to magnesium to aluminium. [4] (NEAB)

40. The following table shows the properties of five substances.

Substance	Melting point (°C)	Boiling point (°C)	Electrical conductivity when		Effect of heating in air
			solid	liquid	
A	800	1470	poor	good	no reaction
B	650	1110	good	good	burns to form a white solid
C	19	287	poor	poor	burns to form carbon dioxide and water
D	114	444	poor	poor	burns to form an acidic gas only
E	1700	2200	poor	poor	no reaction

Each substance can be used once, more than once or not at all to answer the following. Choose from **A** to **E** a substance which is:
a) a metal: [1]
b) a non-metallic element; [1]
c) a molecular covalent compound: [1]
d) an ionic compound; [1]
e) a giant covalent structure. [1] (ULEAC)

41. Questions a) to d) concern the arrangement of the particles in five different substances.

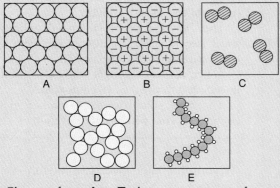

Choose, from **A** to **E**, the arrangement of particles at room temperature that corresponds to
a) a substance that will conduct electricity when molten but not when solid [1]
b) the element mercury [1]
c) a substance whose boiling point is below room temperature [1]
d) a solid metallic element [1] (ULEAC)

42. During the formation of a covalent bond the atoms ...
A gain or lose protons
B share electrons
C gain or lose electrons
D share protons. [1] (NEAB)

43. The formulae of the chlorides of some elements are shown in the table below.

I	II	III	IV	V	VI	VII	O
LiCl	BeCl₂	BCl₃	C ...	NCl₃	OCl₂	FCl	No chloride formed
NaCl	Mg ...	AlCl₃	SiCl₄	PCl₃	SCl₂	Cl₂	

a) What are the formulae of the two missing chlorides? [2]
b) What type of structure will each of the missing chlorides have? [2] (NEAB)

44. The diagrams below show different arrangements of particles in five substances at room temperature. Use them to answer questions a) to d).

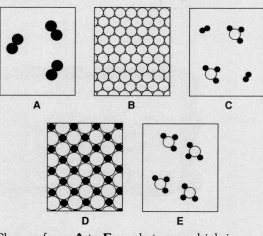

Choose from **A** to **E** a substance which is:
a) sodium fluoride   [1]
b) ammonia   [1]
c) copper   [1]
d) a mixture of ammonia and hydrogen   [1]
                                (ULEAC)

45. The following diagrams represent four different solid structures.

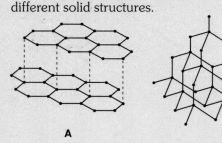

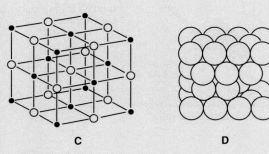

a) Which diagram represents:
   i) diamond; ii) sodium chloride?   [2]

b) Draw a diagram to show the structure of sodium chloride after it has melted.   [1]
c) Explain why sodium chloride has a relatively high melting point.   [2]
d) Describe a test which you could do to show that silver is a metal. Include a diagram and state the result of the test in your answer. [4]
                                (ULEAC)

46. Here is a list of compounds.
   calcium fluoride   carbon dioxide
   sulphur dioxide   potassium chloride
   sodium oxide   nitrogen dioxide
   Choose from the list above:
   a) 3 compounds which have a molecular structure,   [1]
   b) 3 compounds which have an ionic structure.   [1]   (MEG)

Questions 47–50
A simple molecular
B giant covalent
C giant ionic
D giant metallic
Choose from the list A to D the type of structure which is found in
47. zinc.   [1]
48. substances that are gases at room temperature and pressure.   [1]
49. sodium chloride.   [1]
50. sulphur.   [1]   (NEAB)

51. This question is about magnesium and its compounds.
   a) The bonding in magnesium is metallic.
      i) Draw a diagram to illustrate metallic bonding.   [3]
      ii) Use your understanding of metallic bonding to explain why metals can be pulled into wires   [1]
   b) Magnesium chloride $MgCl_2$ is a white crystalline salt similar to sodium chloride. Magnesium is manufactured by the electrolysis of molten magnesium chloride. Why does the magnesium chloride have to be molten and not solid?   [2]
   c) i) Draw a diagram to show the arrangement of the electrons in magnesium oxide, and show the charges on the ions.   [3]
      ii) Suggest a reason why magnesium oxide is used to line the inside of furnaces.   [1]   (NI)

chapter 22

The Atmosphere

Gases in the air

We live in a mixture of gases, called air.
The air makes up the Earth's atmosphere,
and it is essential for life on our planet.

Air is mainly a mixture of 2 gases – **nitrogen and oxygen.**
But do you know which other gases
are all around us?

Look at the table opposite:

There are also tiny amounts of pollutant gases.
Pollution varies from place to place.

Gases in air	% of air
nitrogen	78
oxygen	21
carbon dioxide	0.04
water vapour	varies
argon	0.93 } 1
other noble gases	

Water in the air

The amount of water in the air also varies.
The water cycle shows us how the world's water
moves from place to place:

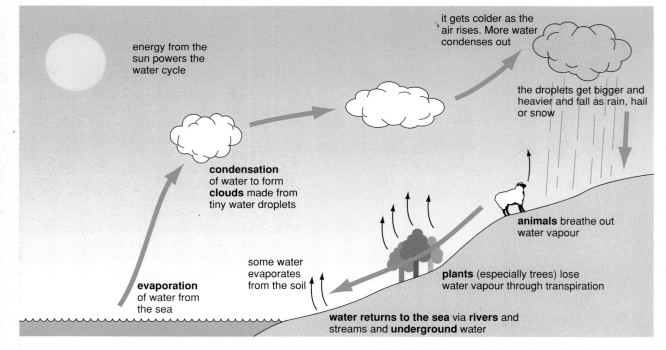

energy from the sun powers the water cycle

it gets colder as the air rises. More water condenses out

the droplets get bigger and heavier and fall as rain, hail or snow

condensation of water to form **clouds** made from tiny water droplets

animals breathe out water vapour

some water evaporates from the soil

plants (especially trees) lose water vapour through transpiration

evaporation of water from the sea

water returns to the sea via **rivers** and streams and **underground** water

- How does water vapour get into the atmosphere?
- Can you explain why it rains when clouds rise?
- Why is it called the water 'cycle'?

▶ Chemistry at work : Uses of nitrogen

You have already seen what an important raw material
nitrogen is. It is used in the Haber process
to make ammonia (see page 217).
But nitrogen has other uses:

Nitrogen for freezing

Liquid nitrogen is very cold. It's almost $-200\,°C$!
Therefore, it can be used to freeze things quickly.
Food can be frozen on a conveyor belt
as it is produced.
Hospitals can use it to store tissues
for many years.

It can also be used to mend leaking pipes.
You can pour liquid nitrogen on the pipe.
It freezes the liquid inside the pipe while
you repair the leak.
This saves money because you don't
have to drain the whole pipe.

Liquid nitrogen can also freeze
marshy ground that is
too wet for mechanical diggers.

*Sperm can be frozen and
stored in liquid nitrogen*

Nitrogen is not reactive

As well as freezing food, nitrogen helps to stop
food 'going off' in another way.
Nitrogen is an un-reactive gas.
So when we pack foods, nitrogen is used
inside the sealed packaging.
This keeps the reactive oxygen gas in the air
away from the food. Bacteria cannot multiply,
and the food stays fresh longer.

Packing peanuts on a production line

There is a risk of fire on the giant ships
that carry crude oil. The vapour from the oil is dense,
and can form an explosive mixture with the air.

It is especially dangerous when oil is pumped ashore,
or when the ship's tanks are cleaned out.
Nitrogen gas is pumped into the tanks to remove
any oxygen. Then an accidental spark will not
result in disaster.

▶ Oxygen gas

Do you know which is the reactive gas in the air?
Think of some reactions we have seen, such as
combustion or oxidation. Which gas is needed
for these reactions to take place?

Oxygen is used up when things burn
or when we breathe.

Look at the reactions below:

> **Remember the test for oxygen:
> a glowing splint re-lights.**

Experiment 22.1   Oxygen and burning
Try the experiment shown with the night-light.

- What happens to the flame?
- What happens to the level of the water in
  the beaker?
- Explain why this happens.
- Wax is a hydrocarbon. What is formed
  as it burns? (see page 177.)

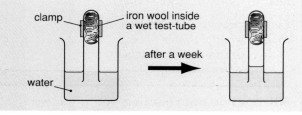

Experiment 22.2   Oxygen and rusting
Set up the apparatus as shown:

Leave it for a week.

- What happens to the level of water in the test-tube?
- Explain why this happens. (see page 90.)

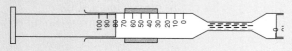

Experiment 22.3   How much oxygen?
Set up the apparatus as shown:

Heat the copper. At the same time,
pass air over it, from syringe to syringe.
Carry on heating until the volume does not
go down any further.
Let the apparatus cool, then read the final volume
of air left.

after the experiment

- How much air is left at the end?
- Explain what has happened (include the word equation:
  copper + oxygen ⟶ copper oxide).
- Why should you let your apparatus cool down
  before taking the final reading on the syringe?

▷ Chemistry at work : Uses of oxygen

About 20 % of the air is made up of oxygen.
Do you know the main difference between
oxygen and nitrogen?
Let's look at some uses of the reactive gas
oxygen:

Oxygen for breathing

We all need oxygen to breathe.
Can you think of any places where you need to take
your own supply of oxygen to survive?
Look at these photos:

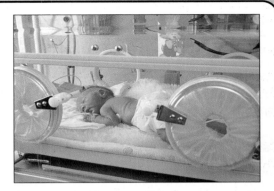

*Premature babies sometimes need oxygen to
help them breathe*

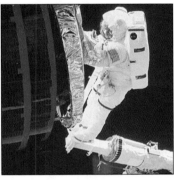

There is no air in space

*The air gets thinner
as you go higher*

Oxygen for burning

Do you remember the fire triangle?
You have already seen how important oxygen is
when we burn things.
Most power stations burn coal, oil or gas
to produce our electricity.

Look at the photo:
Why is oxygen important in welding?
Why is the temperature of the flame so high?

Oxygen is also used in many industrial processes,
such as making **steel** (see page 90).
We also oxidise ammonia in the first stage of
making **nitric acid** (see page 221).
When we make **sulphuric acid**, sulphur is burned
in air. Do you know what is formed when
sulphur burns in air? (see page 153.)

*This welder is burning a mixture of ethyne gas
(a hydrocarbon) and pure oxygen*

▷ Carbon dioxide

You can see from the table on page 272
that air contains about 0.04 % carbon dioxide.
This doesn't seem a lot!
However, 250 years ago there was only 0.028 %.
As you know from page 179, carbon dioxide
is a 'greenhouse gas'. It helps to keep the Earth warm.
But can you remember why people are worried
about the increasing amount of carbon dioxide?

CO₂
- is colourless
- is slightly soluble in water (forming a weakly acidic solution)
- is denser than air
- puts out fires
- turns limewater milky

Carbon cycle

Carbon dioxide is a vital part of the **carbon cycle**.
The carbon cycle shows how carbon is moved
from place to place around the Earth.
Look at the cycle below:

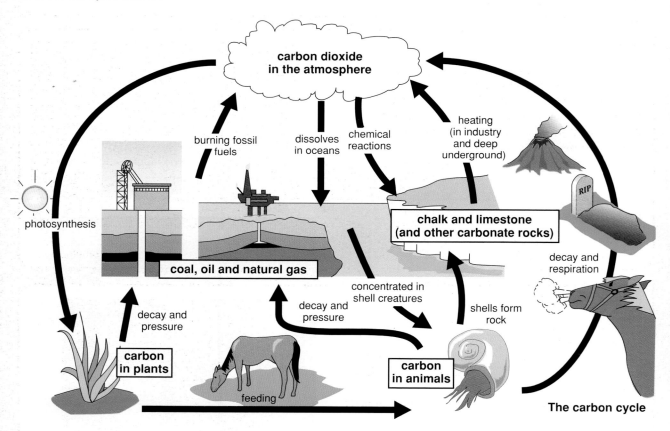

The carbon cycle

Most of the carbon on Earth is in rocks.
The carbon trapped in fossil fuels
is released when we burn the fuels.
The oceans absorb a lot of the CO_2 produced.

Insoluble carbonates and soluble
hydrogencarbonates are formed.
However, the oceans cannot remove all
the extra CO_2 we are now producing.

▷ Chemistry at work : Uses of carbon dioxide

Fizzy drinks

Carbon dioxide gas is slightly soluble in water.
It forms a weakly acidic solution.
Look at the photos :

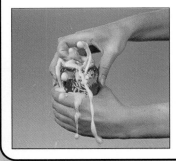

Carbon dioxide puts
the 'fizz' in drinks

Champagne and sparkling wine is bottled before
fermentation has finished (see page 204). The
carbon dioxide builds up pressure in the bottle.

'Dry ice'

If you cool down carbon dioxide gas, it turns
into a solid. It doesn't form a liquid.
The solid carbon dioxide is known as 'dry ice'.
It is much colder than ice. At room temperature,
it sublimes (turns from the solid into a gas).
Look at these uses of 'dry ice' :

Ice cream samples can be
kept cold with 'dry ice'

Lumps of 'dry ice' sublime. This cools down the
water in the air to give smoky effects on stage.

Fire extinguishers

Most things won't burn in carbon dioxide gas.
For example, it puts out a lighted splint.
However, this is **not** the test for carbon dioxide.
Other gases, such as nitrogen, do the same thing.
Do you know the test for carbon dioxide ?
Can you remember why the limewater goes milky ?
(see page 123.)

Carbon dioxide is denser than air. It forms a
'blanket' over a fire. This cuts off the oxygen.
You can read more about this on page 186.

Carbon dioxide puts out most fires

▶ Where on Earth did our atmosphere come from ?

It is hard for us to imagine how old the Earth really is. It might help you to think of the Earth's history as a 24-hour clock. On this scale, humans arrived on Earth at one second to midnight!

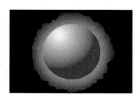

When the Earth was formed (about 4600 million years ago) its atmosphere was probably made from hydrogen and helium, just like 99% of the universe. The Earth itself was a ball of molten rock.

As the ball cooled down, a solid crust formed on the outside. The molten rock underneath often burst through the thin crust. Volcanoes were erupting all over the Earth's new surface. These volcanoes gave out gases, just like volcanoes do today. The gases included **ammonia** (NH_3), **carbon dioxide** (CO_2), **methane** (CH_4) and **steam** (H_2O).

volcanic gases

As the Earth cooled down even more, the steam condensed and fell as rain.
It filled up hollows in the solid crust, and the **oceans** were formed.

first seas and oceans formed

The first **living things** are thought to have developed in the oceans. One theory is that life started near volcanoes on the ocean floor. All the elements needed to evolve into simple cells were there. The first organisms evolved into simple plants, like algae. These used up carbon dioxide during photosynthesis and made the first molecules of **oxygen** gas (O_2).

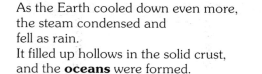

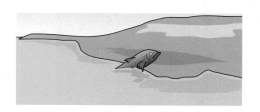

The oxygen was important because some of it turned into **ozone** (O_3). Ozone stops harmful rays from the Sun reaching the surface, and so it became possible to live out of the water.

Some of the oxygen reacted with ammonia, giving off **nitrogen**. More nitrogen was formed by bacteria living in the soil. The levels of methane began to fall as it too reacted with oxygen.

Eventually, about 200 million years ago, the atmosphere reached the mixture we have today of roughly 20% oxygen and 80% nitrogen.

The history of our atmosphere

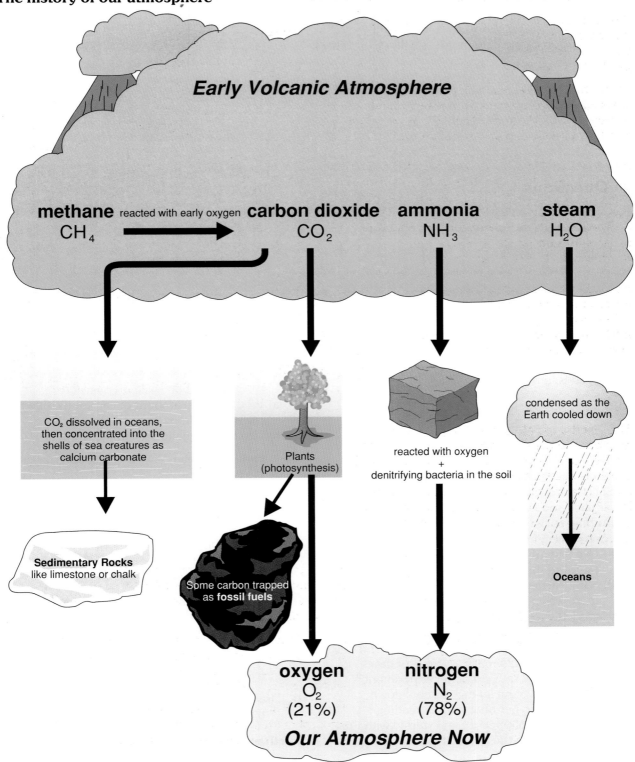

Early Volcanic Atmosphere

methane reacted with early oxygen **carbon dioxide** **ammonia** **steam**
CH_4 CO_2 NH_3 H_2O

CO_2 dissolved in oceans, then concentrated into the shells of sea creatures as calcium carbonate

Plants (photosynthesis)

reacted with oxygen
+
denitrifying bacteria in the soil

condensed as the Earth cooled down

Sedimentary Rocks like limestone or chalk

Some carbon trapped as **fossil fuels**

Oceans

oxygen **nitrogen**
O_2 N_2
(21%) (78%)

Our Atmosphere Now

Summary

- The Earth's early atmosphere contained gases from volcanoes, like carbon dioxide, ammonia, methane and steam.
  As the Earth cooled down, the water in the air condensed to form the oceans.
  The volumes of the other gases gradually got less as the volumes of oxygen and nitrogen grew.
- Our atmosphere today is made up mainly of nitrogen (78 %) and oxygen (21 %).

▶ Questions

1. Copy and complete:
The Earth's atmosphere contains about four-fifths . . . . and one fifth . . . . .
However, its early atmosphere was made up of gases from . . . . These included carbon dioxide, ... , ... and steam. The first oceans formed when the steam . . . . as the Earth cooled down. The first . . . . gas was formed by photosynthesis in plants.

2. Sami did an experiment to find out how much oxygen is in the air.

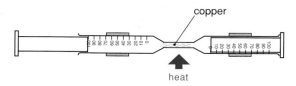
copper
heat

She started with $100 \, cm^3$ of air. She passed the air back and forth over the hot copper by pushing each syringe in turn. She saw the copper turning to black copper oxide.
a) Use a word equation to show how Sami has removed the oxygen from the air.
b) Sami carried on with her experiment until there was no further change in the volume of gas left. Not all the copper had turned black. What volume of air would you expect to be left?
c) Which gas would make up most of the sample left at the end of her experiment?
d) Why should Sami let the gas cool down before taking her final volume reading?
e) What would happen if Sami started with too little copper in the heated tube?

3. a) Why does the amount of water vapour in the air vary?
b) Draw a flow diagram of the water cycle. Include these words:

> clouds, sea, rivers, rain
> evaporates, condenses

c) How do the i) soil, ii) plants and iii) animals, add to the water vapour in the air?
d) Where does the energy for the water cycle come from?

4. Look at the carbon cycle on page 276.
a) Why does the amount of carbon dioxide in the air vary from place to place?
b) The word equation for photosynthesis is:

carbon + water $\longrightarrow$ glucose + oxygen
dioxide

Explain how the carbon in carbon dioxide gets into plants.
c) Explain 4 ways in which the carbon in plants can get back into the atmosphere.
d) What happens to the carbon dioxide absorbed in the oceans?

5. a) Which volcanic gases made up the Earth's early atmosphere?
b) Describe the processes that removed the original gases from the atmosphere. How did this increase the proportions of oxygen and nitrogen in the air?

6. Draw spider diagrams showing some uses of nitrogen, oxygen and carbon dioxide.

Further questions on page 305.

chapter 23

▶ Minerals

Do you remember the difference between an element and a compound? (see chapter 2.)
There are 92 different elements found naturally on Earth. Most of these exist in compounds.
Different elements are chemically bonded together.

Any solid element or compound found in the ground is called a **mineral**.

For example, diamond is a mineral which is an element.
Which element is diamond made from? (see page 248.)
Whereas, rock salt (sodium chloride) is a mineral which is a compound.

Rock salt (or halite) is a mineral

Look at the pie-chart:
It shows the main elements in the Earth's crust.
Silicate minerals (SiO_2) make up most of the rocks on Earth.

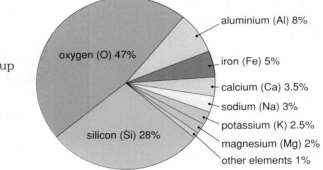

- oxygen (O) 47%
- silicon (Si) 28%
- aluminium (Al) 8%
- iron (Fe) 5%
- calcium (Ca) 3.5%
- sodium (Na) 3%
- potassium (K) 2.5%
- magnesium (Mg) 2%
- other elements 1%

▶ Rocks

Rocks are usually **mixtures of minerals**.
Can you see the different minerals in the rocks shown below?

*The rock **granite** contains the minerals quartz, feldspar and mica*

*The rock **gabbro** contains the minerals feldspar, olivine and augite*

► Weathering

You've heard of the saying 'as hard as rock'.
Yet over thousands of years, the slow process of
weathering wears rocks down.

Sometimes rocks, which were once buried
under the ground, can be exposed.
The layers of rock on top get slowly worn away.

Rocks can be worn away in 3 ways:

- physical weathering,
- chemical weathering, and
- biological weathering.

Edinburgh Castle stands on a 'plug' of granite
that was once inside a volcano! What can you
say about the hardness of granite compared to
the rock on the outside of the original volcano?

► Physical weathering

a) Changes in temperature can break up rocks.
This happens when rocks get very hot in the daytime,
but cool down quickly at night.

Sudden changes in temperature happen in deserts.
During the day, the hot rock expands in the Sun.
Then the rock contracts as it cools down at night.

Most rocks are made from mixtures of minerals.
These expand and contract at different rates.
This causes stress to build up in the rock.
Eventually it will crack.

Look at the experiment below from behind a safety screen.

Rocks in the desert are subjected to extreme
changes in temperature

Demonstration 23.1   Smashing time!

Imagine that the glass rod is a rock.
The change of temperature will be extreme
to speed up the effect.

A glass rod is heated strongly in a Bunsen flame.
Then it is plunged into cold water.

- What happens?

⚠ breaking glass

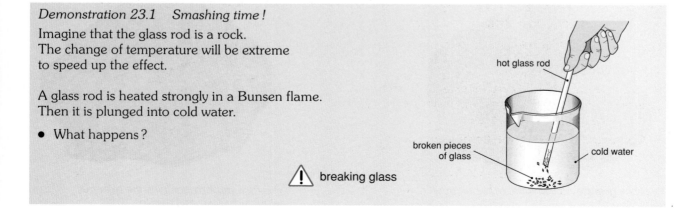

hot glass rod

broken pieces
of glass

cold water

b) In areas where the temperature drops below 0 °C, ice can break apart rocks.

If a rock is cracked, it can fill with water.
Look at the diagrams below:
If it gets cold enough, the water will freeze.
Strangely enough, when water forms ice, it expands.
The force produced in the confined space
can split off pieces of rock.
This is called **'freeze-thaw'**.

You can often see these pieces of rock (called scree)
at the bottom of rocky slopes.

The pieces of rock (scree) at the bottom of the slope have been broken off by 'freeze-thaw' weathering

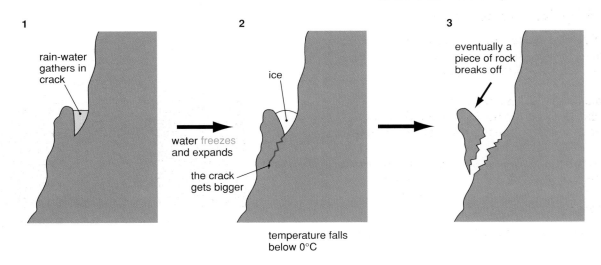

1
rain-water gathers in crack

2
ice

water freezes and expands

the crack gets bigger

temperature falls below 0°C

3
eventually a piece of rock breaks off

Experiment 23.2   Ice-breaker!

Fill a bottle up to the top with water.
Try to make sure that there is no air left
inside the bottle. Screw on the top tightly.
Tie the sealed bottle in a clear plastic bag.

⚠ broken glass

Leave overnight in a freezer.

- What happens?
- In the explanation of frost damage given above
  it says, 'Strangely enough, when water forms ice,
  it expands.' Why is this odd?
- Can you explain why water pipes sometimes
  burst in winter?
- What happens when your milk freezes
  on the doorstep in winter?

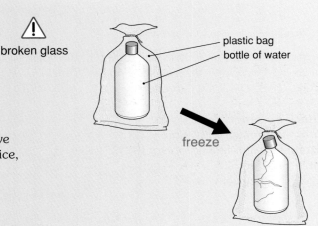

plastic bag
bottle of water

freeze

► Chemical weathering

Acids, water and oxygen can all weather rocks.
They break down rocks by reacting with, or dissolving,
some of the minerals in the rock.
This is called **chemical weathering**.

Acids, water and oxygen can cause chemical weathering

a) Attack by acid

You might think that rain-water is very pure.
In fact it is weakly acidic. Even before people
started polluting our air, rain-water was acidic.
This is because carbon dioxide gas dissolves in rain
as it falls. The weak acid formed (carbonic acid)
attacks rocks, mainly those containing
calcium carbonate (see page 190).

Experiment 23.3   Weathering by acid

You can use dilute hydrochloric acid instead of carbonic acid
to speed up any reaction.

Test the following rock samples with your acid:
marble, granite, sandstone, limestone, chalk, slate.

⚠️
acid

add a few
drops of acid.
Does it fizz?

rock sample

watch glass

- What do you see happen if there is a reaction?
  Do you know the name of the gas given off?
- Which of your rock samples contain calcium carbonate?

The caverns in limestone areas are formed
by this natural chemical weathering.
Calcium carbonate, in limestone, reacts with carbonic acid:

calcium carbonate + carbonic acid ⟶ calcium hydrogencarbonate
$$CaCO_3(s) \quad + \quad H_2CO_3(aq) \quad \longrightarrow \quad Ca(HCO_3)_2(aq)$$

Soluble calcium hydrogencarbonate is formed.
So the limestone is slowly worn away.

Weak acids are also made by leaves rotting in the soil.
This acid (humic acid) is then washed on to
underlying rocks, which it can attack.

b) Attack by water

Water itself can react with some rocks.
For example, water attacks one of the minerals
in granite. The granite breaks down into tiny particles
of clay. Then they get washed away.

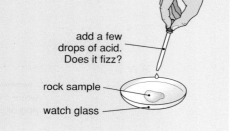

*Limestone is weathered by carbonic acid.
Eventually caverns are formed.*

c) Attack by oxygen

Have you ever noticed the rusty brown streaks
in some rocks? These are iron compounds,
formed in reactions with oxygen.

Oxygen gas in the air can attack some rocks,
especially those containing iron.
This causes weakness in the mineral,
and the rock can wear away.

Chemical weathering is very important in
hot, wet climates. Can you think why?

*Iron in rocks is
attacked
by oxygen*

Investigation 23.4   Chemical weathering

What affects how quickly rocks are attacked by acid?

You can use marble chips as your rock
and dilute hydrochloric acid as your acid.   acid

Plan an investigation into one of the factors that affect
how quickly the acid attacks the marble chips.

- Explain what you think will happen.
- How will you measure the rate of attack?
- How will you make it a fair test? Is it safe?
- How will you get *reliable* results?
- What is the best way to show your results?
- Check your plan with your teacher before you start.

When you have finished your tests;
- How could you improve your investigation?

► Biological weathering

Plants and animals can also help to
break up rocks.

Soil can get trapped in cracks in a rock.
If a seed lands there, plants can grow.
The roots of the plants can then help to
break up the rock.

Look at the photo opposite:

*These tree roots have broken off pieces
of rock*

Burrowing animals also wear away
rocks as they dig.
Some tiny animals *even* feed on rock!

▶ Erosion

The pieces of rock worn away by weathering
are often found a long way from the original rock.

They get moved, or *transported*, either by

- gravity,
- the wind,
- moving water (in rivers or the sea),
- moving ice (in glaciers).

As the rock is carried along it can
wear away other rocks.
This is called **erosion**.

Different sized pieces of rock can be carried along.

a) The *wind* can only carry small grains.
For example, sand is blown about in a desert storm.
Over thousands of years these small grains can still
wear away rocks, especially softer ones.

b) The size of fragments carried by *rivers*
depends on how quickly the water is flowing.
Rivers usually flow quickly near their source
in the mountains. They slow down as they
get closer to the sea.

Fast-flowing rivers can move small rocks and
stones along the bottom. They carve out V-shaped
valleys in the eroded rock.
Slow-moving water can only carry small particles along.

The *sea* also causes erosion.
Waves can smash stones and pebbles against
the coastline.
Cliffs can be worn away at, and below, the water-line.

You will have noticed the smooth, rounded rocks
you find on pebbly beaches. This smoothness
is caused by the constant bashing and rubbing
of the rocks against each other as waves, currents
and tides move them up, down and along the beach.

This constant movement of particles also
sorts them out according to size.

Weathering – breaks off a piece of rock.

transport

Erosion – the piece of weathered rock acts like sand-paper, wearing away other rock and getting smaller itself.

Strange stacks of rock jut out of the desert in Arizona. How do you think they might have formed?

Bits of rock carried by the river have eroded this gorge

Rocks, pebbles and sand carried by the sea erode these cliffs

c) Glaciers are rivers of ice! They move very slowly (only about a metre a day).

However, they are better at eroding the rock, which they pass over, than rivers.

This is because glaciers can carry along rocks of all sizes. They even carry large boulders. These scrape away at the rock along the bottom of the glacier. This forms U-shaped valleys.

Glaciers are good at eroding rock

Investigation 23.5   Which rock is easiest to erode?

You will be given some samples of rock. Plan an investigation, using a file or nail, to see which rock is softest.
- How will you make it a fair and safe test?
- How will you judge the erosion of each rock?
- Check your plan with your teacher before you start.
Put the rocks into order.

Depositing eroded rock

Bits of rock that have been weathered or eroded eventually settle somewhere else. The smaller pieces form the basis of soils. The tiny fragments are usually deposited by rivers.

A river slows down near the end of its journey to the sea. Even small grains of rock sink to the bottom of the river. The bits that settle out are called **sediment**.

As time passes, a river can change its course, or run dry. This leaves the sediments behind.

Some rivers, like the Nile, have flood plains. They regularly overflow into the surrounding fields. When the water retreats, the sediments from the river are left on the land. This forms fertile soil. The type of soil formed obviously depends on the kind of rock the river has flowed over.

The fertile soils on the banks of the River Nile are formed from tiny eroded pieces of rock (called sediment) and organic material (called humus)

Experiment 23.6   Erosion in a river

Set up the apparatus as shown:
You can use a large spoon to stir the water in the trough, making a current.
Take care not to knock over the beaker in the middle as you stir. Once the water is swirling around quite quickly, stop stirring.
- Where is the water moving fastest?
- How does the sand settle out of the water?

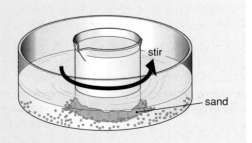

▶ Different types of rock

There are 3 types of rock :
- **sedimentary**
- **metamorphic**
- **igneous**

Sedimentary rocks

As you know, rocks are slowly weathered.
The bits of rock are then carried off
to another place.
Eventually, they settle as sediment.

As time passes, layers of sediment pile up.
The pressure on the older, lower layers builds up.
Any water in between the particles of sediment
is squeezed out. The water often has minerals
dissolved in it. These minerals are left behind
in the sediment, and act like cement.

The pressure (compaction), and mineral 'cement',
stick the particles together.
A **sedimentary** rock is formed.

Sedimentary rocks can be made from clay, silt, sand,
gravel or pebbles.
Look at the table for some examples :

Other sedimentary rocks are made from things
which were once living. Examples are :
- *coal* – made from trees and ferns, and
- *limestone* or *chalk* – made mainly from the shelly
  remains of sea creatures.
  These rocks often contain **fossils**.

Holmes and Watson were looking for clues;
Some old rock samples were making the news.
"It's bitty and gritty," the great man said,
"I think it was formed on an ancient sea bed !
Ages ago, when sediments came to rest,
Layer upon layer, they became compressed.
So you see, dear Watson, it's quite elementary,
This rock before us is clearly ***sedimentary** !"*

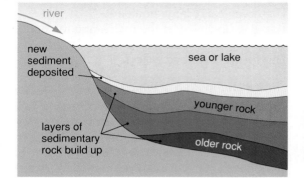

Layers of sedimentary rock forming

Particles	Sedimentary rock
clay ⟶	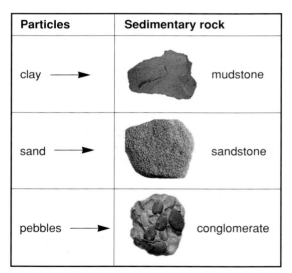 mudstone
sand ⟶	sandstone
pebbles ⟶	conglomerate

Sedimentary rocks : **These form as layers of sediment build up.**
Under pressure, and with mineral 'cement',
the sediment sticks together to form rock.

Metamorphic rocks

Movement of the Earth's crust can bury rock
deep underground (see page 300).
As you go deeper into the Earth's crust,
the temperature gets higher, so does the pressure.

Under these conditions, rocks can have
their mineral structures changed, without actually melting.
The minerals in the rocks line up in
bands or sheets, to form **metamorphic** rock.

Look at the diagram above:

The bands line up at right angles to the pressure
that formed them.
Look at the photo:
Can you see the bands of minerals in this
metamorphic rock called gneiss?

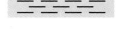

pressure

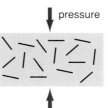

minerals in **mudstone**
are all mixed up

microscopic crystals of
the minerals in **slate**
are all lined up

Gneiss is a very hard metamorphic rock

Rocks can also be 'baked' nearer the surface
by molten rock called **magma**. The molten rock
rises towards the surface through faults in the Earth's crust.

For example, under volcanoes, the rocks
near to the magma get very hot. The temperatures
are high enough to change their structures.

Two examples of metamorphic rocks are:
- *marble* – formed from limestone, and
- *slate* – formed from mudstone.

Have you ever looked closely at a roof tile
made from slate?
It is split into thin sheets.

Metamorphic rocks are hard, but some can be
split (cleaved) along their bands.

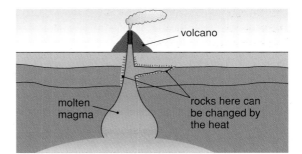

volcano

molten
magma

rocks here can
be changed by
the heat

"And what about this one?" asked Watson of Sherlock,
"It's hard, with bands running right through the rock."
"I deduce it's been baked at one thousand degrees,
Deep underground, rocks on top, they did squeeze."
"And what is its type?" asked the Doctor most humbly,
*"Its **metamorphic**, of course – you can see it's not crumbly!"*

> **Metamorphic rocks : These are rocks that have been
> changed by heat and/or pressure
> (without melting).**

Igneous rocks

When molten rock cools down, it usually forms
crystals. These make up **igneous** rock.
The word igneous comes from the Greek
word for 'fire'. Can you think of any other
words that start with the letters ign . . . . ?

The molten rock comes from deep underground.
It tends to rise to the surface through
cracks in the Earth's crust.
If the molten rock, or **magma**, reaches the surface,
it forms a volcano.

Some igneous rocks are made from small crystals,
like the rock basalt. Others have larger crystals, like granite.
So what affects the size of the crystals in an igneous rock?

Experiment 23.7   Crystal sizes

You cannot melt rocks with a Bunsen burner.
In this experiment you will use a solid called salol to
take the place of rock.
If you look carefully you can see how
the rate of cooling affects crystal size.

Watch the crystals form on the two slides.
You may need to start off the crystals on the
warm slide with a small 'seed' crystal of salol.
You can use a hand lens to observe
the size of the crystals.

● What do you conclude from this experiment?

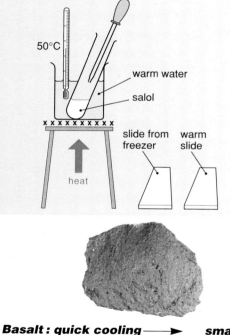

50°C

warm water

salol

x x x x x x x x x x x

slide from   warm
freezer   slide

heat

Molten rock that erupts from a volcano is called lava.
It cools down quickly. This forms rocks with small crystals.
Basalt is the main example.
Most ocean floors are made from basalt.
It is an **extrusive** igneous rock.

Other molten rock rises towards the surface
but never reaches it. It cools down slowly,
surrounded by rocks under the ground.
The solid rock formed has large crystals, like **granite**.
It is an **intrusive** igneous rock.

The granite formed beneath the surface
can later be exposed by Earth movements or
by weathering of the softer surrounding rock.

Basalt : quick cooling ⟶ **small crystals**

Granite : slow cooling ⟶ **large crystals**

> **Igneous rocks : These form when molten rock cools down to form crystals.**

▶ The rock cycle

The 3 types of rock you have now met are recycled
over millions of years. This is shown in the **rock cycle** :

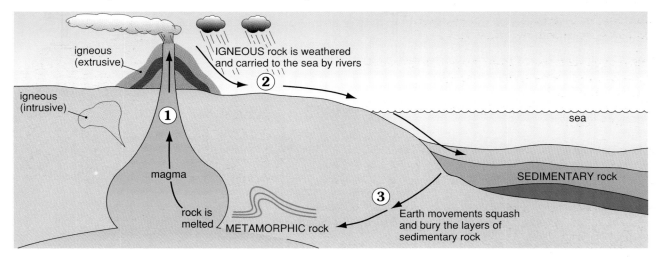

① Molten rock, called magma, rises towards the surface.
When it cools down, it forms igneous rock.

② The igneous rock gets weathered. The bits of rock
are carried away. They settle to form sedimentary rock.

③ Movement of the Earth's crust can bury
the sedimentary rock.
Deep underground, pressure and heat turn the rock
into metamorphic rock.
If the metamorphic rock gets hot enough,
it will melt.
It turns into magma, and the cycle starts again !

Experiment 23.8   Identifying rock types

Use your knowledge of the 3 types of rock to identify some unknown samples.
Remember:
sedimentary rocks can be soft and are often bitty or crumbly (although some are hard),
metamorphic rocks are hard and have bands or sheets in their structure,
igneous rocks are hard and made of crystals.

- Design a simple key you could use to classify rock types.

Summary

- Weathering wears away rock.
  Changes in temperature and 'freeze-thaw' cause **physical weathering**.
  Acids, water and oxygen can cause **chemical weathering**.
  The action of plants and animals cause **biological weathering**.

- Weathered rock particles are transported away by
  gravity, wind, water or ice. As they move along,
  they **erode** away more rock.

- There are 3 types of rock:

sedimentary: Formed from particles that are deposited by
water, wind or ice. They build up in layers.

metamorphic: Formed when rocks (usually sedimentary) are subjected
to heat and/or pressure.

igneous: Formed when molten rock (magma) solidifies into crystals.
Molten rock that cools **quickly** (in air or under the oceans)
forms **small** crystals. For example, basalt is an **extrusive** igneous rock.
Molten rock that cools down **slowly,** under the Earth's surface,
forms **large** crystals.
For example, granite is an **intrusive** igneous rock.

Sandstone is a sedimentary rock

Schist is a metamorphic rock

Granite is an igneous rock

► Questions

1. Copy and fill in the blanks :
   There are 3 types of weathering :
   a) . . . . weathering, which is caused by changes in . . . . and 'freeze- . . . .'.
   b) chemical weathering, which is caused by . . . . , water and . . . . .
   c) . . . . weathering, which is caused by plants and . . . . .
   Weathered bits of rock are transported by gravity, ... , ... or . . . . . They can then wear away more rock. This is called . . . . .
   There are 3 types of rock.
   . . . . rock is formed when particles in a river are . . . . in a lake or on the sea bed.
   . . . . rock crystallises from molten rock as it . . . . down.
   . . . . rock forms when rocks are heated to high temperatures and/or put under high . . . . .
   Fossils, formed . . . . of years ago, are usually found in . . . . rock.

2. a) Describe how frost damage can weather rocks.
   b) Explain how rapid changes in temperature can weather rocks.

3. a) Rocks can be broken down by chemical weathering. How does rain-water become acidic?
   b) Which types of rock are affected most by chemical weathering?

4. Weathered pieces of rock can be transported by wind, rivers and glaciers.
   a) Which one of these can carry along the biggest pieces of rock?
   b) Which one has the greatest eroding power?
   c) What difference would you see between valleys formed by rivers and those formed by glaciers?
   d) An 'erratic' rock is a large boulder, unlike any others in an area. How do you think they happen?
   e) As particles are transported, they get sorted out according to their size. Explain how this sorting happens in a river and on a beach.

5. a) Describe how sedimentary rocks are formed.
   b) Name 3 examples of sedimentary rocks.

6. a) Describe how metamorphic rocks are formed.
   b) Name 2 types of metamorphic rock.
   c) Explain why slate can be split into very thin sheets. Why is this a useful property of slate?

7. a) Describe how igneous rocks are formed.
   b) Name 2 types of igneous rock.
   c) Why do some igneous rocks have large crystals and some have small crystals? Use the words ***intrusive*** and ***extrusive*** in your answer.
   d) You are given a saturated solution of copper sulphate (a solution about to crystallise). How could you investigate how the rate of cooling affects the size of the crystals. ?

8. a) Which layer of sedimentary rock in the picture below is the oldest?

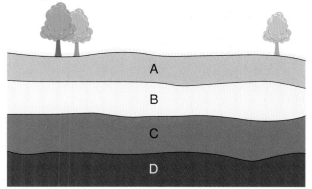

   b) Fossils are often found in sedimentary rock. Why are you unlikely to find fossils in igneous rocks?
   c) Any fossils found in metamorphic rocks are often distorted. Explain why.

9. Draw a simple, labelled flow-diagram of the rock cycle.

Further questions on page 306.

▷ Chemistry at work : Rocks

You have already looked at the world's most useful
rock, limestone, in Chapter 11.
You can see some other uses for materials
that we get from rocks below.

Toothpaste

Have you ever forgotten to put water on your toothpaste?
If you have, you might have noticed its slightly
gritty feel on your teeth. This is powdered limestone!

It is used as an abrasive. Fortunately for us, it is
softer than our teeth so it can't scratch them. It also
helps to neutralise acid that causes tooth decay.

Talcum powder

There is a rock called soapstone which is made
mainly from the mineral talc.
It is used to make talcum powder because it
is soft and is good at absorbing things.
Do you think soapstone is sedimentary,
metamorphic or igneous rock? Why?

Clay

The chemical weathering of certain rocks
produce different types of clay.

When clay is 'fired' in a kiln, its properties change.
It becomes hard. When you add water to it,
it no longer becomes slippy and slimy.

This is how we make pottery and bricks from clay.

Lipsticks and face-creams contain clay.
The slimy texture of clay, plus its ability to
absorb grease, has led to its use as a face-pack.
A clay called fuller's earth is used.
It is also used in cat litter and is added to
paints to make them non-drip.

Plate tectonics

chapter 24

▶ Journey to the centre of the Earth

As you know, the Earth is surrounded by a thin layer of gases. But have you ever wondered what is inside our planet?
If you started digging a hole straight down, about 13 000 kilometres later you would come out in Australia!
But what would you find on the way?

First of all you would go through the Earth's thin **crust**.

It can be as thin as 5 km under the oceans, going up to about 70 km under the continents. The thin crust is the least dense of the Earth's layers.

Under the crust you find the **mantle**. This layer goes down almost half way to the centre of the Earth.

Most of the rock in the mantle is solid, but just under the crust it is almost molten. You can think of the crust as floating on top of very thick treacle!

Next, you reach the **outer core**. This is a dense liquid, made of molten iron and nickel.

Both of these metals are magnetic. They make the Earth behave like a giant magnet itself.

Finally there is the **inner core**. This is the densest part of the Earth. Unlike the outer core it is solid because of the very high pressure. It is also made of iron and nickel.

You would now be almost half way to Australia! In real life, the deepest boreholes ever drilled have not yet pierced the Earth's crust.

crust

mantle

outer core

inner core

There was a young man from Perth,
Who tunnelled for all he was worth.
He became a real bore
As he shot through the core
And came out t'other side of the Earth!

► Our changing planet

We can use the natural radioactivity in rocks to find out how old the Earth is.
It is thought to be about 4 600 000 000 years old!
This vast time-scale is hard for us to imagine.

However, think of the changes described in the rock cycle on page 291.
Great lengths of time are involved.

There has been plenty of time for changes caused by weathering, erosion, volcanoes, and movements of the Earth's crust.
These have re-modelled the surface of the Earth.

New mountain ranges have formed to replace older mountains worn away by weathering.

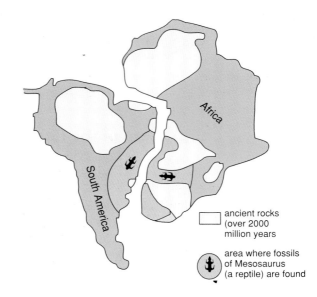

	ancient rocks (over 2000 million years

area where fossils of Mesosaurus (a reptile) are found

The shapes of South America and Africa slot together as in a jig-saw. This gives us evidence that the continents were once joined and must have drifted apart.

Drifting continents

In 1915, a German scientist called Alfred Wegener put forward his ideas about the history of the Earth.
It had already been noticed that Africa and South America looked like two pieces in a jig-saw.
Alfred thought that the two continents were once joined together. Over millions of years they became separated and then drifted apart.

He found that the types of rock match across Africa and South America. So did the fossils.

But he could not explain *how* the continents had moved.

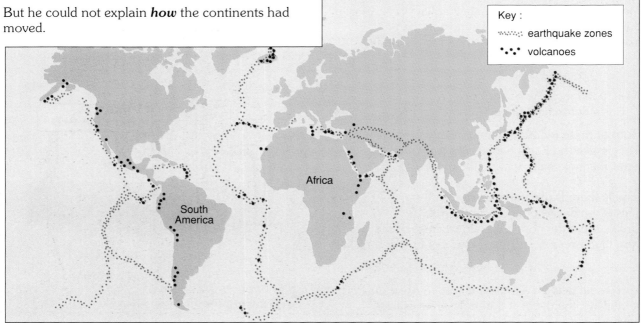

Key :
.... earthquake zones
•.•.• volcanoes

▶ Plate tectonics

Perhaps it was not surprising that other scientists
didn't think much of the 'drifting continents' theory.

People believed that features like mountains,
were formed when the Earth's early crust shrank
as it cooled down (see page 278).
However, after Alfred Wegener's death,
scientists started to notice things that supported his theory.

The same rock and fossil features were found
between *other pairs* of continents. Then explorers of the
oceans discovered evidence that the sea-bed was spreading.
In other words, continents *were* actually moving apart.
At last, people had to take the ideas of Alfred Wegener seriously.
The theory of **plate tectonics** was formed.
This says that the Earth's crust is made up from
huge slabs of rock, called plates, and it explain how they move.

The plates are still moving today, although only a few
centimetres a year. This small movement is enough
to cause earthquakes and volcanoes.

Large earthquakes happen where plates slip a few metres
past each other. Volcanoes appear where molten rock from
beneath the crust rises to the surface through
joints between the plates.

Look at the map on the last page :
It shows areas affected by earthquakes and volcanoes.
You can use these to find the shape of the plates below :

*All the continents were once joined together.
The huge land mass was called Pangaea.*

Key :
- 🟫🟫 mountain ranges
- ▬ plate boundaries
- ➤ direction plates are moving

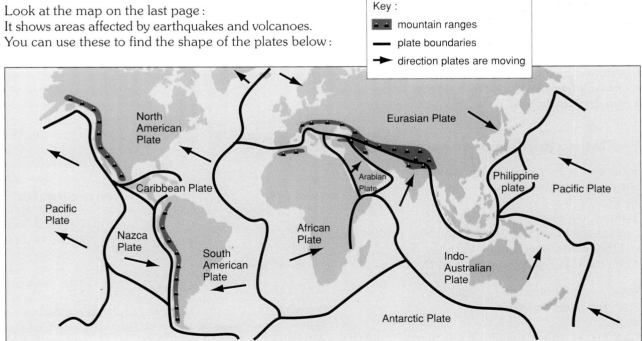

► Moving plates

Nowadays, we can explain why the plates move.
Do you remember what lies underneath the Earth's crust?
It is the upper part of the mantle described earlier as
'very thick treacle'.
You can imagine the plates almost floating
on the mantle. The plates move because of
huge forces caused by **convection currents**
in this partly molten rock.

Experiment 24.1 Convection currents

Set up the apparatus as shown :
Use tweezers to place a crystal of
potassium manganate(VII)
at the bottom of the beaker.

⚠ potassium manganate(VII)

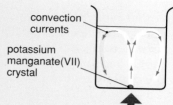

convection currents

potassium manganate(VII) crystal

heat

- Draw a diagram to show what happens.
- Explain how two of the Earth's plates might move apart.

We know it gets hotter the deeper into the Earth we go.
But where does the heat come from?
Natural radioactive atoms are decaying inside
the Earth all the time.
These nuclear reactions give out lots of energy.
They give out enough energy to melt rock, and to set up
the convection currents that move the Earth's plates.

Look at the map on page 297.
It shows the plates and the direction they are moving.

The plates in different parts of the world can be :
- *slipping past* each other,
- *moving towards* each other, or
- *moving away from* each other.

This is the San Andreas fault. You can see where the two plates meet.

► Plates slipping past each other

Some plates are trying to slip past each other.
The most famous example of this is
the San Andreas fault.
It runs down the west coast of the USA.
It marks the boundary between the Pacific plate
and the North American plate.
When the plates slip, there is an earthquake.

As yet, we cannot predict exactly
when the plates will slip.   '
So people in California have to live with
the threat of an earthquake at any time.

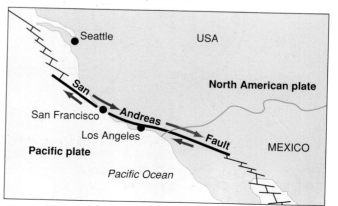

The red arrows show the movement of the plates on either side of the fault

Earthquakes

Have you seen TV pictures after an earthquake on the news?
Look at the photos of the damage they can cause:
As you can see, the shock waves from an earthquake can be very strong.

Friction stops two plates from sliding past each other smoothly.
During an earthquake, the two plates overcome the friction. They slip suddenly.

This happens at the earthquake's **focus**.
The focus may be deep underground.
Then the shock waves spread out in all directions.

The place directly above the focus on the surface is called the **epicentre**.
The waves get weaker as they travel further from the epicentre, but they can still be detected on the other side of the world!

Scientists use a finely balanced instrument called a seismograph to record these vibrations.

Japan lies on the boundary of two plates.
Tall buildings in Japanese cities are now built on giant shock absorbers. Special computers can adjust the shock absorbers to reduce the movement of the building.

Look at the photos:
Can you see the buildings that were designed to withstand earthquakes?

This earthquake in Los Angeles killed 36 people in 1989

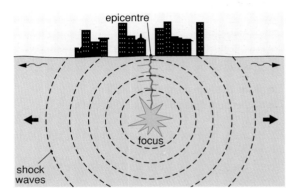

Over 50 000 people died in this earthquake in Armenia

In 1988, an earthquake in Armenia killed over 50 000 people. Most people were crushed as buildings collapsed.
Why do you think so many buildings failed to stand up to the shock waves?

Some buildings in Japan are designed to withstand an earthquake

▶ Plates moving towards each other

There are 2 types of material forming the plates.
In some places the plates are thin and dense.
These are found under the oceans (basaltic crust).
Other plates are thicker and less dense.
These make up the continents (granitic crust).

In some places 2 plates are moving towards each other. Where they meet, the denser oceanic crust slips under the continental crust. This is called **subduction**.

The friction between the plates can cause earthquakes.
The rock can even get so hot that it melts and rises to the surface to form volcanoes.

Look at the map on page 297 :
Can you see where this is happening ?

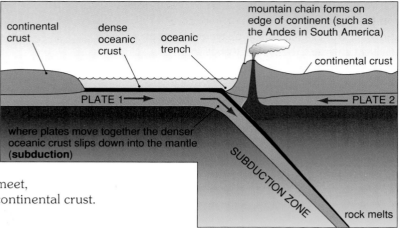

Oceanic plate slipping under continental plate (subduction)

Eventually, the whole oceanic part of the plate slips under the continental crust.
Then the two continental plates collide.
The plates fold upwards, forming mountains.
Metamorphic rocks can form under this great pressure.
The Himalayas and the Alps were formed like this.

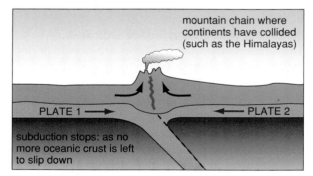

Continental plates colliding

Folds and faults

The great forces involved when plates move can cause layers of rock to snap. This forms a **fault**.
Sometimes the layers bend, forming a **fold**.
Layers can even be turned upside down!

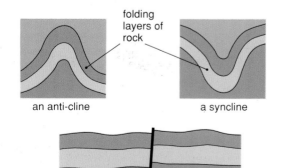

> *Experiment 24.2   Smashing plates!*
>
> Use coloured strips of plasticine to show the layers of rock.
> Move 2 blocks of wood together to show how the layers can fold.
> Use a knife to cut the layers, then move them slightly to form a fault.
>
> ● Can you think of a reason why rocks sometimes form a fold and sometimes a fault ?

▶ Plates moving away from each other

Where plates move apart, magma rises to the surface.
This usually happens under the oceans.
As the molten rock sets, a ridge forms.
An example is the mid-Atlantic Ridge.

Look at the map on page 297 :
Can you see where the mid-Atlantic Ridge is ?

Look at the photo of Iceland :
Iceland is part of the mid-Atlantic Ridge.
Islands are made when the new rock builds up
above the level of the sea.

Sea floor spreading

You have already seen how the continents
were once joined together. Studies of the
ocean floor have given us more evidence
that some plates are moving apart.

The rocks at the ridge contain a lot of
iron compounds. As you know, iron is magnetic.
Its atoms line up when the molten rock sets
on the sea bed. They point towards the North Pole.

However, every few hundred thousand years,
the Earth's magnetic field is reversed.
The South Pole becomes magnetic north.
The rocks on the sea floor show
when these changes happened.

Look at the bands of rock in the diagrams :

They give us evidence that the sea floor is spreading.
In fact, each year you have to travel
about an extra 2 cm to get to America !

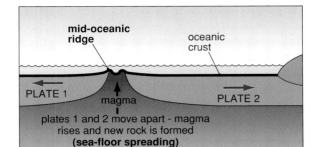

plates 1 and 2 move apart - magma
rises and new rock is formed
(sea-floor spreading)

*Iceland is part of the
mid-Atlantic ridge*

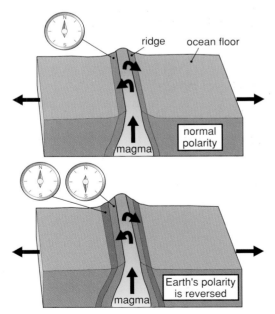

*Stripes of rock with reversed magnetism have
built up on the sea floor (see page 304)*

AIR FARES
GO UP

I'm sorry,
Sir, but it is
further to
America
this year.

301

▶ Volcanoes

You have seen how molten rock, called magma, rises through faults in the Earth's crust. If the magma breaks through to the surface, it is called **lava**.

Volcanoes form where the lava sets into rock. Do you think that the rock formed will be igneous? (See page 290.)

Mount St Helens in the USA. It erupted in 1980.

Lava varies in different places. Some lava is runny, some is thick. This is because magma can have different mixtures of minerals in it.

It can also arrive at the surface at different temperatures, or with different amounts of gases dissolved in it.

All of these affect the thickness (viscosity) of the lava. You can try this investigation:

This lava is viscous (thick)

Investigation 24.3   How does temperature affect the thickness of lava?
You can use treacle instead of lava!

- Plan your investigation.
- Make sure it is a fair and safe test.
- How will you measure the rate of flow?
- Check your plan with your teacher before you start!

The shape of a volcano depends on the thickness of its lava.
Do you think that runny lava will set nearer to a volcano's vent (outlet)?
Thin, runny lava forms a volcano which is very wide, with shallow sides.

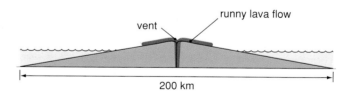

Mauna Loa, Hawaii (a shallow-sided volcano)

Look at the diagrams:

Thicker lava sticks nearer the vent.
It forms a steep sided volcano.
This type of volcano is more dangerous.
The vent can get blocked up by the thick lava.
The pressure builds up inside. Suddenly, we get a violent eruption as the lava bursts through.

What type of eruption would you expect from a volcano with runny lava?

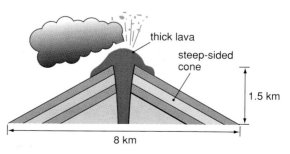

Mount Pelée, West Indies (a steep-sided volcano)

Summary

- The Earth is made from
  - a thin outer **crust**,
  - the **mantle**,
  - the liquid **outer core**, and
  - the solid **inner core**.
- The Earth gets hotter the deeper you go. The energy comes from natural radioactive processes inside the Earth.
- The Earth's crust is made from huge slabs of rock called **plates**. The plates move because of convection currents in the mantle.
- Movement at the boundaries between plates causes earthquakes and volcanoes.

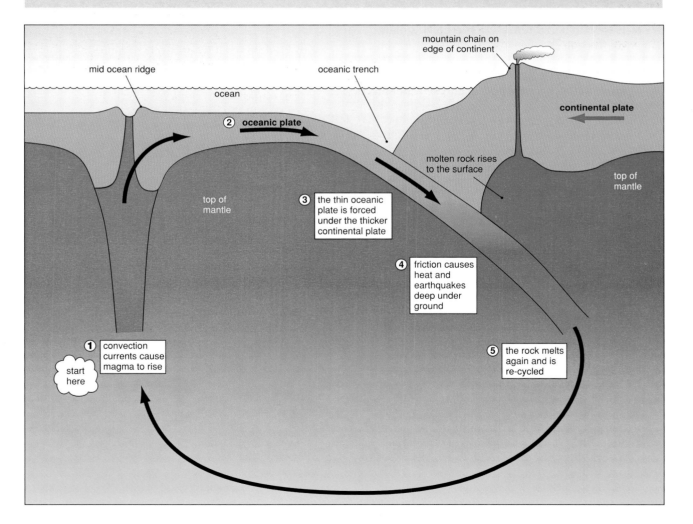

mountain chain on edge of continent

mid ocean ridge

oceanic trench

ocean

continental plate

② **oceanic plate**

molten rock rises to the surface

top of mantle

top of mantle

③ the thin oceanic plate is forced under the thicker continental plate

④ friction causes heat and earthquakes deep under ground

① convection currents cause magma to rise

start here

⑤ the rock melts again and is re-cycled

▶ Questions

1. Copy and complete:
   The Earth is made from a thin outer . . . . , the . . . . , an . . . . liquid core and an inner core which is . . . . . The Earth's crust is made from massive slabs of slowly moving rock called . . . . . They move because of . . . . currents in the . . . . . Where they meet you get . . . . and volcanoes.

2. Imagine that the Earth is like an egg!
   a) Which part of the egg is like the Earth's crust?
   b) Which part of the Earth is represented by the white of the egg?
   c) Give one way in which the egg's yolk is like the Earth's core.
   d) Give one way in which the egg's yolk is different from the Earth's core.
   e) How could you represent the Earth's plates on the egg?

3. a) What evidence did Alfred Wegener put forward for his theory of 'drifting continents'?
   b) At one time all the continents were thought to be joined together in a huge land mass called Pangaea. What evidence is there in this diagram to support this theory?

   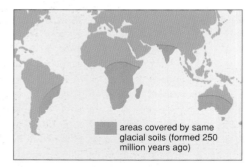

   areas covered by same glacial soils (formed 250 million years ago)

4. a) Trace or get your own printed map of the world and mark on the plate boundaries.
   b) What evidence is there that these boundaries are the places where plates meet?

5. a) Why are San Francisco and Los Angeles prone to earthquakes?
   b) What is the focus of an earthquake?
   c) What is the epicentre of an earthquake?
   d) What precautions could you take against earthquakes if you lived in Los Angeles?

6.

   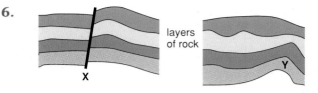

   layers of rock

   a) In the diagram, what is line X called?
   b) Which general type of rock forms the layers shown?
   c) Which is the oldest rock layer shown above?
   d) What happened to the rocks at Y?
   e) What do we call the rock structure at Y?

7. a) What is 'subduction'?
   b) How were chains of mountains, like the Alps and Himalayas formed?
   c) What 'powers' the movements of the Earth's plates?

8. a) Explain what we mean by 'sea-floor spreading'.
   b) Which type of rock will form on the sea-floor at a mid-ocean ridge?
   c) Look at the diagram below:

   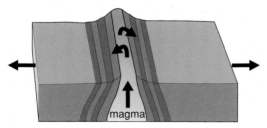

   magma

   Explain the pattern of stripes in the rocks on either side of the ridge.

9. Lava from different volcanoes has different thicknesses. The temperature, dissolved gases, and chemical composition of the lava affect the flow. Look at these two volcanoes:

   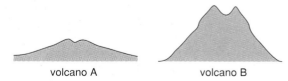

   volcano A   volcano B

   Explain the different shapes of the two volcanoes.

Further questions on page 308.

▶ The atmosphere

1. Clean air is a mixture of gaseous elements and compounds as shown in the pie chart below.

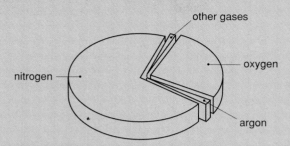

a) Which element is the most abundant in air? [1]

b) Name **two** of the 'Other Gases' referred to in the pie chart. [2] (ULEAC)

2. The diagram below is of the Carbon Cycle.

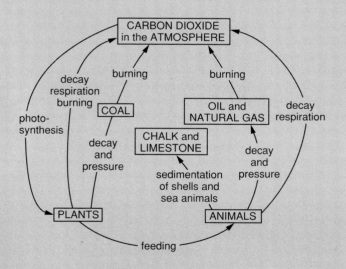

a) Which gas, present in air, provides the plants with the carbon they need? [1]

b) Name the process that plants use to change this gas into carbon compounds. [1]

c) How do animals get the carbon compounds they need? [1] (SEG)

3. The table below gives information about the Earth's atmosphere at various times in its history.

Time	Atmosphere
4500 million years ago	Hydrogen and helium.
3800 million years ago	Mainly carbon dioxide, steam and hydrogen, with small amounts of methane, ammonia and hydrogen sulphide.
2600 million years ago	Carbon dioxide begins to decrease.
1800 million years ago	Oxygen begins to build up.

a) State the origin of the gases present in the atmosphere 3800 million years ago. [1]

b) Suggest what caused:
  i) the decrease in carbon dioxide concentration in the atmosphere 2600 million years ago;
  ii) the build up of oxygen in the atmosphere 1800 million years ago. [2]

c) Use the table above to explain how the oceans formed, and suggest an approximate date for their formation. [3]

d) The table below shows the concentration of carbon dioxide in the air at the Mauna Loa observatory in Hawaii over a period of 30 years from 1958.

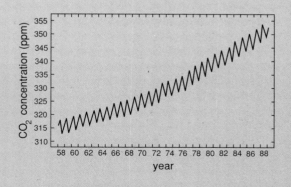

Give, and explain, **two** reasons why the carbon dioxide concentration has been increasing since 1958. [4] (ULEAC)

▶ Rocks

4. a) Rocks can be sorted into three types, sedimentary, igneous and metamorphic. Read the following information about four rock samples.

Basalt is a hard black rock formed from the lava flowing from volcanoes.

Sandstone is soft and has small grains arranged in layers.

Gabbro is a rock made of black crystals and white crystals locked closely together, producing a hard, strong rock.

Marble is a rock found where hot igneous rock has come into contact with limestone. Write down which rock type each sample above belongs to. [4]

b) Rocks are broken down by weathering. One type of weathering process is shown in the diagrams.

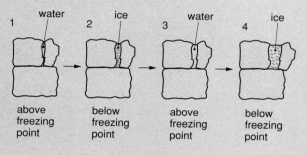

When water freezes, the ice takes up 9% more volume than when the water is not frozen. What volume of ice forms when 100 cm³ of water freezes? [1]

c) Finish the sentences to explain what is happening in the diagrams in b) above. A small crack fills up with i) —————— When this freezes, it takes up more space and ii) —————— against the sides. The gap becomes iii) —————— and fills up with more water. This process is repeated many times until pieces of rock iv) —————— away from the main rock face. [4]   (MEG)

5. a) In which type of rock, igneous, metamorphic or sedimentary are fossils most likely to occur? [1]

b) Why can the presence of fossils be useful in the investigation of rocks? [1]   (WJEB)

6. The diagram shows a section through rocks.

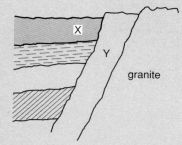

a) There are three main types of rock: igneous   metamorphic   sedimentary. What type of rock is found i) at X   ii) at Y [2]

b) How are metamorphic rocks formed? [2]

c) What metamorphic rock is formed from limestone? [1]

d) How is granite formed? [2]   (ULEAC)

7.

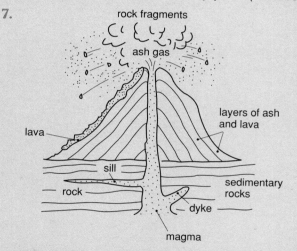

Study the diagram, then answer the questions:

a) i)   Basalt is an igneous rock which has small crystals. Describe where you would expect basalt to be formed on the diagram above. [1]

ii)   How are igneous rocks formed? [1]

iii)   Suggest a reason why basalt has small rather than large crystals. [1]

b) i)   With the aid of a diagram, explain how particles carried by rivers form sedimentary rocks when they reach the sea. [3]

ii)   How would you know if an exposed cliff was made up of sedimentary rock? [1]   (WJEC)

8. The diagram below shows some places where different types of rock are formed.

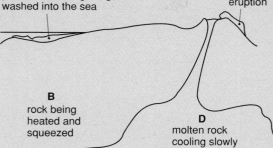

A
particles of rock getting washed into the sea

C
volcanic eruption

B
rock being heated and squeezed

D
molten rock cooling slowly

At which place, **A**, **B**, **C** or **D**, would the rocks described in the table be formed? [4]

Rock	Description
granite	An igneous rock containing large crystals. Often used to decorate buildings.
slate	A metamorphic rock which is easy to split into sheets. Used for roofs.
basalt	An igneous rock containing small crystals. It is used for building roads.
sandstone	A sedimentary rock made up of rounded grains of sand. Sometimes used as lining for furnaces.

9. The diagram below shows the Rock Cycle.

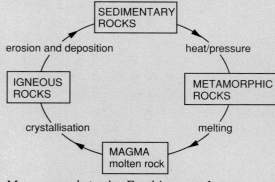

SEDIMENTARY ROCKS

erosion and deposition

heat/pressure

IGNEOUS ROCKS

METAMORPHIC ROCKS

crystallisation

melting

MAGMA molten rock

a) Magma cools in the Earth's crust. It may form granite.
   Is granite an igneous, metamorphic or sedimentary rock? [1]
b) What does granite look like? [2]
c) Describe **one** way granite can be broken down by weathering. [3]   (NEAB)

10. The diagram below shows a section through part of the Earth's crust.

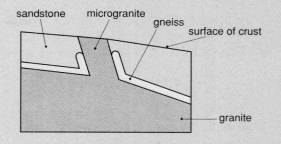

sandstone   microgranite

gneiss

surface of crust

granite

a) Sandstone is a sedimentary rock. Gneiss is a metamorphic rock formed from sandstone.
   Use information from the diagram to explain how the gneiss was formed. [2]
b) Microgranite and granite are both igneous rocks. The crystals which make up microgranite are much smaller than those which make up granite.
   Use information from the diagram to explain why this is so. [3]   (NEAB)

11. The diagram shows some features of the Earth's crust.

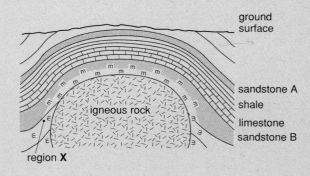

ground surface

sandstone A

shale

limestone

sandstone B

igneous rock

region **X**

a) List the **four layers** of sedimentary rock named in the diagram, in order of age, starting with the oldest. [1]
b) i) What types of rocks are likely to be formed in region **X**? [1]
   ii) Name a rock formed from limestone in region **X**. [1]
c) Describe how a sedimentary rock, such as sandstone, is formed from sediment. [2]
(SEG)

Further questions on Structure of the Earth

▶ Plate tectonics

12. The table below shows the density of the Earth, and of different types of rock from which it is composed.

Type of rock	Density (kg/m³)
Crustal rock	2800
Mantle rock	4500
Average overall density of Earth	5500

Explain what evidence can be obtained from these readings about the nature of the Earth's core.   [2]   (ULEAC)

13. The map below shows the boundaries of the Earth's plates.

- - - - - - - boundary of plate

Use the map to answer the following questions.
a) Explain why the island of Iceland consists almost completely of igneous rock.   [3]
b) Describe how the Himalayan mountains were formed.   [2]   (ULEAC)

14. The theory of plate tectonics is believed to explain why mountains are formed.
a) What are tectonic plates?   [2]
b) Explain, as fully as you can, **one** way in which tectonic plates cause mountains to be formed.   [3]   (NEAB)

15. a) Give **three** features that may be observed at a plate boundary.   [3]
b) What causes the Earth's plates to move? Explain your answer.   [4]   (SEG)

16. The diagram shows how a line of underwater mountains is forming in the middle of the Atlantic Ocean. This is called a mid-ocean ridge.

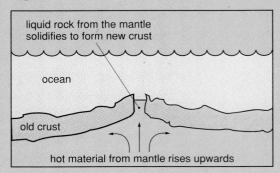

a) Solid rock forms when the liquid from the mantle layer reaches the water.
   i) Which type of rock will form: **igneous**, **metamorphic** or **sedimentary**?   [1]
   ii) Explain why the crystals formed in this rock are very small.   [2]
b) Europe and North America are at opposite sides of the Atlantic Ocean.
Explain why Europe and North America move a little further apart each year.   [2]
         (MEG)

17. The diagram shows a destructive plate margin.

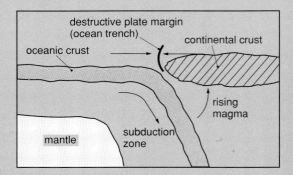

a) Describe how the events at a destructive plate margin lead to the recycling of rocks.   [4]

b) Explain how the events at a destructive plate margin lead to **one** hazard for human populations living near such areas.   [2]   (MEG)

Redox reactions

You have already seen how we extract metals from ores. Often a metal oxide is *reduced*. Look back to page 88.

Whenever a substance is reduced, something else is *oxidised*.
We call the reaction a **redox reaction**.
Can you see why?

Look at an example from the blast furnace on page 89:

iron oxide + carbon monoxide $\longrightarrow$ iron + carbon dioxide
$$Fe_2O_3 \quad + \quad 3\,CO \quad \longrightarrow \quad 2\,Fe \quad + \quad 3\,CO_2$$

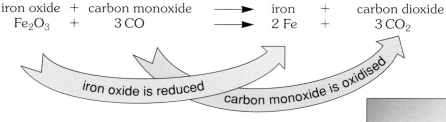

iron oxide is reduced

carbon monoxide is oxidised

Iron oxide is reduced by carbon monoxide. It **loses oxygen**. The carbon monoxide itself gets oxidised. It **gains oxygen**. The carbon monoxide is called a reducing agent.

Can you remember how we extract highly reactive metals. Carbon or carbon monoxide cannot reduce their oxides. We have to use electrolysis.
Look at the extraction of aluminium on page 103.
The aluminium oxide is reduced.

At the cathode (−)

$$Al^{3+} + 3e^- \longrightarrow Al$$

The Al^{3+} ions gain electrons. They are reduced.
So we can say that:

> **Reduction is the *gain of electrons*.**

The Al^{3+} ions have been reduced to Al atoms.

Oxidation and reduction are chemical opposites. So what do you think happens to the number of electrons in an ion that gets oxidised?

> **Oxidation is the *loss of electrons*.**

OIL-RIG will help you to remember!

This blast furnace is about 50 m high. Inside it, iron oxide is reduced to iron.

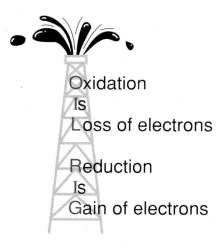

Oxidation
Is
Loss of electrons

Reduction
Is
Gain of electrons

Calculations in Chemistry

On page 34 you saw that we can compare the masses of different elements. Each element has a Relative Atomic Mass (R.A.M. or A_r). The R.A.M.s help us to 'count' atoms.

As you know, atoms are too small to see. So, we have a big problem when we try to count them. However, we can compare numbers of atoms quite easily.

Look at the R.A.M.s in the table opposite: Can you see that oxygen is 16 times as heavy as hydrogen? Therefore, if you have 1 gram of hydrogen and 16 grams of oxygen, you have the same number of hydrogen and oxygen atoms. This is a lot of atoms!

Element	Relative Atomic Mass (R.A.M.)
Hydrogen	1
Carbon	12
Nitrogen	14
Oxygen	16
Fluorine	19

> The number of atoms in 1 gram of hydrogen is called a **mole**.

The mole is a number. It's like 'a dozen' but an awful lot bigger. In fact, in 1 gram of hydrogen there are about 600,000,000,000,000,000,000,000 atoms! No wonder we can't see them! (This number is known as the **Avogadro constant**, and is written 6×10^{23}).

There are huge numbers of atoms even in test-tube reactions. So it is easier to talk about moles than the actual numbers involved. We weigh out a substance, then say how many moles there are.

Learn this equation:

$$\textbf{moles of atoms} = \frac{\textbf{mass}}{\textbf{R.A.M.}}$$

Counting atoms takes its toll. Just weigh them out, then use the mole!

Am I a mole millionaire?

Would you rather win the National Lottery or win a 'mole' of 1p coins?

It's like cashing in 1 p coins at the bank. If you take a thousand 1 p coins to your bank, does the cashier count out each coin? The coins are weighed out on scales. The scales 'know' the mass of one hundred 1 p coins, and tell the cashier how many pounds (£s) are on the scales.

Example

How many moles of atoms are there in 2.4 g of carbon?

$$\text{Moles of atoms} = \frac{\text{mass}}{\text{R.A.M.}} = \frac{2.4}{12} = 0.2 \text{ moles}$$

Now try these yourself (the answers are on page 328).

How many moles of atoms are there in
1. 2 g of hydrogen   2. 36 g of carbon   3. 160 g of oxygen   4. 1.4 g of nitrogen   5. 0.19 g of fluorine?
(R.A.M.s   H = 1, C = 12, O = 16, N = 14, F = 19)

Changing moles to mass

You can re-arrange the equation on the last page:

$$\boxed{\textbf{mass} = \textbf{moles} \times \textbf{R.A.M.}}$$

This tells us the mass of an element, if we know how many moles there are.

> *Example*
> What is the mass of 0.1 moles of carbon atoms?
> mass = moles × R.A.M.
> = 0.1 × 12 = 1.2 g

If you find re-arranging equations difficult, you can use the 'magic triangle'.

Read the question. See what you need to find out.
Cover that part of the triangle with your finger.
Then you have the equation that you need!

Now you can try these:

> What is the mass of
> 6. 2 moles of H atoms   7. 5 moles of N atoms   8. 20 moles of O atoms
> 9. 0.5 mole of F atoms   10. 0.01 mole of C atoms?

*Amedio Avogadro
(1776–1856)*

Moles of molecules

You can use the same ideas for problems about molecules.
Just use the Relative Formula Mass (R.F.M. or M_r) instead of the R.A.M.:

$$\boxed{\textbf{moles} = \frac{\textbf{mass}}{\textbf{R.F.M.}}} \quad \text{or} \quad \boxed{\textbf{mass} = \textbf{moles} \times \textbf{R.F.M.}}$$

So the magic triangle becomes:

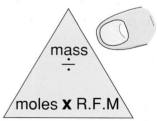

> *Example*
> How many moles are there in 8 g of copper(II) oxide (formula = CuO)?
>
> **Step 1** – Work out the Formula Mass by adding up the R.A.M.s (see page 35):
> Cu = 64
> O = +16
> R.F.M. = 80
>
> **Step 2** – Put information from the question and the R.F.M. into the equation:
>
> moles = $\frac{mass}{R.F.M.}$ moles = $\frac{8}{80}$ = 0.1 mole
>
> Now you can try these. How many moles of molecules are there in:
> 11. 36 g of H_2O 12. 170 g of NH_3 13. 1.6 g of CH_4 14. 0.3 g of C_2H_6 15. 16 g of NH_4NO_3?

Moles of gases

As you know, gases are very light.
It is difficult to weigh them.
However, it is quite easy to measure the **volume** of a gas.

Do you remember your work on rates of reaction
in Chapter 15? Can you think of two ways to measure
the volume of gas given off in a reaction?

Luckily for us, we can change volumes of gas
straight into moles. There is no need to weigh the gas.

At room temperature (25 °C) and pressure (1 atmosphere),
we can say that:
1 mole of any gas takes up a volume of 24 dm³ or 24 litres
(24 dm³ = 24 000 cm³)
Using this information we can write this equation:

$$\text{moles of gas} = \frac{\text{volume of gas (in dm}^3)}{24}$$

It's tricky weighing a gas!

In our experiments in the lab, we usually measure
the volume of gas in cm³. In this case, the equation
becomes:

$$\text{moles of gas} = \frac{\text{volume of gas (in cm}^3)}{24\,000}$$

It's easier measuring volumes.

The magic triangle is:

volume (cm³)
÷
moles **X** 24 000

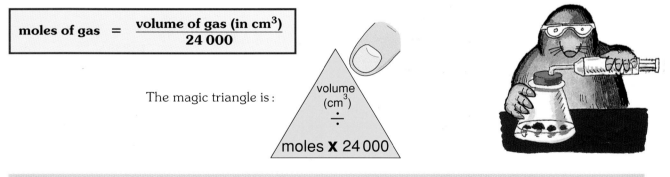

Example
How many moles of hydrogen molecules are there in 24 cm³ of hydrogen gas?

$$\text{moles} = \frac{\text{volume}}{24\,000} = \frac{24}{24\,000} = \underline{0.001 \text{ mole}}$$

Now you can try these:
(Watch out for the units, dm³ or cm³!)
How many moles of gas molecules are there in
1. 24 dm³ of chlorine gas   2. 6 dm³ of hydrogen gas   3. 2.4 dm³ of methane gas
4. 120 cm³ of oxygen gas   5. 48 cm³ of nitrogen gas

Notice that you don't need the Relative Atomic Masses or the Relative Formula Masses of the gases to work out the problems on the last page.

Volumes of gases

You can re-arrange the equations on the last page to get:

| volume of gas (dm³) = number of moles × 24 | or | volume of gas (cm³) = number of moles × 24 000 |

Example
What volume does 0.1 mole of oxygen gas occupy at room temperature and pressure?

$$\text{volume (in cm}^3) = \text{number of moles} \times 24\,000$$
$$= 0.1 \times 24\,000$$
$$= 2400 \text{ cm}^3$$

Now try these:
What volume do these gases occupy
6. 3 moles of hydrogen   7. 5 moles of chlorine   8. 0.1 mole of nitrogen
9. 0.001 mole of hydrogen sulphide   10. 0.005 mole of sulphur dioxide?

You can get more difficult problems which include the mass of the gas.

Example
What volume does 8 g of oxygen gas occupy at room temperature and pressure?

Step 1 – Work out the number of moles of gas molecules.
Remember that the formula of oxygen gas is O_2.
Therefore, the R.F.M. of O_2 is $16 \times 2 = 32$.
So 1 mole of oxygen gas weighs 32 g.

Use the equation $\text{moles} = \dfrac{\text{mass}}{\text{R.F.M.}}$

The number of moles of oxygen $= \dfrac{8}{32} = 0.25$ mole

Step 2 – Now work out the volume of gas.

$$\text{volume of gas (in cm}^3) = \text{moles} \times 24\,000$$
$$= 0.25 \times 24\,000$$
$$= \textbf{6000 cm}^3 \textbf{ of oxygen gas}$$

Now you can try these:
What volume of gas is occupied by these gases at room temperature and pressure.
(You can find the R.A.M.s on page 342.)
11. 4 g of H_2 12. 8 g of CH_4 13. 3.55 g of Cl_2 14. 0.002 g of He   15. 8.8 g of CO_2?

Moles in solution

All bottles of solutions in a lab must be labelled.
Look at a bottle in your next experiment.
You will see that the label has the name of the solution.
Most also show its concentration, such as 1M or 2M.
The concentration is sometimes called the **molarity** of a solution.

1M means that there is 1 mole of the substance dissolved
in $1 \, dm^3$ (or $1000 \, cm^3$) of its solution.

Knowing this, and the concentration, we can work out
the number of moles in any solution.

Let's look at an example:

Example

How many moles of sodium chloride are there in $100 \, cm^3$ of a
2M solution?

2M means that there are 2 moles in $1000 \, cm^3$ of solution.
$100 \, cm^3$ is only a tenth of $1000 \, cm^3$.
Therefore, in $100 \, cm^3$ we will have a tenth of 2 moles,
which is 0.2 mole.

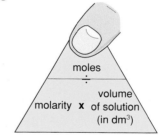

Is this a 1M solution?

This type of logical thinking can be used to solve
any moles calculations.
Here is a more tricky example:

Example

How many moles of sodium chloride are there in $22 \, cm^3$ of a
2M solution?

Here are the logical steps:
In $1000 \, cm^3$ of the solution we have 2 moles.

So, in $1 \, cm^3$ of the solution we have $\dfrac{2}{1000}$ moles

So in $22 \, cm^3$ of the solution we have $\dfrac{2}{1000} \times 22$ moles

$$= \underline{0.044 \text{ mole}}$$

Or you can use a magic triangle
again:

(Don't forget to change any
volumes given in cm^3 to dm^3,
by dividing by 1000)

However, if you prefer to learn equations:

number of moles in a solution $=$ molarity $\times \dfrac{\text{volume of solution (in } cm^3)}{1000}$

So in the first example:
the molarity (concentration) is 2M, and
the volume of solution is $100 \, cm^3$.

Therefore, the number of moles $= 2 \times \dfrac{100}{1000} = 0.2 \text{ mole}$

Now you can try these:
How many moles are there in
1. 2 dm³ of 1M sulphuric acid
2. 500 cm³ of 2M nitric acid
3. 250 cm³ of 1M hydrochloric acid
4. 100 cm³ of 0.5M sodium hydroxide solution
5. 50 cm³ of 0.5M sodium chloride solution?

(Notice that you don't need the formula of the substance because you don't have to work out R.F.M.s.)

Making up solutions

Imagine that you are a lab technician.
You are asked for 250 cm³ of 1M sodium nitrate for a chemistry lesson. How would you make up the solution?

Step 1 – How many moles are needed.
We know that 1000 cm³ of a 1M solution contains 1 mole. But you only need to make up a quarter of this (250 cm³). So you will need to dissolve a quarter (0.25) of a mole of sodium nitrate.

Step 2 – Work out the mass of solid needed.
Find the R.F.M. of sodium nitrate, $NaNO_3$.
$1 \times Na = 1 \times 23 = 23$
$1 \times N = 1 \times 14 = 14$
$3 \times O = 3 \times 16 = +48$
R.F.M. $= 85$
1 mole of sodium nitrate weighs 85 g.
Therefore, 0.25 mole of sodium nitrate weighs $0.25 \times 85 = 21.25$ g
(Remember the magic triangle! mass = moles $\times$ R.F.M.)

So as a technician, you would weigh out **21.25 g** of sodium nitrate, then make it up to 250 cm³ of solution with water.

Now you can try these:
What is the mass of each compound in these solutions.
6. 500 cm³ of 1M sodium chloride, NaCl, solution
7. 100 cm³ of 2M potassium hydroxide, KOH, solution
8. 25 cm³ of 1M sulphuric acid, H_2SO_4, solution
9. 75 cm³ of 0.5M lead nitrate, $Pb(NO_3)_2$, solution
10. 13 cm³ of 0.25M ammonium sulphate, $(NH_4)_2SO_4$, solution?

(R.A.M.s   Na = 23, Cl = 35.5, K = 39, O = 16, H = 1,
S = 32, Pb = 207, N = 14)

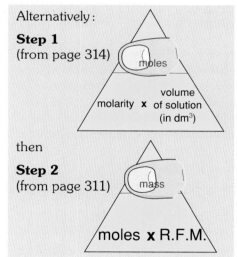

Alternatively:
Step 1
(from page 314)
moles
molarity **x** volume of solution (in dm³)

then

Step 2
(from page 311)
mass
moles **x** R.F.M.

Working out the formula

We can use moles to work out the formula
of a compound.
If we can measure the mass of each element
in a compound, we can calculate its formula.
Let's look at an example :

Example
A compound of nitrogen and hydrogen was broken
down into its elements.
It was found that 1.4 g of nitrogen had combined with
0.3 g of hydrogen in the compound.
What was the formula of the compound ?
(R.A.M.s   N = 14, H = 1)

Step 1 – Work out the **number of moles** of each element in the compound.

Remember that $\text{moles} = \dfrac{\text{mass}}{\text{R.A.M.}}$

moles of N $= \dfrac{1.4}{14} = 0.1$ moles of H $= \dfrac{0.3}{1} = 0.3$

Step 2 – Work out the **ratio** of the number of moles of each element,
to the lowest whole numbers.

N	:	H
0.1	:	0.3
1	:	3

Therefore, we have 3 times as many H atoms as N atoms in this compound.

Its formula must be **NH$_3$**.

Now see if you can work out the formula for each of the compounds
made from :

1. 12 g of carbon and 4 g of hydrogen

2. 414 g of lead and 32 g of oxygen

3. 1.2 g of carbon and 3.2 g of oxygen

4. 11.2 g of iron and 4.8 g of oxygen

5. 3.2 g of copper, 0.6 g of carbon and 2.4 g of oxygen.

(R.A.M.s   C = 12, H = 1, Pb = 207, O = 16, Fe = 56, Cu = 64)

Using results from experiments

You can work out the formula of a compound by
● splitting it up into its original elements, or
● making it from its elements.
In either case you need to measure the mass
of each element in the compound.

Example   Working out the formula of magnesium oxide
A student heated up some magnesium ribbon as shown:
The magnesium ribbons burns in air. It combines with
the oxygen to make magnesium oxide.

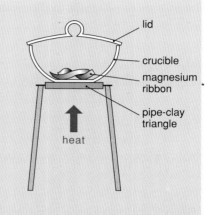

These are her results:

Mass of crucible + lid	= 25.00 g
Mass of crucible + lid + magnesium *before* heating	= 25.24 g
Mass of crucible + lid + magnesium oxide *after* heating	= 25.40 g

Step 1 – Work out the mass of each element in the compound.
Magnesium

Mass of crucible + lid + magnesium before heating	= 25.24 g
Mass of crucible + lid	= 25.00 g
Therefore, the mass of magnesium	= 0.24 g

Oxygen

Mass of crucible + lid + magnesium oxide after heating	= 25.40 g
Mass of crucible + lid + magnesium before heating	= 25.24 g
Therefore, the mass of oxygen in magnesium oxide	= 0.16 g

Step 2 – Change the masses into moles.

$$\begin{array}{cc} \text{Magnesium} & \text{Oxygen} \\ \dfrac{0.24}{24} & \dfrac{0.16}{16} \\ = 0.01 \text{ mole} & 0.01 \text{ mole} \end{array}$$

Step 3 – Work out the ratio of moles of each element.

$$\begin{array}{ccc} \text{Mg} & : & \text{O} \\ 0.01 & : & 0.01 \\ 1 & : & 1 \end{array}$$

Therefore the formula of magnesium oxide is **MgO**.

Experiment   Finding the formula of magnesium oxide
Try the experiment described above.
You will need to lift the lid slightly from time to time with a pair of tongs.
This lets oxygen gas get to the hot magnesium. But try not to let any of the
white smoke produced escape. Why not?
Work out your formula for magnesium oxide.
How do your results compare to the student's experiment described above?

Moles in equations

Imagine that you are the manager of a chemical plant.
When a customer orders some of your product,
you need to know how much raw material you need
to order yourself.

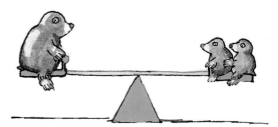

This is where chemical equations help us out.
We can use balanced equations to predict
the masses of reactants and products.
Let's look at an example:

Example
Zinc oxide is heated with carbon in a furnace.
The zinc oxide is reduced to zinc and carbon monoxide is formed.
How much zinc oxide do you need to make 130 tonnes of zinc?
(1 tonne = 1000 kg   Zn = 65, O = 16)

Step 1 – Write the balanced equation.

$$ZnO + C \longrightarrow Zn + CO$$

Step 2 – Write out the number of moles of reactants and products
from the balanced equation.

The equation above means that:
   1 mole of zinc oxide reacts with 1 mole of carbon,
   to make 1 mole of zinc and 1 mole of carbon monoxide.

Step 3 – Circle the information given and what you want to find out.

$$\boxed{ZnO} + C \longrightarrow \boxed{Zn} + CO$$

So 1 mole of zinc oxide is needed to make 1 mole of zinc.

Step 4 – Convert the moles into masses (using R.F.M.s)

$$\begin{array}{ccccc} ZnO & + C \longrightarrow & Zn & + CO \\ (65 + 16)\,g & & 65\,g & \\ 81\,g & \longrightarrow & 65\,g & \end{array}$$

Step 5 – Use logical steps to arrive at your final answer.

If 81 g of ZnO will give us 65g of Zn, then
81 tonnes of ZnO will give us 65 tonnes of Zn.
So how many tonnes of ZnO will give us 130 tonnes of Zn?

$\dfrac{81}{65}$ tonnes of ZnO will give us 1 tonne of Zn.

Therefore, $\dfrac{81}{65} \times 130$ tonnes of ZnO will give us 130 tonnes of Zn
         = **162 tonnes of zinc oxide**

Let's look at another example. Do you remember
the test for a chloride ion? (See page 150.)
You add silver nitrate solution, then see if you get
a white precipitate of silver chloride.

Example

You start with a solution containing 0.95 g of magnesium chloride.
You add a solution of silver nitrate. If all the magnesium chloride reacts,
how much silver chloride could be made?
(Mg = 24, Cl = 35.5, Ag = 108)

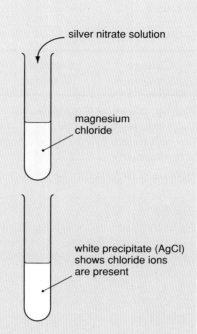

silver nitrate solution

magnesium chloride

Step 1 – Write the balanced equation.

$$2\,AgNO_3 + MgCl_2 \longrightarrow 2\,AgCl + Mg(NO_3)_2$$

Step 2 – Write out the number of moles of reactants and products
from the balanced equation.

   2 moles of silver nitrate react with 1 mole of magnesium chloride,
   to give 2 moles of silver chloride and 1 mole of magnesium nitrate.

Step 3 – Circle the information given and what you want to find out.

$$2\,AgNO_3 + \boxed{MgCl_2} \longrightarrow \boxed{2\,AgCl} + Mg(NO_3)_2$$

So 1 mole of magnesium chloride will give 2 moles of silver chloride.

white precipitate (AgCl)
shows chloride ions
are present

Step 4 – Convert the moles into masses (using R.F.M.s)
   magnesium chloride, $MgCl_2$ silver chloride, AgCl
   $1 \times Mg = 1 \times 24 = 24$ $1 \times Ag = 108$
   $2 \times Cl = 2 \times 35.5 = +71$ $1 \times Cl = +35.5$
   95 143.5

$$2\,AgNO_3 + MgCl_2 \longrightarrow 2\,AgCl + Mg(NO_3)_2$$
$$\;95\,g \qquad (2 \times 143.5)$$
$$\;95\,g \longrightarrow 287\,g$$

Step 5 – Use logical steps to arrive at your final answer.

If 95 g of $MgCl_2$ give us 287 g of AgCl, then

1 g of $MgCl_2$ give us $\dfrac{287}{95}$ g of AgCl.

Therefore, 0.95 g of $MgCl_2$ give us $\dfrac{287}{95} \times 0.95\,g = $ **2.87 g of AgCl**

Now you can try these problems:
1. A student adds 4.8 g of magnesium to excess dilute hydrochloric acid.
   What mass of magnesium chloride would be made? (Mg = 24, Cl = 35.5)
2. If you add 5.3 g of sodium carbonate to excess dilute sulphuric acid,
   what mass of sodium sulphate would be made? (Na = 23, C = 12, O = 16, S = 32)

Moles in electrolysis

You have learned about electrolysis in Chapter 9.
Can you remember what electrolysis means?
When a compound is broken down by electricity,
metals (or hydrogen) form at the negative electrode (cathode).
The non-metals form at the positive electrode (anode).

We can work out how much charge passes around the circuit
during electrolysis using this equation:

> **Charge** = **Current** × **Time**
> (in coulombs)   (in amps)   (in seconds)

You can measure the mass of an element formed at an electrode
in an electrolysis experiment.
You can then work out how much charge would give 1 mole
of the element.

Let's look at an example:

Example

A student set up the circuit as shown:
A current of 0.5 A passed around the circuit for
3860 seconds. The cathode had gained 0.64 g in the
experiment.
How many coulombs of charge are needed to deposit
1 mole of copper?
(R.A.M. of Cu = 64)

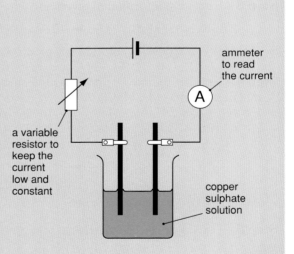

ammeter
to read
the current

a variable
resistor to
keep the
current
low and
constant

copper
sulphate
solution

Use the equation   Charge = Current × Time
$$= 0.5 \times 3860$$
$$= 1930 \text{ coulombs}$$

So 1930 coulombs gave 0.64 g of coper.

Therefore, $1930 \times \dfrac{1}{0.64}$ coulombs will give 1 g of copper.

This means that $1930 \times \dfrac{1}{0.64} \times 64$ coulombs will give 64 g (1 mole) of copper.

193 000 coulombs will produce 1 mole of copper.

Now you can try this example:
1. A current of 2 A is passed through molten sodium chloride
   for 9650 seconds.
   4.6 g of sodium is deposited at the cathode.
   How many coulombs of charge will give 1 mole of sodium?
   (R.A.M. of Na = 23)

Faraday's Law

We have just seen how to work out the charge needed to deposit 1 mole of an element. This information can then be used to tell us the charge on an ion of that element.

The table opposite shows how much charge is needed to deposit 1 mole of the elements. Can you see any pattern?

The famous scientist Michael Faraday did much of the early work on electrolysis. It was a powerful tool in the search for new elements. He found that:

Metal	Charge on ion	Charge needed to deposit one mole (C)
Sodium	1+	96 500
Magnesium	2+	193 000
Aluminium	3+	289 500

Michael Faraday (1791–1867) is sometimes called 'the father of electricity'.

> **96 500 coulombs deposit 1 mole of a metal with a single charge on its ions, e.g. Na$^+$.**

We can calculate the charge on an ion from the results of an electrolysis experiment.

The charge carried by one mole of electrons (96 500 C) is called 1 Faraday. How many Faradays are needed to deposit one mole of magnesium?

Example

A student set up the circuit as shown:
She passed a current of 1 A for 16 minutes.
She collected 1.08 g of silver.
What is the charge on a silver ion?

Charge = Current × Time (in seconds!)
     = 1   × 16 × 60
     = 960 coulombs

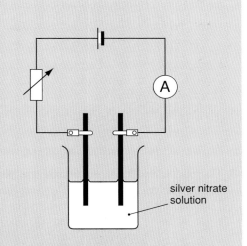

silver nitrate solution

960 coulombs gave 1.08 g of silver.

So $960 \times \dfrac{1}{1.08}$ coulombs will give 1 g of silver.

Therefore, $960 \times \dfrac{1}{1.08} \times 108$ coulombs will give 108 g of silver

     = 96 000 coulombs

If 96 000 coulombs give 1 mole of silver, then the charge on its ions must be 1+.
(This allows for some experimental error.)

Now you try this example:
2. A current of 1 A was passed through molten lead bromide for 1930 seconds.
2.07 g of lead was collected.
What is the charge on a lead ion? (R.A.M. of Pb = 207)

Problems with moles

1. An oxide of copper was reduced (had its oxygen removed)
   in a stream of hydrogen as shown :

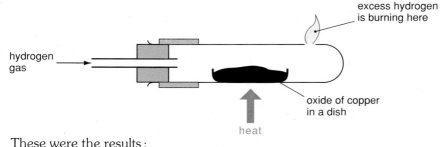

excess hydrogen
is burning here

hydrogen
gas

oxide of copper
in a dish

heat

   These were the results :
   Mass of dish = 25.00 g
   Mass of oxide of copper + dish (before reaction) = 29.0 g
   Mass of copper left + dish (after reaction) = 28.2 g
   Work out the formula of this oxide of copper.

   (Cu = 64, O = 16)

2. Ammonium nitrate fertiliser is made by the following reaction :

$$NH_3 \quad + \quad HNO_3 \longrightarrow \quad NH_4NO_3$$
   ammonia + nitric acid $\longrightarrow$ ammonium nitrate

   How many tonnes of ammonia is needed to make
   2400 tonnes of ammonium nitrate ?
   (1 tonne = 1000 kg)

   (N = 14, H = 1, O = 16)

3. Amy and Hassan are investigating rates of reaction.

   They decide to look at the reaction between
   limestone (calcium carbonate) and dilute hydrochloric acid.
   They want to measure the volume of gas given off in
   a gas syringe. The syringe has a maximum volume of $100 \, cm^3$.

   Oops!

   They plan to follow the reaction until it is complete,
   measuring the volume of gas at regular intervals.
   They will use excess acid.
   What is the greatest mass of calcium carbonate that they
   should start with to avoid the plunger being forced out of the syringe ?
   (1 mole of any gas occupies $24\,000 \, cm^3$ at room temperature and pressure)

   (Ca = 40, C = 12, O = 16)

4. Molten potassium chloride was electrolysed.
   At the end of the electrolysis, 7.8 g of potassium
   had been deposited at the cathode.
   What volume of chlorine gas was given off at the anode ?
   (K = 39, 1 mole of any gas occupies $24\,000 \, cm^3$)

The alternative 'Problem Page'

Can you help these poor, unfortunate souls solve their problems?

1.

Dear Agony Aunt,
I have a terrible compound. It all started with 2.4 g of carbon and 0.8 g of hydrogen. Can you please help me find the correct formula?
(The Relative Formula Mass of the compound is 16.)

Yours hopefully,
Ray C. O.
P.S.   (C = 12, H = 1)

2.

Dear Agony Aunt,
I have been putting aside calcium carbonate for several years now.
I am naturally looking forward to the day when I can roast it all, and change it into calcium oxide and carbon dioxide.
I now have 200 tonnes of calcium carbonate. Can you tell me how much calcium oxide I can expect when I roast it?

Yours elderly,
Mrs L. Kiln
P.S.   (Ca = 40, C = 12, O = 16)

3.

Dear Agony Aunt,
I am studying for my GCSEs, but I am very worried about my concentration. I fear it is too low to ever be successful.
My doctor says that I have 0.585 g of sodium chloride in 250 cm^3 of solution. Please help. Don't try to be kind. I need to know my concentration in moles per dm^3 as soon as possible!

Yours distractedly,
Sol T. Waters
P.S.   (Na = 23, Cl = 35.5)

4.

Dear Agony Aunt,
My daughter recently added 5 g of calcium carbonate to excess dilute hydrochloric acid.
I know this sounds silly, but she forgot to measure the volume of carbon dioxide gas given off. Her lapse was at room temperature and pressure, naturally. Can you help her?

Yours motherly,
Ma Bell
P.S.   (Ca = 40, C = 12, O = 16.
And don't forget 1 mole of gas occupies 24 000 cm^3 at room temperature and pressure.)

These are tricky problems – but you can find my answers on page 328

Molly Cule
Agony Aunt

5.

Dear Agony Aunt,
Last week I found a friend of mine passing 2 amps of electricity through some copper(II) sulphate solution.
She claimed that she had only done it once; and that was only for 5 minutes. However, from the amount of copper deposited, I frankly find this difficult to believe.
Can you tell me how much copper she would get if she is telling the truth?

Yours suspiciously,
Elle Ectrolysis
P.S.   (Cu = 64)

Calculations

1. Which one of the following has the greatest mass?
   (Relative atomic masses: H = 1, O = 16, Na = 23, S = 32, Cl = 35.5)
   A   1 mole Na
   B   0.5 mole NaCl
   C   0.6 mole NaOH
   D   0.2 mole Na_2SO_4 [1]   (NEAB)

2. Which of the following have a concentration of 0.1 mole/litre?
   (Relative atomic masses: H = 1, N = 14, O = 16, Na = 23, S = 32)
   (1) HNO_3(aq) containing 6.3 g/litre
   (2) NaOH(aq) containing 2 g in 500 cm^3
   (3) H_2SO_4(aq) containing 0.98 g in 100 cm^3
                                          [1]   (NEAB)

Questions 3–5
Use pages 342 and 343 to help you.
From the list **A** to **D**,
   A   3
   B   6
   C   9
   D   18
choose the number which is the:

3. mass in grams of water produced when 1 g of hydrogen is burned completely;

$$2H_2 + O_2 \longrightarrow 2H_2O \qquad [1]$$

4. mass in grams of magnesium in 10 g of magnesium oxide, MgO.   [1]

5. number of atoms of beryllium, Be, which have the same total mass as one atom of aluminium, Al.   [1]   (NEAB)

6. Calculate the number of moles of water molecules, H_2O, present in 90 g of ice.
   (Relative atomic masses: H = 1, O = 16)   [1]
                                          (NEAB)

7. 0.5 mole of metal X combine with 1.0 mole of non-metal Y.
   What is the formula of this compound of X and Y?   [1]   (NEAB)

8. Analysis of a sample of the compound sodium oxide, showed that it contained 2.3 g of sodium and 0.8 g of oxygen.
   Use this information to work out the formula of the compound sodium oxide in questions a) to e).
   (You may find it helpful to answer the questions below using moles but use any other method if you prefer.)
   a) What is the mass of each element in the sodium oxide?
   b) What is the mass of 1 mole of each element?
   c) How many moles of each element combine?
   d) What is the simplest ratio?
   e) What is the formula of sodium oxide?
                                 [4]   (NEAB)

9. Joseph Priestley discovered oxygen gas in 1774 by heating mercury oxide.
   A teacher repeated the experiment and found that 2.17 g of mercury oxide decomposed on heating to produce 0.16 g of oxygen.
   Calculate the formula of mercury oxide.
   (Show all your working.)
   (Relative atomic masses: Hg (mercury) = 201, O = 16)   [3]   (NEAB)

10. a) Copper(II) oxide was heated in a stream of hydrogen in a test tube. The word equation for the reaction is given below
      copper(II) oxide + hydrogen $\longrightarrow$
                                 copper + water
      What chemical process has taken place to convert the copper(II) oxide into copper? [1]
    b) The following results were obtained in the experiment
      Before the experiment:
      Mass of test tube + copper(II) oxide = 21.86 g
      Mass of the empty test tube   = 20.60 g
        i)   Calculate the mass of the copper(II) oxide at the start of the experiment. [1]
      After the experiment:
      Mass of test tube + copper produced = 21.72 g
      Mass of the empty test tube   = 20.60 g
        ii) Calculate the mass of copper produced.
                                             [1]
    c) How much oxygen was combined with copper in the copper(II) oxide?   [1]

d) A sample of copper(II) oxide was found to contain 1.92 g of copper and 0.48 g of oxygen.
  i) Calculate the number of moles of copper in 1.92 g [1]
  ii) Calculate the number of moles of oxygen in 0.48 g [1]
  iii) By considering your answers to i) and ii), give the simplest formula of the copper(II) oxide. [1]   (MEG)

11. What mass of copper is formed when 8 g of copper(II) oxide is reduced?
    $$2CuO(s) + C(s) \longrightarrow 2Cu(s) + CO_2(g)$$
    (Relative atomic masses: C = 12, O = 16, Cu = 64)
    A 12.8g
    B 8.0 g
    C 6.4 g
    D 3.2 g   [1]   (NEAB)

12. In the U.K. sulphuric acid is made by the Contact process. The first stage of the process involves burning sulphur to form sulphur dioxide, as shown by the following equation:
    $$S + O_2 \longrightarrow SO_2$$
    Calculate the mass of sulphur dioxide which would be obtained from 160 tonnes of sulphur.
    [Relative atomic mass S = 32, O = 16] [3]
    (ULEAC)

13. Most of the nitric acid that is manufactured is used to make fertilizers such as ammonium nitrate.
    The equation for the reaction is:
    $$HNO_3 + NH_3 \longrightarrow NH_4NO_3$$
    a) Calculate the relative formula masses for nitric acid (HNO_3) and ammonium nitrate (NH_4NO_3).
    (H = 1, N = 14, O = 16). [2]
    b) Calculate the mass of nitric acid needed to make 400 tonnes of ammonium nitrate. [2]
    (MEG)

14. Carbon dioxide may be obtained from marble by strong heating, as shown in the equation
    $$CaCO_3(s) \longrightarrow CaO(s) + CO_2(g)$$
    a) Write down the meaning of both the symbols (s) ands (g). [1]
    b) Calculate the relative formula masses (Mr) of:
        $CaCO_3$ and CO_2 [2]
       (You may find pages 342 and 343 helpful)
    c) How many grams of carbon dioxide could be obtained from 2.5 g of calcium carbonate?
       Show your working. [2]   (WJEC)

15. What mass of chlorine would be needed to make 73 tonnes of hydrogen chloride?
    $$H_2 + Cl_2 \longrightarrow 2HCl$$
    The relative atomic mass (A_r) of chlorine (Cl) is 35.5.
    The relative atomic mass (A_r) of hydrogen (H) is 1.0. [3]   (MEG)

16. What mass of MgO would be produced by burning 12 g of magnesium metal in *excess* oxygen? [2]
    Equation for reaction:
    $$2Mg + O_2 \longrightarrow 2MgO$$ (WJEC)

17. Use the chemical equation to find the mass of carbon which reacts with 223 g of lead oxide
    $$2PbO + C \longrightarrow 2Pb + CO_2$$
    (Relative atomic mass: C = 12; O = 16; Pb = 207)
    A 6g
    B 12g
    C 24g
    D 48 g   (SEG)

18. The equation for the reaction that produces ammonium nitrate is:
    $$NH_3 + HNO_3 \longrightarrow NH_4NO_3$$
    Calculate the number of tonnes of ammonium nitrate that can be made from 68 tonnes of ammonia.
    (Relative atomic masses: H = 1, N = 14, O = 16) [3]   (NEAB)

Further questions on Calculations

19. The balanced symbolic equation for the reaction between ammonia and sulphuric acid is:

$$2NH_3 + H_2SO_4 \longrightarrow (NH_4)_2SO_4$$

How many tonnes of sulphuric acid are needed to exactly neutralise 340 tonnes of ammonia?
(The relative atomic masses are $H = 1$, $N = 14$, $O = 16$ and $S = 32$.)
Show clearly how you obtain your answer. [4]
(SEG)

20. Uranium metal is produced from uranium(VI) fluoride using magnesium.
a) Balance the equation
$$UF_6 + ... Mg \longrightarrow .... MgF_2 + U \quad [1]$$
b) What mass of uranium would be produced from 34.9 g of uranium(VI) fluoride?
(Relative atomic masses: $U = 235$, $F = 19$)
[1]   (NEAB)

21. a) The balanced equation for the reaction between iron(III) oxide and carbon monoxide is

$$Fe_2O_3(s) + 3CO(g) \longrightarrow 2Fe(s) + 3CO_2(g)$$

Calculate the maximum mass of iron that could be obtained from 80 tonnes of iron(III) oxide. (Relative atomic masses: $C = 12$; $O = 16$; $Fe = 56$)   [2]
b) Aluminium can displace chromium from chromium(III) oxide in a redox reaction. Use this reaction to explain the meaning of the word **redox**.   [2]   (SEG)

22. Aluminium oxide is electrolysed to extract aluminium. Oxygen gas is produced at the carbon anode which is then burned away as described in the following equation:
$$C + O_2 \longrightarrow CO_2$$
Given the following relative atomic masses:
$Al = 27 \quad C = 12 \quad O = 16$.
For each 32 tonnes of oxygen used calculate
a) the mass of carbon burned and
b) the mass of carbon dioxide produced.
    Show your working. (1 tonne = 1000 kg) [2]

c) Calculate the mass of aluminium produced from 204 tonnes of aluminium oxide given the equation,
$$2Al_2O_3 \longrightarrow 4Al + 3O_2$$
Show your working.   [2]   (WJEC)

23. 10.6 g of sodium carbonate was added to excess dilute hydrochloric acid. The reaction can be represented by the equation
$$Na_2CO_3(s) + 2HCl(aq) \longrightarrow$$
$$2NaCl(aq) + H_2O(l) + CO_2(g)$$
Which one of the following is the correct volume of gas (measured at room temperature and pressure) produced by the reaction?
(Relative atomic masses: $H = 1$, $C = 12$, $O = 16$, $Na = 23$, $Cl = 35.5$. One mole of any gas occupies 24 litres at room temperature and pressure.)
A   24 litres
B   4 litres
C   2.4 litres
D   1.2 litres   [1]   (NEAB)

24. Sodium reacts with water to produce sodium hydroxide and hydrogen.
$$2Na(s) + 2H_2O(l) \longrightarrow 2NaOH(aq) + H_2(g)$$
Calculate the volume of hydrogen that would be produced, at ordinary temperature and pressure from 3.5 g of sodium.
(Show your working)
(1 mole of any gas occupies $24\,000\ cm^3$ at ordinary room temperature and pressure)
($Na = 23$)   [5]   (NEAB)

25. The equation for the reaction of magnesium with hydrochloric acid is
$$Mg(s) + 2HCl(aq) \longrightarrow MgCl_2(aq) + H_2(g)$$
Use pages 342 and 343 to calculate the relative formula masses (M_r) of:
a) $MgCl_2$ [1]
b) H_2 [1]
c) Calculate the volume of hydrogen (at 1 atmosphere and 25 °C) which could be obtained from 1 g of magnesium reacting with excess hydrochloric acid.
[The relative formula mass of hydrogen measured in grams occupies a volume of 24 litres ($24\ dm^3$) at the above conditions.]
[2]   (WJEC)

326

26. A student heated strongly a known mass of powdered titanium so that all the titanium combined with oxygen from the air. The following results were obtained.

Mass of container + titanium	= 35.9 g
Mass of empty container	= 31.1 g
Mass of container + contents after heating	= 39.1 g

a) What would be a suitable container for the student to use?

b) Calculate the mass of titanium and of oxygen combining in the experiment.

c) Use the table on pages 342 and 343 to write down the relative atomic mass of titanium and of oxygen.

d) Use your answers to parts b) and c) above to calculate the (empirical) formula of the titanium-oxygen compound. You must show your working. [8] (ULEAC)

27. For the reaction between iron and hydrochloric acid:

$$Fe(s) + 2HCl(aq) \longrightarrow FeCl_2(aq) + H_2(g)$$

Use pages 342 and 343 to carry out the following calculations:

a) The **mass** of hydrogen obtained from 56 g of iron. [1]

b) The **mass** of hydrogen obtained from 7 g of iron. [2]

c) The **volume** of hydrogen at 1 atmosphere pressure and 25 °C obtained from 7 g of iron. **Show your working**. (1 mole of any gas occupies 24 000 cm^3 at 1 atmosphere pressure and 25 °C.) [3] (WJEC)

28. The equation for the reaction between sulphuric acid and limestone is
$$H_2SO_4 + CaCO_3 \longrightarrow CaSO_4 + H_2O + CO_2$$
Calculate:

a) the mass of calcium carbonate needed to remove the acidity from a sample of lake water which contains 4.9 g sulphuric acid. (Relative atomic masses: H = 1, C = 12, O = 16, S = 32, Ca = 40) [3]

b) the volume of carbon dioxide, measured at room temperature and pressure, which could be produced in a).
(One mole of any gas at room temperature and pressure has a volume of 24 litres.) [1] (NEAB)

29. The symbol equation below shows the reduction of iron(III) oxide by carbon monoxide.
$$Fe_2O_3 + 3CO \longrightarrow 2Fe + 3CO_2$$

a) Calculate the formula mass of iron(III) oxide. (Use the table on pages 342 and 343) [2]

b) Calculate the mass of iron that could be obtained from 32 000 tonnes of iron(III) oxide. [3] (NEAB)

30. a) Electricity will pass through a solution of copper(II) sulphate (concentration 1.0 mol/dm^3) using copper electrodes. Calculate the mass of copper deposited when 0.5 A of electricity is passed through the solution for 4 hours.
(Relative Atomic Mass (RAM) of copper is 64)
(1 Faraday of electricity is 96 500 coulombs – this is the charge carried by 1 mole of electrons) [3]

b) Explain what happens to the concentration of the copper(II) sulphate solution. [1] (ULEAC)

31. To produce one mole of aluminium metal by electrolysis needs 289 500 coulombs of electric charge. Explain why it only needs 193 000 coulombs to liberate a mole of lead. [2] (MEG)

32. High purity copper is needed because it is used in electrical wires. You get high purity copper by electrolysis using a thin, pure copper cathode and a solution of copper sulphate.
(The Faraday constant (F) is 96 000 coulombs per mole (C/mol). The relative atomic mass of copper is 64.)
A current of 200 amperes (A) is used for 12 hours. What mass of copper is formed at the cathode?
Show clearly how you obtain your answer. [5] (SEG)

Answers to Calculations

Pages 310 and 311
1. 2 moles   2. 3 moles   3. 10 moles
4. 0.1 mole   5. 0.01 mole
6. 2 g   7. 70 g   8. 320 g   9. 9.5 g
10. 0.12 g
11. 2 moles   12. 10 moles   13. 0.1 mole
14. 0.01 mole   15. 0.2 mole

Pages 312 and 313
1. 1 mole   2. 0.25 mole   3. 0.1 mole
4. 0.005 mole   5. 0.002 mole
6. 72 dm^3 (72 000 cm^3)
7. 120 dm^3 (120 000 cm^3)
8. 2.4 dm^3 (2400 cm^3)
9. 0.024 dm^3 (24 cm^3)
10. 0.12 dm^3 (120 cm^3)
11. 48 dm^3 (48 000 cm^3)
12. 12 dm^3 (12 000 cm^3)
13. 1.2 dm^3 (1200 cm^3)
14. 0.012 dm^3 (12 cm^3)
15. 4.8 dm^3 (4800 cm^3)

Page 315
1. 2 moles   2. 1 mole   3. 0.25 mole
4. 0.05 mole   5. 0.025 mole
6. 29.25 g   7. 11.2 g   8. 2.45 g
9. 12.41 g   10. 0.429 g

Page 316
1. CH_4 2. PbO   3. CO_2 4. Fe_2O_3
5. $CuCO_3$

Page 319
1. $Mg + 2\,HCl \longrightarrow MgCl_2 + H_2$
   24 g $\longrightarrow$ 95 g
    1 g $\longrightarrow \dfrac{95}{24}$ g

   4.8 g $\longrightarrow \dfrac{95}{24} \times 4.8$ g = **19 g**

Answer = 19 g

2. $Na_2CO_3 + H_2SO_4 \longrightarrow Na_2SO_4 + CO_2 + H_2O$
  106 g $\longrightarrow$ 142 g
    1 g $\longrightarrow \dfrac{142}{106}$ g

   5.3 g $\longrightarrow \dfrac{142}{106} \times 5.3$ g = **7.1 g**

Answer = 7.1 g

Pages 320 and 321
1. Charge (in coulombs) = $2 \times 9650 = 19\,300$ C
   4.6 g of Na are given by 19 300 C

     1 g of Na is given by $\dfrac{19\,300}{4.6}$

23 g (1 mole) of Na are given by

$$\dfrac{19\,300}{4.6} \times 23\,C = \textbf{96\,500 C}$$

2. Charge = 1×1930 C
   2.07 g of Pb are given by 1930 C

     1 g of Pb is given by $\dfrac{1930C}{2.07}$

207 g (1 mole) of Pb are given by

$$\dfrac{1930C}{2.07} \times 207\,C = 193\,000\,C$$

Therefore the charge on the lead ion is **2 +**.

Page 322
1. CuO
2. 510 tonnes of ammonia.
3. 0.416 g of calcium carbonate
4. 2.4 dm^3 (2400 cm^3) of chlorine gas.

Page 323

Aunt Molly Replies

1. CH_4 – Don't worry, Ray.
   This gas is perfectly natural!
2. 112 tonnes of calcium oxide
   Quite a nest-egg Mrs Kiln!
3. 0.04 moles per dm^3 (0.04M)
   I'm afraid your concentration is weak, Sol.
   But at least the solution is clear!
4. 1.2 dm^3 or 1200 dm^3
   What a forgetful ding-a-ling!
5. 0.2 g (almost!)
   That's not a lot of copper, but it has obviously given you a shock!

Answers to Further questions on Calculations

1. **B**
2. (1), (2) and (3)
3. **C**
4. **B**
5. **A**
6. 5 moles
7. XY_2
8. a) 2.3 g of Na, 0.8 g of O
   b) Na = 23 g, O = 16 g
   c) 0.1 mole of Na with 0.05 mole of O
   d) 2 : 1
   e) Na_2O
9. HgO
10. a) reduction
    b) i) 1.26 g
       ii) 1.12 g
    c) 0.14 g
    d) i) 0.03 mole
       ii) 0.03 mole
       iii) CuO
11. **C**
12. 320 tonnes
13. a) HNO_3 = 63; NH_4NO_3 = 80
    b) 315 tonnes
14. a) (s) = solid
       (g) = gas
    b) $CaCO_3$ = 100; CO_2 = 44
    c) 1.1 g
15. 71 tonnes
16. 20 g
17. **A**
18. 320 tonnes
19. 980 tonnes
20. a) $UF_6 + 3Mg \longrightarrow 3MgF_2 + U$
    b) 23.5 g

21. a) 56 tonnes
    b) chromium(III) oxide is reduced (has its oxygen removed) to chromium, while aluminium is oxidised to aluminium oxide
22. a) 12 tonnes
    b) 44 tonnes
    c) 108 tonnes
23. **C**
24. 1826 cm^3
25. a) 95
    b) 2
    c) 1 litre (or 1 dm^3)
26. a) a crucible
    b) Ti = 4.8 g, O = 3.2 g
    c) Ti = 48, O = 16
    d) TiO_2
27. a) 2 g
    b) 0.25 g
    c) 3000 cm^3 (or 3 dm^3)
28. a) 5 g
    b) 1.2 litres (or 1.2 dm^3)
29. a) 160
    b) 22 400 tonnes
30. a) 2.39 g
    b) It stays the same; as copper ions are removed at the cathode, they are replaced in solution at the anode
31. The charge on the aluminium ion is 3+, whereas the charge on the lead ion is 2+. Therefore it takes (96 500 × 2) coulombs to give one mole of lead, but (96 500 × 3) coulombs to give one mole of aluminium.
32. 2880 g or 2.88 kg

Doing your practical work

GCSE exams have 25 % of the marks awarded for practical work.
Often these marks will be awarded by your teacher while watching
you do experiments or investigations in the laboratory.

Your marks will be awarded under 4 headings:

P   Planning your experimental work
O   Obtaining the evidence
A   Analysing your evidence and drawing conclusions
E   Evaluating your evidence.

When marking you on these skills, your teacher has a checklist
of what to look for. The checklist for 'Planning' is shown below.
Make sure you cover each of the points; starting from 2 marks,
working up the list to the higher marks.

Here are some more details on each of the 4 skill areas:

'Practical skills are important'

P.   Planning your experimental work

• *Fair testing*
Sometimes you will be asked to plan an investigation to solve
a problem or answer a question.
The most important thing here is to devise a ***fair test***.
For example, look at experiment 15.4 on page 192.
In this experiment it is important that the only thing
we change in each test is the size of the marble chips.
We must keep the **same** temperature, the **same** volume
and the **same** concentration of acid in each test.
This is called 'controlling the variables' so that only
one variable changes (the size of the marble chips).

• *Predicting*
Before starting your practical work, you should try to predict
what you think will happen. To gain higher marks it is important
to base your prediction on the science you know.
Say what you think will happen and then ***explain why***.
Remember that you can use text-books and other sources of
information to help you in your predicting and planning.

• *Selecting the most suitable apparatus*
It is important to use the most suitable equipment.
For example, to measure the volume of $100\,cm^3$ of water, you
should choose a measuring cylinder, not a beaker with a $100\,cm^3$
mark on it. (Why?)
To measure a smaller volume of water you should choose a
narrower measuring cylinder. (Why?)

Checklist for skill **P** **PLANNING YOUR WORK**	
Candidates:	Marks awarded
• plan a simple safe method	**2**
• plan a fair test or a practical method, making a prediction if possible • select suitable equipment	**4**

• use scientific knowledge to:
  – plan a method,
  – identify key factors to vary or control,
  – make a prediction if possible
• decide on a suitable number and range of readings (or observations)
	6

• use detailed scientific knowledge to:
  – plan a suitable method,
  – aim for precise and reliable evidence
  – justify a prediction if possible
• use information from other sources, or from preliminary work
	8

• *Deciding the number and range of your readings*

You need to consider **how many** measurements or observations to make in your experiments.
Four is the minimum number of readings if you plan to show your results on a graph.
Aim to collect at least 5 readings.

Your results must also cover a suitable **range** to answer the original question. For example, if you are looking at the effect of temperature on the rate at which water evaporates, would you do tests at 20 °C, 21 °C, 22 °C and 23 °C? This is not a good range.

You also need to decide whether you need to repeat the tests and so get average readings. This can improve the **reliability** of your results.

• *Safety*

The tests that you plan must be safe. You must consult your teacher to ensure that your plan is safe.
You should find out if any chemicals you are using (or any products made in your tests) are dangerous in any way.
These hazard symbols will be useful:

Oxidising
These substances provide oxygen which allows other materials to burn more fiercely.

Highly flammable
These substances easily catch fire.

Toxic
These substances can cause death. They may have their effects when swallowed or breathed in or absorbed through the skin.

Harmful
These substances are similar to toxic substances but less dangerous.

Corrosive
These substances attack and destroy living tissues, including eyes and skin.

Irritant
These substances are not corrosive but can cause reddening or blistering of the skin.

O. Obtaining your evidence

● *Making observations accurately*

Accuracy is important, as well as taking care in checking your readings.
Remember to correct for **zero-errors** (for example, you should check that your balance reads zero before you start to use it).

When reading a scale, make sure you look at right-angles to it, so that you read the correct number.
When using a measuring cylinder, remember to read the **bottom** of the meniscus.

If one of your results seems unusual, make sure you repeat it. If it was an error, you do not have to include it when you consider your results at the end.

● *Recording your results*

Record your results in a table, labelling each column with the **quantity** you are measuring and its **unit**.

Here is a table for the experiment on page 190:
The first column shows the **<u>independent variable</u>**
– this is what you change deliberately, step by step.
The second column shows the **dependent** variable
– the size of this variable depends on the first one.
All other variables must be **controlled** (kept constant).

A. Analysing your evidence & drawing conclusions

● *Drawing graphs and bar-charts*

Having recorded your results, you will often need to draw a graph.
If the first column in your table (the independent variable) can have a continuous range of values, then use a line-graph. However if the first column can only have certain fixed values, then use a bar-chart.

If you draw a line-graph, do it in the steps shown here :

1) Choose simple scales.
   For example, 1 large square = 10 °C
   Never choose an awkward scale like 1 square = 3 °C

2) Plot the points and mark them neatly. Re-check each one.

3) If the points look as though they form a straight line, draw the best straight line through them with a ruler (and pencil). Check that it looks the best line.

4) If the points form a curve, draw a 'free-hand' curve of best fit. Never join the points 'dot-to-dot' with a ruler.

5) If a point is clearly off the line, you should always use your apparatus to repeat the measurement and check it.

Checklist for skill **O**
OBTAINING YOUR EVIDENCE

Candidates :	Marks awarded
● use simple equipment safely	**2**
● make adequate observations or measurements ● record the results	**4**
● make observations or measurements, – with sufficient readings, – which are accurate, and – repeat them if necessary ● record the results clearly and accurately	**6**
● use equipment – with precision and skill, – to obtain and record reliable evidence, – with a good number and range of readings	**8**

Measuring the rate of reaction

Time (s)	Volume of gas (cm³)
0	0
30	
60	
90	

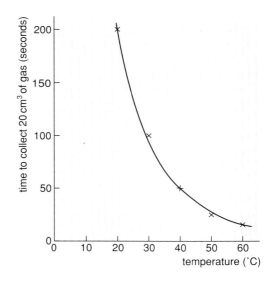

- ### *Drawing a conclusion*

Every experiment has a 'conclusion'. This is a summary of what you found out (or sometimes what you didn't find !). Always look at your results or graph or chart to decide what you have discovered.
What reasonable or 'valid' deduction can be made from your results ? What pattern can you see ?

For example, look at the graph on the last page :
You might conclude :
a) As the temperature increases, the time it takes to collect $20\,cm^3$ of gas decreases.
b) As the temperature increases, the rate of reaction increases.
c) For each 10 °C rise in temperature the time to collect $20\,cm^3$ of gas is halved.

Then use your scientific knowledge to explain your conclusion.

Remember to refer back to your prediction, if you made one, and to **explain** why your results support it or not.

Checklist for skill **A** ANALYSING YOUR EVIDENCE	
Candidates :	Marks awarded
• explain simply what was found out	**2**
• show the results in simple diagrams, charts or graphs • spot any trends and patterns in the results	**4**
• draw and use diagrams, charts, graphs (with a line of best fit), or calculate answers from the results • draw a valid conclusion and explain it using your scientific knowledge	**6**
• use detailed scientific knowledge to explain your conclusion • explain how the results agree or disagree with a prediction made earlier	**8**

E.   Evaluating your evidence

Having drawn your conclusions, you should now think about the **quality** of your investigation.
Ask yourself these questions to see if you could have improved your investigation :
- Were my results accurate ?
- Did any seem strange compared to the others ? These are 'anomalous' results.
- Should I have repeated some tests to get more reliable results ? Could I improve the method ?
- Did I get a suitable range of results ?
- If there is a pattern in my results, is it only true for the range of values I used ? Would the pattern continue beyond this range ?
  How could I develop my investigation to answer these questions, if given time ?
- Are there any other aspects of the original question that I could investigate, if given time ?

Checklist for skill **E** EVALUATING YOUR EVIDENCE	
Candidates :	Marks awarded
• make a relevant comment about the method used or the results obtained	**2**
• comment on the accuracy of the results, pointing out any anomalous ones • comment on whether the method was a good one • suggest changes to improve the reliability of the evidence	**4**

• look at the evidence and :
  – comment on its reliability,
  – explain any anomalous results,
  – explain whether it is good enough to support a firm conclusion
• propose :
  – improvements, or
  – further work,
  that would give more evidence for the conclusion, or extend the investigation.
	6

Helping you investigate !

Use the questions below to help you at each stage in your investigations.

PLAN

Before you start your practical work, think about:

- How can you make your tests *fair*?
- How can you make your tests *safe*?
- Can you *predict* what will happen?
- Can you explain your prediction?
- How many observations or measurements will you make?
- What *range of values* will give suitable results?
- Will you need to repeat results to make them more *reliable*?
- Which apparatus will you choose to get *accurate* results?
- Can you use *other sources of information* to help you plan your tests?
- Should you *try out some tests* to check your ideas before writing down your final plan?
- How will you *record* your results clearly and accurately?

ANALYSE AND CONCLUDE

When you have collected your results, think about:

- Can your results be shown on a *bar-chart or a line-graph*? (Remember to use a line-of-best-fit, and to point out any unexpected results – check these if you have time.)
- Can you see a *pattern* in your results?
- Do your results support your prediction (if you have made one)? Explain why.
- Can you *explain* your results using the work you have done in Science?

EVALUATE

When you have finished your conclusion, think about:

- Can you comment on any *improvements* you could make to:
  - the way you did your tests
  - the accuracy of your readings
  - the reliability of your results (would you get the same results if you were to repeat your tests again?).
- Are there any *results which do not fit in* with the general pattern?
- Are your results good enough to draw a *firm conclusion*? Explain why.
- Can you suggest any *further work* to extend your investigation?

Writing up your practical work

Your coursework will be assessed on its spelling, punctuation and grammar. So take care and check your work before you hand it in.

Suggestions for a revision programme

1. Read the summary at the end of the chapter to gain some idea of the contents.
   Then read through the chapter looking at particular points in more detail, before reading the summary again.

2. Covering up the summary, check yourself against the fill-in-the-missing-word sentences at the end of the chapter.

   Remember to **re-read** the summary and to **review** each chapter after the correct revision intervals of 10 minutes, then 1 day, then 1 week (as explained on page 337). Continue in this way with all the other chapters in the book.

3. While reading through the summaries and chapters like this, it is useful to collect together all the statements in red and yellow boxes that you need to know. At this stage, you will also find the checklists and revision quizzes from the Support Pack useful.

4. While you are going right through the book, attempt the questions on the 'Further Questions' pages for every chapter. These are all GCSE questions from previous years. Your teacher will be able to tell you which are the most important ones for your syllabus.

5. Read the section on 'Examination technique' on page 338, and check the dates of your exams. Have you enough time to complete your revision before then?

6. A few weeks before the examination, ask your teacher for copies of the examination papers from previous years. These 'past papers' will help you to see:
   - the particular style and timing of your examination
   - the way the questions are asked, and the amount of detail needed
   - which topics and questions are asked most often and which suit you personally.

When doing these past papers, try to get used to doing the questions **in the specified time**.

It may be possible for your teacher to read out to you the reports of examiners who have marked these papers in previous years.

The Support Pack contains some extra past paper questions with guidance given on how to answer them.

Revision techniques

Why should you revise ?

You cannot expect to remember all the Chemistry that you have studied unless you revise. It is important to review all your course, so that you can answer the examination questions.

Where should you revise ?

In a quiet room (perhaps a bedroom), with a table and a clock. The room should be comfortably warm and brightly lighted. A reading lamp on the table helps you to concentrate on your work and reduces eye-strain.

When should you revise ?

Start your revision early each evening, before your brain gets tired.

How should you revise ?

If you sit down to revise without thinking of a definite finishing time, you will find that your learning efficiency falls lower and lower and lower.

If you sit down to revise, saying to yourself that you will definitely stop work after 2 hours, then your learning efficiency falls at the beginning but **rises towards the end** as your brain realises it is coming to the end of the session (see the first graph).

We can use this U-shaped curve to help us work more efficiently by splitting a 2 hour session into 4 shorter sessions, each of about 25 minutes with a short, **planned** break between them.

The breaks **must** be planned beforehand so that the graph rises near the end of each short session.

The coloured area on the graph shows how much you gain :

For example, if you start your revision at 6.00 p.m., you should look at your clock or watch and say to yourself, 'I will work until 6.25 p.m. and then stop – not earlier and not later.'

At 6.25 p.m. you should leave the table for a relaxation break of 10 minutes (or less), returning by 6.35 p.m. when you should say to yourself, 'I will work until 7.00 p.m. and then stop – not earlier and not later.'

Continuing in this way is more efficient **and** causes less strain on you.

You get through more work **and** you feel less tired.

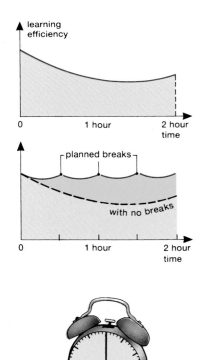

How often should you revise?

The diagram shows a graph of the amount of information that your memory can recall at different times after you have finished a revision session:

Surprisingly, the graph rises at the beginning. This is because your brain is still sorting out the information that you have been learning.
The graph soon falls rapidly so that after 1 day you may remember only about a quarter of what you had learned.

There are two ways of improving your recall and raising this graph.

● 1. If you briefly *revise the same work again after 10 minutes* (at the high point of the graph) then the graph falls much more slowly.
This fits in with your 10-minute break between revision sessions.
Using the example on the opposite page, when you return to your table at 6.35 p.m., the first thing you should do is *review*, briefly, the work you learned before 6.25 p.m.

The graph can be lifted again by briefly reviewing the work *after 1 day* and then again *after 1 week*. That is, on Tuesday night you should look through the work you learned on Monday night and the work you learned on the previous Tuesday night, so that it is fixed quite firmly in your long-term memory.

● 2. Another method of improving your memory is by taking care to try to *understand* all parts of your work. This makes all the graphs higher.
If you learn your work in a parrot-fashion (as you have to do with telephone numbers), all these graphs will be lower. On the occasions when you have to learn facts by heart, try to picture them as exaggerated, colourful images in your mind.

Remember: *the most important points about revision are that it must occur often and be repeated at the right intervals.*

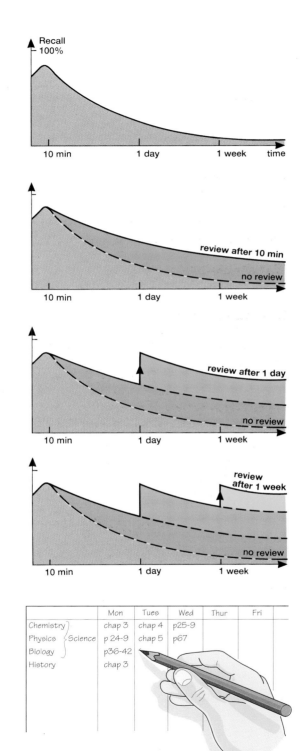

Examination technique

In the weeks before the examinations:

Attempt as many 'past papers' as you can so that you get used to the style of the questions and the timing of them.

Note which topics occur most often and revise them thoroughly, using the techniques explained on previous pages.

Just before the examinations:

Collect together the equipment you will need:
- Two pens, in case one dries up.
- At least one sharpened pencil for drawing diagrams.
- A rubber and a ruler for diagrams.
  Diagrams usually look best if they are drawn in pencil and labelled in ink.
  Coloured pencils are usually **not** necessary (but may sometimes make part of your diagram clearer).
- A watch for pacing yourself during the examination. The clock in the examination room may be difficult to see.
- **A calculator (with good batteries).**

It will help if you have previously collected all the information about the length and style of the examination papers (for **all** your subjects) as shown below:

Date, time and room	Subject, paper number and tier	Length (hours)	Types of question: – structured? – single word answers? – longer answers? – essays?	Sections?	Details of choice (if any)	Approximate time per page (minutes)
4th June 9.30 Hall	Science (Double Award) Paper 2 (Chemistry) Foundation Tier	$1\frac{1}{2}$	Structured questions (with single-word answers and longer answers)	1	no choice	4–6 min.

In the examination room :

Read the front of the examination paper carefully. It gives you important information. How is your examination paper different from the one shown opposite ?

Some hints on answering questions are given in the box below.

In what ways is your examination paper different from this one ?

Answering 'structured' questions :

- Read the information at the start of each question carefully. Make sure you understand what the question is about, and what you are expected to do.

- Pace yourself with a watch so you don't run out of time. If you have spare time at the end, use it wisely.

- *How much detail do you need to give ?*
  The question gives you clues :
  - Give short answers to questions which start : '**State**...' or '**List**...' or '**Name**...'.
  - Give longer answers if you are asked to '**Explain**...' or '**Describe**...' or asked '**Why does**..?'.

- Don't explain something just because you know how to ! You only earn marks for doing exactly what the question asks.

- Look for the marks awarded for each part of the question. It is usually given in brackets, e.g. [2]. This tells you how many points the examiner is looking for in your answer.

- The number of lines of space is also a guide to how much you are expected to write.

- Always show the steps in your working out of calculations. This way, you can gain marks for the way you tackle the problem, even if your final answer is wrong.

- Try to write something for *every* part of each question.

- Follow the instructions given in the question. If it asks for one answer, give only one answer. Sometimes you are given a list of alternatives to choose from. If you include more answers than asked for, any wrong answers will cancel out your right ones !

You can find some structured questions in the Support Pack – together with answers and useful hints on examination technique.

If your exam includes 'multiple-choice' questions :

- Read the instructions very carefully.

- If there is a separate answer sheet, mark it exactly as you are instructed. Take care to mark your answer opposite the correct question number.

- Even if the answer looks obvious, you should look at all the alternatives before making a decision.

- If you do not know the correct answer and have to guess, then you can improve your chances by first eliminating as many wrong answers as possible.

- Ensure you give an answer to *every* question.

Careers

Have you thought what you want to do when you leave school?

Chemistry opens the door to many careers. It is sometimes called 'the central Science', because it lies between Biology and Physics. So if you would like to study these further, Chemistry is a great help.

But hopefully you will want to learn more about Chemistry because you enjoy it!

Here are some careers where further studies in Chemistry will be an advantage, if not a requirement:

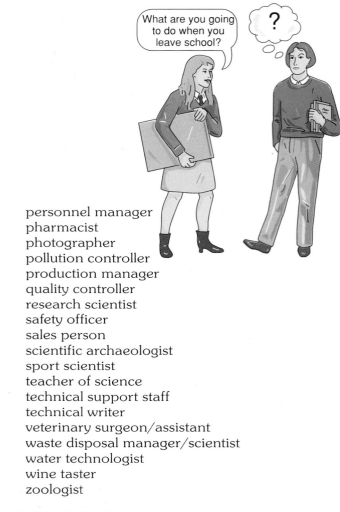

What are you going to do when you leave school?

?

agricultural scientist
animal technician
art restorer
bacteriologist
biochemist
brewer
chemical engineer
chemist
civil engineer
Civil Service science officer
conservationist
cosmetics scientist
dental technician
dentist
doctor
electrical engineer
environmental health officer
food scientist
forensic scientist
geologist
horticulturalist
information scientist
journalist (science)
laboratory technician
lecturer in science
managers in industry
marine scientist
marketing
materials scientist
medical technician
metallurgist
patent lawyer
pathologist

personnel manager
pharmacist
photographer
pollution controller
production manager
quality controller
research scientist
safety officer
sales person
scientific archaeologist
sport scientist
teacher of science
technical support staff
technical writer
veterinary surgeon/assistant
waste disposal manager/scientist
water technologist
wine taster
zoologist

You need a good sense of taste and smell (and chemistry!) to explain about wines

There is a lot of chemistry in developing a photograph (see page 244)

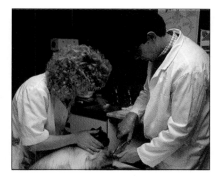

a vet

a research scientist using an electron microscope

a biochemist

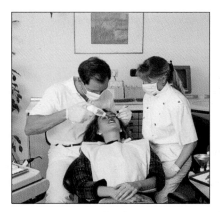

a dentist

an art restorer

an environmental scientist testing water

a cosmetics scientist developing a perfume

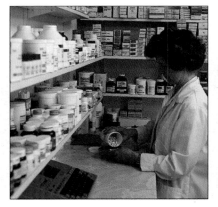

a pharmacist

a brewer testing beer

Table 1   Physical properties of some elements

Element	Symbol	Atomic number	Relative atomic mass	State at 25°C	Melting point (°C)	Boiling point (°C)	Density (g/cm³) (gases at 25°C)
Aluminium	Al	13	27	s	660	2350	2.70
Argon	Ar	18	40	g	−189	−186	0.00166
Arsenic	As	33	75	s	613 (sublimes)		5.78
Barium	Ba	56	137	s	710	1640	3.59
Beryllium	Be	4	9	s	1285	2470	1.85
Boron	B	5	11	s	2030	3700	2.47
Bromine	Br	35	80	l	−7	59	3.12
Caesium	Cs	55	133	s	29	669	1.88
Calcium	Ca	20	40	s	840	1490	1.53
Carbon (diamond)	C	6	12	s	3550	4827	3.53
Carbon (graphite)	C	6	12	s	3720 (sublimes)		2.25
Chlorine	Cl	17	35.5	g	−101	−34	0.00299
Chromium	Cr	24	52	s	1860	2600	7.19
Cobalt	Co	27	59	s	1494	2900	8.80
Copper	Cu	29	64	s	1084	2580	8.93
Fluorine	F	9	19	g	−220	−188	0.00158
Gallium	Ga	31	70	s	30	2070	5.91
Germanium	Ge	32	73	s	959	2850	5.32
Gold	Au	79	197	s	1064	2850	19.28
Helium	He	2	4	g	−270	−269	0.00017
Hydrogen	H	1	1	g	−259	−253	0.00008
Iodine	I	53	127	s	114	184	4.95
Iron	Fe	26	56	s	1540	2760	7.87
Krypton	Kr	36	84	g	−157	−153	0.00346
Lead	Pb	82	207	s	327	1760	11.34
Lithium	Li	3	7	s	180	1360	0.53
Magnesium	Mg	12	24	s	650	1100	1.74
Manganese	Mn	25	55	s	1250	2120	7.47
Mercury	Hg	80	201	l	−39	357	13.55
Neon	Ne	10	20	g	−249	−246	0.00084
Nickel	Ni	28	59	s	1455	2150	8.91
Nitrogen	N	7	14	g	−210	−196	0.00117
Oxygen	O	8	16	g	−219	−183	0.00133
Phosphorus (white)	P	15	31	s	44	280	1.82

Table 1 continued

Element	Symbol	Atomic number	Relative atomic mass	State at 25°C	Melting point (°C)	Boiling point (°C)	Density (g/cm³) (gases at 25°C)
Platinum	Pt	78	195	s	1772	3720	21.45
Potassium	K	19	39	s	63	777	0.86
Rubidium	Rb	37	85	s	39	705	1.53
Scandium	Sc	21	45	s	1540	2800	2.99
Selenium	Se	34	79	s	220	685	4.81
Silicon	Si	14	28	s	1410	2620	2.33
Silver	Ag	47	108	s	962	2160	10.50
Sodium	Na	11	23	s	98	900	0.97
Sulphur	S	16	32	s	115	445	1.96
Strontium	Sr	38	88	s	769	1384	2.6
Tin	Sn	50	119	s	232	2720	7.28
Titanium	Ti	22	48	s	1670	3300	4.51
Uranium	U	92	238	s	1135	4000	19.05
Vanadium	V	23	51	s	1920	3400	6.09
Xenon	Xe	54	131	g	−112	−108	0.0055
Zinc	Zn	30	65	s	420	913	7.14

Table 2 Charges on some ions

Positive ions			Negative ions		
Charge	Name of ion	Formula	Charge	Name of ion	Formula
1+	ammonium	NH_4^+	1−	bromide	Br^-
	copper(I)	Cu^+		chloride	Cl^-
	hydrogen	H^+		hydroxide	OH^-
	lithium	Li^+		fluoride	F^-
	potassium	K^+		iodide	I^-
	silver	Ag^+		nitrate	NO_3^-
	sodium	Na^+			
2+	barium	Ba^{2+}	2−	carbonate	CO_3^{2-}
	calcium	Ca^{2+}		oxide	O^{2-}
	copper(II)	Cu^{2+}		sulphate	SO_4^{2-}
	iron(II)	Fe^{2+}		sulphide	S^{2-}
	lead(II)	Pb^{2+}			
	magnesium	Mg^{2+}			
	nickel(II)	Ni^{2+}			
	strontium	Sr^{2+}			
	zinc	Zn^{2+}			
3+	aluminium	Al^{3+}	3−	nitride	N^{3-}
	iron(III)	Fe^{3+}		phosphate	PO_4^{3-}

Periodic Table of the elements

1	2												13	14	15	16	17	18
																		4 **He** 2
7 **Li** 3	9 **Be** 4												11 **B** 5	12 **C** 6	14 **N** 7	16 **O** 8	19 **F** 9	20 **Ne** 10
23 **Na** 11	24 **Mg** 12												27 **Al** 13	28 **Si** 14	31 **P** 15	32 **S** 16	35 **Cl** 17	40 **Ar** 18
39 **K** 19	40 **Ca** 20	45 **Sc** 21	48 **Ti** 22	51 **V** 23	52 **Cr** 24	55 **Mn** 25	56 **Fe** 26	59 **Co** 27	59 **Ni** 28	64 **Cu** 29	65 **Zn** 30		70 **Ga** 31	73 **Ge** 32	75 **As** 33	79 **Se** 34	80 **Br** 35	84 **Kr** 36
85 **Rb** 37	88 **Sr** 38	89 **Y** 39	91 **Zr** 40	93 **Nb** 41	96 **Mo** 42	99 **Tc** 43	101 **Ru** 44	103 **Rh** 45	106 **Pd** 46	108 **Ag** 47	112 **Cd** 48		115 **In** 49	119 **Sn** 50	122 **Sb** 51	128 **Te** 52	127 **I** 53	131 **Xe** 54
133 **Cs** 55	137 **Ba** 56	139 **La** 57	178 **Hf** 72	181 **Ta** 73	184 **W** 74	186 **Re** 75	190 **Os** 76	192 **Ir** 77	195 **Pt** 78	197 **Au** 79	201 **Hg** 80		204 **Tl** 81	207 **Pb** 82	209 **Bi** 83	210 **Po** 84	210 **At** 85	222 **Rn** 86
223 **Fr** 87	226 **Ra** 88	227 **Ac** 89																

140	141	144	147	150	152	157	159	163	165	167	169	173	175
Ce	**Pr**	**Nd**	**Pm**	**Sm**	**Eu**	**Gd**	**Tb**	**Dy**	**Ho**	**Er**	**Tm**	**Yb**	**Lu**
58	59	60	61	62	63	64	65	66	67	68	69	70	71
232	231	238	237	242	243	247	245	251	254	253	256	254	257
Th	**Pa**	**U**	**Np**	**Pu**	**Am**	**Cm**	**Bk**	**Cf**	**Es**	**Fm**	**Md**	**No**	**Lr**
90	91	92	93	94	95	96	97	98	99	100	101	102	103

(The mass numbers shown are those of the most common isotope)

'Ode to Dmitri'

The Periodic Table was a scientific break-through.
For chemistry made sense, it was easier too.
A Russian named Dmitri was first to spot the pattern,
But some elements were wrong in the spaces they sat in.
"I know," thought Dmitri, "I'll just leave some gaps."
And a stroke of genius had just come to pass.
Some of the elements were as yet undiscovered
So he made predictions from the properties of others.

A few years later when germanium was found,
Scientists agreed his ideas were sound.
Even now we use the Table on which we never dine,
Still based on that discovery in 1869.

New elements

Over 110 elements have now been discovered. However, the new atoms are unstable, often existing only for a split second.

The International Union of Pure & Applied Chemistry (IUPAC) confirm that from now on elements discovered will be named according to the following format:

element No. 104 is called
UNNILQUADIUM
1   0   4
UN   NIL   QUAD   IUM

element No. 105 is called
UNNILPENTIUM
1   0   5
UN   NIL   PENT   IUM

etc...

Index

Acknowledgements

I would like to thank the science staff and students (particularly Rebecca Henry, Tamara Ranatunga and Richard Secker) at Bramhall High Scool for their help in developing material for this book. I must also thank Geoff Bailey, John Bailey, Gareth Bell, Peter Borrows, Phil Bunyan, Alan Goodwin, Janet Hawkins, Sandra Humphries, Alan Jackson, Steve Lund, Claire Penfold, Gordon Sutton, Malcolm Tomlin and Adrian Wheaton. Their comments and suggestions have been invaluable. Finally, my thanks go to Keith Johnson for his advice and insight into the way we learn and what makes a good text book.

Acknowledgement is made to the following Examining Bodies for permission to reprint questions from their examination papers:

MEG   Midland Examining Group
NEAB   Northern Examinations and Assessment Board
NI   Northern Ireland Schools Examinations Council
SEG   Southern Examining Group
ULEAC   University of London Examinations and
        Assessment Council
WJEC   Welsh Joint Education Committee

Illustration acknowledgements

Adams Picture Library: 109B, 121C, 309, 340L, 341BC, J. Howard 225B, 277CR, 341TL   J Allen Cash Photolibrary: 92CR, 122, 206, 261B   Ancient Art & Architecture Collection: 259   Barnaby's Picture Library: 90B, 154T   BASF: 216C   BOC: 273T, 277CL   British Airways: 260T   Britstock-IFA: E Bach 286T   Bubbles Photolibrary: F. Rombout cover C, 53, 130R   Martyn Chillmaid: 10, 18, 21T, BR, 23, 35, 56, 64TL, B, 65, 77BL, 90L, 91, 100, 106, 109T, 118B, 121T, 128T, 129, 130T, 131T, 140T, 141, 145, 157, 165, 166, 172e, g, 174, 175, 177T, 180, 186C, 189L, R, 196, 198, 202, 204, 205T, 206B, 208, 214, 222, 242, 244, 246, 248B, 249, 250T, 251T, 277TL, 294T, C, BL, 314, 340R   Bruce Coleman Limited: CM Pampaloni 144, J Cancalosi 158, K Burchett 172h, A Davies 178C   Collections: R Weaver 127, A Sieveking 172f, 177B   Mary Evans Picture Library: 14, 216T, B, 243   Eye Ubiquitous: D Cumming 67CL, T Hawkins 92T, S Passmore 109TR, J Reid 176B, L Fordyce 285T, 286C, J Dakers 299 BR   Leslie Garland Picture Library: I Cartwright 93TR   Geoscience Features Picture Library: 77TR, TL, BR, 86TL, 121B, 143, 226, 275, 281 (3), 283, 287B, 288 (4), 289T, 290, 292R, L, 301, 302   Robert Harding Picture Library: 250C   Grant Heilman Photography: Barry L Runk 205B, 220   Holt Studios International: N Cattlin 142, 218   ICI: 112, 115, 225T   Images Colour Library: 151, 186T, 192   Image Bank: M Regine 21B, Barros & Barros 154CL, A Van der Vaeren 167, W Bokelberg 244T   Impact Photos: T. Webster 148, R Scruton 341CR, M George 341CC, R Roberts 341 BL, C Bluntzer 341BR   Mike Inglis: 277B

Johnson Matthey: 59R, 178B   KP Foods: 273   Frank Lane Picture Agency: J Zimmermann 172a   Aaron M Levin: 251B   Magnum Photos: 175BR   Mary Rose Trust: 173T   Mile post 92$\frac{1}{2}$: 81   National Medical Slide Bank: 250B   Panos Pictures: S Sprague 65T   The Photographers Library: 118T, 186B, 341CL   Photri Inc.: 57   Photo Library International: 46T, 67CR, 251C   Pictor International: 21C, 125B, 261C   Paul Popper Ltd: Reuter 168T, 277TR   Science Photolibrary: 212, 311, NASA 4B, 119T, 275TL   E McNulty 52, CNRI 58B, T Beddow 59L, J Greim 67T, W & D McIntyre 67BR, 131B, S. I. U. 93TL, S Terry 128B, P. Jude 130L, M Brodsky 140B, Biophoto Associates 149, Dr J Burgess 154B, E Schrempp 176T, H Schneebell 260B, H Morgan 273C, S Grand 275TR, National Library of Medicine 321   Sporting Pictures: 168B   Still Pictures: 175BL   Tony Stone Images: 67BL, 113, 172b, 183B, 287T, D Austen 282B, P Tweedie 4T, 172C, A Sacks 92CL, M Lewis 130CL, A Husmo 145T, B Forster 154CT, 178T, K Wood 159, H Staartjes 160, C Keeler 172d, J Riley 204T, R Frerk 248T, S & N Geary 258, L Stone 282, H R Johnston 286B, R Rusing 294B, J Balog 298, R Iwasaki 341TR   Sygma: 275CR   Telegraph Colour Library: cover T, back cover, Rapho 46B, VCL 48, E. Hesser 64TR, D James 86TR, P Ward 93B, P Tweedie 103, P Boulat/Cosmos 118C, Space Frontiers 119B, J Moss 147, D Ellison 162, Masterfile 183T, S Benbow 189B, M Fielding 341TC   Topham Picture Source: 124, 125T, 299T, BL, Press Association 186 TR;   Viewfinder: 92B, 109C, 285B   Tony Waltham Geophotos: 289B, 292C   World Gold Council: 261T   Jennifer Wright: 58T   Zefa Pictures: Studio Benser 284